Midway

Oahu HAWAIIAN ISLANDS
Hawaii

ake I.

NORTH PACIFIC OCEAN

Wotje MARSHALL Is
· Maloelap
uit ·
Makin· GILBERT Is
Tarawa·

·Fanning I.
· Christmas I.

ru Ocean I.

PHOENIX Is

· ELLICE Is

N Is.

NTA CRUZ Is

MARQUESAS
Is

SAMOA

FIJI

SOCIETY
Is

TONGA

COOK Is

TUBUAI Is

IA

SOUTH PACIFIC OCEAN

Norfolk I.

Auckland

EA

NEW ZEALAND
Wellington
Christchurch

JECTION

THE WAR
WITH JAPAN

Sinai Hospital operated on 25th

Happy Birthday to my Husband
Earl
From
Helen

THE WAR
WITH JAPAN

A Concise History

BY CHARLES BATESON

MICHIGAN STATE UNIVERSITY PRESS
1968

*The photograph on the front of the jacket is by Douglass Baglin
and those on the back come from the Australian War Memorial*

★
  ★
★
  ★

★

ACKNOWLEDGMENTS

The author and publishers would like to express their gratitude to the following for giving us permission to quote various extracts from their publications:

The Australian War Memorial for permission to quote from *The Japanese Thrust* by Lionel Wigmore.

Cassell and Company Ltd, Publishers, London, for permission to quote from *Defeat Into Victory* by Field Marshal Viscount Slim.

Chatto & Windus Ltd, Publishers, London, for permission to quote from *The Jungle is Neutral* by Spencer Chapman.

Collins Publishers, London, for permission to quote from *Orde Wingate* by Christopher Sykes.

Mr Allan Dawes for permission to quote from his book *Soldier Superb,* published by F. H. Johnston Publishing Co., Sydney.

Duell, Sloan & Pearce, Publishers, New York, for permission to quote from *General Kenney Reports*: *A Personal History of the Pacific War* by George S. Kenney.

Eyre & Spottiswoode (Publishers) Ltd, London, for permission to quote from *The War in Malaya* by Lieutenant-General Percival.

William Heinemann Ltd, Publishers, London, for permission to quote from *Retreat from Kokoda* by Raymond Paull.

Mr W. B. Russell for permission to quote from his book *The 2/14 Battalion,* published by Angus & Robertson Ltd, Sydney.

The United States Naval Institute for permission to quote from *Midway! The Battle that Doomed Japan* by Mitsuo Fuchida and Masatake Okumiya. Copyright © 1955 by U.S. Naval Institute, Annapolis, Maryland.

The Viking Press, Inc, Publishers, New York, for permission to quote from *Our Jungle Road to Tokyo* by Robert L. Eichelberger. Copyright 1949, 1950 by Robert L. Eichelberger.

We should also like to thank the Australian War Memorial and the United States Navy and Marine Departments for their kind co-operation in our search for the illustrations reproduced in this book.

CONTENTS

ILLUSTRATIONS

MAPS

PREFACE

I have attempted to tell, within the compass of a single volume, the story of the war with Japan on land and sea and in the air, both for those who lived through or actively participated in World War II and for the generations which have grown up since.

My thanks are due, in particular, to Mr. Gavin Long, General Editor of *The Australian Official History of World War II,* for encouragement and much wise counsel. Without his active help many factual errors would have crept into the text, and the unstinting manner in which he gave both his time and knowledge was heart-warming. I have also to thank the unnamed members of the editorial staff of the Michigan State University Press and its Director, Dr. Lyle Blair, for many valuable and constructive suggestions.

I owe a debt to all the official historians, Australian, American, Indian, British, Canadian and Japanese, whose exhaustive histories of every phase of the war against Japan alone have made possible this one-volume history.

Lastly, the book could not have been completed but for the forbearance and active encouragement of my wife, Ann, who remained undismayed at the numerous upsets caused by its research and writing.

CHARLES BATESON.

INTRODUCTION

by Gavin Long, General Editor of the
Australian Official History of World War II

A short and comprehensive history of the war on which
Japan recklessly embarked in December 1941 is long overdue.
Every large episode of that war and many small ones have
been examined and re-examined in print. The Western govern-
ment-sponsored histories — political, strategical, logistic, naval,
military and air — from the United States, Great Britain, India,
Australia, New Zealand and Canada run to about eighty
volumes. Books telling authentic stories of units, ships and
individuals, and histories and memoirs translated from the
Japanese are vastly more numerous. Charles Bateson has not
been daunted by the task of telling, between two covers and
for the general reader, the story of this strange new war.

In a coalition war each ally, and particularly each larger ally,
is inclined to see his successes somewhat larger than life, his
setbacks somewhat smaller. As an Australian, Mr Bateson
views the drama from a position that was geographically both
central and close to action, and from the relatively detached
standpoint of a citizen of one of the smaller nations of the

alliance. Thus he should be the better able to observe the whole picture in perspective. Some of his assessments may give a mild shock to a few of his readers, and the weight he gives to some episodes may occasionally ruffle preconceived notions on both sides of the Atlantic.

The Japanese war against the West was indeed both new and strange. It was one thing for the Japanese Navy in 1905 to lie in wait for and destroy a bumbling European fleet. It was another for a Japanese Navy and Army in a hundred days to destroy European and American power throughout the Far East and Western Pacific, and establish a new imperial frontier stretching from the Kuriles to Burma and embracing south-east Asia and the Indies.

The war the Japanese Army leaders engineered in 1941 was also a new kind of war; but its shape had not been unforeseen. In public, Western writers, and in private, Western strategists, had predicted that, with the West engaged in an internecine struggle, Japan would advance against the West's east Asian bridgeheads, would overcome their naval bases from the landward side and seize their colonies; and that it would take a few years for Western power, and the United States Navy in particular, to lop off these gains and restore the status quo. Some Japanese naval leaders, notably Admiral Yamamoto, shared the opinion that in the final reckoning Japan would be defeated. But such voices were quelled by the over-stimulated generals who had gained control of the Tokyo government.

As Mr Bateson shows, the initial Japanese offensive was ably planned, and for the most part admirably executed by leaders and men of well-trained and indoctrinated sea, land and air forces, the sea and air forces at that stage being far better armed and exercised than those of their adversaries. But, as Yamamoto had foreseen, the initial victories could not be sustained. Once their first objectives had been reached the Japanese Army feared to go much farther, half its strength being engaged in a hopeless effort to break the heart of the Chinese people, and a quarter of its strength nervously awaiting a Russian onslaught from Siberia. Therefore, the generals decided to station garrisons round the perimeter of their new empire and hope that their enemies, lacking Japanese stamina, would go home and allow them to keep the spoils.

Within five months after December 1941 it was evident to the Japanese in Tokyo that they had missed the bus, and within six months that they had lost command of the sea and the outer skies, and therefore their enemies could henceforth attack their frontier when and where they wished. After their Midway disaster, or at the latest after the Japanese Navy had lost the long campaign of attrition round Guadalcanal, commonsense — a quality as rare then as now among politico-military strategical advisers — should have suggested making peace. But the Japanese generals were disinclined to confess incompetence and, to save face, they had at their command an obedient nation of heroes, whose youngsters in the next two years and a half fought hopeless battles in which few ever surrendered. On this return journey, as Mr Bateson shows, men of equal calibre on the other side, at last better led and trained, and equipped on a crescendo scale, won back (for a time) Japan's Great East Asia Co-Prosperity Sphere.

Aging warriors on the three sides in the conflict — counting as the third the Asian nationalists — and their sons are still entangled in the consequences of Japan's war. To two generations Mr Bateson presents a brief account, timely and authentic, of Japan's war against the West.

GAVIN LONG.

Canberra, 1967.

one

PEARL HARBOUR

The date: November 26, 1941. The time: 0600-0900.[1]

Hitokappu Wan or Tankan Bay, on the southern coast of Etorofu, largest of the thirty-two islands of the lonely Kuriles to the north of Japan, lay wreathed in fog. It shrouded the island's forest-clad mountain slopes and rocky coastline, hiding the few indications of human occupation — the small concrete pier, the tiny, triple-masted radio station, the three fishermen's huts.

The steady throb of engines carried dully on the heavy air, and presently grey shapes loomed out of the fog as ship after ship moved cautiously from the normally unfrequented anchorage toward the open sea. Once clear of the island, the fleet of twenty-eight large and small surface vessels manœuvred into formation and headed at thirteen knots toward the south-east through the lonely waters between the Aleutians and Midway Island.

Japan's Pearl Harbour Striking Force, commanded by Vice-Admiral Chuichi Nagumo, had assembled at Hitokappu in great

secrecy and had now begun the sortie which was to widen the
war ravaging Europe into a global struggle and bring bitter
conflict to the vast waters and many islands of the Pacific
Ocean.

Some 200 miles off, three submarines scouted ahead of
Nagumo's fleet. Much closer, but still well in advance of the
main body, a line of nine destroyers led by a light cruiser was
stationed to give warning of any stray ships that might be
encountered, and far out on each flank steamed a heavy
cruiser. The main body of six aircraft carriers and two battleships moved in line ahead in two parallel columns, with the
carriers in the lead. Behind them came the train of eight
tankers, whose slow speed regulated the rate of advance of the
entire fleet. The normal complement of aircraft aboard the
carriers had been augmented by air groups from two other
carriers, so that between them they carried the unusually large
total of 450 planes.[2] The pilots, each of whom averaged better
than 800 hours' flying time, had undergone intensive training in
horizontal and dive bombing and in the technique of torpedo
attack in shallow water.[3]

The success or failure of Nagumo's mission depended largely
upon secrecy. Elaborate ruses were practised to prevent the
concentration of the fleet being detected and to lull the Americans into a sense of false security. Of the three alternative lines
of approach to Hawaii, the most northerly was chosen because
it lay farthest from the normal shipping lanes. It involved a
voyage of some 3,000 miles, much of it through seas often
tempestuous, but in these remote waters the Japanese ships,
blacked out, under strict radio silence and taking special precautions to reduce telltale smoke and waste tracks, were unlikely
to be seen. To minimize the risk that heavy weather might
prevent refuelling at sea, thousands of barrels of fuel oil were
crammed into every available vacant space above and below
decks in the combat ships. If the worst happened, the big ships
were under orders to dispense with their screening destroyers.
Any British, American or Dutch merchantman unlucky enough
to stray across the fleet's line of advance was to be sunk out
of hand and any neutral vessel boarded promptly and its wire-

less put out of commission. In the event, however, only one ship was sighted and she flew the Japanese flag.

Nagumo's command comprised an odd mixture of new and old vessels. The aged battleships *Hiei* (32,156, 1914) and *Kirishima* (26,300, 1915) had been converted to oil burners after World War I and in the 1930s had been completely modernized. They carried 14-inch guns and had a speed of 26 knots. The light cruiser *Abukuma* (5,170, 1925), leading the destroyers, had been recently modernized. In contrast, the heavy cruisers *Tone* (8,500, 1938) and *Chikuma* (8,500, 1939), mounting 8-inch guns and capable of 33 knots, and the large aircraft carriers *Shokaku* (20,000, 1941) and *Zuikaku* (20,000, 1941) were new vessels only recently added to the Japanese Combined Fleet. The smaller carriers *Hiryu* (10,050, 1939) and *Soryu* (10,050, 1937) had been completed in the late 1930s, but the carriers *Akagi* (26,900, 1927) and *Kaga* (26,900, 1928) had been converted respectively from a battle-cruiser and a battleship.

On December 2, Nagumo received from the flagship of Admiral Isoroku Yamamoto, Commander-in-Chief of the Combined Fleet, the code signal 'Niitaka Yama Nobore' ('Climb Mount Niitaka'), intimating that the attack was to proceed. Later that day the date of the attack was confirmed — December 8 Tokyo time, December 7 Hawaiian time. Intelligence reports from Japanese Imperial General Headquarters indicated that seven battleships and seven cruisers were at Pearl Harbour, but no carriers. The *Enterprise* and *Lexington* were engaged on aircraft delivery missions to Wake and Midway. The Japanese erroneously believed four carriers were based on Hawaii, but there were only *Enterprise* and *Lexington,* and their whereabouts was as much a mystery to the Japanese as was the sudden disappearance of the Japanese carrier divisions to the Americans.

Having successfully refuelled,[4] the Striking Force reached the meridian — longitude 158° — of Oahu at 2100 on Saturday, December 6 Hawaiian time, and being now less than 500 miles north of the island, altered course to due south. Leaving the tankers to proceed to an appointed rendezvous, the

carriers and their escorts increased speed to twenty-six knots
for the final approach to the selected launching spot 200 miles
north of Pearl Harbour. The Japanese were confident they
were undetected and that the Americans were oblivious of the
approaching danger. The tone of broadcasts from stations KGU
and KGMB in Hawaii, to which the Japanese had been listening
carefully, was normal and by intercepting the messages of
United States patrol aircraft, whose code they could not read,
and fixing their position by radio bearings, the Japanese knew
that the patrols were all concentrated to the south-westward of
Oahu.

It was a dark, thick night, with a rising sea, but the Striking
Force maintained its course and speed and arrived in position
on schedule next morning. Two reconnaissance aircraft, which
later confirmed the absence of the United States carriers, were
catapulted from the cruisers at an early hour, and at 0600 the
first attack wave of more than 180 aircraft under the command
of Captain Mitsuo Fuchida began roaring into the twenty-knot
north-east trade wind from heavily pitching flight decks. This
first wave comprised 90 Kate single-engined bombers, 40 of
which carried torpedoes and the remainder armour-piercing
bombs, 51 Val two-seater dive-bombers and 43 Zeke single-
seater fighters. Climbing above the overcast, they levelled off
at 9,800 feet and sped toward their target.

Oahu was sighted just before 0740. Clouds wreathed Waianae
and Koolau mountains, but the sky was clear and although a
thin film of morning mist hugged the earth the Japanese pilots
could see the green fields of sugar cane in the valley of Aiea.
Over Pearl Harbour, its surface dotted with naval vessels, were
only a few stray wisps of cloud. It was a pleasant and peaceful
scene, with no indication that the Americans were forewarned.
At 0749 Fuchida gave the signal to attack, and as the first
aircraft swooped from southward toward their appointed targets
he notified his superiors by radio that complete surprise had
been achieved.

The Americans should have been alert and waiting. They
had received ample warnings, but, as Admiral Ernest J. King
later stressed, 'an unwarranted feeling of immunity from attack

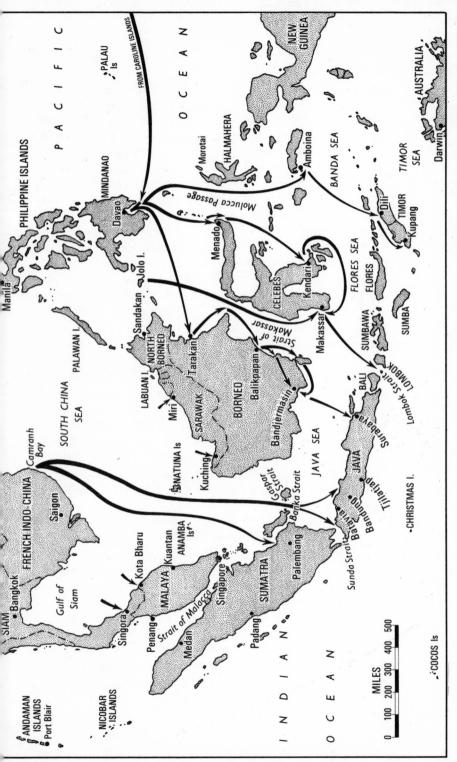

1. The lines of the Japanese southward thrusts

seems to have pervaded all ranks at Pearl Harbour, both Army and Navy'.[5] He might with justice have added that a similar feeling held sway in Washington. Yet the possibility, perhaps even probability, of a surprise attack on Oahu, with or without any prior declaration of war, had been studied frequently by high-ranking United States service chiefs and as far back as 1936 had formed the basis of war games and drills.[6] Even earlier, in 1924, Brigadier-General William Mitchell, Assistant Chief of the Army Air Corps, had stressed that Oahu formed 'an easy, compact and convenient object for air attack'.[7]

In Hawaii itself Brigadier-General Frederick L. Martin, commanding the Army Air Forces, and Rear-Admiral Patrick N. L. Bellinger, commanding the Naval Air Arm, had issued on March 31 1941, a secret joint report in which they asserted that 'the most likely and dangerous form of attack on Oahu would be an air attack', launched from one or more carriers within a range of 300 miles, that if launched at dawn there would be a high probability that the attack would come as a surprise, and that 'a single submarine attack might indicate the presence of a considerable undiscovered surface force probably composed of fast ships accompanied by a carrier'.[8] On April 1 Admiral Harold R. Stark, the U.S. Chief of Naval Operations, warned all commanders to be particularly alert at week-ends. Later, on August 20, Martin informed General Walter C. Short, Commanding General of the Hawaiian Department, that the most probable line of approach of a Japanese carrier force would be from the north-westward.

The Japanese changed the call signals of their naval vessels on November 1 and again on December 1, although normally these changes were made only at six-month intervals. 'The fact that service calls lasted only one month', reported Lieutenant-Commander Joseph J. Rochefort, in charge of the Navy's Combat Intelligence at Hawaii, 'indicates an additional progressive step in preparing for operations on a large scale'.[9]

The many appreciations and discussions and the reports of the various intelligence departments, of which the above are typical, were underlined by grave warnings from Washington as the diplomatic situation deteriorated and it became clear that the negotiations being conducted through the Japanese Ambassador, Kichisaburo Nomura, and Japan's special envoy, Saburo Kurusu, had failed. The Americans enjoyed the tremendous advantage of having cracked the principal Japanese diplomatic ciphers, including that known as Purple, the most important of these. They were thus able to read the most private communications passing between the Japanese Government and its ambassadors, consuls, military attachés and secret agents throughout the world. The process by which the Japanese messages were decoded and distributed was known as Magic, and the Magic messages gave — or should have given — the Americans a prescience that made surprise impossible.

Many of the Magic messages, however, did not find their way to the theatres, either paraphrased or in their original text, or if forwarded were not necessarily disseminated both to the Army and the Navy. Thus, on September 24, a Tokyo message to the Japanese Consulate at Honolulu divided the waters of Pearl Harbour into five areas and requested periodic reports as to the location of warships in port, particularly requesting that mention be made of two or more vessels alongside the same wharf. Five days later another message set up codes for designating the location of vessels in Pearl Harbour, and on November 15 a message, which was not deciphered by the Americans until some days later, stated that relations between Japan and the United States were most critical and directed that the 'ships in harbour' report be sent irregularly, but at least twice a week.[10] These messages, since similar ones were being sent to other places, were considerd routine requests and, incredibly, were not even passed on to Hawaii.

On November 27 Stark sent the following message to the commanders in Hawaii and the Philippines:

> This dispatch is to be considered a war warning. Negotiations with Japan looking toward stabilization of conditions in the Pacific have ceased. An aggressive move by Japan is expected within the next few days. The number and equipment of Japanese troops and organization of naval task forces indicate an amphibious operation against either the Philippines, Thai or Kra Peninsula or possibly Borneo. Execute

> an appropriate defensive deployment preparatory to carrying out the tasks assigned in WPL-46. (The war plan.)

In the absence at Army manœuvres of General George C. Marshall, Chief of Staff of the U.S. Army, the Chief of the War Plans Division, Brigadier-General Leonard T. Gerow, sent a similar but less strongly worded message to Short. This read:

> Japanese future action unpredictable but hostile action possible at any moment. If hostilities cannot be avoided, the United States desires that Japan commit the first overt act. This policy should not be construed as restricting you to a course of action that might jeopardize your defence. Prior to hostile Japanese action you are directed to undertake such reconnaissance and other measures as you deem necessary, but these measures should be carried out so as not to alarm civil population or disclose intent. Report measures taken.

At about the same time as this message reached him, Short also received from Army Intelligence in Washington the following warning:

> Japanese negotiations have come to practical stalemate. Hostilities may ensue. Subversive activities may be expected.

As events transpired, it was unfortunate that these two messages arrived almost simultaneously, since they channelled Short's thoughts toward the danger of sabotage rather than of air attack.

On November 28, in consequence of these warnings, Admiral Husband E. Kimmel, Commander-in-Chief of the Pacific Fleet, who had been elevated to that post over the heads of thirty-two admirals,[11] and Short placed their commands in the lowest condition of combat readiness. With the Navy this was No. 3, with the Army, No. 1. The latter provided for defence against sabotage and uprisings, but not against threat from without, and although the Army was responsible for the defence of Pearl Harbour as a naval base no Army anti-aircraft guns were manned or supplied with ready ammunition. Short, however, did alter the monitoring hours of the six mobile radar sets, which were under the control, not of the Army Air Forces, but of the Signal Corps and which, as the permanent installation had not been completed, were all that was available at Oahu. He ordered them manned from 0400 to 0700 daily instead of from 0600 to 1130, but did not explain he made the change because he considered the earlier period 'the most dangerous hours' for a carrier-borne air attack, and the radar personnel concluded the change was merely to avoid wear and tear of the equipment. Army, Marine and Navy aircraft were drawn up on the airfields in rows, to all intents wing-tip to wing-tip, as a precaution against sabotage, it being more economical of manpower to guard them concentrated than dispersed.

In the Fleet, under condition of readiness No. 3, one in every three machine-guns was manned, although the ready ammunition remained in locked boxes, the keys to which were held by the officer of the deck. The main and 5-inch batteries, the plotting rooms, directors and ammunition supplies were unmanned.

No alterations in the condition of readiness of either service and no additional precautions of any importance followed the receipt of further messages revealing the rapidity with which the situation was deteriorating. A spate of messages giving news of Japanese troop and fleet movements, almost all to the southward, flowed steadily into Oahu's intelligence sections, and on December 3 came two messages from Washington reporting that the previous day urgent instructions had been sent to Japanese diplomatic and consular posts to destroy most of their codes and ciphers and to burn all other confidential and secret documents. Three days later, Kimmel, in view of the international situation and the exposed position of America's outlying Pacific islands, was empowered to authorize the destruction of secret and confidential documents 'now or under conditions of greater emergency'.

Incidents at Hawaii itself during the night of December 6-7 might, at the last moment, have deprived the Japanese of surprise had that 'unwarranted feeling of immunity from attack' not pervaded all ranks. Twenty-seven Japanese submarines, eleven equipped with small reconnaissance aircraft and five with midget submarines, had left Kure and Yokosuka between November 18 and 20, and most of these, about December 5, took up scouting and patrolling positions around Hawaii. The five midgets were launched off the entrance to Pearl Harbour in the early hours of December 7.

At 0342 the minesweeper *Condor* (165, 1941), making a routine sweep about 1,000 yards from the entrance, sighted a suspicious object, and promptly alerted the destroyer *Ward* (1,060, 1918), also on patrol, that she believed a submarine was in the area, an area in which U.S. submarines were prohibited from operating except on the surface. *Ward* made a sonar search for an hour without success, but then learned she had gone in the opposite direction to that taken by the suspected submarine when last sighted.[12] Neither *Condor* nor *Ward* reported this incident to the Harbour Control Post ashore. At 0447 the anti-torpedo net protecting the harbour entrance was opened to admit the minesweeper *Crossbill* (165, 1941), and as other vessels were due to arrive or leave at intervals of thirty to forty-five minutes over the next few hours it was allowed to remain open.

A few minutes after 0630 a small submarine was detected trying to enter the harbour in the wake of the target ship *Antares* (4,800, 1922). The midget was sighted by those aboard *Antares* and *Ward* and by a patrolling Catalina of the Navy's dawn patrol. *Ward* attacked with gunfire and depth charges and the Catalina with bombs or depth charges. The destroyer reported her attack to the Harbour Control Post in two messages radioed at 0651 and 0653 and the officer on duty passed on these reports to various naval officers but not to the Army. There was some delay in the passing on of the messages and before orders were issued for the ready-duty destroyer *Monaghan* (1,345, 1935) to get under way and assist *Ward* and for the stand-by destroyer to raise steam. The pilot of the Catalina made his report in code at 0700, but delays in decoding and telephoning meant that the staff duty officer of the Naval Air Force did not begin circulating the message until

about 0730. It reached Kimmel ten minutes later, but again
nobody thought to inform the Army.[13] Although the nerve
centre for emergency signals, the Harbour Control Post that
morning was manned by one reserve officer and an inexperienced and untrained telephone operator.

Even stronger if later evidence that something unusual was
afoot came the Army's way fortuitously, only to be ignored
because of unpreparedness. A mobile search radar on Kahuku
Point, the northern extremity of Oahu, from 0645 to 0700
tracked one of the Japanese float aircraft reconnoitring ahead
of the bombers. This contact was promptly reported to the
Information Centre, which as promptly disregarded it.[14] As the
breakfast truck was late, an Army private, under instruction by
a fellow private, continued his training beyond 0700 and at
0702 picked up a large flight of planes some 137 miles to the
north of Oahu. After some argument between the two men,
neither of whom had ever seen such a large plot, the contact
was reported about 0720. The Information Centre had closed
down at 0700 and the only officer the telephone operator could
find was an Army Air Corps lieutenant on duty for training and
observation. In the absence of any air liaison officer he imagined
the plot came from Flying Fortresses staging into Oahu en
route to the Philippines and decided to take no action. The
two privates tracked the aircraft until, twenty-two miles out,
nearby hills blacked them off the screen. Pearl Harbour had
forfeited its last-minute opportunity to avoid or minimize
surprise.

The Japanese air armada now swooped down to deliver its
devastating blow. This first attack, of which the world learnt
within a few minutes through the terse but dramatic broadcast,
'Air raid, Pearl Harbour — this is no drill', was directed principally at the airfields and battleships. It lasted from 0755 to
about 0825 and did tremendous damage. Because of the danger
of smoke obscuring the battleships after the airfield attacks, the
Japanese torpedo-bombers launched their torpedoes at a longer
range and several minutes earlier than had been planned, but
this did not affect the accuracy of their aim. The stabilizers
with which they had been specially fitted prevented the tor-

pedoes dropping harmlessly to the bottom in the narrow, shallow waters of Pearl Harbour, and, launched at low heights, they sped true to their stationary targets. The ground and air opposition was pitiful and for thirty minutes the Japanese bombed and strafed virtually at will. The Fleet's manned machine-guns began firing within a few minutes, but all naval anti-aircraft batteries were not in action until ten minutes after the opening of the attack. The Army failed to get a single anti-aircraft gun firing during the first raid.[15] The few fighters which got into the air were quickly shot down without inflicting much loss on the enemy, as were five of the eight aircraft which arrived from the carrier *Enterprise* during the attack.

The second wave of Japanese aircraft began their attack at 0840. The 54 Kate high-level bombers, 81 Val dive-bombers and 36 Zeke fighters met stronger anti-aircraft fire than had Fuchida's squadrons, but it came mostly from the ships. Only three Army anti-aircraft units were ready to fire before the attack terminated around 0945, and hardly any fighter planes got airborne.

In Washington that morning further Magic messages had been deciphered. Two in particular were significant. The first directed the Japanese Embassy to destroy at once its cipher machine and secret documents; the other instructed the ambassador to deliver the Japanese Government's final reply to the United States at 1300 Washington time, the equivalent of dawn in Honolulu. The Army and Navy had received translations of these messages by 1000, but nobody realized their significance until Marshall read them on reaching his office at 1115. He at once sent the following warning to the Philippines, Panama, Hawaii and San Francisco:

> The Japanese are presenting at 1 p.m. Eastern Standard Time today what amounts to an ultimatum. Also they are under orders to destroy their code machine immediately. Just what significance the hour set may have we do not know, but be on alert accordingly.

Although Marshall thrice sent officers to ensure this message was expedited, the breakdown of Army radio communications, due to atmospherics, resulted in it being sent by commercial channels via San Francisco, and it was not even marked urgent. It arrived in Honolulu at 0733 and was handed to a bicycle messenger for delivery. Delayed by the Japanese attack, he did not reach Short's headquarters until 1145 and the message was not decoded until 1458 — just seven hours after the Japanese attack.[16]

The U.S. Navy and Marine Corps at Pearl Harbour lost 2,117 officers and men killed or fatally wounded and 779 wounded. The Army's casualties were 218 killed and 364 wounded, making the total losses 2,335 killed and 1,143 wounded. In addition, 68 civilians were killed and 35 wounded.[17] The battleships *Arizona* (32,000, 1916), *California* (32,300, 1921) and *West Virginia* (31,500, 1923) were sunk, *Oklahoma* (29,000, 1916) capsized, and *Nevada* (29,000,1916), *Maryland* (31,500, 1921), *Pennsylvania* (32,600, 1916) and *Tennessee* (32,300, 1920) damaged. Thus, half the eight battleships in port had been sunk and the remainder damaged. In addition, the target ship *Utah,* an old battleship, and the minelayer *Oglala* (1,400, 1917) were sunk, and the light cruisers *Helena* (10,000, 1939), *Raleigh* (7,050, 1924) and *Honolulu* (9,475, 1938), the destroyers *Shaw* (1,450, 1936), *Cassin* (1,450, 1936) and *Downes* (1,450, 1937), the repair ship *Vestal* (6,525, 1913) and the seaplane tender *Curtiss* (8,671, 1940) damaged. Ninety-two Navy and 96 Army aircraft, a total of 188, were destroyed and others damaged. Naval and Army installations, especially at airfields suffered severely. Only one airfield, Haleiwa, was not attacked.

On the other hand, the Japanese escaped lightly. Their total casualties were under 100 and they lost only 29 aircraft and all 5 midget submarines. The Japanese task force, after a proposal for a third air strike had been rejected, escaped to the Inland Sea without being attacked.

Gifted with hindsight and possessing all the facts unearthed by no fewer than eight separate official investigations, it is difficult to objectively assess responsibility for the American defeat. The Magic and other decoded messages, standing starkly alone instead of being viewed with all the other deciphered messages and information from a wide variety of sources, point so irresistibly to the Pearl Harbour attack that it is inconceivable anybody could have failed to forecast the Japanese move. However, for those charged at the time with the task of sifting the mass of material being received, these messages did not speak with the same clarity or force. Moreover, everybody did not have access to all the relevant messages. For security reasons Magic messages were zealously guarded and their distribution restricted to a few officials and officers of the highest rank, and even they had to read them while the delivering officer waited to take the copies away for immediate destruction. Other information, because of service jealousies, clashes of personality and faulty liaison, did not always gain a sufficiently wide distribution. Deliberately or inadvertently, the interchange of information and intelligence between the Army and the Navy, even between different departments and sections of the same service, fell far short of what was necessary. So also, especially in Washington, did the definition and delegation of responsibility. These and many other factors render difficult the apportionment of blame.[18]

The one indisputable truth about Pearl Harbour is that both the Americans and the Japanese allowed themselves to be mesmerized by events elsewhere. This was the essential cause of the American miscalculations and of the Japanese reaping no more than a tactical victory.

The service chiefs in Washington, and Kimmel and Short in Hawaii, were convinced that war was imminent and unavoidable, but, the wish being father to the thought, they believed the Japanese would strike against Thailand, the Netherlands East Indies and Malaya, and possibly also at the Philippines, Wake and Guam. As the spate of reports of Japanese troop and convoy movements southward in the Western Pacific flowed in, the naval and military commanders, who only a few months earlier had regarded an attack on Pearl Harbour as a serious possibility, forgot their earlier fear. They decided that Japan had neither the effrontery nor the resources to attack Pearl Harbour from the air or to seek its capture by an amphibious operation, in addition to aggressive moves else-

The aftermath of the Japanese attack on Pearl Harbour. USS *Cassin,* lying on her side, and USS *Downes,* left, were badly damaged, while behind them USS *Pennsylvania,* flagship of the American Pacific Fleet, suffered only slight damage

During the Pearl Harbour attack USS *Maryland*, left, was only slightly damaged and was one of the first ships to rejoin the fleet. But USS *Oklahoma*, right, capsized

where. The warnings Washington sent Hawaii were strongly coloured with this delusion.

The commanders at Pearl Harbour were similarly mesmerized. Kimmel and Short, momentarily forgetting that battles are won by surprise and that commanders need to anticipate the unexpected as well as the probable, adopted the view that an attack on Pearl Harbour was improbable if not impossible. They had the excuse that in this they were echoing the conclusions of their better-informed superiors in Washington, but as the custodians of America's most important fleet and base in the Pacific their failure to alert both against at least air attack is incomprehensible. Despite widespread rumours to the contrary at the time, the personal relations of Kimmel and Short were friendly, but co-operation between the two services at Hawaii was lamentable. Their mistakes, however, do not exonerate those in Washington, who were equally to blame, particularly as the War Department was aware Short had merely alerted his command against sabotage and yet made no effort to advise him that in the circumstances this was inadequate.

For their part, the Japanese conceived the attack on Pearl Harbour as an integral part of their southward operations. They regarded the elimination of the U.S. Pacific Fleet, so that it could neither threaten nor intervene against these operations, as a necessary and vital prelude. Their strategic thinking was simply short-range, the securing of an immediate advantage. To eliminate ships, guns and aircraft from immediate calculations, they made the Pacific Fleet and the airfields their primary targets, ignoring the more vital ship repair and maintenance facilities and the great dumps of oil fuel above ground, the destruction of which would have profoundly affected the development of American sea and air power and delayed by many months the American deployment in the Pacific. The crippling of the Pacific Fleet was a brilliant tactical victory that greatly facilitated operations elsewhere, but it gained the Japanese no worthwhile strategic advantages, particularly as the all-important carriers escaped. Further, Pearl Harbour achieved overnight what no other event could have brought about so quickly — the stamping out of the vociferous and influential advocates of a policy of non-intervention and the uniting of all Americans behind President Franklin D. Roosevelt in the vigorous prosecution of the war.

Thus, ironically, what at the time seemed an overwhelming Japanese victory in fact sealed Japan's fate and ensured an ultimate Allied victory.

NOTES AND REFERENCES

1. Tokyo time, the equivalent of 1030-1330 25th November in Hawaii, 1600-1900 25th November in Washington, 2100-0000 25th November in Greenwich, and 0700-1000 26th November in Sydney and Melbourne.
2. Samuel Eliot Morison, *History of U.S. Naval Operations in World War II,* III *The Rising Sun in the Pacific 1931-April 1942,* 85.
3. *The Army Air Forces in World War II:* I *Plans and Early Operations January 1939 to August 1942,* 195.
4. Accounts differ as to whether the refuelling was accomplished easily or with difficulty. The report of the Congressional Investigation states that the weather was uniformly calm, and that the anticipated refuelling difficulties did not arise. (Inquiry Report, 57.) Col. T. N. Dupuy, Pearl Harbour: Who Blundered? (*American Heritage,* XXIII, (February 1962) 72) says the attempts at refuelling continued for several days under almost heartbreaking conditions of bad weather.
5. Morison, op. cit., III, 138.
6. Roberta Wohlstetter, *Pearl Harbour: Warning and Decision,* 68.
7. *American Heritage,* XXIII (February 1962), 74.
8. *U.S. Army in World War II: The War Department: Chief of Staff; Pre-war Plans and Preparations,* by Mark Skinner Watson, 476.
9. Woh'stetter, 41, citing Pearl Harbour Hearings, pt. 17, 2636.
10. Inquiry Report, 516.
11. Walter Lord, *Day of Infamy,* 7.
12. Evidence of Captain William W. Outerbridge, commander of the *Ward,* in Hans Louis Trefousse, *What Happened at Pearl Harbour?* 104-5.
13. Wohlstetter, 15-18. Compare Morison, 96-97, where it is stated the *Ward's* report was also sent in code.
14. Morison, 138.
15. Inquiry Report, 67.
16. Watson, *Chief of Staff,* 514; Trefousse, 67.
17. I have followed the casualty figures as given by Morison, 126.
18. On this subject generally, see Wohlstetter, passim.

FURTHER READING:

The best popular account of Pearl Harbour for the general reader is Walter Lord, *Day of Infamy* (London, 1957). Professor S. E. Morison's *The Rising Sun in the Pacific, 1931-April 1942* (London, 1948), volume 3 of his *History of U.S. Naval Operations in World War II,* will appeal equally to the general reader and the student. The evidence and findings of the eight official inquiries are published in forty volumes, of which the first, *Report of the Joint Committee on the Investigation of the Pearl Harbour Attack* (Washington, 1946), gives a detailed summary of the whole. Several volumes of selected and abridged extracts from the evidence at the inquiries have been published, of which H. L. Trefousse, *What Happened at*

Pearl Harbour? (New York, c. 1958) is one. Roberta Wohlstetter, *Pearl Harbour: Warning and Decision* (Stanford, 1962),
ably discusses the causes of the American failure, both at Pearl
Harbour and in Washington. Background information of pre-
war plans and events leading to the attack will be found in
several of the volumes in the American official histories — *U.S.
Army in World War II* and *The Army Air Forces in World
War II*. A. A. Hoehling, *The Week Before Pearl Harbour*
(London, 1964), dealing with the personalities and events of
the week before the attack, provides useful general reading.
For the Japanese side, the U.S. Strategic Bombing Survey's
The Campaigns of the Pacific War (Washington, 1946), Masa-
nori Ito and Roger Pineau, *The End of the Japanese Imperial
Navy* (London, 1962), Mitsuo Fuchida and Masatake Oku-
miya, *Midway: The Battle that Doomed Japan* (Annapolis,
1955), Mochitsura Hashimoto, *Sunk: The Story of the
Japanese Submarine Fleet 1942-1945* (London, 1954), and
Masatake Okumiya, Jiro Horikoshi and Martin Caidin, *Zero!
The Story of the Japanese Naval Air Force 1937-1945*
(London, 1957) should be consulted. The memoirs and bio-
graphies of several officers refer briefly to Pearl Harbour, but
the only one which requires mention is H. E. Kimmel, *Admiral
Kimmel's Story* (Chicago, 1955).

two

THE JAPANESE
FORCES AND PLANS

Japanese aggression in Asia, cleverly adjusted to meet the changing winds of the international situation, was of long standing. Her defeat of China in 1894 and of Russia in 1904-5 was followed in 1910 by her annexation of Korea. Her militarists emerged from these adventures with their prestige greatly enhanced and their ambitions whetted. Yet on the outbreak of war in 1914 their influence was insufficient to prevent Japan adhering to the Anglo-Japanese Alliance, first signed in 1902 and renewed in 1905 and again in 1911, and entering the conflict in support of the Allies. The pro-German Japanese Army, which had studiously modelled itself on Prussia, but not the Navy, whose instructors had been British, would have preferred to support the Central Powers.

As events transpired, Japan gained considerably through her adherence to the Allies. At the peace treaty she was given a mandate under the League of Nations over the German colonial possessions she had occupied in the Marianas, the Carolines and the Marshalls, strategically important island groups in the

Pacific, and she was allowed also to retain the German concession at Tsingtao, on the Shantung Peninsula in China, which her troops had captured in the first days of the war.

With Germany's defeat, Prussian militarism was discredited and a wave of democratic sentiment, the natural consequence of the universal revulsion at the carnage of the war years, swept the world. Even Japan felt the stimulation of these cleansing winds and, as elsewhere, they led to the temporary eclipse of militarism. Despite the clumsiness and complexity of her political structure — which gave the militarists direct access to the Emperor, obliged them to select the War and Navy Ministers from high-ranking officers on the active list and enabled them to unseat Cabinets by inducing one or other of these ministers to resign — Japan was led from 1921 onwards by liberal and mainly civilian governments, pledged to maintain peace. She accepted the naval limitations of the Washington Treaty of 1922 and of the London Conference of 1930 and signed also both the Four Power Treaty, confirming the *status quo* in the Pacific, and the Nine Power Treaty, guaranteeing the integrity of China, to whom she had to restore Tsingtao.

The economic unrest which followed the world depression, coupled with Japanese discontent at the naval limitations of the 1930 London Agreement, gave the militarists, long waiting in the wings, their opportunity. They seized it quickly and firmly, seeing in foreign adventures the road to national aggrandizement, loot and glory, and the solution to Japan's pressing economic problems.

In 1931, on a specious pretext, Japan struck at Manchuria. Defying the League of Nations, from which she withdrew in 1933, she set up the puppet State of Manchukuo and forced China to cede control of the adjoining province of Jehol. Japan also withdrew, as she was entitled to do, from the naval limitation agreements, which thereupon expired in 1936, and, ignoring the conditions of her tenure, refused access to her mandated islands, thus leading the world to conclude that she was busily fortifying them. Hitler meanwhile had risen to power and in November 1936 Germany and Japan signed the Anti-Comintern Pact.

Japan was now on the march in Asia as the Nazis were in Europe and there was no holding back the militarists. In 1937, following an incident which was almost certainly stage managed by the Japanese Army, the undeclared war against China, with all its attendant affronts to the British and the Americans, was launched. In the face of the storm clouds gathering over Europe, Japan's leaders correctly divined that neither Britain nor America would actively intervene in Asia, however much both might chide and condemn. They therefore continued unmolested their plans for expansion. The war was extended to south China in May 1938, when Japanese troops landed at Amoy, some 300 miles north-east of Hong Kong; in October, landing a force at Bias Bay, only thirty-five miles north-east of Hong Kong, the Japanese advanced westward and occupied Canton, and in February 1939 they seized the island of Hainan, within easy striking distance of Indo-China.

Hitler's invasion of Denmark and Norway in April 1940, his conquest of Holland and Belgium in May and the surrender of France on June 21, were followed in Japan by the appointment of Prince Fuminaro Konoye, who had been Premier at the time of the Japanese invasion of China in 1937, as Prime Minister, with General Hideki Tojo, leader of the powerful Army group determined to conquer East Asia, as War Minister, and the aggressive nationalist, Mr Yosuke Matsuoka, who had led Japan from the League of Nations, as Foreign Minister. With the acquiescence of the French Government, the new Japanese administration quickly moved troops into northern French Indo-China.

These events heightened tension between Japan and the United States, and in the same month that the Konoye Government took office the Americans abrogated their commercial treaty with Japan. Following this, President Roosevelt, exercising powers conferred on him by Congress, stopped the export of scrap iron, aviation fuel, machine tools and other war materials to Japan and at the same time stepped up American aid to China. In September, Germany, Italy and Japan concluded the Tripartite Pact and in April 1941, shortly before Hitler's attack on Russia, Japan signed — for what it was worth — a neutrality pact with the Soviet Union. In July, again with French approval, the Japanese occupied southern Indo-China, whereupon America, Britain and the Netherlands froze all Japanese assets and imposed an oil embargo. With the imposition of these economic sanctions, war became inevitable unless Japan was prepared to relinquish her ambition of establishing a Co-Prosperity Sphere in East Asia, and the chances of this became remote on October 17, when the Japanese Government was reconstructed with General Tojo as Prime Minister.

The four years war with China, which Japan had been vigorously but vainly seeking to bring to an end, had witnessed a great expansion of Japan's armed services and of her industrial capacity to wage war. Economically, however, she was still incapable of sustaining a long war against a first-rate power because, first, she lacked access to vital raw materials; second, her industrial resources were inadequate; and third, her merchant marine was barely sufficient to satisfy her peacetime needs. Her stockpiles of oil and other essential war materials, for the most part, would not last more than two years, but as her armed services were already on a war footing and were adequately equipped, with sufficient immediate reserves, she was as prepared as she ever would be for a short war even against opponents possessing enormous resources and great industrial potential.

The Japanese Army at the time of Pearl Harbour consisted of fifty-one active service divisions, ten depot divisions serving as training units, and probably the equivalent of twenty-nine or thirty divisions in the form of independent brigades and garrison troops. She thus already had trained and mobilized between a million and a million and a quarter men, while conscription, with its two-year period of service, had given her an immediately available trained reserve not far short of two million men. As with the Navy and Air Force, most of her Army units and a substantial part of her reservists had seen recent active service in China and were experienced and battle-tested.

The individual Japanese soldier was fanatically brave, obedient, inured to hardship and capable of great physical endurance, but the officers lacked initiative and when plans went awry were often at a loss how to act. Intelligence, communications and supply were spheres in which the Japanese were weak, but their engineers were efficient, particularly in speedy road-making and bridge-building, and all branches of the Army were skilled in amphibious and landing operations, for which the shipping branch of the engineers had developed a variety of landing craft which they handled efficiently.

As the official Australian historian stresses:[1] 'The tactics and equipment, the strengths and weaknesses of the Japanese Army of 1941 were products largely of the long war in China against stubborn soldiers lightly armed and generally ill-led, but cunning guerillas fighting in terrain which presented immense difficulties to the movements of mechanized forces. Hence, largely, came the Japanese skill in landing operations and road-making and bridging; their changing organization and tendency towards forming *ad hoc* forces; their relatively light equipment and reliance on mortars and small guns rather than on the standard field-gun, and on light tanks; their emphasis on envelopment tactics; partly also their development of a large and grimly efficient corps of military police (Kempei Tai) possessing wide powers and trained to employ those powers ruthlessly.'

As with its American counterpart, the Japanese Air Force was not a separate service, the Army and the Navy each having its own independent force. The Army Air Force, primarily responsible for ground support to the land forces, had a strength of about 2,000 first-line aircraft and 2,500 pilots, of whom about half had seen combat in China or against the stronger Soviet Air Force in the Manchurian border fighting of May-September 1939. The Army pilots, who received about 300 hours' training before being posted to tactical units, had not been trained to operate over water. The Navy Air Force, charged with supporting the surface fleets and responsible for coastal defence, sea reconnaissance, antisubmarine patrols and convoy protection, had an operational strength of some 3,000 aircraft and 3,500 pilots, of whom the élite were the carrier pilots. About 10 per cent of the land-based naval pilots had combat experience in China.

Co-operation between the two Air Forces was weak in all spheres. For the most part, the Army aircraft were regarded and handled as tactical weapons for the close-range support of ground forces. The Navy, although it took a broader view, did not appreciate the strategic potentialities of air power. As a result there had been little development of aircraft for troop-carrying or supply-dropping and no attempt to establish a bomber force for long-range, sustained attacks on rear areas. The division of the forces extended into the production field, where both competed for production facilities and raw materials and neither made much effort to exchange information for the benefit of the aircraft industry. The latter was incapable of supplying a continuous flow of new aircraft to replace wastage and maintain reserves. The training organizations, of which the Navy's was the better, were likewise inadequate.

Of the Japanese aircraft only one was outstanding. This was the fast, highly manœuvrable but somewhat vulnerable single-seater Mitsubishi A6M Zero-Sen fighter, the carrier-borne version of which became known to the Allies as the Zeke and the land-based as the Zero. It was common to both the Army and the Navy, and the model employed at the outbreak of war was armed with two 7.7-mm. machine-guns and two 20-mm. cannon, had a speed of 336 m.p.h. at 19,685 ft., and a service ceiling of 33,790 ft. It had a range of 1,580 miles.[2]

The Japanese Navy, lavishly modernized in the years immediately before the outbreak of war, possessed eleven battleships, six fleet and four light aircraft carriers, eighteen 8-inch gun cruisers, twenty-one light cruisers with 6-inch or smaller guns, one hundred destroyers, of which about half were vessels of from 1,300 to 2,000 tons built in the 1930s, and sixty-three submarines, of which forty-two were large vessels of between 1,600 and 2,400 tons. In the battleship *Yamato,* laid down in 1937, Japan possessed the largest and most heavily armed ship in the world. She had an overall length of 866 ft., a standard displacement of 63,700 tons, and mounted nine 18.1-inch guns in her main armament. Her sister, *Musashi,* was not commissioned until 1942. The earlier battleships, two of which mounted 16-inch and the remainder 14-inch guns, were unremarkable vessels, but generally faster than their opposite numbers in the Allied fleets. The Japanese cruisers were both faster and more powerfully gunned, though less well protected, than their Allied counterparts. By Western standards all ships were extravagantly manned, but as recruitment was by conscription no manning difficulties were experienced. Training was rigorous and thorough. During the China war the Navy had built up an invaluable fleet of small transports, patrol craft and gunboats, and had developed efficient and flexible Special Naval Landing Forces, the equivalent of marines in the opposing navies.

Like the aircraft industry, the shipbuilding industry was insufficiently developed to replace losses of warships and merchantmen, even had the supply of steel and other materials been adequate. Repair and maintenance facilities were likewise deficient. The merchant navy had been substantially modernized during the 1930s, old and slow vessels being replaced by new and fast ones. After 1938, however, merchant shipbuilding had declined sharply because of the need to divert steel and shipyards to naval construction. At the outbreak of war the Japanese merchant fleet totalled 5,916,000 tons of steel vessels of 500 tons gross and over, and just under 2,000,000 tons of wooden junks.

The strengths and weaknesses of the Japanese armed services had been accurately assessed by military and naval observers, but these reports were largely ignored. As a result, the ability and efficiency of the Japanese in war constantly surprised and confounded the Allies in the first months of the war.

The Japanese Higher Command was complex. Japanese Imperial Headquarters, formed late in 1937, was headed by the Chiefs of Staff of the Army and Navy and was concerned primarily with operational plans. Each service planned its own operations, subject to the Emperor's approval, and to ensure co-operation and co-ordination between them there had to be mutual agreement between the two Chiefs of Staff. If this were not forthcoming, inaction resulted. Cabinet had little or no control over operational planning and was merely responsible

for the economic and political administration of the nation and
for the provision of the material and manpower required by
the armed services. On the naval side, however, the Commander-in-Chief of the Combined Fleet also originated
operational plans, although ultimately he was required to win
the approval of the Chief of the Naval General Staff before
these could be put into action. The Supreme War Council,
composed of members of the Board of Field Marshals and
Admirals, the War and Navy Ministers, the Chiefs of Staff of
the Army and Navy, and other high officers appointed by the
Emperor, was unwieldy and purely advisory.

Japanese peacetime planning, like that of the United States
and the British Commonwealth, was based until at least the end
of 1940 on fighting one adversary—the British Commonwealth,
the United States or the Soviet Union separately—not any two
or all three. Early in 1941 planning was placed on a more
realistic basis. The securing of the Southern Area, vital to
Japan if she were to obtain the natural resources and raw
materials essential to her expansionist policy, was now planned
on the basis that she would have to fight simultaneously the
British Commonwealth, the United States and the Netherlands.
Not until July, however, did the planners assume that war
would occur before the year's end.

Meanwhile, Admiral Yamamoto conceived the idea of a
carrier-borne attack on Pearl Harbour. He was convinced that
the United States would enter the war no matter what happened
and for this reason believed it essential the U.S. Pacific Fleet
should be prevented from intervening against Japanese operations in the Philippines, Malaya and the Netherlands East
Indies. In January 1941 he directed a preliminary study to be
made of the operation. The first planning was carried out in
great secrecy and the project was not disclosed to Admiral
Osami Nagano, Chief of the Naval General Staff, until September. Nagano and his staff at first strongly opposed the plan
on the ground that the operation would be certain to bring the
United States into the war against Japan, but Yamamoto convinced him this was inevitable in any event, and Nagano then
approved the proposal.

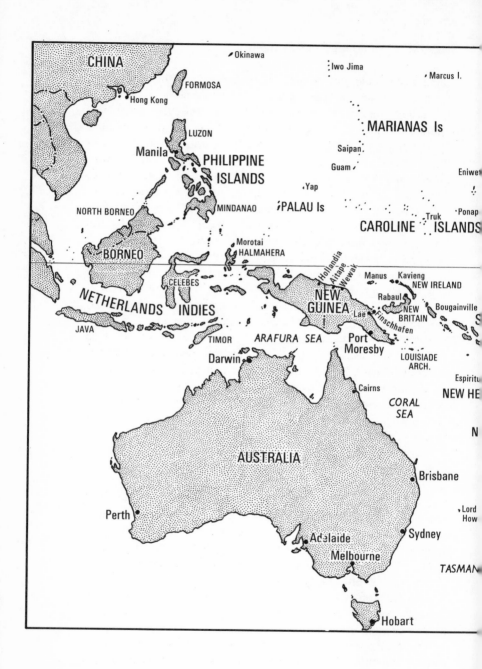

· Midway

·• Oahu HAWAIIAN ISLANDS
ke I.   ⊛ ⚬·⚬
                        🐚 Hawaii

N O R T H   P A C I F I C   O C E A N

Wotje MARSHALL Is   ·
·⁝·
·.   · Maloelap
t ·.   ·⁝·
·,
Makin·   ·Fanning I.
Tarawa· GILBERT Is   • Christmas I.
·⁝·   ·   EQUATOR
◄ Ocean I. ·.·
                 · ·.   ·
                 ·⁝ PHOENIX Is   ·
N Is.   ·⁝ ELLICE Is
            ·,·
TA CRUZ Is   ·⁝·
                                               ·⁝·
                   ⊸SAMOA ·   MARQUESAS
                    ·⁝·   Is   ·
FIJI⊸ ·⁝·   ·⁝   SOCIETY ·· ·.   ·
🝆🝆 ·   ·   Is ·.·
 o   ·⁝·
                 ·⁝ TONGA   ·⁝·
IA   ·   COOK Is
                              TUBUAI Is

S O U T H   P A C I F I C   O C E A N
orfolk I.   ·
                        ·

      ⬧Auckland
A   ⬧
      ⬧NEW ZEALAND
      ⬧Wellington
      ⬧Christchurch·   MERCATOR'S PROJECTION

2. The Pacific Ocean theatre

The plan for the advance into the Southern Region was completed quickly. It was governed by three important factors — first, the need for continuing the war against China and for guarding the Manchurian border so long as Soviet divisions were stationed there; second, the necessity of capturing early and if possible undamaged the oil-producing centres in Borneo and Sumatra; and third, weather conditions over the widely separated areas of operation. The first, coupled with the shortage of merchant shipping, reduced to eleven divisions and about 1,200 aircraft the forces available for the capture of the Southern Region, necessitating the employment of the same formations in successive operations and thus calling for a carefully integrated time-table. The second meant that economic rather than strategical considerations determined the first points of attack and the order in which different operations were carried out and placed the emphasis on surprise throughout. The third dictated the timing. The campaign had to start before the north-east monsoon in the South China Sea and the winter gales in the North Pacific reached their full force, and occupation of the Southern Region must be completed before the end of the Manchurian winter, since during those months attack by the Soviet was unlikely, if not impossible. The planners chose early December for the commencement of the war and provided for the occupation of the Philippines in fifty days, of Malaya in one hundred, and of the Netherlands East Indies in one hundred and fifty.

After considerable discussion the Army and Navy agreed to attack the Philippines and Malaya simultaneously, at the same time staging the air attack on Pearl Harbour, to then advance southwards and capture the Netherlands East Indies from the east and the west, and finally, to occupy Burma. The seizure of the Southern Region accomplished, a strong defensive perimeter was to be formed and consolidated against Allied counter-attacks. This perimeter was to run from the Kuriles through Wake Island, the Marshall and Gilbert Islands, the Bismarck Archipelago, New Guinea, Timor, Java, Sumatra and Malaya to Burma and the Indian border. How this plan was carried out and the forces arrayed against the Japanese are dealt with in the subsequent narrative.

NOTES AND REFERENCES

1. Lionel Wigmore, *The Japanese Thrust*, 117.
2. William Green, *Famous Fighters of the Second World War* (London, 1960), 50-6; William Green, *War Planes of the Second World War, Fighters* (London, 1960), III, 43-6; Okumiya, Horikoshi and Caidin, *Zero* (London, 1957), 350.

FURTHER READING:

The Japanese armed services and plans are described fully in the official histories, of which the most readable are Major-General S. Woodburn Kirby's *The Loss of Singapore* (London, 1957); the first volume of the British official history, *The War Against Japan;* Lionel Wigmore's *The Japanese Thrust* (Canberra, 1957), in the Australian Official History series; and Professor S. E. Morison's *The Rising Sun in the Pacific, 1931-April, 1942* (London, 1948), the third volume of his *History of U.S. Naval Operations in World War II. The War Department Chief of Staff: Pre-War Plans and Preparations,* by M. S. Watson (Washington, 1950), in the *U.S. Army in World War II* series, *The Army Air Forces in World War II,* I, *Plans and Early Operations, January, 1939 to August, 1942* (Chicago, 1950), and *The Campaigns of the Pacific War* by the Naval Analysis Division of the U.S. Strategic Bombing Survey (Washington, 1946) should also be consulted. On the naval side, the relevant volumes of the British and Australian Official Histories — Captain S. W. Roskill's *The War at Sea,* I (London, 1954) and II (London, 1956) and G. Hermon Gill's *Royal Australian Navy, 1939-1942* (Canberra, 1957) — will be found useful. *How the Jap Army Fights* (London, 1943), although propagandist, furnishes much useful information.

three

THE FALL
OF THE PHILIPPINES

Before the bombs fell at Pearl Harbour other Japanese air units had begun attacking widely scattered targets thousands of miles from Hawaii, and Japanese convoys stood off their selected landing beaches, steamed secretly along the high seas or prepared to leave port. In a vast, intricate and carefully synchronized movement of troops and equipment, the Japanese employed over 500 merchant vessels, totalling almost 1,500,000 tons. Tens of thousands of men, with all the paraphernalia of modern war, were, for the first time, on the move in Asian seas.

The unfortified outpost of Guam, situated in the jaws of the hungry enemy, was quickly swallowed. Its small garrison, lacking air and artillery support, was attacked by aircraft from Saipan as early as 0830 on December 8. That day and the next the Japanese pilots bombed and strafed at will, and on the 10th an invasion force landed in overwhelming strength. The fighting lasted 25 minutes and when it ceased the flag of the Rising Sun floated over Guam, the first U.S. territory to be captured by the Japanese.

At Wake Island, 1,300 miles away to the east, 36 Japanese bombers swept in at noon of the 8th under cover of a rain squall. Being without radar, the garrison had no warning of their approach, and seven of Wake's twelve obsolete Grumman Wildcat (F4F) fighters, which had been flown in from the carrier *Enterprise* as recently as December 4, were destroyed where they stood on the air strip. The Pan-American Airways flying-boat station on Peale Island, one of the three islands of the Wake Group, was severely damaged and ten civilians killed, but the white-hulled clipper riding the calm waters of the lagoon, although riddled by machine-gun bullets, was able to take off that afternoon, overloaded with civilians, on the 1,025-mile flight to Midway. The air attacks continued on the following two days and before 0500 on the 11th a small invasion fleet was off Wake, the ships rolling and pitching in the seas whipped up by the strong north-east trade wind.

The garrison's 522 men, mostly Marines, were armed with 3-inch and 5-inch guns emplaced in three strongpoints, but half the 3-inch batteries lacked crews to man them and only one had its full allowance of fire control equipment. Contemptuous of the atoll's defences, the expedition's commander, Rear-Admiral Sadamichi Kajioka, began his bombardment and closed to within 4,500 yards of the shore. The reply of the 5-inch batteries was prompt and effective. The admiral's flagship, the light cruiser *Yubari* (3,500, 1923), was hit and then forced to retire, the destroyer *Hayate* (1,270, 1925) was blown up, sinking immediately, and both the remaining destroyers and one of the transports were damaged. Four Wildcats, the only aircraft remaining to the defenders, bombed and strafed the retiring enemy ships and blew up the destroyer *Kisaragi* (1,315, 1925), from which there were no survivors.

Having lost two destroyers and over 500 men, Kajioka withdrew to Kwajalein, whence he had sailed so confidently on the 9th, to repair his ships and reorganize and strengthen his force for a second attempt to capture Wake. Spurred on by their loss of face, the Japanese moved swiftly and determinedly. The 450 troops of the Special Naval Landing Force in the first expedition were raised to a strength of 2,000 in the second; the tempo of the raids by land-based aircraft was increased and, to lend added weight to the air pounding, the carriers *Soryu* and *Hiryu,* with an escort of heavy cruisers and destroyers, were diverted from the returning Pearl Harbour Striking Force. So quickly did the Japanese act that Kajioka sailed again on the 20th.

Immediately after the Japanese repulse and before his removal on the 17th from active service in the Navy, Admiral Kimmel, realizing the Japanese would return to Wake, organized three carrier forces to evacuate the island's garrison. After the debacle of Pearl Harbour he hoped to restore his reputation by winning a battle over the enemy's covering forces or at least by smashing his light forces and transports off the beaches. On paper the plan held promise, but its execution was bungled. The American task force commanders moved too slowly and their leadership lacked drive and determination. When the operation was abandoned on the 22nd — the 23rd at Wake — the task force which should have been off the island was still almost 400 miles away.[1]

Kajioka launched his second attempt before dawn on the 23rd. This time, in an effort to secure tactical surprise, he delivered no preliminary bombardment. The troops landed simultaneously on Wilkes, the third island of the Group, and the southern shore of Wake at first light. The 100 men who landed on Wilkes, where the defences were least advanced, were almost wiped out, but on Wake the enemy made a firm lodgment and built up strength rapidly. Without air support, its last two Wildcats having been shot down in a carrier-borne raid the previous day, its slender defences were battered by the air pounding. Heavily outnumbered, the garrison surrendered at 0730, although fighting on Wilkes continued until the afternoon. Fifty-two U.S. servicemen and 70 civilians had been killed; 470 officers and men of the armed services and 1,146 civilians, principally aircraft construction workers, were taken prisoner. Total Japanese losses were 820 killed and 333 wounded.

In the Philippines, Kimmel's 0800 broadcast of the Pearl Harbour attack was received at 0230 on the 8th. Here, late in July, 61-year-old Major-General Douglas MacArthur had

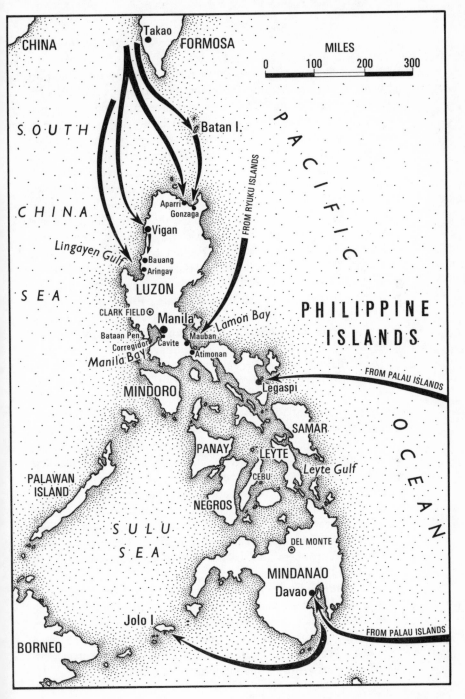

CHINA

Takao

FORMOSA

MILES

0   100   200   300

S O U T H

P A C I F I C

Batan I.

C H I N A

FROM RYUKU ISLANDS

Aparri
Gonzaga

Vigan

Lingayen Gulf

Bauang
Aringay

S E A

LUZON

CLARK FIELD⊙   Manila

PHILIPPINE

Lamon Bay

ISLANDS

Bataan Pen   Mauban
Corregidor Cavite
Manila Bay   Atimonan

MINDORO

Legaspi

FROM PALAU ISLANDS

O C E A N

SAMAR

PANAY   LEYTE

PALAWAN
ISLAND

CEBU

Leyte Gulf

NEGROS

SULU

DEL MONTE ⊙

SEA

MINDANAO

Davao

Jolo I

FROM PALAU ISLANDS

BORNEO

3. The Japanese landings in the Philippines

been recalled to active service in the U.S. Army from his post as military adviser to the Philippine Government. On July 26, President Roosevelt had issued a decree bringing the armed forces of the Philippines into the service of the United States, and the same day the U.S. Army Forces in the Far East had been formed, with headquarters in Manila and with MacArthur as Commander-in-Chief, with the rank of Lieutenant-General. The Americans had promised the Filipinos their independence in 1946, and to enable them to assume responsibility for their defence MacArthur had been engaged in creating land, sea and air forces, which by Independence Day were to comprise a small regular army of 10,000, backed by a conscript reserve of 400,000, an air force of 100 fast bombers supported by fighter and reconnaissance aircraft, and in place of a navy an off-shore patrol of 36 fast torpedo-boats. Progress toward the attainment of these forces had been slow and when war came the Philippine armed services were small numerically and, for the most part, poorly trained and equipped.

Anticipating heavy air raids at daybreak on the 8th, the American-Filipino garrison took up its battle stations immediately. But dawn broke without any appearance of the enemy, except far to the south over Davao Gulf, in Mindanao, where the anchored seaplane tender *William B. Preston* (1,190, 1940) was attacked ineffectually by carrier-based dive-bombers and their fighter escorts.[2] Not until about 0930 did the first Japanese aircraft appear over Luzon, the principal island of the group, and they struck not at Manila and its nearby airfields, but at Tuguegarao, an airfield in central northern Luzon, and at military installations in the summer capital of Baguio. As these bombers flew in toward Lingayen Gulf, fighters took off to intercept them and the heavy bombers were sent aloft, so as to avoid destruction on the ground.

The comparative peacefulness of the skies over Luzon was not of the enemy's making. Unknown to the Americans, fog had closed the crowded Japanese airfields less than 700 miles away on Formosa and the bombers and fighters, which were to have taken off at dawn to raid the Philippines, were grounded.

MacArthur's air commander, Major-General Lewis H.

Brereton, was at Far East headquarters by about 0500. He wanted to beat the Japanese to the punch and sought permission to raid the Formosan airfields or the port of Takao in southern Formosa with the 18 Flying Fortresses (B-17's) still at Clark, the remaining 17 having recently been moved to Del Monte, in Mindanao. The later recollections of those concerned — Brereton, MacArthur and the latter's chief of staff, Brigadier-General Richard K. Sutherland — conflict sharply as to what transpired and the contemporary written record is defective, but there is no doubt that the impatient Brereton was told to wait. Less than three hours later he again pressed his request and was again refused permission. Apparently Sutherland considered a reconnaissance essential before a raid could be undertaken with any prospect of success, while a radio signal he sent later that day indicates that MacArthur was thinking in terms of a raid the following morning. However, about 1010 Brereton was told he might prepare for a reconnaissance mission and an hour later was authorized to bomb Formosa, although Sutherland later claimed Brereton subsequently cancelled the operation.

The concept behind the air strategy of the United States in the Philippines was to utilize it as a base for offensive operations against Japan, for which purpose 165 modern heavy bombers were to be stationed there. At the outbreak of war, however, only 35 had been delivered. Formosa lay beyond the range of the American land-based fighters of the day and no attempt had been made to provide fighter escorts by adding a carrier to the Asiatic Fleet, which was based on Manila. However, the Flying Fortress had been designed expressly for operating beyond fighter range and although the number at Brereton's disposal did not constitute a decisive striking force, the alternatives to their offensive employment were their evacuation from Luzon, or even from the Philippines, or their destruction on the ground. One would therefore expect Brereton to suggest bombing Formosa, for which operation he considered his somewhat scanty target data sufficient.

Whether with his small force the risk was justified, whether the bombers would have located the fog-enshrouded Formosan airfields or the ports in which the invasion fleets were assembling and loading, and whether they would have inflicted any worthwhile damage or been blasted out of the air by fighters and anti-aircraft fire are questions for intriguing but unprofitable speculation. MacArthur said the raid would have been suicidal and denied ever having spoken to Brereton about it.[3] However, the Japanese feared such a raid and anxiously sweated it out on the ground until, with the clearing of the fog, they at last got their aircraft into the air and, later, their convoys out of their ports.[4]

Whatever the precise course of events that morning, the die had been cast by 1100. The Japanese planes which had raided Tuguegarao and Baguio had left for home and the plotting board at Air Headquarters on Nielson Field was clear of bandits. With the sounding of the all clear, the American planes began to land — the fighters, which had failed to intercept the raiders, to refuel, and the bombers to prepare for the afternoon's strike, should it eventuate. By 1130 almost all American aircraft were back on the ground.

It was then that a large blip of incoming aircraft appeared on the only two operational radar sets and simultaneously reports began to flow in by telephone and telegram from postmasters who formed Luzon's observer corps. The enemy planes were successively reported all along the north-west coast. The Americans had ample warning, but, due to inexplicable bungling, Clark Field, the most important of the airfields around Manila, either received no warning of the approaching raid or did not heed it, and fighters at Del Carmen, ordered to cover Clark Field, did not take off because of a thick dust haze.

The time at which the first Japanese bombers appeared over Clark is a matter of controversy, but it was somewhere between 1215 and 1240. Whatever the exact time, the Flying Fortresses were still refuelling and loading their bombs, and the fighters were preparing to take off again when the first Japanese formation of 27 planes bombed from 22,000 to 25,000 feet. A second similar formation followed immediately, and 34 Zeros then strafed at low level. The attack lasted an hour. Three or four Curtiss Warhawks (P-40's) managed to get airborne, but five others were blasted by bombs as they taxied for take-off. The squadron of obsolete Republics (P-35's) at Del Carmen belatedly beat the dust haze and, though hopelessly inferior to the Zero, got into action, but by then Clark Field was a shambles of shattered and blazing buildings and wrecked aircraft. At Iba, the other field attacked, 12 Warhawks, low on fuel after a fruitless patrol over the South China Sea, were landing to refuel as 54 twin-engined bombers and 50 Zeros swept in, and all but two were destroyed. Fighter opposition at Clark and Iba, as it had also been at Pearl Harbour, was negligible, and the relatively light anti-aircraft defences were ineffective. The anti-aircraft guns could not reach the high-flying bombers and there was a high percentage of duds in their ammunition, one observer stating that of every six shells fired only one actually exploded.[5]

At the time of these attacks the U.S. Far East Air Force possessed about 150 aircraft suitable for combat, including the 35 Flying Fortresses and 104 P-40 fighters. When the raiders headed for home only 17 of the Flying Fortresses remained operational, and 53 P-40's, three P-35's and about 30 other aircraft had been destroyed and many others seriously damaged. Casualties totalled 80 killed and 150 wounded, while buildings and installations on both fields had been destroyed, burnt out or heavily damaged. The Japanese lost seven fighters.

The enemy air attacks continued on the following days. Only on the 11th, when bad weather over Formosa kept the Japanese grounded, was there a brief respite. Nichols and Nielson Fields, two other important bases near Manila, were hit as heavily as Clark and Iba, and by December 17, American air strength in the Philippines had been whittled down to a mere handful of fighters. The Flying Fortresses were withdrawn to Darwin, in Australia, where fourteen landed at Batchelor Field between December 16 and 21. Despite the ample warning the Americans had received and the fog over Formosa on the 8th, which should have robbed the Japanese of tactical surprise, the enemy air force had attained results far beyond its expectations.

Within a week of the outbreak of hostilities American air

power in the Philippines had been rendered impotent and the great natural harbour of Manila, with its extensive facilities, made untenable as a base for the U.S. Asiatic Fleet. The enemy air blows against the Navy had been as disastrous as those against the Air Force. Cavite naval yard, with its repair shops, warehouses, barracks, radio station and other installations, had been gutted by a fire which had raced through it out of control, the submarine *Sealion* (1,450, 1939) had been sunk, 230 torpedoes, vital for the continuance of offensive operations by the twenty-seven submarines based on Manila, had been blown up, and all seven aircraft of a Catalina (PBY) squadron at Olongapo had been destroyed at their moorings in a single raid, thus depriving the Navy in one swoop of a third of its reconnaissance aircraft. By the 14th the units of Admiral Thomas C. Hart's Asiatic Fleet, except the submarines and a few motor torpedo-boats, gunboats and other small craft, had fled south to distant British and Dutch bases. The 4th Marines, who, except for detachments at Peking and Tientsin, had been transferred from Shanghai to the Philippines only a few days before Pearl Harbour, were handed over to MacArthur to serve as ground forces. The merchant shipping in Manila Bay, which had not been seriously attacked, began to put to sea on the 9th, all but one of the 40 or 50 vessels, many loaded with valuable cargoes, finally escaping.

The first Japanese landings, made by small forces for the sole purpose of seizing airfields for their short-range fighters, began as early as the 8th. At dawn that day defenceless Batan Island, to the north of Luzon between Luzon Strait and Bashi Channel, was occupied and from its airfield near Basco Japanese fighters operated next morning to protect the dawn landing of Colonel Toru Tanaka's 2,000 men at Aparri, a port at the mouth of the Cagayan River less than 300 miles from Manila. Having landed only two companies, the enemy was forced by the strong north-east wind and heavy seas to transfer landing operations to a more sheltered anchorage at Gonzaga, 20 miles along the coast to the east, but the Filipino garrison failed to exploit this opportunity and tamely retired southwards without firing a shot.

The rest of the Japanese got ashore at Gonzaga, where an attack by P-40's and five B-17's set off the depth charges of a minesweeper and forced her to beach, but it was 1300 before they joined their comrades in Aparri. However, so swiftly did the Tanaka Detachment then move that by 0530 on the 12th it had won Tuguegarao airfield, 50 miles to the south.

The weather also interfered with the landing of the 2,000-strong Kanno Detachment at Pandan, on the north bank of the Abra River, on Luzon's western shore. Only a few men were ashore when landing operations were suspended, but no Filipino troops were near and by 1030 the Japanese had occupied the port of Vigan, three miles north of Pandan and 220 miles from Manila. Raids by Flying Fortresses and escorting fighters inflicted casualties, sunk a minesweeper and so severely damaged the transports *Oigawa Maru* and *Takao Maru* that both had to be beached. However, the Kanno Detachment completed its landing and by the evening of the 11th had advanced 50 miles to seize the provincial capital of Laoag and its airfield, whither the Japanese airmen moved next day.

In south Luzon Major-General Naoki Kimura's detachment, 2,500 strong, came ashore at Legaspi, near the tip of the Bicol Peninsula, in Albay Gulf, early on the 12th and, there being no American troops within 150 miles, secured the airfield and the terminus of the Manila railway by 0900. Later landings at Davao, in Mindanao, and at Jolo, in the Sulu Archipelago, cut Luzon's communications to the south, but their real object was to facilitate the invasion of Borneo and the Netherlands East Indies, and they played no part in the conquest of Luzon.

The air attacks and the preliminary Luzon landings clarified the pattern of Japanese strategy in the Philippines. MacArthur realized that serious invasion was at hand. Lieutenant-General Masaharu Homma's XIV Army, part of the powerful Southern Army under General Count Hisaichi Terauchi, would land on Luzon in strength now that its Army and Navy air components, respectively the 5th Air Group under Lieutenant-General Hideyoshi Obata and the 11th Air Fleet commanded by Vice-Admiral Nishizo Tsukahara, had shattered the U.S. Far East Army Air Force, had occupied airfields on Luzon and had driven the Asiatic Fleet from Filipino waters. The landings could be expected somewhere along the 120-mile long eastern shore of Lingayen Gulf, to the north of Manila, and to the south at Batangas Bay, on Luzon's south-west coast. At both places the beaches were suitable for landings and, once ashore, the enemy could launch a two-pronged drive for Manila by direct routes over favourable terrain.

Following his appointment as Commander-in-Chief, MacArthur had revised America's pre-war plans for the defence of the Philippines. He had decided that instead of fighting a defensive battle and slowly withdrawing into the Bataan Peninsula, as previously had been planned, he would take the offensive and defeat the Japanese on the beaches. His optimism was infectious, and his plan was endorsed by Washington. More and more reinforcements and more and more equipment were diverted to the Philippines, but although MacArthur's command was markedly strengthened between July and December, when war came, the bulk of the promised reinforcements of men, aircraft, guns, vehicles and other equipment were on the high seas or still scheduled for early shipment from the United States.

MacArthur, supremely confident of his ability to hold the Philippines for at least three months, vigorously but unsuccessfully urged a reversal of the fundamental basis of Allied global strategy, so that instead of first defeating Germany and Italy the main weight of American armed might would be thrown firstly against the Japanese in the Pacific. He repeatedly urged Washington to organize a relief expedition and to push it across the Pacific. With the resources then available, adoption of this plan was impossible.

Like almost every other Allied leader, military and civilian, MacArthur underrated Japan's ability to wage a far-ranging offensive war of short duration. In October he had informed an Australian Minister, Sir Earle Page, that after five years intermittent war in China, Japan was over-extended and incapable of undertaking another major struggle without a long period of recuperation.[6] He likewise under-estimated the fighting capacity and skill of the Japanese and valued too highly the fighting worth of his treasured Philippine Army, which, despite its shortcomings in leadership, training and equipment, he considered capable of repelling the Japanese.

For the defence of the Philippines MacArthur had a regular garrison of 31,000 officers and men, including the Philippine Scouts, a locally enlisted corps about 12,000 strong, which was part of the United States Army, and the Philippine Army, which within a week of the outbreak of hostilities totalled 102,000 men. A large part of the latter, however, was but partially trained, many of its units never having even fired a rifle, and the whole was deficient in equipment. In particular it lacked machine-guns, automatic rifles, mortars and artillery — at the end of September it had possessed only forty-eight 75-mm. guns of World War I vintage and eight delivered to one division on December 7 incredibly had neither sights nor fire control equipment. The largest unit composed entirely of Americans was the 2,000-strong U.S. 31st Infantry Regiment, which with the Philippine Scouts formed the well-trained but not fully equipped Philippine Division.

The North Luzon Force, commanded by Major-General Jonathan M. Wainwright, was composed of the 11th, 21st and 31st Philippine Army divisions, with a Philippine Scout infantry battalion, the 26th Philippine Scout cavalry, two batteries of 155-mm. guns and one battery of 2.95-inch mountain guns. A fourth Philippine Army division, the 71st, was in reserve under MacArthur's own hand. Despite MacArthur's determination to defeat the Japanese on the beaches and his conviction that the enemy would land in Lingayen Gulf, little had been done to provide defences. At the beaches where the Japanese landed underwater and anti-tank obstacles had not been erected, wire had not been strung, mines had not been laid, pillboxes and trenches had not been constructed, and everywhere there was a shortage of medium and heavy guns.

The South Luzon Force, under Brigadier-General George M. Parker, Jr., was smaller and his two Philippine Army divisions — the 41st and 51st — were even less trained and equipped than Wainwright's divisions.

On the 10th the incursion into Lingayen Gulf of a Japanese

motor boat on reconnaissance led to widely publicized reports
that an invasion attempt had been defeated,[7] but the truth is
there was no battle of Lingayen Gulf. Reports of the approach
of an invasion force did not start to reach MacArthur's headquarters until December 18; and on the evening of the 20th,
units guarding the Lingayen beaches were warned that the
convoy could be expected off the mouth of the Gulf next
evening. Yet when the Japanese landed the Filipinos were
waiting on the beaches only at Bauang. The invasion force,
which had loaded, in some confusion and in much trepidation
of American bombers, at the Formosan ports of Kirun and
Takao, and at Mako in the Pescadores, was divided into three
groups, each of which was to land at a different place. The
76 Army and 9 Navy transports possessed 199 large and small
landing craft and carried a total of 43,110 Army, shipping
and Army Air Force personnel.

With their naval escort of 2 light cruisers, 16 destroyers and
numerous smaller craft, whose guns were to cover the landing,
the transports anchored in Lingayen Gulf between 0110 and
0430 on the 22nd. In the darkness of the wet night the ships
overshot their anchorages, so that, strung out over about 20
miles, they were some 8 miles farther from the selected beaches
than intended.[8] Heavy seas made the launching and loading of
the landing craft hazardous and gave the troops a rough trip
to the shore. The men were drenched by flying spray on the
way in and by the surf as they waded ashore. Many landing
craft were overturned and others driven so firmly on the beach
that they could not be refloated for hours. These difficulties
and mishaps dislocated the landing schedules, so that the second
waves could not be brought in on time, heavy equipment could
not be landed, and many transports had to seek more sheltered
anchorages. The experienced and hard-working shipping units,
however, managed during the day to land more men and also
mountain artillery and some armour.

Ashore on a 15-mile strip of coast from Bauang in the north,
to Agoo in the south, the Japanese met light and spasmodic
opposition, which was heaviest initially at Bauang. Here light
and heavy machine-gun fire met the invaders as they came

ashore, but the Filipinos had few machine-guns, their ammunition was largely defective, and they were quickly driven from their positions. Reinforced by the Tanaka Detachment — which after its landing on the 9th had proceeded to Vigan, where it picked up the Kanno Detachment and then had marched southwards down the coast — the Japanese fanned out to the east and south and by evening had a tenuous hold of the narrow coastal corridor between the sea and the Cordillera central range for 20 miles from Bauang southwards to Damortis and Rosario.

The Filipinos lacked the skill, determination and weapons necessary for the delivery of the strong, co-ordinated counter-attacks which alone at this critical stage might have thrown the Japanese back into the sea. The weather continued to hamper the enemy more than the defenders, but they contrived during the next three days to build up their forces ashore and with air support drove ahead. Here and there a Filipino formation fought staunchly, but the majority fled to the rear, disorganized and panic-stricken, as soon as the Japanese pressed them. By Christmas Eve the enemy held northern Luzon firmly and, having debouched on to the broad central plain, was preparing to march in strength on Manila.

During this period the invasion fleet offered a tempting and profitable target, but the Americans had little with which to hit it. Four 155-mm. guns at San Fabian and Dagupan ineffectively shelled the southernmost ships when they moved into the inner bay and the only air attack, made by four Flying Fortresses from Darwin, caused merely a few casualties and slight damage. Five submarines arrived when the Japanese Fleet was already in the Gulf and found the reef-snarled entrance so well guarded by destroyers that only the *S-38* (850, 1923) succeeded in entering. The shallow-draught transports presented difficult targets and the submarine's torpedoes proved defective, running four feet lower than the depth for which they were set. In consequence, *S-38* sank only the 5,445-ton converted mine-layer *Hayo Maru*. The *S-38* was under almost continuous attack and thrice ran aground, but escaped from the Gulf and returned safely to Manila. Outside the Gulf, near Vigan, the submarine *Seal* (1,448, 1938) sank the 850-ton freighter *Hayataka Maru,* but these were - the only vessels sunk by American submarines in Filipino waters — a humiliating result for an arm from which so much had been expected.[9]

The southern invasion force, numbering about 7,000 men under Lieutenant-General Susumu Morioka, commander of the 16th Division, dropped anchor in Lamon Bay, off the east coast, at 0130 on December 24. Originally, the Japanese had intended landing in Batangas Bay, on the south-west coast, where MacArthur expected them to come ashore and where the main body of the South Luzon Force was stationed. However, because of commitments elsewhere, the Japanese were compelled to reduce the air forces supporting the Philippines invasion and lack of air cover induced Southern Army head-quarters to transfer the southern operation to Lamon Bay. The beaches here were less suitable and the roads to Manila, running through mountainous country, less direct, but the selection of Lamon Bay secured for the Japanese the inestimable advantage of surprise.

The landings were made at dawn at three points — Mauban, in the north; Atimonan, 20 miles to the south, and Siain, seven miles further south. At Mauban and Atimonan the Filipinos fought stubbornly, but, too few in numbers and without artillery, were soon forced back. At Siain the enemy got ashore without difficulty, but did not link up with the Kimura Detachment, which had landed at Legaspi on the 12th, until the 27th. Nevertheless, the first day's operations put the Japanese firmly ashore and gained them a secure hold on the roads leading westwards across the Tayabas Mountains. Thus, by Christmas Eve the Japanese were poised, both north and south of Manila, for their drive on the capital.

By the 23rd MacArthur realized his plan to defeat the Japanese on the beaches had failed ignominiously. At 1100 next day he announced his adoption of the earlier plan of withdrawing into the Bataan Peninsula for a last ditch stand, so that use of Manila Bay might be denied the enemy as long as possible. President Manuel Quezon's government, the United States High Commissioner's office and MacArthur's headquarters moved at once to the fortified island of Corregidor, near the harbour entrance and close to the Bataan shore, and the work of improving defences and building up supplies began. Curiously, the Japanese strategists, in their pre-war planning, had disregarded the possibility of the American and Filipino forces falling back into the Bataan Peninsula and, believing the decisive battle of the campaign would be fought in front of Manila, had made no preparations to counter such a move.

This major change in MacArthur's tactics meant that supplies, stores and equipment of all kinds in Bataan and Corregidor required to be augmented. Hasty efforts were made to transfer stocks of food, ammunition, fuel and other necessities, as well as vehicles, guns and weapons, to Corregidor and Bataan and to destroy everything that could not be moved. Time was short and the confusion and muddle great. As there was only one road into Bataan, most supplies were moved by sea, but the units and labour which, under pre-war plans, were to have effected the transfer were in many instances no longer available now that battle had been joined. The shortage of manpower, vehicles and vessels often necessitated hurried improvisation and constantly caused delay.

Further, since civilian officials and some military personnel were not yet geared to the realities of war, their leisurely peace-time thinking caused mistakes. The order waiving a regulation prohibiting the removal of rice and sugar from one province to another was so long in arriving that 10,000,000 lb. of rice in the Government Rice Central at Cabanatuan could not be transferred before the town fell to the enemy. Again, Japanese-owned stocks in Manila warehouses might easily have been removed, but MacArthur's headquarters prohibited their seizure and instead of swelling the supplies in Bataan they had to be destroyed at the last moment to deny them to the enemy. Much that might have been removed was left behind and much that should have been destroyed fell intact into enemy hands. Pre-war plans to keep civilian refugees out of Bataan were never implemented, so that thousands more had to be fed than had been forecast. Yet a large quantity of stores and supplies was transferred to Bataan and Corregidor in the course of a few days.

On Boxing Day, MacArthur declared Manila an open city. Many of its inhabitants had already fled and now a new stream of refugees crowded the roads, complicating alike the movement of troops and the transference of supplies. Next day, Japanese bombers attacked the harbour area, doing great damage to port installations and wrecking many of the buildings in the Intramuros, the ancient walled city of the Spaniards. Manila, deserted and forlorn, its shops mostly shuttered and its empty streets littered with uncollected garbage, was ringed by flame and smoke as quantities of abandoned stores and equipment and stocks of oil blazed fiercely, and it reverberated to the thump of explosions as installations were demolished.

The withdrawal of the North and South Luzon Forces into Bataan demanded precise timing and close co-operation. It was fraught with danger. To reach the one road leading into the peninsula (except for a secondary road in the west, available to Wainwright's left wing alone), every man, gun and vehicle both north and south of Manila had to pass through the road junction of San Fernando, in Pampanga province. Here highways 3 and 10 met, and if the Japanese could seize the road junction quickly they might cut off a large proportion of both American Forces.

MacArthur's orders to Wainwright were to deny San Fernando to the enemy until January 8 by falling back slowly from one defensive position to another, delaying the enemy on each for as long as possible without risking destruction or jeopardizing a further retirement. Meanwhile, the South Luzon Force, adopting similar tactics, was to skirt Manila and march up Highway 3 to clear San Fernando in the early hours of the 8th.

The withdrawal of the North Luzon Force almost ended in disaster. Possessing air superiority, the Japanese gave the Americans and Filipinos no respite. On December 26 they hustled the defenders out of their line behind the Agno River, second of the five positions which had been reconnoitred and selected in peacetime and to which they had withdrawn on

When Japanese aircraft sank the battle cruiser HMS *Repulse,* above, and battleship HMS *Prince of Wales,* below, the British received a crippling blow to their defence of Malaya

Australian War Memorial

Above, '*Riding three or four abreast and talking and laughing, just as if they were going to a football match.*' A correspondent's description of the Japanese infantry's bicycle advance through Malaya. Below, Japanese soldiers in Kuala Lumpur

Australian War Memorial

Christmas Eve. A determined night attack smashed Wainwright's right flank, driving it back 10 miles, and in the evening
his centre was shattered. Extricating themselves with difficulty
and heavy loss, the Americans were too disorganized to stand
on the third line and by the morning of the 28th were holding
the fourth position, situated just below the centre of the North
Luzon plain. It ran for 25 miles from Tarlac in the west, to
Cabanatuan in the east, and was only some 30 miles north of
San Fernando. Wainwright ordered it held at all costs.

Homma paused to bring up armour, guns and more men.
He massed his main strength on his left and when his troops
attacked with skill and determination on the 29th their progress
was rapid. The American right was outflanked and forced back,
Cabanatuan being captured that night. In a vigorous pursuit
next day, the 30th, the Japanese by late afternoon had driven
14 miles down Highway 5, which, passing to the east of
Mount Arayat (3,867 ft.) and the 20-mile long Candaba swamp,
joined Highway 3, leading to Manila, south of Plaridel. Simultaneously, other forces struck westward from Cabanatuan,
caused heavy casualties to Wainwright's centre and threatened
to outflank his left, where Tarlac fell at noon. The entire
American-Filipino line was unhinged and the tired troops retired
to their last defensive position, barely 20 miles in front of San
Fernando.

In six days the North Luzon Force had been driven back
50 miles. Its men, worn out by heavy fighting and constant
marching, and subject to continuous strafing and bombing, had
suffered considerable casualties and were dispirited. Some units
had retired precipitately without firing a shot and the premature
blowing of bridges had cut off others, sometimes with heavy
casualties and the loss of valuable tanks, guns and vehicles.

The new line, running for 15 miles from Bamban in the
west, to Mount Arayat in the east, lay to the west of the
Candaba Swamp, and, when the retiring troops occupied it in
some confusion on the morning of the 31st, it was already in
danger. During the night an enemy mechanized force under
Colonel Seinosuke Sonoda daringly pushed down Highway 5
and, meeting no opposition, by afternoon was massing at

Baliuag, five miles north-east of Plaridel, preparatory to attacking. If it could capture Plaridel, it would be in position to seize the road and rail bridges over the Pampanga River at Calumpit, on Highway 3, six miles north-west of Plaridel, thus cutting off the South Luzon Force from Bataan Peninsula. Moreover, at Calumpit, to which a road ran from Plaridel, it would be far in the rear of the Bamban-Mount Arayat line and only a few miles south-east of San Fernando, the early capture of which would jeopardize the retreat from the front line.

MacArthur had foreseen this envelopment threat when the Japanese had broken through at Cabanatuan on the 30th and had taken steps to meet it. The South Luzon Force, whose commander, Parker, having been given the task of preparing the Bataan defences, had been replaced by Major-General Albert M. Jones, had begun to retire on Christmas Eve. On the narrow mountain roads, obstacles, blown bridges and other demolitions had slowed the Japanese pursuit. There had been little fighting and contact with the enemy had soon been lost. MacArthur now ordered Jones to hasten his retreat and to clear the Calumpit bridges by 0600 on the 1st, a week ahead of schedule. At the same time he ordered its nearest units to join other troops in the defence of the Plaridel-Calumpit area and placed Jones in command of these operations.

A tank counter-attack, supported by self-propelled guns, saved the day for the Americans. There was confused fighting as the tanks, under cover of artillery fire, broke into Baliuag, a village of nipa huts and narrow streets. When the Americans withdrew at dusk eight enemy tanks had been knocked out and Sonoda's advance effectively, if momentarily, stopped. By 0600 next morning the South Luzon Force and the troops in the Plaridel-Calumpit area had passed over the Calumpit bridges, both of which were blown 15 minutes later.

Throughout New Year's Day the road from Calumpit to San Fernando and thence south to Bataan was packed tight with tanks, guns, vehicles of all types, troops and refugees, but the Japanese Air Force passed up this splendid target, thus throwing away the opportunity of seriously hampering the retreat into Bataan.

The Bamban-Mount Arayat line was evacuated that night and shortly after 0200 on the 2nd, when the tank rearguard had passed through San Fernando, the bridge across the San Fernando River was demolished six days earlier than MacArthur had planned. The Japanese, delayed by road blocks and blown bridges and the difficult crossing of the Pampanga River at Calumpit, did not enter San Fernando until 1830, three-quarters of an hour after their first troops, marching by Highway 3, had entered Manila.

Homma was now supremely confident. Believing he was confronted by a demoralized army, he considered victory was simply a matter of drawing tight the strings of the sack into which he thought the Americans and Filipinos were tumbling. He was very nearly right. On the 3rd the Japanese shattered the American left, driving a wedge into it. With smoke billowing up from the burning canefields around them, the defending infantry broke, streaming to the rear in panic. For six hours, firing at point-blank range over open fields, the artillery beat off one Japanese attack after another, halting the enemy and giving time for the panic-stricken troops to be rallied and reorganized. On the 4th the Japanese effort was switched to the American right, which was driven back in confusion by a succession of attacks spearheaded by tanks and supported by artillery. Despite severe losses, the Tanaka Detachment, in bright moonlight, persisted in its attack until 0500 on the 5th, but failed to rout the Americans and Filipinos.

However, these attacks drove the defenders behind the Gumain River in the utmost confusion, with their units irretrievably intermingled. Having suffered heavy losses and with several gaps in their line, they could scarcely have withstood a determined assault; had the Japanese been capable of another effort that day, Homma might have won the decisive victory he was seeking. That night the Americans withdrew farther, but the Japanese, having recovered their breath, followed up and on the 6th again penetrated the American-Filipino line, driving MacArthur's men back in disorder and forcing them under cover of darkness to withdraw into the peninsula proper.

In two weeks of fighting the Americans and Filipinos had

been bottled up in the Bataan Peninsula. The North Luzon
Force had lost some 12,000 men, and the South Luzon Force
about 1,000, mostly Filipinos who had deserted and returned
to their homes, but the number of killed and wounded in these
totals is unknown. The Japanese, from their first landing, had
lost 627 killed, 1,282 wounded and 7 missing. They had
captured Manila and all of Luzon except Bataan and the fortified islands in the Bay, but they had failed by a narrow margin
to smash MacArthur's Army in the field, and until they did
they could not make use of Manila Bay.

The Japanese planners had estimated the Philippines would
be captured in fifty days, by January 27, and because of
their limited resources had arranged for the 48th Division,
Homma's best formation, to be then relieved by a garrison
force, the 65th Brigade, so as to free the division for the
invasion of Java. On the 2nd, however, Homma was notified
by Southern Army Headquarters that the Java operation had
been advanced a month ahead of schedule and that consequently he would lose the 48th Division and most of the
5th Air Group earlier than had been arranged. The 6,500-
strong 65th Brigade, whose commander, Lieutenant-General
Akira Nara, deemed it 'absolutely unfit for combat duty', began
to disembark at Lingayen Gulf on the 1st, and seven days later
completed its relief of the 48th Division. At the same time,
Homma's air support was reduced to fewer than 70 fighters,
bombers and reconnaissance aircraft. The XIV Army commander did not protest at the loss of these forces ahead of
schedule, for he still believed the Americans defeated and that
the mopping-up of the peninsula would be easy.

The Abucay line, which the Japanese now faced, was divided
into two sectors. On the east, forming the American right, was
the II Philippine Corps of about 25,000 men under Parker. Its
positions ran from Mabatang, on Manila Bay, westwards across
low, swampy ground, mainly given to rice-growing, to the rocky
north-east slopes of Mount Natib, an extinct volcano 4,222
feet high. The mountainous, wooded western sector, the American left, was held by Wainwright's I Philippine Corps, 22,500
strong, and ran from the slopes of Mount Silanganan (3,620 ft.)

to Mauban, a village on the shores of the South China Sea. Thus, the American line, 20 miles long from east to west, was split in the centre by the volcanic mass of Mount Natib and Mount Silanganan, with their steep and jagged peaks and their densely timbered slopes, which made physical contact between the two corps impossible.

The Japanese attacked the II Philippine Corps on the 9th, but Nara's frontal assault down the east coast road under cover of artillery and mortar fire stalled hopelessly, and gradually he shifted the weight of his pressure westwards into the rugged slopes leading to Mount Natib. The Japanese were handicapped by their inaccurate maps, whose small scale continually misled them. Nevertheless, by the 15th, having drawn Parker's corps reserve into the battle, they were threatening a break-through in the American centre, at the point of junction between two of Parker's divisions, the 41st and 51st Philippine Divisions. The position was so critical that MacArthur's Headquarters released additional troops to meet the threat, and as they moved into position Parker ordered a dawn counter-attack on the 16th to restore the position. Jones, who now commanded the 51st Division, protested vigorously against this order, claiming that the weakened state of his division made the operation 'extremely hazardous'. Parker, however, insisted it be carried out. Although it met strong resistance, it made progress, but then miscarried, creating a dangerous salient of which the Japanese took immediate advantage. The Filipino troops of the 51st Division, attacked simultaneously on three sides, fled in disorder. The exposure of their flanks by this debacle caused neighbouring units to pull back. Many of the men, becoming separated in the jungle, lost their way, and some made a long and weary march through the difficult country to the west coast, living on leaves, shrub roots and boiled snails.

The immediate danger passed, however, because the local Japanese commanders failed to exploit their advantage. Colonel Susumu Takechi, who had been ordered to turn the American flank, was misled by his imperfect maps, which caused him to confuse two river valleys. He began a wide sweep into almost impenetrable country that was to take him out of action for several days. Colonel Takeo Imai, becoming suddenly over-cautious, failed to attack his most profitable objective and suffered a repulse. Nara threw in fresh reinforcements and continued the pressure against Parker's left flank, and by the evening of the 21st the Japanese, with overwhelming air and artillery support, were in a position to roll back the American line to the shores of Manila Bay.

MacArthur ordered I and II Corps to begin withdrawing from the Abucay line after nightfall on the 23rd. The Japanese pursued boldly and vigorously and their pilots strafed and bombed the retreating troops throughout the daylight hours. The II Corps suffered heavily, but I Corps, which had been less strongly attacked, and whose right flank had been turned by Japanese infiltrators through the forests and over the rugged mountain slopes, disengaged with less difficulty.

By the 26th the Americans were occupying their last defence line in Bataan, running from Orion in the east, to Bagac in the west. In the centre they were less than 20 miles from the peninsula's tip, and 80,000 soldiers, of whom 13,000 were Americans, and 26,000 civilians were now compressed into 200 square miles of mostly rugged, mountainous, forest-clad country. Here they subsisted on an inadequate and unbalanced ration, sweltering by day in a heat of 95° and shivering with cold at night.

From the moment they had retired into the peninsula Mac-Arthur's commanders had feared Japanese landings in the rear of their forward positions. To meet this threat the southern part of Bataan, at first known as the Service Command Area, had been placed under the command of Brigadier-General Allen C. McBride, MacArthur's deputy for the Philippine Department. It was divided by the Paniguian River, flowing down the centre of the peninsula into Mariveles Bay, into two sectors, an eastern and a western, the latter of which was defended by a mixed force of sailors, marines, airmen, constabulary and Philippine Army troops, few of whom knew anything of infantry tactics and many of whom had never fired a rifle.

As early as the 14th, when the attack on the Abucay line did not appear to be progressing, Homma had suggested to

Kimura the advisability of staging an amphibious operation against Bataan. Kimura took command of the forces attacking I Corps on the 18th and three days later decided to land a battalion at Caibobo Point, five air miles south of Bagac, the next night. The operation, mounted hurriedly with inadequate preparation, went wrong from the start. Two of the barges were sunk by an American motor torpedo boat, *PT34,* as the flotilla made its way down the western shore of Bataan. With defective charts and poor maps, and encountering a tide running more strongly than they had anticipated, the Japanese were split into two groups and lost their bearings. One group, 300 strong, landed at Longoskawayan Point, toward the tip of the peninsula and 10 air miles south-east of Caibobo Point. The second and stronger force, numbering 600, came ashore at Quinauan Point, seven miles to the north of Longoskawayan Point.

The landings took the Americans by surprise. They learnt of the one at Quinauan Point before 0230 on the 23rd, but that at Longoskawayan Point was not reported until six hours later. The Japanese, however, were not able to exploit the advantage of surprise because they themselves were at first bewildered as to their whereabouts. Kimura, although he later knew of the Quinauan Point landing, remained until the end ignorant of the landing at Longoskawayan Point, never dreaming that his men had got so far south.

When discovered, the Japanese at Longoskawayan Point had moved inland and taken possession of Mount Pucot (617 ft.). They were, however, driven from this dominating height by a detachment of seamen and marines and by nightfall of the 24th were bottled up in the woods of 700-yard long Longoskawayan Point. The scratch forces brought against them could make no progress in eliminating them, the Japanese making full use of the cover in which they found themselves and fighting a skilful defensive battle. The area in which they were hiding was plastered by 75-mm. guns, pack howitzers and mortars, including eight 12-inch mortars on Corregidor, but the American advance was halted. Not until the 29th, after further shelling and when trained infantry had been put into the fight, was this pocket of 300 Japanese liquidated.

The jungle at Quinauan Point also favoured the Japanese, who fought as fanatically as their comrades nearer the tip of the peninsula. Around 0300 on the night of the 26th-27th an attempt was made to reinforce this landing. A force of 200 Japanese came ashore on a beach between the Anyasan and Silaiim Rivers, 2,000 yards short of Quinauan Point, and although the beach defenders fled without firing a shot, the landing failed. Morioka, who had replaced Kimura as commander of the operations against Wainwright's I Corps, dropped supplies from the air, but most of the parcels fell in the American and Filipino lines. Another attempt to reinforce Quinauan Point with men and supplies was made on the evening of 1st February, but having advance information of it the Americans were ready. The dozen barges were shelled by shore batteries and bombed and strafed by four P-40's, all that remained of the Far East Army Air Force. The convoy turned back, but not until it had landed about half its force on the Anyasan-Silaiim beach.

Tanks and infantry were called in, but the Japanese at Quinauan Point, although half starved, continued to resist. 'The sight and stench of death was everywhere,' wrote one participant.[1] 'The jungle, droning with insects, was almost unbearably hot.' In these conditions the Japanese were slowly pressed back and by nightfall of 4th February had been compressed into an area 100 yards wide and 50 yards from the cliff edge. Some Japanese ripped off their uniforms and jumped over the cliff, but most scrambled down the steep face and holed up in caves, from which they were dynamited in a land-sea operation on the 8th.

By then the Americans were also making progress in reducing the survivors of the Anyasan-Silaiim landing. In two attempts at evacuation, the enemy succeeded in taking out only 34 wounded, but at dawn on the 12th 200 gaunt, half-starved Japanese, in a desperate counter-attack, broke through the encircling troops. They were, however, rounded up by fresh troops, although one party of 80 escaped northwards. When located seven miles from Silaiim Point it took two days to destroy this party.

In these mismanaged, hastily staged landings behind the American lines, the Japanese lost about 1,800 men and the Americans nearly 200 killed and over 500 wounded.

Meanwhile, on January 28, Japanese infantry had opened a gap in the Orion-Bagac line on the west and established two strongpoints behind the I Corps front. These were known as Little Pocket and Big Pocket. An attempt on February 8 to reinforce them was halted only 800 yards short of Big Pocket and the salient which on this occasion was driven into the American lines was dubbed the Upper Pocket. All three pockets were in jungle and the fighting to eliminate them was as savage as that of the Points, the enemy resistance being as determined and the American progress as slow. During the night of the 8th-9th the Japanese evacuated Little Pocket undetected, but its survivors were located as they attempted escape and, refusing to surrender, were annihilated. The survivors from Big Pocket slipped through the encircling Americans, but of the 1,000 Japanese who had effected the break-through, only 377 rejoined their own forces. In Big Pocket alone they left 300 dead and 150 graves. The Upper Pocket salient was now squeezed out and by the 17th the Americans had restored their main line of resistance.

Meanwhile Homma had decided on the 8th to break off his offensive. Without difficulty he pulled back his men to a position where they could rest and reorganize. His army was in bad shape. It had lost 2,700 killed and over 4,000 wounded, while between 10,000 and 12,000 men were ill with malaria, beriberi, dysentery and other diseases. American resistance had been far stronger than Homma had anticipated, and to bring the siege of Bataan to a successful conclusion he was forced to request substantial reinforcements.

The plight of the Americans and Filipinos was even more desperate. Since January 5 they had been on half rations, the distribution of which had been difficult and haphazard, especially to front-line formations, so that while some units ate reasonably well others ate very poorly. 'There is nothing quite

so controversial as the Bataan ration,' wrote one officer.[11]
'Some units get corned beef, others none. Some had corned
beef hash in lieu of fish. Some got eight ounces of rice, others
3.7. Some got flour in place of bread, some hard tack. But
there is nothing controversial about the fact that the ration was
grossly inadequate.' As the food stocks dwindled, the ration
was reduced still further, and the front-line troops, because of
supply difficulties, suffered most. Weakened by malnutrition,
they soon were incapable of sustained physical effort, particularly after the opportunities to supplement the ration by jungle
foods disappeared.

From the first the Filipinos had obtained chickens, pigs,
sweet potatoes, bamboo shoots, mangoes, bananas, dogs, monkeys, snakes and iguanas in order to supplement their rations,
and the Americans quickly followed their example. 'I can
recommend mule,' wrote one American officer.[12] 'It is tasty,
succulent and tender — all being phrases of comparison, of
course. There is little to choose between calesa pony and
carabao.[13] The pony is tougher but better flavour than carabao.
Iguana is fair. Monkey I do not recommend. I never had
snake.' Soon, however, these supplementary foods began to
disappear. 'Monkeys and iguanas are scarce,' wrote an officer
on March 15, 'and about all we have is rice.'[14] The constant,
never-ending search for food led some to eat poisonous berries
and the toxic wild carrot, leading to illness and sometimes
death.

The lack of mosquito nets and the inadequacy of the supply
of quinine caused a marked increase in malaria, so that soon
there were 750 cases daily. Dengue, scurvy, beri-beri, hook-
worm and dysentery were also common, for all of which the
supply of medicines and drugs was inadequate.

Efforts to get supplies to the beleaguered garrison were frequent but largely unsuccessful. The *Pensacola* convoy, carrying
4,600 troops and much ammunition and equipment, as well as
18 P-40's and 52 single-engined Dauntless dive-bombers
(A-24's), was *en route* to Manila when war occurred. It was
diverted to Brisbane, in Australia, where efforts to get the more
urgently needed items to the Philippines failed. Large sums

were made available for the purchase of food and the charter of ships, but the Japanese steadily tightened the blockade. Of the vessels which sailed from Australia, *Coast Farmer,* which reached Mindanao 15 days after leaving Brisbane, and *Dona Nati* and *Anhui,* which reached Cebu in mid-March, were the only three to get through. The others were bombed and sunk or driven ashore, or, as happened with two Chinese ships on British registry which sailed from Fremantle, their crews mutinied on reaching dangerous waters and took the vessels back to an Australian port.

Barely 1,000 of the 10,000 tons of food, ammunition and supplies landed by the three vessels that successfully ran the blockade reached Bataan or Corregidor; for the smaller inter-island traders which carried the cargoes on from Mindanao or Cebu were under constant attack and 10 were sunk by the enemy or scuttled by their crews to avoid capture. Ten air deliveries of medical supplies, including much needed morphia and quinine tablets, ammunition and signal equipment were made, but again little reached Bataan. Ten supply submarines brought in only 53 tons of food, 3,500 rounds of 3-inch anti-aircraft, 37 tons of .50-calibre and one million rounds of .30-calibre ammunition and about 30,000 tons of diesel oil.

Homma's cessation of his attacks led to rumours that he had committed suicide because of his failure to win victory. The troops and MacArthur's Headquarters alike believed he had committed *hara-kiri* and morale improved. Despite the shortage of food and the hardships they were enduring, the rank-and-file believed they had the measure of the enemy and that before long the promised relief expedition would arrive. However, with the departure for Australia of MacArthur on March 12, it became evident no help was to be expected and morale slumped. Suffering from malnutrition and tropical diseases, gaunt skeletons whose tattered clothes hung loosely on their emaciated frames, the men felt they had been deserted:

> We're the battling bastards of Bataan;
> No mama, no papa, no Uncle Sam;
> No aunts, no uncles, no cousins, no nieces;
> No pills, no planes, no artillery pieces
> . . . And nobody gives a damn.

MacArthur left the Philippines under a presidential order from Roosevelt, and took with him, in addition to his wife, young son and the latter's Chinese nurse, seventeen selected officers. The party left Corregidor in four PT boats on the evening of March 12, holed up next day on an uninhabited island of the Cuyo group in the central Philippines and reached Mindanao at daybreak on the 14th to find that of four Flying Fortresses dispatched from Australia two had been forced to return through engine trouble and a third had crashed. The fourth reached Del Monte airfield in Mindanao, but was in such poor mechanical condition that MacArthur refused to fly in it. Three more B-17's were dispatched from Australia in response to his radio appeal and two of these landed safely at Del Monte by midnight of the 16th. They at once set out on the return journey and MacArthur and his party landed in Australia at 0900 next morning. The ailing Quezon, dying of tuberculosis, reached Australia by submarine before the end of the month.

On leaving Corregidor, MacArthur had announced he would continue to exercise command from Australia, 4,000 miles away. He proposed to do this through Colonel Lewis C. Beebe, whom he promoted Brigadier-General and appointed Deputy Chief of Staff of the United States Army Forces of the Far East. The defenders of Bataan he designated the Luzon Force, command of which he gave to Wainwright, who was relieved as commander of I Corps by Jones. MacArthur did not inform the War Department of these command arrangements, which seem to have been designed by MacArthur against the eventuality of part of the Forces in the Philippines having to surrender. So long as there were only local commanders they could surrender only the troops under their immediate control. However, MacArthur's command set up was unacceptable to Washington and after a few days of confusion Roosevelt and Marshall promoted Wainwright to Lieutenant-General and made it clear that he had succeeded MacArthur as commander of all the Forces in the Philippines, although still nominally subordinate to MacArthur. On March 21 Wainwright pinned on his third star and established the Headquarters of the United States

Forces in the Philippines on Corregidor. He appointed Major-General Edward P. King, Jr., as his successor in command of the Luzon Force.

Strong infantry, artillery and air reinforcements having reached him, Homma in mid-March began the preparations for his final offensive. Although his Force was able to shell, bomb and strafe the American positions at will, his earlier optimism had given way to pessimism, and he estimated the reduction of Bataan would occupy a month.

At 1000 on April 3 — Good Friday — the Japanese laid down a devastating barrage from 150 guns, the majority of which concentrated on the 5,000-yard sector of II Corps' extreme left. The barrage was reinforced by bombing and strafing attacks by Homma's reinforced air force, which dropped 60 tons of bombs this day, mainly on the same small sector of the American-Filipino line. After five hours of bombardment, the infantry attack, led by tanks, jumped off at 1500. The half-starved Filipinos, dazed by the bombardment and bewildered by the smoke and dust from the tinder-dry cogon grass and bamboo thickets, which had been set alight by the shelling and strafing, turned and fled. By the evening of Easter Saturday the Japanese had secured the entire main line of resistance in the area of the attack and on the 5th they gained the summit of Mount Samat (1,920 ft.), where American artillerymen rolled their guns over the cliffs to prevent their capture.

During the next three days the Luzon Force disintegrated in chaos, and in the early hours of the 9th two officers entered the Japanese lines under a white flag. At 1230 that day King surrendered unconditionally. In six days Homma had achieved what he had expected would take him a month!

The Manila Bay forts — Fort Mills on Corregidor, Fort Hughes on Caballo, immediately south of Corregidor, Fort Drum, four miles farther south, and Fort Frank on Carabao, close to the shoreline of Cavite Province — were still in American hands. They had been under intermittent air attack since December 29 and had been shelled at intervals since February 6. The bombardment of them was now increased, and although casualties were light, damage to the batteries and installations was heavy. Ammunition dumps and magazines, penetrated by shells from 240-mm. howitzers, were blown up, and by 5th May, except for three 155-mm. weapons, Corregidor's guns had been silenced. Despite the network of tunnels under Malinta Hill, on Corregidor, in which life was uncomfortable, if less precarious than outside, the number of casualties steadily increased toward the end of the bombardment.

The Japanese assault was delivered on the night of May 5. The enemy landed on the wrong beaches and came ashore in the wrong order, largely because the tide at Corregidor flowed in the opposite direction to that expected, but the beach defences no longer existed and the Americans could offer little resistance. By the morning of the 6th it was all over. Wainwright tried to surrender only Corregidor and the Bay forts, but the Japanese insisted he surrender all the Forces remaining in the Philippines, and to avoid further bloodshed he agreed. Distributing the surrender order to the troops in the Visayas and on Mindanao took time and the final surrender on Luzon did not take place until June 6. A few small units and a number of individuals took to the hills to wage guerilla warfare, but apart from these the Americans and Filipinos had by then laid down their arms.

When King surrendered on Bataan about 64,000 Filipinos and 12,000 Americans became prisoners of the Japanese. On April 10 they began the 55-mile march from Mariveles to San Fernando that has become known in the chronicles of infamy as the Death March of Bataan. Because they had expected to take only 20,000 to 25,000 prisoners, the Japanese arrangements for the transporting and feeding of the prisoners broke down. Denied food and water, compelled to march under a tropical sun with few rest periods, often clubbed or bayoneted, thousands of the prisoners died by the roadside or in the crowded rail trucks which carried them from San Fernando to Capas, a journey of three or four hours. From Capas they marched the final eight miles to their prisoner-of-war compounds at Camp O'Donnell. Between 7,000 and 10,000 men, including 2,330 Americans, died during the Death March of Bataan from disease, starvation, exhaustion or brutality.

NOTES AND REFERENCES

1. Morison, *Rising Sun in the Pacific*, 235-44.
2. Toland, *But Not in Shame*, 41, says the radio station at Aparri, on Luzon's north coast, was attacked by Zeros about the same time, but the official histories make no mention of this raid.
3. MacArthur, *Reminiscences*, 120.
4. For this controversy, see Brereton, *Diaries*, 36 et sq.; Craven and Cate, *The Army Air Forces in World War II*, I, 204-9, and Morton, *The Fall of the Philippines*, 81-4, 88-9.
5. Morton, 86.
6. Wigmore, *The Japanese Thrust*, 93-4.
7. MacArthur, 123, repeats the canard that the Japanese attempted a landing in the Lingayen area, but it was repulsed with severe loss by a Philippine Army division.
8. Toland, 93.
9. Theodore Roscoe, *U.S. Submarine Operations in World War II* (Annapolis, 1954), 23 et seq.
10. William E. Dyess, *The Dyess Story*, 43.
11. Colonel Richard C. Mallonee, *Diary*, II, 11, quoted by Morton, 371, from a photostat copy on file in the office of the U.S. Chief of Military History.
12. Ibid., quoted by Morton, 370.
13. A working animal, similar to a working bullock or ox.
14. Major Achille C. Tisdelle, *Diary*, 15th March 1942, quoted by Morton, 370. Tisdelle's Diary was published in *Military Affairs* (U.S.), XI.

FURTHER READING:

The fullest and most readable account of the Philippines campaign is Dr Louis Morton's indispensable *The Fall of the Philippines,* in the official U.S. Army History of World War II (Washington, 1953). Morison's *The Rising Sun in the Pacific, 1931-April, 1942,* and Craven and Cate's *The Army Air Forces in World War II,* I, *Plans and Early Operations, January, 1939, to August, 1942,* supplement it on the naval and air side. The Japanese plans are given in *The Campaigns of the Pacific War.* An account of the campaign for the general reader will be found in John Toland's *But Not in Shame* (New York, 1961). Of the personal accounts of participants, the most important are *General Wainwright's Story* (New York, 1946), Ernest B. Miller's *Bataan Uncensored* (Long Prairie, Minn., 1949), which needs to be read as a corrective to Wainwright's volume, Major-General Lewis H. Brereton's *The Brereton Diaries* (New York, 1946), Lieutenant-Colonel Allison Ind's *Bataan, The Judgment Seat* (New York, 1944) and Lieutenant-Colonel William E. Dyess' *The Dyess Story* (New York, 1944). The Death March of Bataan is described in S. L. Falk's *The March of Death* (London, 1964). The taking of Wake is told in *The Defence of Wake,* by Lieutenant-Colonel R. D. Heinl, Jr., a Marine Corps monograph (Washington, 1947).

four

THE CONQUEST OF MALAYA

Contrary to popular belief, the first Allied shots in the war against Japan were not fired at Pearl Harbour but near Kota Bharu, a small village on the east coast of Malaya. Here three Japanese transports, carrying an invasion force of 5,500 men, and their naval escorts anchored offshore at 2200 on December 7, the equivalent of 0410 on the 7th in Hawaii. British batteries opened fire, to which the Japanese escorts replied, and Hudsons of an Australian squadron bombed and strafed the enemy ships and landing-craft, inflicting casualties and damage. When the enemy infantry began landing at 0030 on the 8th, meeting heavy rifle and machine-gun fire from Indian troops dug in along the beach, there was still an hour and a quarter to go in Honolulu before the first bomb would fall on Pearl Harbour.

News of the Kota Bharu landing was received in Hong Kong, 1,450 miles to the north of Singapore, at 0800 on the 8th. It was then 1130 on the 7th in Pearl Harbour, an hour and three-quarters after the end of the second Japanese air attack.

The British Crown Colony of Hong Kong, 80 miles south-east of Canton, comprised the rugged island itself, on which was situated the city and port of Victoria, the concession of Kowloon on the mainland opposite and, beyond Kowloon, leased territory extending 17 miles to the north to the general line of the Sham Chun River. In 1941 the total population, predominantly Chinese, was 1,250,000. Until its removal to Singapore, the headquarters of the Royal Navy's China station had been located at Hong Kong, but the colony's importance as a naval base had diminished greatly with Japan's incursion into China and her acquisition of bases on Hainan Island, Formosa and the Pescadores, the nearest of which was only 300 miles away.

The British Chiefs of Staff recognized that in the altered circumstances, and in an era when the range of aircraft had been so greatly extended, an isolated and exposed Hong Kong weakened rather than strengthened the Allied position in the Far East. In August 1940 they described Hong Kong as an outpost of no vital importance and incapable of prolonged resistance, and they warned against reinforcing it. On November 11 1940 Air Chief Marshal Sir Robert Brooke-Popham reached Singapore as Commander-in-Chief of the Far East. His optimism was as great as MacArthur's but a good deal less infectious. In February 1941 he told the Australian Chiefs of Staff that Hong Kong could defend itself for four months,[1] although five weeks earlier, in a memorandum of January 7, Winston Churchill, in reply to Brooke-Popham's recommendation that Hong Kong be reinforced, had with blunt commonsense declared:

> This is all wrong. If Japan goes to war with us there is not the slightest chance of holding Hong Kong or relieving it. It is most unwise to increase the loss we shall suffer there. Instead of increasing the garrison it ought to be reduced to a symbolical scale. . . . Japan will think long before declaring war on the British Empire, and whether there are two or six battalions at Hong Kong will make no difference to her choice.[2]

On this occasion reinforcement was summarily rejected, but the matter was again raised before the year's end. On July 20

Major-General C. M. Maltby relieved Major-General A. E.
Grasett as military commander at Hong Kong. Grasett returned
to England by way of Canada, his native country, and there
told General H. D. G. Crerar, Chief of the Canadian General
Staff that 'the addition of two or more battalions to the forces
then at Hong Kong would render the garrison strong enough to
withstand for an extensive period of siege an attack by such
forces as the Japanese could bring to bear upon it.' On his
arrival in England he urged this view strongly on the Chiefs of
Staff and suggested Canada be asked to furnish the reinforcements. He won over the Chiefs and inexplicably Churchill
allowed himself to be drawn from his earlier firm stand. On
September 19 the Dominions Office asked Canada to furnish
two battalions because this reinforcement 'would reassure
Chiang Kai-shek as to the genuineness of our intention to hold
the colony and in addition would have a very great moral
effect throughout the Far East'.[3] The idea that the arrival of
two battalions would exercise an important deterrent effect
upon Japan was, in the words of the official Canadian historian,
an 'egregious absurdity'.

The Canadian Government agreed to the British request and
Crerar selected as the reinforcing battalions the Royal Rifles of
Canada and the Winnipeg Grenadiers, both of which had been
on garrison duty and neither of which had received any intensive tactical training. They arrived at Hong Kong, without their
carriers or lorries, on November 16. Their arrival brought
the garrison to a strength of six battalions, two of which were
British, the 2nd Royal Scots and the 1st Middlesex, and two
Indian, the 5/7th Rajput and the 2/14th Punjab. Including
the numerically small Hong Kong Volunteer Defence Corps
and the Hong Kong and Singapore Royal Artillery, a regular
Army unit whose ranks included Britishers, Indians and local
Chinese, the garrison's combatant strength was almost 12,000.
There were shortages of equipment, notably anti-aircraft
weapons, artillery, mortars, transport and some types of
ammunition. Three obsolete Vildebeeste torpedo-bombers and
two Walrus amphibians constituted the Air Force. All that
remained at Hong Kong of the Royal Navy's China Squadron

were the destroyer *Thracian* (905, 1920), a flotilla of eight motortorpedo boats and a few old gunboats.

Its geographical position made Hong Kong more aware of the menace of Japanese aggression than more distant Allied territories, but even here, on the enemy's doorstep, there was complacency, a conviction of Japanese inferiority and a belief that Japan would not go to war. Soon after their arrival, Canadian officers attending a lecture were told by a British officer that opposite the frontier the Japanese had only 5,000 ill-equipped troops, with very little artillery, that they were inexpert at night fighting, that their aircraft for the most part were obsolete and their pilots myopic, which prevented them carrying out dive-bombing. There was also a belief that they were addicted to stereotyped methods and plans and that their automatic weapons were neither so numerous nor modern as the British.[4]

In the face of such wishful thinking, the energy and skill of the Japanese, the strength and accuracy of their artillery, the effectiveness of their bombing and low-level air attack, the stealth and competence of their night fighting, their intimate knowledge of the colony's defences, and the thoroughness of their planning, which was revealed by the provision at the right places of the precise quantities of materials required for the repair of demolitions, came as an unpleasant shock.

However, as news of Japanese troop concentrations opposite the frontier came in, even though these were thought to be exaggerated, all battle stations were manned and by the 7th the garrison was alert and ready. By 0730 on the 8th all demolitions along the frontier, including the blowing up of the road and rail bridges across the Sham Chun River, had been carried out. At 0800 came the first air raid. A force of 36 bombers and 12 fighters attacked the airfield at Kai Tak, on the mainland, and the adjoining seaplane base in Kowloon Bay, destroying all five R.A.F. and eight civilian aircraft.

On the frontier Japanese bridging teams went to work immediately and during the day the enemy advanced on a broad front toward the British defensive position, known as the Gindrinkers' line. Eleven miles long and only three miles north

of the city and port of Kowloon, this ran from Gindrinkers'
Bay on the west, along the heights of Golden Hill and Smugglers'
Ridge, thence along the southern shore of Tide Cove and
across the hills to Port Shelter on the east. Essentially a delaying position, Maltby expected to hold it for no longer than
from seven to ten days while installations on the mainland
were destroyed and supplies ferried across to the island.

The Japanese advanced swiftly and in a brilliant assault on
the night of the 9th-10th Colonel Teihichi Doi's 228th Infantry
Regiment, its commander gaining some unpopularity by his
disregard of regimental boundaries, seized Shing Mun Redoubt
at the northern end of Smugglers' Ridge. The five pillboxes of
the Redoubt, linked by fire trenches and tunnels, and surrounded by barbed wire, covered 12 acres of rocky hillside.
The leading Japanese troops, wearing rubber-soled canvas
shoes, crept up to it and dropped grenades down the ventilating
shafts of the tunnels at the north end. Fighting in the underground tunnels lasted an hour, while resistance on the surface
was not overcome until 0200, three hours after the assault
began.

The loss of this key position imperilled the Gindrinkers' line
and the demolitions around Kowloon were hastened. On the
night of the 11th-12th most of the Mainland Brigade was
withdrawn to the island and the rearguard followed next morning, its last elements being back on the island by 0930.

Hong Kong now came under heavy artillery and air bombardment, which steadily mounted in intensity as the Japanese got
more guns into position. Demands on the 13th and 17th for
surrender were curtly rejected, although by the latter date
many of the defence positions along the northern shore, including most of the pillboxes, had been knocked out. On the
evening of the 18th, with the tide favourable and the moon not
due to rise until midnight, the Japanese launched their assault.
Thick smoke from burning oil tanks and a blazing paint factory,
and from the brief but heavy pre-assault artillery bombardment,
shrouded the enemy's approach. The first wave, crossing the
harbour in collapsible assault boats, were assisted by Fifth
Columnists who cut the beach wire. The Japanese came ashore

at the north-east corner of the island, between Causeway Bay in the west and Pak Sha Wan in the east, and, by-passing centres of resistance, advanced rapidly inland along all routes leading to commanding heights. The brunt of the attack fell initially on the 5/7th Rajput, who fought gallantly and suffered heavy casualties.

At the time it was thought the Japanese employed three divisions in the attack, but actually there was only one, the 38th, commanded by Lieutenant-General Tadayoshi Sano, from Lieutenant-General Takashi Sakai's XXIII Army. Its three infantry regiments, the 228th, 229th and 230th, were not greatly superior numerically to the garrison, but the division had been strongly reinforced in artillery, mortars and specialist categories, particularly engineers, and it possessed very strong air support. Nor did it have to guard its rear — a special force, the Araki Detachment, had been provided to ward off possible interference by Chinese armies.

Maltby had divided the island into two sectors, an eastern and a western, each defended by a brigade, but fearful of a seaborne landing along the southern shore, and having no reconnaissance aircraft or naval patrols seawards to warn of the approach of a hostile fleet, he did not deploy his whole force against the imminent invasion from the mainland. In both sectors the Canadians guarded the southern shoreline. This dispersion weakened the defence. It left insufficient troops immediately available for counter-attacking and it meant that the battalions least trained for mobile warfare, the Canadians, eventually had to be used offensively in an attempt to restore the situation. Even had Maltby disregarded the threat from the sea, it is doubtful if different dispositions would have much prolonged the defence of the island in view of the enemy's overwhelming artillery and air support.

The fighting throughout was bitter and disjointed. Small detachments, often surrounded and always outnumbered, fought heroically and held their positions for long periods until at length overrun. By dawn on the 20th the Japanese had driven a wedge between Maltby's two brigades. Local counter-attacks, often hastily organized, rarely co-ordinated and sometimes ambushed as they set out, achieved no more than to momentarily check the enemy's advance. They failed to break through to their objectives or to link up the two brigades again.

The British, Canadians, Indians and loyal Chinese had no reply to the enemy's artillery and mortar fire or to his bombing and low-level strafing attacks, and by Christmas Eve, worn out with fatigue, short of water and having suffered heavy casualties, their plight was desperate. At 1515 on Christmas Day Maltby informed the Governor, Sir Mark Young, that further effective resistance was impossible, and at the Peninsula Hotel, in Kowloon, that night Sir Mark unconditionally surrendered. It had taken Japan eighteen days to conquer her first defended British territory. Some acts of wanton barbarism, including the murder of prisoners, followed the capitulation.

Total British battle casualties were approximately 4,400, of whom 955 all ranks were killed and 659 were missing. The Canadians alone lost 23 officers and 267 other ranks killed or died of wounds and 28 officers and 465 other ranks wounded out of a force about 1,800 strong. The fighting and surrender together involved the loss of 11,848 combatants. Japanese casualties were officially given as 675 killed and 2,079 wounded.

While Hong Kong was being bludgeoned into submission and the Americans and Filipinos driven into Bataan, the Japanese invasion of Malaya was proceeding swiftly.

Some 400 miles long and varying in breadth from 60 to 200 miles, Malaya is divided down its centre by a jungle-clad range of mountains towering from 4,000 to over 7,000 feet in height. The western coastal plain is narrower but more densely populated and with more developed communications than the eastern. Sandy beaches line both coasts, those on the west being more frequently interspersed with mangrove swamps. Except for the areas cultivated for rubber, rice, coconut or other crops, the land is mostly covered by jungle, in which visibility even in daytime is very limited. The climate, humid the year long, is enervating. Rainfall is heavy and during the north-east monsoon, which lasts from November to March, much of the low-lying ground, especially in the eastern coastal belt, becomes waterlogged. The jungle itself, eerily silent except for the buzz

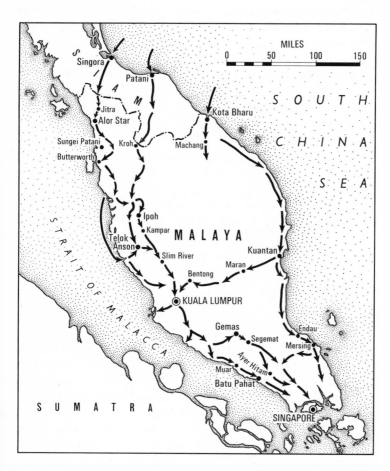

4. The lines of the Japanese advance in Malaya

of insects, is oppressive and movement in it difficult and exhausting.

Captain F. Spencer Chapman, who had been an instructor at commando and guerilla warfare schools and was to make reconnaissances behind the Japanese lines, has given a memorable picture of this difficult fighting country[5]:

> By the middle of the day the atmosphere was exactly that of the Orchid House at Kew, except that not only did the heat seem to rise up and strike us from the ground but a burning sun shone mercilessly everywhere but in the thick jungle. Our clothes were soaked with sweat which, in that already saturated air, could not evaporate, and we were tortured with thirst. It was as if every dram of energy was being sucked away, and all we wanted to do was to lie down and sleep — which, as a matter of fact, we did whenever we stopped to rest . . . Rain was terrific. Within half a minute we were soaked to the skin, and having been unbearably hot all day were now equally disconsolate with cold. The rain came down so hard that it actually hurt our bare heads and hands, and we had to take shelter under a grove of coconut palms. The huge drops splashed up from the ground in a pale knee-deep mist; the roar of the rain on the leathery leaves above our heads was so loud that we had to shout to make each other hear; and the small stream between us and the road rose visibly, as we watched it, to become a turbid flood.

The population of Malaya in 1941 was nearly 5,500,000, of whom 720,000 lived in Singapore. Malays, Chinese and Indians formed the principal racial groups, both Europeans and Japanese being few in numbers. Politically, the country was divided into a number of federated and unfederated states, which meant a multiplicity of civilian administrations.

Everywhere complacency and wishful thinking reigned. In Singapore the gay social round and the sharp peacetime demarcations between the different races and social groups held sway to the end, as though no enemy stood at the gates. The wives and families of service personnel and of European civilians had not been compulsorily evacuated, as they had been from Hong Kong, and this task, with its time-consuming practical difficulties and its human problems, had to be carried out after battle had been joined. The war in Europe had seemed so curiously remote that a solid body of opinion, service as well as civilian, considered that Japan would not resort to war or, if she did, would not invade Malaya.

Most British officers, especially in the higher ranks, regarded the Japanese as inferior antagonists, and the same miscalculations of the enemy's strength, skill, and economic and technological capabilities flourished in Malaya as in Hong Kong and the Philippines, only to a greater degree.

When Brooke-Popham conferred with the Australian Chiefs of Staff on February 14 1941 he confidently predicted that even if Johore, the mainland state adjoining Singapore Island, was captured and the facilities of the naval base were lost, the island itself could continue to hold out. He depreciated the Japanese Air Force, stating that its training was neither as thorough nor as sound as that of the Allied Air Forces and its aircraft less efficient. He added specifically that Japanese fighter planes were not as good as the Brewster Buffalo, and forecast that the Air Force in Malaya would cause the Japanese Air Force such losses as to prevent it putting the British Forces out of action.[6] At that time, of course, Chungking had not reported on the armament and tankage of a Zero shot down over China, nor furnished the aircraft's estimated performance figures, but as these accurate and illuminating reports, when they came to hand in July and September respectively, were pigeon-holed by Far East Air Headquarters without any action being taken, it is unlikely they would have tempered Brooke-Popham's optimism.

The country lived in such an atmosphere of false security that nowhere was there any sense of urgency. Inter-service jealousies, particularly between the Army and the Air Force, hampered planning, and the lack of harmony and understanding between the military and civilians made the implementation of defence measures difficult and sometimes impossible. Repeatedly assured by their political and military leaders of Singapore's impregnability, that it was the 'Gibraltar of the East' or a 'bastion of Empire', and knowing how disdainful serving officers were of Japanese military equipment and fighting prowess, civilians took the threat of Japanese aggression lightly and saw no reason to disturb their pleasant daily routine or to risk their personal interests to further defence measures. The inadequacy of the air raid precautions in Singapore is one example of the consequences of this attitude. Other difficulties arose from Britain's decision that Malaya's dollar-earning, which came principally from the export of rubber and tin to the United States, should have priority over defence measures. This largely nullified the expansion and training of the Malay Volunteers because the men who should have provided the corps with its officers and N.C.O's. could not be released from the rubber plantations and the tin mines.

The decision to build the £60,000,000 Singapore naval base was taken originally in 1921, but was reversed three years later, and when on a change of government it was again decided to proceed with it, financial and political considerations delayed its construction. There was no unanimity as to its desirability or effectiveness, and not until February 1938 was it officially opened. The Chiefs of Staff in 1937 estimated that it would have to withstand attack from 70 to 90 days before it could be relieved by a fleet from European waters, but in 1939 this estimate was increased to 180 days.

The truth, of course, is that between the time when the base was begun and the date of its completion the strategical situation had altered. Instead of being confronted with a prostrate and exhausted Europe, Britain had to meet the menace of Nazism and Fascism and of a less friendly and more aggressive Japan, and in the same period the range and hitting power of aircraft had increased tremendously. The naval base had been planned, sited and constructed to provide defence against attack from the sea, and its defence had been based on the assumption that a powerful Far Eastern Fleet would be based on it, a hypothesis which by the time of its completion was no longer tenable if, as seemed probable, a Pacific coincided with a European war. All its great guns pointed seawards. The likelihood of attack through its back door, by an assault from the land was forcibly raised by Major-General W. G. S. Dobbie, the Army commander in Malaya, in 1937-38, following an appreciation written by his Chief of Staff, Colonel Arthur Ernest

Percival. He reported that the greatest potential danger lay in an attack on Singapore from the north and he demonstrated in manœuvres the falsity of the comfortable assertion, first, that landings on the mainland were impracticable during the period of the north-east monsoon and, second, that the jungle in Johore was mainly impassable for infantry.

The tardy realization that Singapore was not as impregnable as had been claimed came too late, in view of events in Europe, for effective remedial measures to be taken. It led naturally to a reorientation of Malayan strategy, since the provision of a powerful fleet, the first prerequisite of a successful defence of the base, was now impracticable. In the absence of a battle fleet, chief reliance was placed for defence upon air power, which meant that airfields had to be constructed, manned and defended throughout Malaya. The defence of Singapore had therefore to be extended to the defence of the whole of Malaya. Little, however, was done to prepare defensive positions against a possible offensive down Malaya against Singapore Island, although much might have been done in this direction if the local command had more keenly appreciated this danger or displayed greater energy.

In agreeing, after the fall of France and Holland, that the whole of Malaya should be held, the Chiefs of Staff estimated that a total of 336 first-line aircraft and a minimum garrison of six brigades would be required. However, in October 1940 the commanders of the three services at Singapore jointly reported that 566 first-line aircraft and a garrison of 26 battalions — 200 more aircraft and eight more battalions than the Chiefs of Staff had estimated — would be needed to ensure a successful defence.

For the British Commonwealth, with all its commitments, the provision of forces on this scale was impossible. Such reinforcements as could be scraped from the bottom of the barrel were rushed to Singapore, but many of them were poorly trained and all ill-equipped. The story in Malaya was much the same as the story in Hong Kong and the Philippines. Peacetime neglect could not be remedied overnight and time was needed to rectify the shortages of essential weapons and equipment and to train adequately the various units — and time the Japanese would not allow.

When war came the Malayan garrison numbered about 88,600 — 37,000 Indians, 19,600 British, 16,800 locally recruited and 15,200 Australians. The Army's strength was much below the minimum set by the local commanders almost a year earlier, its training left a great deal to be desired, there was a shortage of anti-tank and anti-aircraft guns, and although tanks had been asked for as early as 1937 none had yet arrived. Under Brooke-Popham as Far East Commander-in-Chief, the Army commander in Malaya was Percival, now holding the rank of lieutenant-general, a not very forceful or impressive man of 52. He had under him as commander of the III Indian Corps, comprising the 9th and 11th Indian Divisions, Lieutenant-General Sir Lewis Heath, and Major-General H. Gordon Bennett, commander of the 8th Australian Division.

The gravest weakness in Malaya, however, was the inadequacy of the Air Force, which had nothing approaching the 336 first-line aircraft laid down by the Chiefs of Staff as the minimum requirement, much less the total of 556 requested by the commanders on the spot. There is some variation in the figures of first-line aircraft strength as given by different authorities, but the total certainly did not exceed 160 and there were only 88 reserve aircraft, of which no fewer than 21 Buffaloes were temporarily unserviceable because of trouble with the valve gear on a new make of engine.[7] Many of the aircraft were obsolete or outmoded, and only the Hudsons and Blenheims could be regarded as modern. The Buffaloes were inferior in all respects to the Zero, and even when the weight of their armament, ammunition and fuel was reduced, effecting some improvement in performance, they were still slower and less manœuvrable than the Zero. Six Australian-built Beauforts, far superior to the Vildebeeste as a torpedo-bomber and more effective as a bomber than most of the Blenheims in Malaya, arrived at Singapore early in December, but had not been armed and five were returned to Australia for this reason, the sixth being retained in the hope that it would prove useful for photo-reconnaissance work. Difficulties had been experienced in constructing airfields, mainly owing to the shortage of earth-moving and other mechanical equipment and the difficulty of procuring labour, but about 23 had been completed, of which 15 were grass surfaced, a grave defect in a country with such a heavy tropical rainfall as Malaya. Communication channels were inadequate and ground-to-air radio equipment obsolete, unreliable and of limited range. Most of the airfields outside Singapore Island lacked essential facilities and those which possessed any anti-aircraft defences were protected by an insufficient number of weapons. The northern airfields, lacking camouflage, stood out prominently from the surrounding jungle, presenting splendid targets from the air, and the dispersal arrangements on all were poor. The Air Force commander was Air Vice-Marshal C. W. H. Pulford, who had served as a naval pilot at Gallipoli in 1915, and his assistant was Air Vice-Marshal P. C. Maltby.

The Far Eastern Fleets of the Allies were widely dispersed, and the only ships immediately available for the defence of Malaya, apart from submarines, were the battleship *Prince of Wales* (35,000, 1941), the battle-cruiser *Repulse* (33,250, 1916) and some not very modern destroyers. *Prince of Wales* and *Repulse,* sent to Singapore on Churchill's insistence and against the Admiralty's advice, had arrived on December 2. They were to have been accompanied by the new aircraft carrier *Formidable* (23,000, 70 aircraft, 1941), but she had grounded when entering Kingston, Jamaica, while on working-up trials and, requiring repairs, had been unable to join the other ships. Admiral Sir Thomas Phillips, as Commander in Chief, Eastern Fleet, flew his flag in *Prince of Wales,* and his principal assistant was Vice-Admiral Sir Geoffrey Layton, who until succeeded by Phillips had been Commander in Chief, China.

Southern Army Headquarters had assigned the XXV Army, under Lieutenant-General Tomoyuki Yamashita, to the conquest of Malaya. It consisted of the Imperial Guards, 5th, 18th and 56th Divisions. Excluding the latter, which in the event was not required in Malaya, but including Yamashita's specialist and service troops, the XXV Army had a strength of 125,408 men, of whom 36,719 were in lines of communication units. It possessed over 7,000 vehicles and more than 11,500 horses, and was equipped with at least 90 medium and 100 light tanks. Yamashita's front-line troops were superior to the divisions employed in the Philippines. With the exception of the unblooded Imperial Guards Division, they were battle-tested troops who had been intensively trained in jungle fighting. In the air this formidable invasion force was backed up by the 3rd Air Division and the 22nd Air Flotilla, the former with 354 first-line aircraft, the latter with 180. In addition, three seaplane tenders, with a total of 30 aircraft, were employed. Of the 560 operational aircraft available to Yamashita, about 180 were fighters.

A dawn reconnaissance on the 8th revealed that the Japanese main landings had taken place during the night at Singora and Patani, in Thailand. Land fighting during the day was restricted primarily to the Kota Bharu area, but the Japanese Air Force was active, striking particularly at the airfields in northern and central Malaya. Considerable damage was done and many aircraft were destroyed on the ground.

Singapore was raided by 17 bombers at about 0400. Radar gave the defence 30 minutes warning of the attack, but the defending fighters were refused permission to take off because it was feared they would interfere with the effectiveness of the anti-aircraft barrage and when an attempt was made to contact the civil defence authorities, it was discovered that Air Raid Precaution Headquarters was not even manned! The street lights remained blazing throughout the attack because the holder of the key of the central switch could not be located.[8] As the raid was made in tropical moonlight, this may not have helped the Japanese pilots, but along with the failure to sound the sirens it had a serious psychological effect on the civilian population. Civilian casualties totalled almost 200, although the main attacks had been on the airfields.

At 1735 on the 8th, Phillips sailed from Singapore with *Prince of Wales* and *Repulse,* accompanied by the destroyers *Electra* (1,375, 1934), *Express* (1,375, 1934), *Tenedos*

(1,000, 1919) and *Vampire* (1,090, 1917), the latter a unit of the Royal Australian Navy. His plan was to raid the Japanese transports and warships off Singora, where he expected to arrive at dawn on the 10th. He had requested Pulford to furnish air reconnaissance ahead of his ships on the 9th and fighter cover off Singora at dawn on the 10th and subsequently during his retirement that day. The reconnaissance was promised, but Pulford said it was most unlikely fighter protection could be provided and later, as the ships passed Changi signal station, confirmed it was impossible. 'Well,' remarked Phillips, with a shrug of his shoulders, 'we must go on without it.'[9]

By steering a course that added 250 miles to the 450-mile route from Singapore to Singora, and given during the daylight hours the usual low cloud, rain squalls and poor visibility of the monsoonal weather, Phillips gambled on evading detection from the air during the 9th. He believed he would thus have the advantage of surprise at Singora.

There seems no doubt that Phillips, like other commanders, underestimated the Japanese. He probably believed he would be out of range of Japanese torpedo-bombers for the greater part of the sortie and, even if he were not, that the Japanese pilots would attack neither resolutely nor skilfully in the face of the anti-aircraft barrage from his ships. A successful attack on the invasion fleet might have seriously dislocated Japanese plans, and the Navy could hardly stand idly by when the Army and Air Force were being assaulted, but the big ships were too valuable as the nucleus of a powerful Fleet for future operations to be risked in a blind stab at the invasion fleet without fighter cover. Nevertheless, the ships could not remain at Singapore or in Malayan waters without being in constant danger of destruction from the air, and having regard to his knowledge at the time and the poor opinion of the Japanese common to all the services, Phillips's action in carrying out the sortie is understandable, but it was not justified.

Late on the afternoon of the 9th Japanese aircraft were sighted shadowing the Fleet, and Phillips, knowing he had lost all chance of surprise, decided to turn back after dark. Although he did not know it, a Japanese submarine had reported his course at 1400, but had made an error of 140 miles in his position.[10] This message was not received at Saigon, where the 22nd Air Flotilla was loading its aircraft with bombs for a raid on Singapore, until 1600. Rearmed with torpedoes, the planes took off for a night attack, but failed to locate their target and returned to base about midnight.

At 2015 the Fleet reversed course for the return run to Singapore. Because of her limited fuel endurance, *Tenedos* had been detached earlier, at 1835, to return independently to Singapore, and Phillips had given her commander a signal to send at 0800 on the 10th to the effect that his Force would be off the Anambas Islands not earlier than 0600 on the 11th. This message, of course, was drafted before the shadowing aircraft had been sighted and when Phillips still expected to make the run-in to Singora.

Shortly before midnight Phillips received a radio signal stating that the enemy were reported landing at Kuantan and about 0100 on the 10th he altered course for there. He did not break wireless silence to advise Singapore of his discontinuance of his Singora operation or of his decision to close Kuantan. This was unfortunate, as half-a-dozen fighters had been found and they were ready to take off if Phillips had requested air cover. While closing Kuantan, the Fleet was sighted by another Japanese submarine, which fired five torpedoes that went astray. She then surfaced and made a sighting report, which was received at Saigon at 0315. Ten aircraft were promptly dispatched to make a sector search for the British ships and they were followed by a strike of bombers and torpedo-bombers.

The Kuantan report proved false and when Phillips reached there all was quiet. He was investigating a tug towing some barges when the Japanese search aircraft, which had flown further south without seeing him and were now returning northwards, sighted him. They summoned the strike force, and both big ships were attacked by high-level bombers and torpedo-bombers from about 1100 onwards. The pilots of the torpedo-bombers attacked determinedly and skilfully, flying into the ships' anti-aircraft barrage without flinching. Two torpedoes

Australian War Memorial

Above, British firefighters try to control the blaze at the Singapore docks caused by the Japanese bombardment. Below, Singapore is taken and victorious Japanese troops march through the streets

Australian War Memorial

Elated Japanese troops in Singapore

hit *Prince of Wales,* causing great damage and putting her out of control. Unable to take evading action, she was soon struck by four more torpedoes in rapid succession and later received a bomb hit. As she settled rapidly in the water, listing heavily to port, *Express* ran alongside and took off her wounded and those men not required to fight her. At 1320 she turned turtle and sank.

Repulse had sunk almost an hour earlier, after a hit had jammed her steering gear and three torpedoes had slammed into her. Much older and less substantial than the flagship, she could not take such punishment and rolled over at 1233. The destroyers rescued 2,081 officers and men, but 840 were lost — 513 from *Repulse* and 327 from *Prince of Wales.* Six Australian Buffaloes arrived at the scene during the rescue operations and their pilots were impressed by the courage of the men in the oil-smeared waters, who waved and gave thumbs up signs as they awaited rescue. Phillips was among those who died.

While the Japanese Air Force was delivering this crippling blow and reducing the Allied Air Force almost to impotency, the Japanese XXV Army launched its drive for Singapore with speed and resolution. In addition to the 5,500 men landed at Kota Bharu, the enemy put ashore 13,500 at Singora and another 7,550 at Patani during the same night. The British, expecting the enemy to land at these places in Thailand, had drawn up a plan, to which they gave the code name of Matador, for the defence of Singora and Patani. It was fatuous and unrealistic to imagine this plan was practicable, since the British must not in any circumstances appear to be the aggressor. Therefore they could not cross the frontier into Thailand unless the Japanese first violated Thai territory or the British had unimpeachable evidence that the enemy was about to land at Singora and Patani. Apart from the fact that Matador offered no prospect of prolonged defence of Singora and Patani, since Japanese landings further south would outflank the British force and cut it off, the British had no chance of forestalling the Japanese unless they were the first to invade Thailand, and at that many hours ahead of the Japanese.

Yet despite its impracticability, the British clung to Matador until the last moment. On the 6th the 11th Indian Division, charged with the defence of northern Malaya, was placed on 30 minutes notice to undertake operation Matador. In drenching rain the Indians stood by with three battalions near trains that were to take them forward, two in camp with their trucks ready loaded and one forward near the frontier. Japanese convoys were sighted on the 7th, but Brooke-Popham could not determine their destination, and although he decided he could not authorize Matador he did not cancel it until about 1000 on the 8th. Even then Malaya Command creaked rustily into action. At 1130 Percival issued orders to III Indian Corps to cancel Matador and occupy defensive positions astride the roads running southwards from the frontier and to dispatch mobile columns into Thailand to disrupt and delay the Japanese advance, but it was 1300 before III Indian Corps received these orders and another 30 minutes before they reached the division.

The Japanese were thus given a flying start of 10 hours, while the 11th Indian Division, physically wearied and its morale lowered by the abrupt change to a defensive role after its long stand-by for an offensive move, arrived at its Jitra position to find its gun pits and trenches waterlogged from the heavy rain. Because they had been packed for the forward move under Matador, their wire had not been strung and their mines not laid, and the troops had to turn round and prepare the position against attack.

Krohcol, the mobile force assigned the task of seizing The Ledge, a narrow defile on the Patani-Kroh road 30 miles inside the Thai frontier, and the only good defensive position in front of Kroh, failed to appreciate the need for speed. Against resistance by the armed Thai constabulary it moved forward at such a leisurely pace that when it camped for the night on the evening of the 8th it had penetrated only three miles inside the frontier. On the 9th, although Thai resistance collapsed suddenly in the afternoon, its unhurried advance carried it only to Betong, some 20 miles short of its objective. Next day it drove forward in lorries to within six miles of The Ledge and after advancing another mile on foot ran into enemy tanks. With 75 miles to cover from Patani to The Ledge, the Japanese had forestalled the British by vigorous, determined action.[11] The other mobile columns sent forward by the British did no more than destroy some bridges.

Lightly accoutred, unhampered by extensive administrative services and ignoring, almost recklessly, normal security precautions, the Japanese drove down the roads leading to Singapore. The initiative lay with them and both on the east and west coasts they called the tune, giving the British no respite. Their leading infantry used bicycles freely to push ahead and when forward units flagged from fatigue or casualties, fresh troops were leap-frogged through them to maintain unslackened the momentum of advance. When opposition on the roads was encountered, the Japanese took to the jungle trails and by enveloping and infiltrating tactics crushed or by-passed the resistance, in the latter case setting up strong road blocks in the rear of the by-passed troops. They employed the same tactics against the defence of tactical features, such as hills and rivers. Further forces on one axis of advance manœuvred skilfully to produce an enveloping threat against the British resisting on another line of advance. In this way the British were hustled out of one defence line after another.

Amphibious landings behind the defenders — and the British commanders, like their American counterparts in Bataan, were constantly looking over their shoulders — were often planned, but were carried out in only a few instances, as such operations were generally rendered unnecessary by a further British withdrawal.

Chapman, on a reconnaissance behind the enemy lines in front of the Perak River at Christmas, watched the advancing Japanese as he lay hidden in the jungle by the roadside, and his description recreates the feverish atmosphere of the advance:

> We lay only 100 yards from the road and could see the enemy, hundreds and hundreds of them, pouring eastwards towards the Perak River. The majority were on bicycles in parties of 40 or 50, riding three or four abreast and talking and laughing, just as if they were going to a football match. Indeed, some of them were actually wearing football jerseys; they seemed to have no standard uniform or equipment, and were travelling as light as they possibly

could. Some wore green, others grey, khaki, or even
dirty white. The majority had trousers hanging loose
or enclosed in high boots or puttees; some had tight
breeches, and others shorts and rubber boots or gym.
shoes. Their hats showed the greatest variety: a few
tin hats, topees of all shapes, wide-brimmed terai or
ordinary felt hats, high-peaked jockey hats, little caps
with eye shades, or even a piece of cloth tied round
the head and hanging down behind. Their equipment
and armament were equally varied and were slung
over themselves and their bicycles with no apparent
method. We noticed with delight that their weapons
—tommy-guns and rifles (either our own Service rifle
or the long Jap Meije)—were usually tied on the
frames of the bicycles, so that they would have taken
some time to go into action had they been suddenly
attacked. Every now and then a convoy of staff cars
and lorries would go past, heavily camouflaged with
palm fronds.

The general impression was one of extraordinary
determination: they had been ordered to go to the
bridgehead, and in their thousands they were going,
though their equipment was second-rate and motley
and much of it obviously had been commandeered
in Malaya. Their cooking gear was also of the
lightest, and they were living off the country by
collecting rice, fowls, and vegetables from the roadside villages. We saw several parties cooking their
evening meal. Each man produced a cigarette tin
with a loop of wire over the top and, cutting a stick,
he hung his tin and boiled his rice over a communal
fire. Some of those we watched produced a small tin
of fish or other concentrated food, while others
seemed to eat the rice alone. The whole meal took
only a quarter of an hour to prepare and eat.

All this was in very marked contrast to our own
front-line soldiers, who were at this time equipped
like Christmas-trees with heavy boots, web equipment, packs, haversacks, water bottles, blankets,
ground sheets and even great-coats and respirators,
so that they could hardly walk, much less fight.[12]

Handicapped by elaborate administrative services, cautiously
adhering to text-book security measures and overloaded with
personal equipment, the British and Indians were slow in their
movement over the ground and in their mental reactions. The
Indian units had been denuded of the greater proportion of
their experienced officers and N.C.O.'s to provide cadres for
the new units of the rapidly expanding Indian Army, and con-

sequently their standard of subordinate leadership was uneven. This, coupled with inadequate peacetime training, especially in jungle fighting, and the failure to develop sound aggressive tactics to meet the enemy's methods, in great measure explain the British failure.

It was not, as propaganda asserted at the time, that the defenders were heavily outnumbered and that there were Japanese in overwhelming strength in every direction. Repeatedly British and Indian units were defeated by numerically inferior forces. At the start of the campaign the 11th Indian Division was forced out of its Jitra position by only the advanced guard of the Japanese 5th Division, and later, the Slim River disaster was the work of a single tank company, with an infantry battalion and some engineers, who virtually destroyed two Indian brigades.

Failing to think and act aggressively, the British did not attempt to ambush the onrushing Japanese or even to harass them with patrols. If the firing of infiltrators was heard on the flanks or in the rear of a position, the immediate reaction was to withdraw. Seldom was an attempt made to ascertain the strength of the infiltrators or to counter-attack, and more often than not the defenders retired before they were seriously attacked. As the retreat continued, frequently in confusion, the morale of the troops was lowered further. The men lost confidence in their leaders and themselves, and the Japanese gained a moral ascendancy that was never shaken.

The policy of fighting for almost every inch of ground, irrespective of its tactical value, led to British and Indian units being frequently overrun or cut off. Communications, which were never good, sometimes failed at critical moments, adding to the confusion and uncertainty of front-line troops and resulting in platoons, companies and even battalions being left isolated and unsupported. Orders, which were often suddenly and repeatedly changed, did not always get through to the front-line troops.

Percival's primary purpose in defending northern and central Malaya, apart from the defence of the naval base, was to deny the enemy those airfields from which his aircraft might interfere with the convoys bringing reinforcements and supplies to Singapore. He wished to keep the Japanese Air Force as far away as he possibly could. The airfields, however, had been sited without reference to the best positions for their tactical defence, and as a result the Army often found itself called upon to stand on a position which was defensively weak.

Under these conditions, fighting and marching by day and night, the British and Indians were soon left physically and mentally fatigued, so that they became an even easier prey to their enemy. 'Officers and men moved like automata and often could not grasp the simplest order', an eye-witness said of the men of the 12th Indian Brigade, but his remark might have been applied with equal force to almost every unit of III Indian Corps.

On the west coast, where the main Japanese effort was made, the campaign opened badly for the British. The Japanese advance was made along the trunk roads running down Malaya from Singora and Patani, and the Indians, most of whom had never even seen a tank, fled when a Japanese column of tanks and motorized infantry burst through the outpost line in front of the waterlogged Jitra line. The enemy was only halted on the main line of resistance after fierce fighting. On the Patani road, driving back the Krohcol force, the Japanese advance threatened the British communications farther westward, and this threat was sufficient to compel the evacuation of the Jitra position. As some of the troops were being withdrawn they were mistaken for the enemy and the bridge over which they were to have passed to safety was blown up, causing many vehicles and eleven anti-tank and mountain guns to be lost. A counter-attack to check the enemy saw the Jats mistake the Punjabis for Japanese, so that they fired upon one another, and it ended in failure, with severe losses. By the 23rd, having retreated some 150 miles, the 11th Indian Division, its strength depleted, was back behind the Perak River.

Although not a strong position, since it did not run at right angles to the trunk roads, Yamashita expected the line of the Perak River to be defended, but to his astonishment it was evacuated and his troops crossed it unopposed. The British fell back south of Ipoh, but the Japanese followed hard on their heels and by the 29th had forced them back to a position astride the trunk road at Kampar.

There was one effort at offensive action behind the Japanese lines. The Perak Flotilla, comprising the destroyer *Scout* (1,000, 1918) and some light craft, had been formed originally to stop enemy landings in northern Sumatra and later had been given the task of countering Japanese seaborne landings between the Krian and Perak Rivers. On December 28 it was used to transport 'Roseforce', a party of 50 Australians organized by the Royal Navy to disrupt enemy communications west of the Perak River, behind the enemy's lines. Some of the motor-boats broke down, but the party, although thus reduced in number, landed successfully near Trong and ambushed and destroyed some motor transport and staff cars on the coastal road. This raid, which had no effect on the campaign but which showed what might have been done had such forces been organized on a large scale before the war, brought an immediate reaction from the enemy. The flotilla's base depot ship, lying at Port Swettenham, was bombed and sunk, and soon afterwards five fast motor-boats on their way north to reinforce the flotilla were sunk or driven ashore by enemy aircraft.

The Japanese force which had landed at Kota Bharu, on the east coast,[13] had seized the airfield there by the end of the first day's fighting and before the end of the month the British had retired to Kuantan. Here Yamashita planned to seize the airfield by a seaborne landing, but cancelled the operation when he decided it could be captured by an overland advance. On the night of January 3, when the British defenders finally withdrew, part of their rearguard was cut off and only 40 men succeeded in fighting their way back through the two road blocks established by the enemy, although a few small parties rejoined later.

As the Japanese Army advanced down both coasts the dwindling British Air Force was driven back from one airfield to another. All its forward airfields were relinquished to the enemy in the opening days of his attack. In some instances they were vacated in confusion and near panic, with British and Australians fleeing southwards without waiting for orders. The pre-war denial plans were so inadequate that in the prevailing confusion large stocks of aviation fuel, petrol, ammunition and other supplies fell into enemy hands. In this rainy country piles of road metal had been accumulated alongside airfields for their maintenance. The Japanese thus had immediately at hand the materials needed for the repair of damaged runways and, with abundant local labour available, captured airfields were quickly repaired and put into use.

Similar confusion occurred on Penang Island when, after heavy Japanese air raids — there were some 2,000 civilian casualties in the first raid on Georgetown — all Europeans, but no Asians, were evacuated by midnight of December 17-18. The broadcasting station fell intact into enemy hands and was used by the Japanese to spread anti-British propaganda through-out the Far East, while in the harbour he captured 24 self-propelled vessels of varying sizes and numerous large junks and barges.

The British aircraft were no match for the Japanese planes and the number operational dwindled until so few remained that they had to be husbanded for essential reconnaissance and for protecting the convoys bringing reinforcements to Singapore. A few bombing raids, carried out by up to half-a-dozen aircraft at a time, were made against shipping or enemy airfields, but these puny efforts, despite the gallantry with which they were carried out, caused few casualties and little damage and had no appreciable effect on the campaign. After the first few days of the fighting, the Air Force could give little support to the ground forces, and it was rarely that a British plane was seen by the front-line troops. The Japanese pilots bombed and strafed the retreating British without meeting any opposition, but, as in the Philippines, their direction was faulty; their attacks were not systematic or delivered against road junctions or focal points through which the retreating traffic flowed.

By December 19 the British Air Force had been driven back to Kuala Lumpur, against which increasingly heavy air attacks were now launched. So effective were these that by the 22nd No. 453 R.A.A.F. squadron had only three of its 15

Buffaloes still fit for combat and next day the squadron vacated the airfield.

In the Slim River area, to which the 11th Indian Division had retreated after a seaborne landing at Utan Melintang and Telok Anson had outflanked its position at Kampar, disaster again struck on January 7. At 0330 that morning a Japanese column of tanks and motorized infantry began a drive down the west coast trunk road. The enemy by-passed resistance by using loop roads which had been left when the trunk road had been straightened to eliminate a number of bad bends and which had been neither mined nor blocked. There were three of these loop roads at intervals and although they were in poor condition for traffic the Japanese proved that all were passable.

By 0700 the Japanese column had seized Trolak, where they captured the bridge undamaged when the demolition charge failed to explode. They then swept on southward. The 28th Indian Brigade, which had been resting and reorganizing, was moving up to occupy its positions in the Slim River area when the enemy caught it on the road in column of route. Owing to faulty communications, no word of the enemy column's advance had been received by the rear units and the brigade was scattered like chaff in a strong breeze and suffered heavy casualties. The enemy spearhead — a solitary tank company with a battalion of infantry and some engineers — captured the vital Slim River bridge intact and was only halted, having driven forward for six hours, when a battery, although taken by surprise, managed to get a 4.5-inch howitzer into action and stopped the leading tank at a range of 30 yards. The Japanese were now 20 miles behind the British front-line and had almost wiped out two brigades, the 12th and 28th, each of which had lost all its transport, most of its guns and equipment, and on the 8th could muster between them only approximately 1,173 all ranks. This enemy break-through was almost identical with, but more disastrous than, that which Homma's army achieved at Cabanatuan, in the Philippines, on December 29-30.[14]

'It would be easy to lay the blame for this disaster on the failure to organize adequate anti-tank defence, or to warn the troops in rear of what was happening, or to blow the bridges,' wrote Percival, long after the event,[15] 'but to do so would divert attention from the real cause, which was the utter weariness of the troops, both officers and men. They had been fighting and moving by day and night for a month and few of them had any proper rest or relief. To their physical fatigue was added a mental fatigue brought about by the enemy's complete supremacy in the air and on the sea and by a general sense of futility. In the exhausting and enervating climate of Malaya this was too great a test of human endurance, and the troops had reached a stage when their reactions were subnormal. It was not unexpected.'

Few will quarrel with this judgement, but the real failure lay with Malaya Command. Percival left III Indian Corps to fight one rearguard action after another for too long instead of relieving it with fresh troops from Singapore or making a large-scale withdrawal to a feasible line of resistance in Johore. General Sir Archibald Wavell, who arrived in Singapore on the day of the Slim River disaster, immediately realized this and acted promptly, although by then it was perhaps too late for the position to be retrieved.

At the Arcadia Conference in Washington late in December Roosevelt and Churchill decided, at the insistence of Marshall, on the appointment of a Supreme Commander for the Far East. The job went to Wavell, and his command was known as A.B.D.A. Burma, the Andaman and Nicobar Islands, Malaya, the Netherlands East Indies, the Philippines, and Christmas and Cocos Islands were constituted the area over which A.B.D.A. — initials which stood for American, British, Dutch and Australian forces — was to exercise command. Australia, New Zealand and China were excluded, although Chinese forces, if they came to fight in Burma, would be under the A.B.D.A. Supreme Command and later, so as to provide responsibility for the defence of Darwin, Australia northwards of a line running from Onslow on the west coast to the southeast corner of the Gulf of Carpentaria, was added to the area. 'I have heard of men having to hold the baby, but this is twins,' remarked Wavell, when offered the post of Supreme

Commander. When he called at Singapore on 7th January he was on his way to Java to open his new headquarters.

On the 8th he visited the front line. His visit convinced him that III Indian Corps, and in particular 11th Indian Division, was at the end of its tether. He decided the division's fighting value was now almost negligible and that if it were not rested and reorganized it would disintegrate. He ordered Percival to withdraw the corps by road and rail into Johore and to defend the north-west frontier of that State with the 8th Australian Division, which had been guarding the Mersing area on the east coast, where an enemy seaborne landing had always been feared. One Australian brigade group was to temporarily remain at Mersing, but Wavell directed it was to be relieved and rejoin its Division as soon as the 53rd British Infantry Brigade reached Singapore. In the event, Wavell's order was not executed. The 8th Australian Division, the best-trained formation in Malaya and the only one which might have appreciably slowed the Japanese, never fought in Johore as a complete unit, but was used piecemeal on three different fronts.

Even before the battle for Johore opened, the confident Japanese began preparing for their invasion of the Netherlands East Indies by securing the northern approaches to the Strait of Macassar and the Molucca Passage. After Japanese landings, British North Borneo, where the oilfield equipment had been destroyed as early as December 8, was surrendered on January 19. The small Indian garrison of Kuching, its rearguard having been overwhelmed, crossed into Dutch Borneo on December 27. At Tarakan on January 10, billowing smoke proclaimed to the Japanese landing force that it had arrived too late and that the oilfields had been set on fire. The Dutch garrison, having delayed the invaders until the last demolitions had been carried out, laid down its arms on the 12th. In the northern Celebes the enemy landed at Menado and Kema before dawn on the 11th and a few hours later, in an attempt to seize the airfield south of Menado, employed paratroops for the first time. The drop was made from too great a height and, with the strong wind blowing, the 334 paratroopers were widely scattered on landing, so that an additional 185 men had to be dropped next morning. However, by the evening of the 12th the enemy had control of the whole area and on the 24th the 21st Air Flotilla was operating from the airfield. By the capture of the Tarakan and Menado airfields the Japanese had advanced their air bases 300 miles farther south.

In Northern Johore the British forces, now known as 'Westforce', were commanded by Bennett, the aggressive-minded commander of the 8th Australian Division, a non-regular, who had led a brigade in France in World War I. His 27th Brigade, with Indian forces in support, was astride the trunk road at Gemas, while in his rear his left flank was guarded in the Muar River area on the coast by the poorly equipped and semitrained 45th Indian Brigade, which had reached Singapore in the first reinforcement convoy on 3rd January. Instead of concentrating this brigade for the defence of the main coastal road and against possible seaborne landings south of the Muar River, so as to protect his communications, Bennett dispersed it on a 24-mile front along the river. Failing to appreciate how poorly trained the brigade was, he insisted upon it placing an outpost line north of the river, but the outpost units were unfit to carry out the aggressive patrolling and ambushing which he seems to have had in mind. Apart from this weakness, the brigade was not sufficiently strong in numbers for the task assigned it.

For the Australians the battle opened auspiciously. An ambush had been set in front of Gemas, at a spot where the road crossed a bridge, and at 1600 on the 14th a company of the 2/30th Australian Battalion sprang this trap on the Mukaide Detachment, a bicycle-mounted infantry battalion, a tank regiment and some artillery and engineer units which had been sent forward to make contact with the British line. After a considerable number of Japanese had been allowed to pass over it the bridge was blown up and the Australians, concealed in the jungle alongside the road, opened fire. A telephone link to the artillery, having been poorly concealed, had been spotted and cut by the Japanese, which prevented the Australian artillery entering the action. Nevertheless, Japanese losses were heavy. Finally, the Australians, not without difficulty, returned to their own lines. Next day, although the forward troops were forced into the perimeter, Japanese tank and infantry attacks were beaten off.

On the coast, however, things went badly from the start. Here Yamashita employed the *élite* Imperial Guards Division, which had not fought in China and was receiving its baptism of fire. On the morning of January 15 it surprised and over-ran two companies of the 7/6th Rajputana Rifles north of the river and then moved into Muar. That night a few men in small boats, crossing the river, collected all the native craft moored to the south bank, and using these the Japanese effected a crossing before dawn. An Indian patrol which encountered a party of the enemy on the south bank inexplicably failed to report the crossing, and before the Rajputana Rifles realized the enemy was across, another of their companies had been surprised and destroyed.

Further inland, by the 16th, the 4/9th Jats were isolated, with a strong enemy road block in their rear, and reports of enemy landings south of the Muar River and around Batu Pahat were coming in. Only the two leading companies of the Jats eventually broke through the road block, while a counter-attack to take Muar came to nothing, the 5/18th Royal Garhwal Rifles being ambushed as they moved forward to deliver it and suffering such heavy casualties that they were reduced to some 400 all ranks.

Bennett, whose headquarters was somewhat isolated from the coastal front by the intricate nature of the country and the poorness of communications, was slow to appreciate the gravity of the threat on the Muar front, and, believing the enemy only numbered about 200, sent only a small force, most of his reserve battalion, the 2/29th of 27th Australian Brigade, to restore the position. Percival was more alert to the danger and ordered to the west coast the 53rd British Infantry Brigade, which had landed only three days earlier after eleven weeks in crowded transports, and the 2/19th Battalion of the 22nd Australian Brigade at Mersing. At 2145 on the 18th he trans-ferred the command of the Muar area to III Corps, and Bennett did not assume command again until 1200 on the 21st, when the battle had been lost, but when he was in a better position to again exercise control.

The Japanese on the Muar front would not be denied, and on the 19th the threat against 'Westforce's' communications had developed to such an extent that Percival decided a general retirement was unavoidable. Without much difficulty Bennett's forces in the Gemas area fell back to new positions, but on the coast the 45th Brigade and the two Australian battalions, the 2/19th and 2/29th, lost heavily as they tried to fight their way out of the Japanese encirclement. In the end, having destroyed all their heavy arms and equipment, some 500 Australians and 400 Indians found their way back to the British lines. The wounded, who had been abandoned in the charge of volunteer attendants, were nearly all massacred by the enemy.

On the 20th Wavell paid another visit to Singapore. He now saw little chance of the Japanese being held in Johore. On his previous visit he had ordered that defences be prepared along the northern shore of Singapore Island, but he found little had been done to carry out his order and reiterated that the work must be put in hand at once. By now, however, the almost continuous Japanese air raids on Singapore meant that civilian labour for this work was no longer available and little could be done.

On the east coast Australian patrols clashed with the enemy north of Endau on January 14, but the Japanese moved toward Mersing cautiously and not until the 24th did the Australians and Japanese face one another along the line of the Mersing River. Before any heavy fighting developed, continued disaster on the west coast had compelled 'Westforce' to again fall back, and the Australians at Mersing also had to withdraw, since it was now clear Johore had been lost and the final stand would have to be made on Singapore Island. A 'box' ambush by the 2/18th Australian Battalion to cover the Mersing retirement took such heavy toll of the Japanese 55th Infantry Regiment that it fell back in turn to await strong reinforcements ordered to the area by Yamashita.

On the 26th a convoy was sighted 20 miles north-east of Endau and was heroically attacked by Hudson, Vildebeeste and

Albacore aircraft, escorted by Buffaloes and Hurricanes. Eighteen of the latter had arrived at Singapore in crates on the 20th and had been assembled and were flying within 48 hours, but although the Hurricanes were masters of the Zero at heights above 22,000 feet they were slower and less manœuvrable below this height and, in any event, were too few in numbers to seriously challenge Japanese air supremacy. The attacks against the convoy did little damage, largely because bombs were carried instead of torpedoes, but British losses were heavy. In two attacks 10 Vildebeestes, two Albacores and one fighter were shot down.

On the west coast on the 26th the 15th Indian Brigade defending Batu Pahat was cut off. It was unable to break through the enemy's road blocks, and a column of artillery, armoured cars, carriers and lorries which tried to reach it was overwhelmed and destroyed. Only one carrier, having hurtled through six road blocks, reached the Indians, who thereupon destroyed their guns, vehicles and equipment and tried to make their way back by jungle trails. One party of 1,200 men did so, but the rest had to be evacuated over several nights by the gunboats *Dragonfly* (585, 1938) and *Scorpion* (700, 1937), assisted by small craft from Singapore. In all, 2,700 men of the Brigade reached safety.

By 0815 on January 31 the last troops had passed from Johore on to Singapore Island and a 70-foot section of the 1,100-yard long, 70-foot wide Causeway linking the island to the mainland was demolished. However, it remained fordable, since the demolished section was covered at low tide by but four feet of water.

Percival had about 85,000 men, of whom 15,000 were base, administrative or non-combatant troops, with which to defend Singapore Island, but many of his units had been badly mauled in the mainland fighting and some of the reinforcements — convoys had reached Singapore on January 3, 13, 22, 24 and 29 and February 5 with the loss of only one transport, sunk by enemy bombers — were poorly trained. The 44th Indian Brigade, which arrived on January 22 with 7,000 Indian reinforcements, was no better trained than the 45th

which had suffered so heavily on the Muar front, and the reinforcements were almost raw recruits. The 2/4th Australian
Machine-gun Battalion, which arrived on the 24th, was well
trained, but many of the 1,900 Australian reinforcements who
arrived with it, due to bungling by the Australian military
authorities, had been dispatched within a fortnight of enlistment
and had not even learnt how to handle their weapons. The 18th
British Division, whose main body did not reach Singapore until
the 29th and the last elements of which were rescued, except
for a small number, from the bombed transport during the
night of February 4-5, was a very valuable and powerful
reinforcement, but its training had been designed to fit it for
desert fighting in the Middle East and the men had been at sea
for many weeks.

Moreover, after the retreat down Malaya morale was scarcely
high, and it was further lowered as the naval base was destroyed
by demolitions. To the men, as they saw oil tanks set on fire
and heard the roar of explosions as the base was blown up, it
seemed that the High Command had lost all faith in the impregnability of Fortress Singapore.

Wavell believed the Japanese would land on the north-west
of the island and he considered this sector should be the most
strongly defended. Percival, however, disagreed, believing that
the assault would be against the north-east section and his
dispositions were based on this appreciation. He divided the
27-mile long coastline of the island into three sectors. The
Northern, embracing the north-east coast from Changi to the
Causeway, was assigned to III Corps (11th Indian and 18th
British Divisions) and was the most strongly held, both as
regards infantry and artillery. The Western, extending from
the Causeway along the north-west coast to the Jurong River,
was placed under Bennett, with the 8th Australian Division and
the 44th Indian Brigade. The Southern, running along the
southern coast from the Jurong River to Changi, was defended
by the 1st and 2nd Malaya and Straits Settlements Volunteer
Infantry Brigades, which had not yet seen action but which
were to fight staunchly, under the Fortress Commander, Major-
General F. Keith Simmons. Percival's main reserve was the

12th Indian Brigade, whose two battalions had a combined strength of less than 1,000 men.

The Japanese launched their assault on the evening of February 8 under cover of an artillery bombardment, to which mortars firing from moored landing craft contributed. The 5th and 18th Japanese Divisions, employing 21 battalions, of which only five were in reserve, came ashore on a narrow front of some six miles between Tanjong Buloh on the east, and Tanjong Murai on the west. The artillery and air bombardment over the previous days had cut most of the communications within the Western area, which prevented defensive artillery fire being brought down until S.O.S. light signals went up from the forward infantry positions and rendered it impossible for rearward headquarters to gain a clear picture of the fighting. Indeed, throughout the battle the 'fog of war' was dense.

The first Japanese to land suffered heavily, particularly from machine-gun fire, and at several points a landing was effected only at the second or third attempt, but the sheer weight of the attack was too much for the thinly spread defenders. The Japanese, once ashore, moved quickly forward into the gaps between the Australians' widely separated defended localities and were soon attacking them from all sides. The remnants of the forward troops retired to their battalion perimeters, but in the darkness, and closely engaged, the withdrawal was carried out with difficulty and in much confusion. Throughout the 9th the Australians were incessantly dive-bombed and strafed, and by nightfall they had been driven back to the Bulim position, near Tengah Airfield and the Choa Chu Kang-Panjang road.

About 2100 that evening the Japanese launched a second assault. The men of the Japanese Guards Division came ashore between the Causeway and the Kranji River, but met stiff opposition from the 27th Australian Brigade and made little progress. Indeed, in the early hours of the 10th the position seemed so critical to the division commander, Lieutenant-General Takumo Nishimura, that he sought Yamashita's permission to call off the attack and to land his division in the rear of the 5th Division, on his right. A senior officer from Army Headquarters was sent across to make a personal reconnaissance and about 0430, finding that resistance had suddenly slackened, reported that the landing should continue.

The explanation for the weaker Australian resistance was that the local commander, learning about 0400 that vital oil tanks had been destroyed, had ordered both the 2/26th and 2/30th Battalions to fall back. At the time the three forward companies of the 2/26th, much depleted in numbers, were holding a strong position across the neck of the Kranji peninsula, 500 yards in from the shore, and had repelled every Japanese attempt to dislodge them. Their commander believed they must soon be overwhelmed, but had he delayed his withdrawal order only a little longer the Japanese might have withdrawn. As it was, the Australian withdrawal created a dangerous gap between the right of the 27th Australian Brigade and the left of the 11th Indian Division.

On the 9th Percival had issued a secret and personal instruction to his senior commanders, announcing his intention, if it became necessary, to fall back on a narrow perimeter around Singapore City. Bennett's headquarters issued a normal operation order based on this instruction, thus giving it a wider circulation than Percival had intended. As with the destruction of the naval base, the knowledge that Percival was thinking in terms of a last-ditch stand in front of the city had a bad psychological effect, since it tended to channel the thoughts of commanders towards retreat. This may not have been so disastrous if the instruction had been confined to those senior officers for whom it was intended, but its wider distribution by Western Area headquarters had far-reaching consequences. In at least one instance the limited nature of the order, which stipulated that no action except reconnaissance was to be taken, escaped the notice of a brigadier receiving it, and, reading it as an order to be immediately obeyed, he ordered a further withdrawal.

On the afternoon of the 10th the defence began to disintegrate. An Indian company withdrawing hurriedly along the Jurong Road with a few men from the British battalion, and a false report that the latter had retired, started a rearward movement that it was impossible to check, and by dusk the easily defended Jurong line had been abandoned. Soon afterwards an enemy attack down the Choa Chu Kang Road, spear-headed by tanks, broke through and by midnight had captured the road junction at Bukit Timah. Percival, not having accumulated a sufficient reserve, could not intervene to influence the battle and the Australians, Indians and British continued to fall back under pressure.

By the morning of the 13th the defenders had been forced back into the 28-mile long perimeter around Singapore, but it obviously was only a matter of time before they were overwhelmed. Armed deserters were already looting in Singapore or seizing small vessels at rifle point in an effort to escape, and their numbers were growing steadily. At 1810 on the 15th Percival unconditionally surrendered and at 2030 that night fighting ceased. Singapore had fallen after a campaign of 70 days, 30 fewer than the Japanese had estimated would be needed. British losses totalled 138,708, of whom over 130,000 were taken prisoners. In the fighting and capitulation the Indians lost 67,340, the British 38,496, the Australians 18,490 and the local volunteers 14,382. The official total of Japanese casualties was only 9,824.

Although the defeat of the British, in the circumstances, was inevitable, Percival's dispositions made the Japanese task easier. His main strength in infantry and artillery was not concentrated in the area where the assault was delivered, and he committed his force to a static defence role, depriving himself of a strong mobile reserve with which to try to influence the course of the battle once Japanese intentions had become clear. Moreover, he clung to his belief that a landing would occur on the north-east shore of the island, so that even after the Japanese had stormed ashore in the western sector he was slow to transfer troops from III Corps to the threatened area.

During Singapore's dying hours a stream of large and small ships, all crowded with civilians and military personnel, fled for Java, Sumatra, Australia or wherever their optimistic navigators believed they could make a landfall. In two days more than forty were sunk by bomb or gunfire, with heavy loss of life. A few reached safety, but many others were wrecked, among them a motor launch carrying Pulford, Rear-Admiral

E. J. Spooner, and a number of officers and men. After being bombed, it was beached on a small, malarial island 20 miles north of Banka. Here the party was marooned for two months, during which time eighteen, including Spooner and Pulford, died, and when the survivors eventually crossed to Sumatra in a native boat they had no alternative but to surrender to the Japanese. The small auxiliary patrol vessel *Li Wo,* running into a Japanese convoy on February 14, attacked with her single 4-inch gun and then rammed the nearest transport amidships before being sunk at point-blank range by an enemy cruiser. When the facts became known after the war, this exploit won for the *Li Wo's* commander, Lieutenant T. Wilkinson, R.N.R., the award of a posthumous V.C.

Some who successfully reached Sumatra or Java were overtaken by disaster at a later stage of their escape. Thus, one party left Padang in a small ship for Colombo, but it was torpedoed by a Japanese submarine when half-way to its destination. A single lifeboat, with 135 people in it or clinging to its sides, escaped and after 26 days under the tropical sun drifted ashore on a lonely island 60 miles west of Sumatra. There were only four survivors — a Scottish soldier, a Chinese woman and two Javanese seamen.

Bennett, accompanied by Major Charles Moses and Lieutenant Gordon Walker, left Singapore in a native craft with some planters of the Malaya Volunteers, sailing about 0100 on February 16. They reached the east coast of Sumatra and then crossed to Padang, on the west coast. Thence they were flown to Java, where Bennett picked up a commercial airline flight to Australia. He received a cool welcome from the Chief of the Australian General Staff, Lieutenant-General Vernon Sturdee.[16] During the war he was not again employed in an overseas command, and late in 1945 a Commissioner was appointed to investigate the circumstances of his escape. After hearing much evidence, the Commissioner, Mr Justice Ligertwood, found that Bennett had not had the permission of any competent authority to escape, since there existed no such authority to give him permission, that when he left Singapore he was not a prisoner of war in the sense of being a soldier under a duty to escape and that he was not justified in relinquishing his command and leaving Singapore. However, the Commissioner also found that Bennett, having acquired valuable information and experience in Malaya and believing Australia was in peril, felt that it was of vital importance that he should return to take a leading part in its defence, that Bennett genuinely, but in the Commissioner's view mistakenly, believed that he was a prisoner of war under a duty to escape, and that his decision involved no reflection on his personal courage and was inspired by patriotism.[17]

The fighting in Johore and on Singapore Island was still in progress when the Japanese, continuing their preliminary moves for the invasion of the Netherlands East Indies, strengthened their positions in Borneo and the Celebes and began to seize the stepping-stones to Java — Amboina, Sumatra, Bali and Timor.

On January 20 a force left Tarakan to move down the Borneo coast to Balikpapan, where the oilfields had already been destroyed. Dutch aircraft sank one transport as the convoy moved down Macassar Strait and a Dutch submarine a second, while a night attack was delivered by the United States Striking Force under Vice-Admiral W. A. Glassford. On this sortie, the cruiser *Boise* (10,000, 1939) struck an uncharted pinnacle rock in Sape Strait and had to return. The cruiser *Marblehead* (7,050, 1924), after arranging a rendezvous with the destroyers, doubled back with her. The destroyers *John D. Ford, Parrott* and *Pope* (each 1,190, 1920) and *Paul Jones* (1,190, 1921) found the enemy ships at Balikpapan silhouetted against the light of the burning oilfields and for almost an hour attacked with torpedoes and, later, gunfire. Believing the attack was being made by submarines, the Japanese commander, Rear-Admiral S. Nishimura, led his destroyers out into the strait to hunt them, thus leaving the transports at the mercy of the Americans. Despite the favourable conditions, the results were disappointing, only four transports out of twelve and a converted 750-ton torpedo boat being sunk and a few other ships superficially damaged.

By the evening of the 24th the Japanese had occupied Balikpapan. The same day Kendari, in the Celebes, was captured by the force which earlier had taken Menado, and by February 4 the Dutch and Australian forces garrisoning Amboina had surrendered to the Japanese 228th Infantry Regiment, which had participated in the conquest of Hong Kong.

Reports of a new Japanese convoy assembling at Balikpapan induced Rear-Admiral K. W. F. M. Doorman, the Dutch commander of A.B.D.A.'s Combined Striking Force, to set out from Bunda Roads at midnight on February 4. Flying his flag in the Dutch cruiser *De Ruyter* (7,548, 1936), he was accompanied by the United States cruisers *Houston* (9,050, 1929) and *Marblehead* (7,050, 1924), the small Dutch cruiser *Tromp* (3,350, 1938) and four American and three Dutch destroyers. There is some doubt as to who planned and ordered the sortie,[18] but considering the distance the ships had to steam the operation was foolhardy, as the route chosen invited air attack. At 0949 four Japanese formations, each of nine bombers, appeared from the east, and, the lesson of the value of concentrated anti-aircraft fire having yet to be learned, the ships scattered. *Marblehead* was severely damaged, but, shepherded by the other ships, made port safely. She had to be sent to the United States for repair. *Houston's* triple 8-inch after turret was put out of commission and *De Ruyter* had her anti-aircraft fire control knocked out, but both remained operational. *Tromp* and the destroyers were not seriously attacked. Casualties were unexpectedly light — 60 killed in *Houston* and 15 in *Marblehead*.

By nightfall on February 9 Macassar had surrendered to a seaborne landing force and next day Bandjermasin was occupied by an overland expedition. The Japanese then struck at Sumatra, where, early on the 14th, 260 paratroopers were dropped on the P1 airfield at Palembang and another 100 a few miles away near the oil refineries at Pladjoe and Soengi Gerong. Another 100 paratroopers were dropped on the airfield next morning. At dawn that day the seaborne invasion force entered the Moesi River in landing-craft against strong resistance, and in the evening joined up with the paratroopers in the outskirts of Palembang. The paratroopers, having surprised the garrison, had captured the oil refinery at Pladjoe, and although they were later driven out, the denial scheme could not be put into effect, with the result that production was quickly restored. By the 17th all Allied forces had withdrawn from Sumatra to Java.

On the 18th the Japanese landed at Bali. Doorman struck at this convoy, but, never favoured by fortune, he had to leave the Dutch destroyer *Kortenaer* (1,310, 1928) behind when she grounded in leaving Tjilatjap. He lost the Dutch destroyer *Piet Hein* (1,310, 1927), sunk by torpedoes or gunfire, while *Tromp* was so badly damaged that although she made port she had to be sent to Australia for repair. A Japanese transport and a destroyer were damaged. The latter, although suffering loss of half her crew, was successfully towed to Macassar.

The same day, the 18th, an Allied convoy bound for Timor returned to Darwin, having been ordered back by Wavell, who considered an enemy attack on Timor imminent. Early on the 19th this convoy was caught in harbour when 188 carrier-borne aircraft bombed Darwin, bringing war to Australian soil for the first time in her history. A second attack about midday was delivered by 54 land-based aircraft from Kendari. The United States destroyer *Peary* (1,190, 1920), four American transports, a British tanker and two large and two small Australian ships were sunk and 10 aircraft destroyed. Casualties totalled 238 killed, including 35 civilians.[19]

The attack on Timor took place next morning, when the Japanese 228th Infantry Regiment from Amboina landed and paratroops were dropped. At 1000 on the 23rd the garrison of Kupang surrendered on finding itself surrounded, but the Australian Independent Company and some Dutch soldiers, who had been garrisoning Dili, in Portuguese Timor, withdrew to the centre of the island and continued to wage guerilla warfare until evacuated in January 1943.

With the conclusion of these preliminary operations and the fall of Singapore, the Japanese were ready to invade Java. Their Eastern Force, its principal unit the 48th Division from the Philippines, embarked in 41 transports at Jolo Island, in the Sulu Archipelago, while the Western Force, comprising the 2nd

Division from Japan and the 230th Infantry Regiment which had taken part in the subjugation of Hong Kong, assembled in 56 transports at Camranh Bay. On February 25, when it was obvious invasion was near, Wavell dissolved his headquarters and returned to his former post of Commander in Chief, India. A.B.D.A. Command had been formed far too late and its task from the outset had been hopeless. The defence of Java was essentially a matter for the Dutch, with General H. ter Poorten as army commander, Major-General L. H. van Oyen as air commander, and Admiral C. E. L. Helfrich as naval commander in chief. The Dutch regular Army numbered about 25,000 and their home guard, only partly trained, about 40,000. The British had a token force of a squadron of the 3rd Hussars with 25 light tanks, and the Australians were represented by two well-trained and experienced battalions from I Australian Corps, which had fought in Syria. The air force — Dutch, American, Australian and British — had been fighting continuously since the invasion of Malaya, and although on paper it perhaps mustered almost 200 aircraft, the number operational, including obsolete types, was about 80, of which fewer than 30 were fighters. Helfrich's command comprised 8 cruisers, 12 destroyers and 32 submarines, besides auxiliary vessels.

The initial sweeps by the Allied naval forces were abortive, neither the western nor eastern convoys being located, and it was not until 1616 on the afternoon of February 27 that Doorman clashed with Rear-Admiral T. Takagi's two heavy cruisers and 14 destroyers escorting the Eastern Force. Doorman, still flying his flag in *De Ruyter,* had with him the Dutch cruiser *Java* (6,670, 1921), *Houston,* whose after turret was still out of action, the Australian cruiser *Perth* ex *Amphion* (6,980, 1936) and the British cruiser *Exeter* (8,390, 1931), with nine destroyers, Dutch and American. Such a mixed force, assembled hurriedly, without any prior opportunity to exercise together and lacking both a common code of signals and a common tactical doctrine, was at a great disadvantage.

In the battle of the Java Sea the opponents fought one another intermittently for seven hours. The Japanese, greatly helped by three spotter planes, scored an overwhelming victory, sinking both Dutch cruisers, the British destroyers *Electra* and *Jupiter* (1,760, 1939) and the Dutch destroyer *Kortenaer*. They lost no ships, although one destroyer was badly damaged. Doorman went down with his ship. The same day, the United States aircraft tender *Langley* (11,050, 1912), attempting to deliver 32 Kittyhawk (P-40) fighters to Tjilatjap, was scuttled after being badly damaged by land-based bombers.

Houston and *Perth* reached Batavia at 1330 on the 28th and after refuelling sailed that evening for Tjilatjap. They surprised some Japanese transports in Bantam Bay, just east of the entrance to Sunda Strait, and destroyed four loaded vessels, of which three managed to beach themselves, before the *Houston* and *Perth* were in turn sunk by the Japanese covering force of three cruisers and nine destroyers. The Dutch destroyer *Evertsen* (1,310, 1927), following in the wake of the two cruisers, was so badly damaged that she had to be beached. Next day *Exeter* and the destroyers *Encounter* (1,375, 1934) and *Pope,* which had been delayed at Surabaya patching up damage to *Exeter,* were also, sunk. Allied naval vessels paid heavily in the defence of Malaya and the Netherlands East Indies. Among the ships that escaped in the final days were four United States destroyers which successfully reached Fremantle, in Western Australia, and the Australian cruiser *Hobart* ex *Apollo* (7,105, 1936), the British cruisers *Danae* (4,850, 1918) and *Dragon* (4,850, 1918) and the British destroyers *Scout* and *Tenedos,* all of which fled into the Indian Ocean.

The naval actions delayed the Japanese landings in Java by 24 hours, but during the night of February 28-March 1 the enemy came ashore simultaneously in eastern and western Java. Although the Australians held up the enemy for four days, the issue was never in doubt and on the 12th Allied forces surrendered. The same day the Japanese Guards Division sailed from Singapore and by the 28th had completed the occupation of Sumatra. The remnants of the Indian garrison of Kuching, in British Borneo, were among those who surrendered after Java's formal capitulation on March 12. After crossing into Dutch Borneo,[20] they had set out from Leda in two columns for

Sampit and Pangkalanboeoen, on the south coast, in an attempt to reach Java. After great hardships in passing through the unexplored jungle and swamps of southern Borneo, the western column reached Pangkalanboeoen on February 24 and joined the Dutch garrison there. The other column arrived at Sampit on March 6, a day after the Japanese landed.

Japan's swift conquest of Hong Kong, Malaya and the Dutch East Indies was achieved at a cost of approximately 15,000 casualties. Allied losses in killed, missing and captured, excluding the Dutch, totalled 166,500, most of whom became prisoners. At Hong Kong 11,848 combatants were lost, in Malaya 138,708, and in the naval and air actions and in the Netherlands East Indies 15,958. At a time when Allied, and more particularly British Commonwealth, manpower resources were strained to the limit, this huge loss was a grievous blow.

NOTES AND REFERENCES

1. Wigmore, 56.
2. W. S. Churchill, *The Second World War*, III: *The Grand Alliance* (London, 1950), 157.
3. C. P. Stacey, Canadian Official History, I: *Six Years of War: The Army in Canada, Britain and the Pacific*, 439-41.
4. British Official History of the War Against Japan, I: *The Fall of Singapore*, 116-7.
5. F. Spencer Chapman, *The Jungle is Neutral*, 27, 29.
6. Wigmore, 58; D. Gillison, *Royal Australian Air Force, 1939-42* (Canberra, 1962), 151.
7. Gillison, 204-5, gives a total of 164; the British Official History, 162, and Wigmore, 121 n., place it as 158, including 24 obsolete Vildebeeste torpedo-bombers; and J. M. S. Ross, *Royal New Zealand Air Force* (Wellington, 1955), 83, puts the total at as low as 144. Denis Richards and Hilary St. George Saunders, *Royal Air Force 1939-45*, II (London, 1954), 10, merely say there were eight squadrons of bombers and four of fighters.
8. Frank Owen, *The Fall of Singapore*, 36.
9. Grenfell, *Main Fleet to Singapore*, 114.
10. Gill, *Royal Australian Navy 1939-42*, 478.
11. The Japanese realization of the need for speed is well brought out in Masanobu Tsuji, *Singapore The Japanese Version*, 86, et seq.
12. Chapman, 27-8.
13. Ante, 80.
14. Ante, 65.
15. A. E. Percival, *The War in Malaya*, 206.
16. Bennett, *Why Singapore Fell*, 217.
17. The full findings of the Commissioner are given in Wigmore, 650, et seq.
18. See Gill, 555.
19. Wigmore, 493. Cf. Gill, 594-5, and Gillison, 430.
20. Ante, 107.

FURTHER READING:

The literature on Malaya is very extensive. The various official histories, naval, military and air, both British and Australian, are indispensable, but are so detailed, especially the military volumes, that they are not always easy reading. The general reader may prefer Lieutenant-General A. E. Percival's *The War in Malaya* (London, 1949), Lieutenant-General H. Gordon Bennett's *Why Singapore Fell* (Sydney, 1944), Frank Owen's *The Fall of Singapore* (London, 1960), Kenneth Attiwill's *The Singapore Story* (London, 1959), Ian Morrison's *Malayan Postscript* (London, 1942), and, for Hong Kong, Tim Carew's *The Fall of Hong Kong* (London, 1960). *The Jungle is Neutral,* by F. Spencer Chapman (London, 1952), gives a splendid picture of the difficulties of the jungle and the climate and of reconnaissance behind the enemy lines. For the Japanese side, *The Campaigns of the Pacific War* mentioned in earlier reading guides should be supplemented by Masanobu Tsuji's *Singapore The Japanese Version* (Sydney, 1960). John Toland's *But Not in Shame,* mentioned in the guide to further reading on the Philippines campaign, deals briefly with the fall of Hong Kong and at greater length with the conquest of both Malaya and the Netherlands East Indies. The sinking of the *Prince of Wales* and the *Repulse* is the subject of Captain Russell Grenfell's *Main Fleet to Singapore* (London, 1951), Bernard Ash's *Someone Had Blundered* (London, 1960), and Richard Hough's *The Hunting of Force Z* (London, 1963). Morison's *The Rising Sun in the Pacific,* mentioned in previous reading guides, as well as the official histories, deal fully with the naval actions. Escape stories include *Let's Get Cracking,* by Athole Stewart (Sydney, 1943), while prisoner-of-war books are numerous. A list of some appears in Wigmore, *The Japanese Thrust* (Canberra, 1957), but Rohan Rivett, *Behind Bamboo* (Sydney, 1946), R. H. Whitecross, *Slaves of the Son of Heaven* (Sydney, 1951), W. S. Kent Hughes, *Slaves of the Samurai* (Melbourne, 1946), Betty Jeffrey, *White Coolies* (Sydney, 1954), Laurens van der Post's semi-fictional *The Seed and the Sower* (London, 1963), John Coast, *Railroad of Death* (London, 1946), and A. J. Sweeting's part 3 of *The Japanese Thrust* may be mentioned.

five

THE FALL OF BURMA

In all main essentials but one, the story of Burma was that of Malaya all over again.

After the country's separation from India in 1937 serious invasion of this long, narrow land, mountainous and jungle-clad, with few and poor communications, was considered improbable by soldiers and civilians alike. For this reason and because of limited finance, Burma's armed forces were organized, equipped and trained rather as a police force responsible for maintaining internal order and controlling the frontier tribes than for repelling an external enemy. On the outbreak of war in Europe the strengthening of Burma's forces practically ceased, since she then dropped to the bottom of the priority list for weapons, equipment and men, naturally enough in view of the straitened resources of the British Commonwealth and the universal belief that she was in no danger of attack.

The military view was that at worst Burma faced heavy air attack and sporadic raids by land and sea. Even when the Far East war clouds darkened this forecast was not revised, and neither the weight nor the direction of the Japanese attack were foreseen. It is true that a defence conference at Singapore in October, 1940, warned that while attacks on eastern Burma might at first be confined to raids, a Japanese advance from Chiengrai, near the Indo-China border, into the southern Shan states was a feasible undertaking for a large force, but it placed more emphasis on air attacks on the docks and oil refineries at Rangoon and on land, seaborne and air attacks on Tenasserim — Burma's long, thin tail, stretching 400 miles to the south and with an average width of about 40 miles — to capture or destroy airfields on the route to Singapore. The Chiefs of Staff decided the conference had over-estimated both the scale of attack and the forces required to meet it. Not until after the outbreak of war with Japan, when the enemy stood at the gates of Burma, was an accurate estimate made of the available Japanese forces, though not of the direction in which they would strike, and then it was too late.

Nevertheless, despite the tendency to underrate the Japanese, which was as prevalent in India and Burma as in Hong Kong and Malaya, the complacent belief that Japan would not attack and the strident demands of Singapore for reinforcement, some attempt was made in 1941 to strengthen Burma's defences. Additional troops at least were sent and when war broke out the 16th Indian Brigade was still landing at Rangoon.

The concentration of Japanese forces in Thailand was regarded as a threat to Malaya rather than Burma, but the latter's strategic importance, if not her vulnerability, was recognized. Clearly Burma constituted a bastion against invasion of India's eastern frontiers. If the country were lost, Calcutta and the industrial north-east of India, with its many munition factories, would be exposed to air attack, and in Burma the enemy would hold a well-stocked base from which to launch an invasion of India. Further, through Burma ran China's so-called 'lifeline', the 750-mile Burma Road by which her armies were supplied and the United States air bases in China maintained. These supplies entered Burma across the docks at Rangoon, were carried up the Burma railway and highway to Lashio, and then over the road to China. A variety of factors — the bottleneck of the Gokteik gorge between Mandalay and Lashio, the multiplicity of Chinese agencies controlling the road, corruption, theft and embezzlement and the necessity of the lorries carrying their own petrol — curtailed the tonnage which might have been carried and reduced drastically the quantity of goods actually delivered. Yet if Burma were captured, China would be isolated and her resistance might collapse, releasing Japanese armies for employment in the Pacific.

The armed forces in Burma were numerically weak, poorly equipped and only partly trained. They lacked specialist categories and administrative services, and were mostly young and untried, without any training in jungle fighting. The British and Indian units were short of experienced officers and N.C.O.'s. No anti-aircraft guns reached Burma until after the outbreak of war, and artillery, mortars, mortar ammunition, machine-guns, automatic weapons, rifles, anti-tank mines, motor and pack transport and many other essential items were in short supply. The Burma Command — a war office and army and corps headquarters rolled into one — was too small and inexperienced to discharge its varied functions successfully and was without an intelligence staff.

The Air Force was almost non-existent. On the outbreak of war it possessed 37 first-line aircraft instead of the 280 planned. Apart from a communications unit flying Moth-type planes, there were only two fighter squadrons in the country — one an R.A.F. unit with 16 Buffaloes and the other an American Volunteer Group with 21 Tomahawks, the latter lent by Chiang Kai-shek for the defence of Rangoon. These forces later were reinforced by some Blenheims, Hurricanes and army co-operation Lysanders, which from necessity were employed also as light bombers. Considerable progress, despite a lack of mechanical equipment, had been made in the construction of airfields and strips, but many of the former had been built in the wrong places. The warning system, largely improvised and tied to telephone and telegraph lines because radio sets had not been provided, was inadequate. The only naval forces consisted of a flotilla of five motor launches and a few auxiliary vessels.

The inadequacy of these forces was underlined by the difficulty of the political situation. In 1941 Burma had a population of almost 17,000,000, of whom about 10,000,000 were Burmans and 4,000,000 Karens of the eastern hills. The Shans, Kachins, Nagas and Chins, all hill people, made up the rest of the indigenous population. The Indians, about 1,000,000 strong, and the Chinese, probably totalling rather under half a million, were numerically the most important non-indigenous elements of the population. The Governor, Sir Reginald Dorman-Smith, believed that once the Japanese crossed the frontier the Burmese would rise in their wrath against the invaders, but this was wishful thinking. The uneducated masses were probably neither pro-British nor pro-Japanese, but almost certainly would support whichever side appeared to be winning. The hill folk were, on the whole, loyal to Britain, but the educated Burmans, despite the many political factions and personal jealousies which had prevented the country securing a stable government, were united in their determination to achieve complete independence. If Britain had given Burma independence, she might have won the country to her side. As it was, the nationalistic Thakin Party, pro-Japanese because such a policy promised freedom from the British yoke, had won more widespread support than the British authorities realized or than some British historians have since admitted. Its violently anti-British attitude created a considerable Fifth Column, led to large-scale desertion from the armed services and made possible the appearance, within a few weeks of the opening of hostilities, of the Burma Independent Army in active support of the Japanese.

Another factor which contributed materially to Burma's unpreparedness was the fact that Burma was an unwanted baby, shuffled by the British Government from one reluctant father to another. Before separation, Burma, operationally and administratively, was for defence purposes the responsibility of India. After separation, the British War Office assumed operational control, and the administration of the armed services was shared by the British Government and the subordinate Defence Department in Burma. India had neither a share in this defence nor a say in it.[1] Then, in November 1940, on the creation of the Far East Command, with headquarters at Singapore, Burma was included among Air Marshal Brooke-Popham's many responsibilities, except that Army administration remained with the War Office. Successive Commanders in Chief of India urged that the defence of Burma, since it formed an integral part of the defence of India, should be placed under Delhi, both operationally and administratively, but these representations, logical though they were, failed to bring about any change. Not until December 11 1941 after the outbreak of war with Japan, was Burma hurriedly dumped into India's lap. However, she was not allowed to remain there for long. As soon as the A.B.D.A. Command was formed, Burma, for operational purposes, became Wavell's responsibility despite his vigorous protests, the remoteness of his headquarters in Java and the difficulties of communication. Administratively, however, Burma remained under India, and not until February 22 1942 was operational control again transferred back to Delhi.

These changes in the supreme command, and the separation, for most of the time, of the operational and administrative functions into different hands, prevented a consistent policy being pursued, interfered with planning and rendered reinforcement and the strengthening of Burma's defences more difficult. It was Wavell's realization that Burma's military system required overhauling and reorganizing that induced him to replace Lieutenant-General D. K. McLeod, the General Officer Commanding in Burma, by India's Chief of Staff, Lieutenant-General Thomas J. Hutton, a brilliant staff officer. Hutton assumed command on December 27, but he was denied by the enemy the time he needed to reorganize the defence of Burma.

The Japanese assigned their XV Army, under Lieutenant-General Shojira Iida, to the conquest of Burma. Like the forces in the Philippines and Malaya, it came under the Southern Army. The XV Army initially was composed of Lieutenant-General Shoso Sakurai's seasoned 33rd Division, which had been serving for almost two years in China, and the 55th Division, commanded by Lieutenant-General Yiroshi Takeuchi. These two divisions had a strength of rather over 35,000 men, but after the fall of Malaya the Army was substantially rein-

Australian War Memorial

Above, General Yamashita, far left, accepts the surrender of Singapore in 1942 from the British commander, Lieutenant-General Percival. Below, three years later events turn full circle as Japanese commanders surrender Singapore to the British on board HMS *Sussex*

Australian War Memorial

Australian War Memorial

A Japanese medium tank destroyed by anti-tank fire in Malaya

Indian troops using ponies as transport in Burma

Australian War Memorial

forced by the transfer to Burma of the 18th and 56th Divisions, with certain tank, anti-aircraft and artillery units, all of which reached Rangoon in March and April. Air support was at first given by the 10th Air Brigade, but following the fall of Manila, Obata's 5th Air Division, with the 4th Air Brigade, was moved to Thailand and, taking the 10th Air Brigade under command, furnished the XV Army with its air support throughout the Burma campaign.

Japan's first operations were designed to secure the airfields along the Tenasserim coast, so that their fighters might operate from them to escort bombers raiding Rangoon. Obviously untenable by the British it was purposeless for the Army to defend them, and when a small Japanese force crossed into Tenasserim on December 11, the British garrisons were evacuated by sea. By the 24th the airfields of Victoria Point, Mergui and Tavoy were in enemy hands.

The British began the war with a 'needless and blundering operation'[2] into Thailand. This operation was designed to demolish two bridges on the Bangkok-Malaya railway, but it foundered through the use of maps made in 1909, for the country had so changed in appearance in the interval, the tidal river having been reclaimed and converted into paddy fields, that the bridges could not be found!

The war was six weeks old when on January 20 the Japanese 55th Division began to move into Burma in strength and, employing the envelopment and infiltration tactics which had proved so successful in Malaya, quickly forced the 16th Indian Brigade out of Kawkareik. The retiring brigade had to cross the Gyaing River, but the ferry was sunk by an over-loaded ammunition truck and the greater part of the force was stranded east of the river. Most of its vehicles and supporting weapons had to be destroyed, and the men, their morale shaken although having suffered few casualties, marched down the river for two days until picked up by steamers and taken to Martaban. On the 30th, under heavy Japanese attack, the 12-mile perimeter around Moulmein, at the mouth of the Salween River, began to crumble and early next day the garrison was evacuated in fifteen river steamers, only one of which was sunk by enemy gunfire. Martaban, on the Salween opposite Moulmein, was evacuated on February 9, the garrison reaching Thaton two days later after a 50-mile march. The same day the Japanese 33rd Division, launching an offensive from Pa-an, seized Kuzeik and established a bridgehead west of the Salween River.

Major-General J. G. Smyth, V.C., whose 17th Indian Division had been entrusted with the task of stopping the Japanese drive on Rangoon, decided on the evening of the 14th to withdraw to the line of the Bilin River in view of a Japanese threat to outflank him. His decision did not meet with the approval of Wavell, far away at his headquarters in Java, and the A.B.D.A. Supreme Commander cabled Hutton that 'continued withdrawal, as experience of Malaya showed, is most damaging to morale of troops, especially Indian troops,' and added, 'Time can often be gained effectively and less expensively by bold counter-offensive. This especially so against the Japanese.'[3] Wavell, despite what had happened in Malaya, still believed that the Indian and Burmese troops, ill-trained and ill-equipped, were yet capable of defeating the tough, well-trained enemy infantry. His failure to accurately evaluate the fighting ability of the Japanese troops contributed to the disaster that followed. Later, he was to admit a serious error of judgement in underestimating the danger to Burma and in failing to appreciate the weakness of the British troops.[4]

Hutton's problem was similar to Percival's: to keep the Japanese as far from Rangoon as possible so that reinforcements might land. With the optimistic Wavell emphasizing the danger of continued withdrawal, and talking, as he did after visiting the Salween front on February 6, of taking the offensive and inflicting a heavy defeat on the enemy,[5] Hutton, like Percival, felt obliged, perhaps against his better judgement, to fight for every inch of ground, with similar disastrous results. Smyth, realizing that the easily fordable Bilin River was not a naturally strong position, wished at one bound to fall back behind the wider, swift-flowing Sittang River, a more formidable obstacle, but Hutton ordered the line of the Bilin to be held and said it was to be relinquished only with his permission.

The 17th Indian Division, whose brigades were drawn from

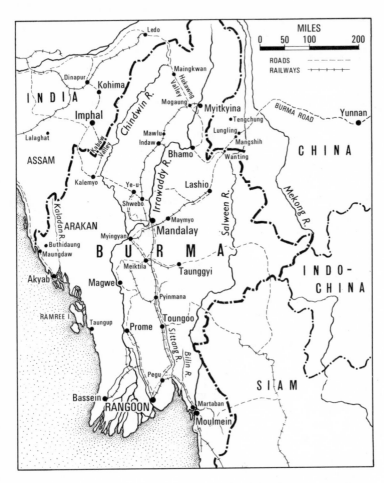

5. The Burma war theatre

different formations and had never trained together as a division, was outnumbered, but despite its many deficiencies fought well. It held up the Japanese advance for four days and compelled the leading enemy division to deploy almost its entire strength. By February 18, however, the enemy not only held a bridge-head across the river in the centre of the British line but was threatening both its flanks, particularly Smyth's left. Next day Hutton gave Smyth permission to withdraw. Unfortunately, some formation or unit issued the withdrawal orders by radio in clear and this message was intercepted by the Japanese. Sakurai seized the opportunity thus presented and ordered the 215th Infantry Regiment to move across country at top speed and seize the Sittang River bridge before the main body of the retiring British could reach it.

During the night of the 20th the British broke contact on the Bilin River, but, weary and hungry, fell back only to within some 15 miles of the bridge. On the 21st the retreat was resumed in great heat and, again, without any feeling of par-ticipating in a race for the bridge, although the flank guards were heavily engaged in the jungle on both sides of the road during the day. Clouds of red dust clearly marked the line of retreat, and Japanese aircraft bombed and machine-gunned the retiring columns unceasingly. They were also attacked, as a result of a faulty briefing following a false report of an enemy column of 300 lorries, by Allied planes. The air attacks, British and Japanese, were accurate, caused heavy casualties and delayed the withdrawal. Mules stampeded with their loads into the jungle, lorries, ambulances and guns were overturned, vehicles set on fire.

All three brigades of the 17th Division had to cross the single-lane bridge over the Sittang, and as unwanted transport had not been sent back in advance, the congestion was great. In fact, the retreat was badly mismanaged by the divisional staff, but the confusion along the bomb-cratered road leading to the bridge was increased by an accident which occurred at a critical moment in the early hours of the 22nd. A 3-ton lorry crashed through the temporary decking of the bridge and, becoming jammed, brought all traffic to a halt The accident occurred at

0300 and, lacking recovery apparatus and unable to jettison the lorry since it was a girder bridge, the engineers took three hours and a half to clear the obstruction and restart traffic across. By then the crowded road for miles back was blocked with stationary vehicles, often double-banked. In consequence, only a part of the leading brigade was safely across when from the jungle north-east of the bridge the Japanese 215th Regiment attacked at 0830. The 3rd Burma Rifles gave way at once and momentarily it seemed that the enemy's attempt to rush the bridge would succeed, but, fortunately for the British, an immediate counter-attack restored the bridgehead line.

Throughout the day there was fighting in the bridge-head, and British and Indians were under attack from the air and from troops off the road in the jungle, while a strong road block established in the gap between two of the brigades was the scene of fierce fighting and delayed the retreat. These attacks had an adverse effect on morale and the 8th Burma Rifles had nearly 200 desertions. The fighting continued during the night, and early on the 23rd, when it was reported the bridgehead could not be held much longer, Smyth ordered the bridge to be blown up, leaving the bulk of his division on the eastern bank. As the roar of the demolition explosion died away a hush settled momentarily on the battlefield, as though both sides were stunned by the knowledge that the bridge had gone.

Under air and ground attack, the British, Indians and Burmese made their way to the river bank as best they could. 'Here there was chaos and confusion,' said Brigadier R. G. Ekin, of the 46th Indian Infantry Brigade, in describing the scene[6]; 'hundreds of men throwing down their arms, equipment and clothing and taking to the water . . . some bringing their arms with them on improvised rafts . . . As we crossed, the river was a mass of bobbing heads . . . Although it was a disastrous situation there were many stout hearts and parties shouted at each other, egging on others to swim faster, with jokes about the boat race.' The tide had come in and at places the river was a mile and a half wide. Some men were shot by enemy snipers or killed by machine-gun fire from the air; others were swept away by the swift current and drowned. The wounded, wherever possible, were ferried across on rafts, and some of their rescuers swam the river more than once to help their less fortunate comrades. A lifeline rigged across the fallen spans of the bridge saved the lives of some 300 non-swimmers despite enemy fire.

In the disaster of the Bilin River the 17th Division lost some of its guns, most of its transport and much other equipment, and on the 24th its infantry mustered only 80 officers and 3,404 other ranks, of whom but 1,420 still had their rifles.

Hutton, knowing the battle was going against him and that his forces were too weak to hold Rangoon, said so frankly in a realistic report on February 18, before the Bilin River disaster. His appreciation was soundly based and accurate, as events were to prove, but it was unwelcome. Wavell and senior officers in India concluded the constant failures and retreats of the Burma Army were due to Hutton's indifferent generalship. On the day he forecast the probable loss of Rangoon, the Viceroy of India, the Marquess of Linlithgow, cabled London that the troops in Burma were 'not fighting with proper relish' because of lack of drive and inspiration from the top. In consequence of this message and with Wavell's approval, the War Cabinet on the 22nd informed Hutton that he was to be superseded by General Sir Harold Alexander, but was to remain on in Burma as Alexander's Chief of Staff. However, in April, at his own request, he was relieved as Chief of Staff by Major-General T. J. W. Winterton. In mid-March, when it was decided to set up a corps headquarters for which Hutton had asked in vain, Lieutenant-General William J. Slim was appointed corps commander. Alexander had commanded a division in the B.E.F. in France and Slim had led a brigade in operations in Abyssinia and a division in Iraq and Syria.

These changes, particularly the appointment of Slim, had in them the seeds of future success and were to pay big dividends, but it is impossible not to sympathize with Hutton, who, with wholly inadequate forces and despite a near escape from death in an aircraft crash in which his pilot was killed, had displayed vigour and foresight and had resolutely refused to indulge in wishful thinking.

In Malaya local air superiority over Singapore was never held by the British, but in Burma, small as was the Air Force, local air superiority over Rangoon was secured at the outset and retained despite desperate enemy challenges. The American Volunteer Group Squadron were primarily responsible, but they were stoutly supported by the R.A.F. pilots.

The first raid on Rangoon had taken place on December 23, when some 60 bombers, escorted by fighters, attacked Mingaladon airfield, the docks and congested parts of the city. Military damage was not heavy, but the naive and uninstructed civilians, flocking into the streets to watch the bombing and the aerial combats, suffered severely. Some 1,250 were killed on the spot and another 600 died in hospital.[7] A second attack by 100 bombers and fighters was made on Christmas Day. On this occasion only 60 civilians were killed and 40 wounded,[8] although another source[9] claims about 5,000 were killed. A respite followed this raid, allowing aircraft reinforcements and anti-aircraft guns to arrive. The air commander in Burma, Air Vice-Marshal D. F. Stevenson, used the new arrivals — a squadron of Blenheim bombers and some 30 Hurricanes — offensively, the Blenheims dropping 11,000 lb. of bombs on the chief Japanese air base at Bangkok within a few hours of their arrival from the Middle East and the fighters strafing the advanced enemy airfields and giving some support to the Army on the banks of the Salween.

From January 23 to 29 there was continuous day fighting over Rangoon as the Japanese attempted to wrest air superiority from the Allies. They failed and suffered heavy losses. On one day alone a squadron of heavy bombers from the 14th Air Regiment was completely destroyed, and in the seven days the Japanese are believed to have lost 50 bombers and fighters as against 10 R.A.F. and two American aircraft. His losses caused Obata to abandon daylight attacks in favour of sporadic night raids, but on February 24 and 25 he again attempted to secure local air superiority. This second effort also failed, with severe losses, but the Allies had little left and when the Air

Force flew out, with the fall of Rangoon imminent, it had only 3 Buffaloes, 4 Tomahawks and 20 Hurricanes to move northwards.

Stevenson's valiant stand, however, had enabled all reinforcements and supplies reaching Rangoon to be landed without serious interruption by the enemy air force, but the port and city lost almost its entire labour force. After the first raid the dead lay unburied for three days, shops closed, food supplies broke down, mail deliveries ceased and public transport came to a halt. When the Christmas Day raid took place three-quarters of the city's population had already left. Many people returned to the city during the subsequent lull, but whenever the sirens sounded 'all those who possessed cars jumped into them and drove madly for the open country at the highest possible speed. The remainder downed tools and hid themselves in the nearest ditch or drain. For a few moments there was complete pandemonium as the carriage folk shrieked their way through the main streets; then there was a still and deathly silence through which the noise of the engines of the approaching planes sounded like the sound of impending doom.'[10]

The renewal of the air fighting over Rangoon and the night raids led to another exodus from the city, so that by mid-February little civilian labour was left. Looting and arson in the almost deserted city were checked by military patrols and by compelling the offenders to work at the docks under guard. Tens of thousands of men, women and children were trekking northwards to walk over the jungle trails crossing the Arakan Yomas to Taungup in the hope of obtaining passage by country craft to Chittagong or to follow the steep Chindwin routes into Assam. The ranks of the refugees, who suffered every imaginable hardship and died in great numbers, were constantly swelled as the Japanese thrust deeper into Burma.

On March 5 Alexander reached Rangoon. The Japanese, having forced the crossing of the Sittang, were vigorously attacking the British around Pegu and were also attempting to cut the road to Prome, Rangoon's only escape route. He at first hoped to save Rangoon, but the hope was short-lived. He ordered forward the 63rd Indian Brigade, which had just arrived, but in negotiating a Japanese road block, after having made a reconnaissance to Pegu, the Brigadier and his three battalion commanders were all killed or wounded, so that even before it became engaged the brigade lost all its senior officers. The British were forced out of Pegu and suffered severe casualties in breaking through the enemy road block on their line of retreat. Late on the 6th Alexander decided to evacuate Rangoon, but in the time available the small force of engineers could not complete the denial scheme, and large supplies of timber, coal, steel rails and bridging material, hundreds of river craft and intact warehouses, wharves and rice and timber mills fell into the enemy's hands.

But for Sakurai's rigid adherence to his plan, which was to cross the Prome road and take Rangoon from the north-west — a direction which was likely to achieve tactical surprise — the bulk of the British forces in the Rangoon area might have been cut off and destroyed. To protect their flank as the 33rd Division crossed the road, the Japanese established a strong road block a few miles north of Taukkyan. On the 7th the retreating British came up against it, and two tank-supported attacks failed to break through. By evening the British position seemed desperate, and plans for a deliberate attack next morning, supported by artillery and armour, were made. However, having crossed the road during the night, and believing the British main body was still garrisoning Rangoon, for which they expected to have to fight, the Japanese withdrew their road block, which had served its purpose as a flank guard. In the morning the British were able to resume their retreat and at midday the Japanese entered Rangoon to find it deserted.

With the loss of Rangoon, and except for such supplies and reinforcements as could be flown in, the British Army in Burma was cut off and the Chinese isolated. The Japanese, anxious to complete the conquest of the country, brought in strong reinforcements, since they knew Chinese armies were coming to the assistance of the British. The 18th and 56th Divisions, fresh from the conquest of Malaya, and additional tank, artillery and specialist units were shipped to Rangoon. Alexander concentrated the British, Indian and Burmese forces in the Irrawaddy valley around Prome, leaving to the Chinese the defence of the direct road and railway up the Sittang valley to Mandalay and the prevention of any enemy thrust into the Shan States from Indo-China. The Chinese V and VI Armies, each about the strength of a British division, were commánded by Lieutenant-General Joseph W. Stilwell, an unconventional, Chinese-speaking American officer, who had been appointed Chief of Staff to Chiang Kai-shek and whose acid tongue and critical outspokenness had earned him the nickname of 'Vinegar Joe'. He was hampered by the independence of the Chinese generals, who often refused or neglected to carry out his orders, and the absence among the Chinese of a staff system, which meant their units were incapable of quick movements in an emergency. However, the Chinese fought well and stubbornly, although their co-operation was often faulty and they frequently missed opportunities for offensive action.

Lacking an adequate warning system and based too far forward, the depleted Allied Air Force was shattered, so that when the Japanese advanced they held complete control of the air and were free to give every support to their ground forces. The Japanese attempt to trap the British in the loop of the Irrawaddy failed, as also did their efforts to get across the lines of retreat by a wide enveloping movement. The Chinese, whose stubborn defence held up the Japanese advance along the Sittang valley for a fortnight, were very roughly handled. Their armies disintegrated under constant attack and they suffered severe losses before making a disorderly retreat into China, except for their 38th Division, which retreated westward into India.

By April 30, the day after the Japanese capture of Lashio, terminus of the Burma Road, central Burma had fallen to the enemy. That night the British crossed to the north bank of the Irrawaddy and the great Ava bridge was destroyed at midnight. The retreat of the British, at first made in intense heat, was orderly and well managed, and in its later stages developed into a race for Shwegyin, where troops, guns and vehicles were to be ferried up the Chindwin to Kalewa. Although the British won the race, the Japanese were hard on their heels and by May 10 had seized a hill overlooking the embarkation area.

The result was that most of the Army's tanks, guns, vehicles and equipment had to be destroyed, while the men climbed the narrow, precipitous track to Kaing. On the 12th the monsoon broke, adding to the misery of the exhausted troops on the last section of their 900-mile retreat.

'From then onwards,' says Slim, in his account of the Burma campaigns,[11] 'the retreat was sheer misery. Ploughing their way up slopes, over a track inches deep in slippery mud, soaked to the skin, rotten with fever, ill-fed and shivering as the air grew cooler, the troops went on, hour after hour, day after day. Their only rest at night was to lie on sodden ground under the dripping trees, without even a blanket to cover them. Yet the monsoon which so nearly destroyed us and whose rain beat so mercilessly on our bodies did us one good turn — it stopped dead the Japanese pursuit. As the clouds closed down over the hills, even their air attacks became rare.'

On May 19 the rearguard reached Tamu and next day Alexander's command was dissolved, all his troops being placed under IV Corps, charged with the defence of India's frontier in this area. The retreat of over 900 miles had occupied three months and a half. Only 50 lorries, 30 jeeps and 28 guns were brought back by the Army, whose total casualties in the campaign were 13,463. The British and Indians lost 3,670 killed and wounded and 6,366 missing, while Burmese units had 363 killed and wounded and 3,064 missing. As the retreat continued many of the Burmese personnel were dismissed to their homes. They took their rifles and ammunition with them and many, especially the hill people, waged guerilla warfare against the Japanese. The Allies lost 116 aircraft, of which 65 were destroyed in aerial combat. Japanese casualties were 4,597 killed and wounded, while they lost 117 aircraft, 60 of them destroyed in the air.[12]

About 400,000 refugees, of whom almost 200,000 reached Imphal by way of Tamu and 100,000 crossed the Arakan Yomas and arrived at Calcutta by ship from Akyab, reached India, but many thousands died on the way.

While these events were taking place, the defences of India were being strengthened and it was being built up as a great base from which future offensive operations against the Japanese could be launched. At the time it seemed that an attack on India or Ceylon was imminent, but in actual fact the Japanese had decided not to extend their sphere of conquest westward. With a view to securing the lines of communication in the Indian Ocean, a British plan for the seizure of the air and naval base of Diego Suarez, in Vichy-controlled Madagascar, was drawn up. The attack was made on May 5 and achieved surprise, and on the 7th the city surrendered. The price was small, casualties being 100 killed and nearly 300 wounded, with the loss of a minesweeper and five aircraft. Before the end of the month, however, a daring and skilful attack by two midget submarines sank a tanker and damaged the British battleship *Ramillies* (29,150, 1917), which, however, was able to make her own way to Durban for repairs. Largely at the suggestion of South Africa's Prime Minister, General J. C. Smuts, the south of Madagascar was later occupied, the final capitulation taking place on November 6.

Early in April British and Japanese warships played hide-and-seek in the Indian Ocean as the Japanese struck from the air at Ceylon and raided shipping in the Bay of Bengal. These operations were designed by the Japanese to cover the arrival of their reinforcement convoys at Rangoon. The rival fleets failed to locate one another, which was probably fortunate for the inferior British Eastern Fleet under its new commander, Admiral Sir James Somerville. Nagumo, who had led the Pearl Harbour attack, had five fleet carriers, supported by four battleships, two heavy and one light cruiser and eight destroyers. On April 5, from about 300 miles south of Colombo, he launched 53 bombers, 38 dive-bombers and 36 fighters against that port. As at Pearl Harbour, it was a Sunday and the attack, starting about 0800, lasted 35 minutes. Thirty-six Hurricanes and 6 Fleet Air Arm Fulmars, although they had little warning of the raid, took off and attacked the enemy formations. Although the loss of life was small, severe damage was done to the harbour area and the railway workshops, but the airfield was only slightly damaged. The destroyer *Tenedos,* which was refitting, and an armed merchant cruiser were sunk, a submarine depot ship was holed and a merchant vessel damaged by fire. Two Catalinas, 15 Hurricanes, 4 Fulmars and 6 Swordfish, the latter armed with torpedoes and *en route* from Trincomalee to Colombo, were shot down. The defences claimed 24 enemy aircraft shot down, but the Japanese, who said they shot down 41 British planes, admitted the loss of only 7 aircraft.

The same day, when speeding to a rendezvous with the rest of the Eastern Fleet, the cruisers *Dorsetshire* (9,975, 1930) and *Cornwall* (10,000, 1928) were found by enemy aircraft and sunk by bombs. *Dorsetshire,* struck by at least nine bombs, capsized and sank within eight minutes of the first bomb falling, and she was followed beneath the waves by *Cornwall.* A total of 1,122 officers and men out of 1,546 were rescued, but they were not picked up in the normally shark-infested waters until late the following afternoon, when a cruiser and two destroyers reached the scene.

The second raid against Ceylon was directed at Trincomalee, where the dockyard and China Bay airfield were the principal targets for the enemy carrier-based planes in a raid that began at 0725 on April 9. The 17 Hurricanes and 6 Fulmars, which were all the fighters the British had and all of which were airborne when the raid began, were hopelessly outnumbered and 8 of the Hurricanes and 1 Fulmar were shot down. Damage both to the dockyard and the airfield was severe. Nine Blenheims located and bombed the enemy fleet, but, apparently, did not score a single direct hit, and only four of the bombers, all damaged, returned to base.

The losses at sea following this raid were heavy. The harbour had been cleared as soon as a reconnaissance Catalina reported the presence of a fleet in the vicinity. The ships which had taken to the ocean in an effort to evade the bombers were caught by the enemy as they began to set course back to harbour. The small aircraft carrier *Hermes* (10,850, 1924), attacked by 90 bombers and fighters, was sunk in 20 minutes, and her escort, H.M.A.S. *Vampire,* was also sunk. Through a tragic breakdown of communications, orders to fighters at Colombo and Trincomalee to cover the two ships did not reach the airfields. The hospital ship *Vita,* which chanced to be on passage, picked up 600 survivors, and others reached the shore in small craft or by swimming, but 19 officers and 283 ratings from *Hermes* and 1 officer and 7 ratings from *Vampire* lost their lives. A tanker, a corvette and a fleet auxiliary were also sunk by Japanese aircraft, but as the last-mentioned vessel was sinking 8 Fulmars reached the scene and shot down at least 3 bombers for the loss of 2 of their own planes. Total Japanese losses in all these operations are now known to have been only 17 aircraft. There were no further attacks against Ceylon.

Vice-Admiral Jisaburo Ozawa's Malaya Force, which carried out the raid on shipping, sank no fewer than 23 ships, totalling 112,312 tons, between April 4 and 9, while on India's west coast enemy submarines sank about 32,000 tons of merchant shipping. These losses for a time practically halted all shipping, but although the British did not know it, a Japanese fleet was not again to venture into the Indian Ocean.

NOTES AND REFERENCES

1. *The Retreat from Burma 1941-42* (Calcutta, 1959), XXV.
2. Ibid., 70.
3. *India's Darkest Hour* (London, 1958), 46.
4. J. R. M. Butler, *Grand Strategy*, III, pt. II, 466. (London, 1964.)
5. Ibid., Smyth, *Before the Dawn*, 162.
6. Quoted in *India's Darkest Hour*, 72.
7. *The Retreat from Burma*, 74.
8. Ibid., 74.
9. Royal Air Force History, II: *The Fight Avails* (London, 1954), 56.
10. Smyth, 123.
11. Slim, *Defeat into Victory*, 109.
12. The casualty figures are those given in the British official history, *India's Darkest Hour*. They vary slightly from those in *The Retreat from Burma*. Figures of Chinese losses, which were heavy, are not recorded.

FURTHER READING:

Again, the official histories, British, Indian and American, provide the greatest detail about the campaign in Burma, the air raids on Ceylon and the naval hide-and-seek in the Indian Ocean, but the only volume so far published in the official Australian naval history stops short of the incursion of Nagumo and Ozawa into the Indian Ocean and Bay of Bengal. Compton Mackenzie's *Eastern Epic,* I, *Defence, September 1939-March 1943* (London, 1951) devotes considerable space to Burma, but a more readable popular account is Field-Marshal Sir William Slim's *Defeat into Victory* (London, 1956), although he devotes only 121 pages to the first Burma campaign. An account of the sinking of the *Dorsetshire* and the *Cornwall* will be found in Carl Olsson's *From Hell to Breakfast* (London, 1943), 75-81.

six

THE CORAL SEA
AND MIDWAY BATTLES

While these events were taking place, the conversion of Australia into a base for future offensive operations was under way. The process began, somewhat uncertainly, even haphazardly, under the spur of the wish to reinforce the Philippines, particularly with aircraft. The *Pensacola* convoy,[1] *en route* to Manila when war broke out, was diverted to Brisbane, in Australia, on December 12, and over the next five days General Marshall ordered four additional shipments of fighters and ammunition sent to Australia, bringing the total of fighter aircraft dispatched to 248. These planes were all intended ultimately for the Philippines, although at the time of their dispatch Washington was far from clear as to how they were to be got to General MacArthur, and, in the event, the Japanese blockade of Luzon prevented their arrival.

On the 14th Marshall directed Brigadier-General Dwight D. Eisenhower, soon to become Supreme Commander of the European Theatre of Operations, to study the advisability of establishing an advanced American base in Australia.[2] On the 17th

Australian War Memorial

Well-camouflaged Japanese troops advance through Gemas

American planes in action over the Pacific. Above, a Dauntless on a bombing raid on Wake Island. Below, a Helldiver climbs away after successfully hitting a Japanese transport ship

Australian War Memorial

Bombs from RAAF Liberators land perilously close to the Japanese cruiser *Isuzu* as she alters course to avoid them

RAAF transport planes return after dropping supplies to forward areas in New Guinea

Australian War Memorial

In the battle of the Coral Sea, which turned the tide in the Pacific and saved Port Moresby, USS *Lexington,* above, exploded after being struck by a number of bombs and torpedoes

An aerial view of a Pacific battle between Japanese planes and American ships and aircraft

Marshall approved Eisenhower's plan and ordered him to implement it. It provided for what was essentially an air base, using the men and aircraft in the convoys already ordered to Australia as the nucleus of the new command. Major-General George H. Brett, who at the time of these decisions was attending an Allied conference in Chungking, was selected to command the United States Army Forces in Australia.

The creation of this force necessarily implied the willingness of the United States, in association with its allies, to defend the South-West Pacific, and as the Japanese advance continued it was used to this end, but in December its primary and immediate object remained that of getting vital supplies to the Philippines. By Christmas Eve it had been decided that the United States Army Air Forces in Australia should comprise two heavy, two medium and one light bomber and four fighter groups, and that of this force — 'the largest projected concentration of American air power outside the Western Hemisphere'[3] — one medium bomber and two fighter groups should go to the Netherlands East Indies.

The Central Pacific air supply route from the United States to Australia was unusable because of its proximity to the Japanese air bases on their mandated islands and the loss of Wake and Guam, and at all cost the alternative and hitherto subsidiary South Pacific route had therefore to be developed, kept open and protected throughout its length against attack. This in itself was a major undertaking. Airfields had to be built or improved between Hawaii and Australia, port facilities created, aviation fuel, guns, ammunition and other essential supplies and equipment furnished, and provision made for the quartering and feeding of air and ground crews, anti-aircraft units and garrisons. The Free French port of Bora Bora, in the Society Islands, where the United States Navy wished to establish a refuelling base, also had to be garrisoned. Since local resources were limited, almost all the constructional workers and *matériel,* as well as equipment and supplies, had to be shipped from the United States. Local resources in Australia were greater, but *matériel* and equipment in considerable quantities were needed there also, and since the attrition rate of Brett's command was likely to be high initially, a steady flow of replacements of men and aircraft was necessary to maintain the United States Army Air Forces in Australia at strength.

All this involved the provision of an enormous quantity of merchant shipping and a large number of escort vessels. To lift the same number of troops and their equipment to Australia, because of the great distances in the Pacific, required twice the shipping tonnage used on the shorter Atlantic crossing. Sufficient transports were needed to lift 37,000 men immediately, with a further 10,000 to follow, and to house and feed these forces, and to supply them with all their needs, after making allowance for what was available locally required merchantmen capable of transporting more than 500,000 tons of cargo. The provision of shipping on such a scale, at a time when resources were already stretched, required the intervention of the Arcadia Conference,[4] but Churchill and Roosevelt approved the plan as necessary to give effect to the Allied strategy of containing the Japanese while defeating Germany and Italy and ordered the necessary ships to be found, even to the serious detriment of commitments elsewhere.

Apart from a field artillery brigade which chanced to be in the *Pensacola* convoy, United States Army ground forces were not being committed by these decisions to strengthen Australia's defences. The United States War Department's policy was not to send Army ground forces to Australia, but the march of events caused an abrupt change. Japanese successes in Malaya, the Indies, Burma and the Philippines brought closer the possibility of invasion of Australia and India or of one or the other. To Allied strategists, and even more to uninformed and dismayed civilian populations which had never expected the Japanese to advance so fast or so far, the course of events in the first months of 1942 seemed to be bringing the world toppling about their heads and to indicate clearly that invasion of Australia and India was imminent and inevitable. If Allied strategy were to succeed, if the Japanese were to be contained while the war against Germany and Italy was won, the Pacific flanks, Australia and New Zealand on the one side and India and China on the other, must be held; for these were the spring-boards from which the Japanese could later be smitten. The risk that one or the other might be lost simply could not be taken.

In anticipation of the early fall of Singapore, Wavell on February 13 suggested that the loss of Sumatra and Java was now also inevitable and that therefore Australian divisions released from the Middle East should be sent either to Burma, where Rangoon had not yet fallen, or Australia. He followed this warning message on the 16th with a long report to London on the general situation. In this, after warning how vital it was to hold the flanks, he recommended that the 7th Australian Division, part of which was then approaching Ceylon, should land in Burma in an effort to save Rangoon and that if it were necessary to reinforce Australia, United States ground forces should be sent. Churchill and Roosevelt made personal appeals to the Prime Minister of Australia, John Curtin, to agree to the Australians going to Burma, but the Australian Labour Govern-ment, acting on the advice of General Sturdee, their Chief of Staff, refused, much to Churchill's chagrin, and maintained its refusal in the face of a further appeal. The strongly worded messages which Churchill and Curtin exchanged on this occa-sion formed, in Churchill's words, 'a painful episode', with the result that 'amid the stresses of the time bitter feelings swept our circle, military and political, in London.'[5] The British Prime Minister had been so certain that Australia would agree that he had turned the convoy around without informing Curtin!

With the full knowledge of events we now possess, Curtin and Sturdee were undoubtedly right. Their refusal was, indeed, a morally courageous step that later was to have far-reaching, perhaps decisive, influence on the course of operations in the South-West Pacific.[6]

The 7th Australian Division would have arrived at Rangoon piecemeal, a brigade at a time, with the men in different vessels from their vehicles and heavy weapons, and they may well have had to land under heavy and sustained enemy air attack. In these circumstances, and having regard to the earliest dates on which each brigade could have arrived, the division could not have turned the tide in Burma and saved Rangoon. At best, almost certainly at heavy cost, it might have delayed Rangoon's capture for a day or two, but inevitably what then remained of the division would have joined the Burma Army in its withdrawal to India and been lost, as last-minute reinforcements thrown into Singapore had been lost, to the Allied cause without compensating advantage.[7]

What effect Wavell's warning message may have had on American military thinking remains a matter of speculation, but significantly on February 14, the day after his first signal and before his longer report of the 16th sparked the controversy over the employment of the Australian division, the War Department in Washington had decided to send combat ground troops to Australia in addition to Army air units. By the 19th the necessary shipping had been found for the transfer to Australia of the triangular 41st United States Division, 15,000 strong, a tank destroyer battalion of 800 men, and 8,000 service troops.

The convoys to Australia were protected by task forces formed round the United States fleet carriers *Enterprise* (19,800, 1938), *Lexington* (33,000, 1925), *Saratoga* (33,000, 1927) and *Yorktown* (19,900, 1936), the latter transferred to the Pacific from the Atlantic after Pearl Harbour. However, on January 11, a Japanese submarine scored a torpedo hit on *Saratoga* and she had to be sent to the west coast of America for repair and modernization. When they were not engaged in covering convoys, these task forces bombed and bombarded enemy positions in the Marshalls and the Gilberts and on Manus and Wake Islands. These raids, the first offensive moves by the United States Navy, caused little damage and inflicted few casualties, but they had a beneficial effect on morale, both in the fleet and among Allied civilians, and were invaluable in the tactical lessons they taught and the experience they gave air and ship crews.

The incident regarding the employment of the 7th Australian Division and the fall of Singapore yielded far-reaching strategic decisions. They directed Roosevelt's thoughts, first, to the need of ensuring the defence of Australia, whose industrial capacity, although still weak and undeveloped, was potentially great and whose trained manpower, with one division lost in Malaya and three others still overseas, was temporarily depleted, and, second, to the desirability of setting up a simplified but effective system of command. On February 20, in a message to Curtin, Roosevelt said that because of their geographical position 'we Americans can better handle the reinforcement of Australia and the right flank'. He had made this suggestion to Churchill two days earlier and when its reception was favourable he put forward command proposals which Eisenhower had drafted. The ensuing discussions between Roosevelt and Churchill resulted in an agreement for a world-wide division of strategic responsibility, under which the United States assumed responsibility for the Pacific and Britain for the Indian Ocean and Middle East. Both theatres, as well as the European, which was to be a joint Anglo-American responsibility, were to be under the direction of the Combined Chiefs of Staff in matters of grand strategy, with the United States Joint Chiefs of Staff exercising operational control in the Pacific and the British in the Indian Ocean and the Middle East.

The United States Joint Chiefs of Staff divided the Pacific theatre into two principal areas — the South-West Pacific, which embraced Australia and the islands to the north and north-east as far as the Philippines (the Solomons, the Bismarcks, New Guinea and the Netherlands East Indies, except Sumatra, which fell into the Indian Ocean area), and the Pacific Ocean, comprising the remainder of the Pacific except the waters east of the meridian 110° west guarding the Panama Canal approaches and the west coast of South America, which constituted the minor South-East Pacific area.[8] The South-West Pacific area was to be an Army, and the Pacific Ocean area a Navy, responsibility, with Marshall, as Chief of Staff, acting as executive agent for the former and King, as Commander in Chief of the United States Navy, for the latter.

Through Brett, Roosevelt suggested to Curtin that the Australian Government should nominate MacArthur, who had reached Australia on March 17, for selection as Supreme Commander of the South-West Pacific, and this was done. Admiral Chester W. Nimitz, Commander in Chief, United States

Pacific Fleet, was appointed Commander in Chief, Pacific Ocean area, which was divided into three sectors — the North Pacific, the Central Pacific and the South Pacific.[9] Despite the protests of Australia and New Zealand, the latter and New Caledonia, held by the Free French, instead of being included with Australia in the South-West Pacific area, were brought within the South Pacific sub-area on the ground that both properly belonged to the lines of communication, which was a naval responsibility.

MacArthur, who elected to call himself Commander in Chief rather than Supreme Commander, and Nimitz received their directives on April 4. These required them to hold key military positions in their respective areas, to check the Japanese advance, to prepare major offensives against the enemy and to support, and co-operate fully with, one another and with their Allies in the Indian Ocean. MacArthur was informed that in addition to the 41st Division, the 32nd United States Division, with supporting troops, was assigned to his area and that his two heavy, two medium and one light bomber and three fighter groups would be brought to full strength. For the time being, however, commitments elsewhere and the critical shortage of shipping prohibited further United States forces being sent to the South-West Pacific. The structure of MacArthur's headquarters and Australia's contribution to the forces under his supreme command are described in the next chapter.[10]

During April both MacArthur and Curtin pressed for the allocation of additional forces, air, ground and naval, but these requests, understandably, were rejected. Out of some 132,000 Army personnel embarked in the United States for overseas destinations between the beginning of January and the middle of March no fewer than 90,000 had gone to the Pacific. Of this total, 79,000 left for the South-West Pacific, 57,000 of them for Australia. Admittedly, 2,000 were killed, missing or taken prisoners in the Netherlands East Indies, 3,000 had gone to India to form the Tenth United States Air Force, and the garrison of New Caledonia, which at the time numbered 17,000 and soon was increased to more than 22,000, had been transferred to the South Pacific sub-area. The islands forming the stepping stones of the supply route from Hawaii across the South Pacific to Australia — Palmyra, Christmas Island, Canton Island, Bora Bora, Samoa, the Fiji Islands and New Caledonia — had been garrisoned and additional bases established at Tongatabu, in the Tonga Islands, and at Efate, in the New Hebrides.

The substantial reinforcement of the Pacific had been carried out at the expense of other theatres. So long, however, as the defeat of Germany and Italy remained the first object of the Allies, this process could not continue indefinitely. Once the Combined Chiefs of Staff were satisfied that there were sufficient forces to halt the headlong Japanese onslaught, the European and Middle East theatres must be reinforced and the flow of supplies to Russia, and, if possible, also to China, increased. The battle of the Atlantic was clearly moving to a climax; for having found new and profitable hunting grounds through America's entry into the war, U-boats were sinking an increasingly greater tonnage of Allied shipping. There were fears that the Russians, who were calling vociferously for the establishment by their Allies of a 'second front' in Europe, would be unable to withstand the impending German summer offensive, and in the Middle East, with Malta under incessant air attack, there were indications that General Erwin Rommel was about to launch a thrust for Cairo. China, through the fall of Burma, was now cut off from Allied help from the south and a doubt existed whether she would be able to continue in the war. Although MacArthur urged that the 'second front' should be in the Pacific, and called for ground, air and naval reinforcements for an all-out attack on the Japanese, his appeals, in view of the critical position in other theatres, were without avail. As Roosevelt told him in a personal message on May 6, the Russian armies were 'killing more Axis personnel and destroying more Axis *matériel* than all the other 25 United Nations put together', and it therefore seemed logical to support the Russians 'in every way we possibly can, and also to develop plans aimed at diverting German land and air forces from the Russian front'.[11]

It is necessary now to see what had happened in the New

Guinea area from the beginning of the year. After repeatedly raiding Rabaul, situated at the north-eastern tip of New Britain and the capital of Australia's mandated territory of New Guinea, the Japanese landed in overwhelming strength during the night of January 22-23. By the evening of the 23rd all organized resistance by the small Australian garrison of some 1,400 men had ceased. About 400 of the garrison escaped to Australia; the remainder were killed or taken prisoners, 150 of the latter being massacred by the Japanese. On the 21st Kavieng, at the north-western extremity of neighbouring New Ireland and 125 miles north-west of Rabaul, was raided by about 60 bombers and fighters and on the night of the 22nd-23rd it also was occupied. A lull then followed until March 2, when Lae, Salamaua, Wau, Bulolo and Port Moresby were made the targets of heavy air raids. In the early hours of the 8th, army troops occupied Salamaua, on the western coast of New Guinea, and a naval detachment occupied Lae, 18 miles to the north. Neither landing was opposed. While the Japanese developed Rabaul as a major naval and supply base, only isolated clashes occurred in the New Guinea coastal areas as Japanese patrols pushed inland in search of Australian observation posts and individual coast-watchers. This game of hide-and-seek, with death as the penalty for any coast-watcher or member of the New Guinea Volunteer Rifles who was caught, makes a stirring and adventurous page in the history of operations in this area, but lies outside the scope of this book.[12]

If the speed and extent of the Japanese conquests had startled Allied military leaders and dismayed civilian populations, it had also surprised the Japanese themselves. Although aware of the fatal weaknesses of the Allied defence, they had neither expected resistance to crumble and collapse so dramatically nor to achieve their object at such small cost. The Army's casualties, considering the extent of territory conquered and the number of prisoners captured, were extraordinarily light, and the Navy, instead of the losses of 20 or 30 per cent it had forecast, had lost a mere 23 vessels, of a total of 26,441 tons and none larger than a destroyer. Sixty-seven transports and merchant ships totalling 314,805 tons had also been lost.

Nagumo's carrier forces had struck Pearl Harbour, Darwin and Ceylon devastating blows without losing a major warship and at the cost of few aircraft and air crews.

Once the Southern Region had been conquered, the Japanese war plan provided for its immediate consolidation and the organization of a strong defensive perimeter to protect the region from any counter-offensive. Only when this had been achieved were moves to be made against New Guinea, New Britain, Fiji, Samoa, the Aleutians, Midway and important points in the Australian area. The Army, which had been so insistent that Japan should embark upon war, was now hesitant about undertaking new commitments. It desired to hold its gains and to transfer some divisions from the Southern Army to China, Manchuria and Japan. The Navy, which had reluctantly agreed to war, was now the eager and adventurous partner, anxious to speed up the time-table. It wanted to at once extend the defensive perimeter by fresh conquests to ensure defence in depth so as to delay the expected counter-offensive. The question was, where should this be done?

Plans to strike westward into the Indian Ocean and seize Ceylon were prepared by the staff of the Combined Fleet, but were rejected by Imperial Headquarters, the Army and Navy Chiefs of Staff agreeing that the time was unsuitable and that sufficient forces were not available. The Navy was divided as to Japan's best course. Nagano, Chief of the Naval Staff, urged an advance to the south-east, so as to cut the lines of communication from the United States to Australia. Yamamoto, conscious that Japan's industrial capacity could not match that of the United States once the latter was placed on a war basis, insisted that the prime consideration was bringing the United States Pacific Fleet to battle before it could rebuild its strength. He proposed an expedition to seize Midway Island.

On February 2, in issuing orders for the occupation of Salamaua and Lae, Imperial Headquarters had referred to moves against Port Moresby, on the south-west coast of Papua, of which it was the capital, and Tulagi, in the southern Solomon Islands, but had given no specific orders for these operations.

This silence arose from the difference of opinion among the naval leaders as to the best strategy to pursue.

On March 15 the Army and Navy sections of Imperial Headquarters met to determine what action should be taken in this area. Both were concerned at the extent to which Australia was being reinforced from the United States. The Navy's solution was to seize Australia, but the Army successfully maintained that Japan did not have 'the munitions, the reinforcements or the ships' for such an operation. It was therefore agreed, as already planned, to seize Port Moresby, which would safeguard Rabaul, provide a base for neutralizing airfields in North Australia, and guard the flank for later operations to the south-east, aimed at occupying the southern Solomons and isolating Australia by the capture of Fiji, Samoa and New Caledonia. If this plan succeeded, the invasion of Australia might follow whenever the time seemed opportune and the necessary forces were available.

While this decision settled the course of events in the South-West Pacific and South Pacific, it did not resolve the broader issue raised by Yamamoto of bringing the United States Pacific Fleet to action. Discussions on this proposal were still proceeding when the Allies dramatically, if unwittingly, intervened to force a decision.

Early on the morning of April 18, some 650 miles east of the coast of Japan, 16 United States Army Air Force B-25's took off from the decks of the newly commissioned carrier *Hornet* (20,000, 1940). They were led by Lieutenant-Colonel J. H. Doolittle and shortly after noon 13 of them bombed Tokyo, while the other three dropped incendiaries on Nagoya, Osaka and Kobe. The aircraft were to have flown off from *Hornet's* deck much closer to their targets, but the carrier and its escorts, forming Vice-Admiral William F. Halsey's *Enterprise* task force, were sighted by a Japanese reconnaissance plane. The Mitchells were thereupon launched immediately, as the risk of air attack on the task force only a few hundred miles from the Japanese mainland could not be accepted. In any event, the bombers did not have the range to return to their carrier and they were to fly on to friendly airfields in China. Because of the premature take-off, and the strong head wind they encountered, none was able to make it. One landed near Vladivostock, four crash-landed in China, and the crews of the other 11 bombers baled out, in darkness and rain, over Chinese territory. Three were captured and executed by the Japanese and five others killed, but the remaining 72 men, cared for by Chinese peasants, reached Chungking and eventually returned to the United States. *Enterprise* and *Hornet*, evading a pursuing fleet, reached Pearl Harbour safely.

The Doolittle raid inflicted little material damage, but its effect on morale was considerable. Its daring and spectacular nature, capturing the public imagination, served as a tonic to the Allied nations at a time when spirits were low, while in Japan, although possibly relatively few civilians knew Tokyo had been bombed, it created alarm for the safety of the homeland. More important, the bombing of Tokyo showed Japan's military and naval leaders that a gap existed in her defences and strengthened support for Yamamoto's argument that a forward base at Midway must be seized and the United States Pacific Fleet brought to action and decisively defeated. As a consequence, Imperial Headquarters reached agreement that, in addition to the isolation of Australia, an expedition should seize Midway and another should land in the Aleutians.

Thus, the Japanese plan now was to capture Port Moresby in May, to seize Midway and the Aleutians in June, and in July to move against Fiji, Samoa and New Caledonia. It was thought that the capture of Midway, by threatening Hawaii, would force a fleet action on the Americans while the odds were still in Japan's favour. In the final plans the seizure of the western Aleutians, besides blocking the shortest route from the United States to Japan, would serve as a diversion for Midway, while the aircraft of the carriers sent into the Coral Sea, after seeing the invasion force landed at Port Moresby, were to bomb Townsville, Brisbane and other Allied bases in Queensland, Australia.

The Allies had attempted already to strike at the Japanese so busily developing Rabaul as a base. Late in February Vice-Admiral Wilson Brown's *Lexington* task force had set out to raid Rabaul, but was detected when it met enemy twin-engined bombers, most of which were shot down, and, running low on fuel, turned back without attacking. A second attempt was made early in March to cover the transfer of American troops to New Caledonia. On this occasion Brown commanded the *Lexington* and *Enterprise* task forces and an Australian cruiser squadron under Rear-Admiral J. G. Crace, R.N. While *en route* Brown learned of the Japanese landings at Salamaua and Lae and, abandoning the Rabaul strike, decided to attack shipping off both ports. In the Bay of Papua he launched over 100 aircraft, which, flying through a gap in the rugged Owen Stanley Mountains, bombed Salamaua and Lae. Allied aircraft based in Australia — B-17's and Hudsons — followed up the carrier-borne raids. The enemy was taken by surprise, but the results were disappointing—three ships sunk and four damaged, with 130 Japanese troops killed and 245 wounded.

What added a touch of lustre to American generalship in the Pacific, both on land and at sea, was the American ability to read not only Magic messages[13] but also to decode Japanese naval signals. The Japanese naval code had been 'cracked' shortly after Pearl Harbour, and the enemy command, oblivious to the last that their top secret messages were being read by the Allies, did not change their code, although from the outset King hourly expected them to do so. As a result, every top level Allied admiral and general in the Pacific was aware broadly, and often in considerable detail, of what was going on 'on the other side of the hill'.[14] The Allies thus possessed the most reliable and comprehensive intelligence service any belligerent has ever enjoyed, and it enabled each Japanese move to be countered as it was made. To those who did not know what was going on, it made Allied, and more particularly American, generalship appear both prescient and omniscient. Nimitz has testified that if it had not been for this ability to intercept and decipher the enemy's radioed orders and reports, American ships would have been thousands of miles away when the Japanese moved against Port Moresby, and the battle of the Coral Sea, which turned the tide in the Pacific and saved Port

Moresby, would never have been fought. The same remark applies with equal force to the battle of Midway.

The Japanese forces for the capture and occupation of Tulagi and Port Moresby assembled at Truk, in the Carolines, and on April 30 sailed southwards for Rabaul, where the troops were to embark. Task Force 'MO' was under the overall command of Vice-Admiral Shigeyoshi Inouye, Commander in Chief of the Japanese Fourth Fleet, who remained throughout the operations aboard his flagship at Rabaul. He had five separate naval forces to control and co-ordinate, as well as the land-based air support provided by Rear-Admiral Sadayoshi Yamada's reinforced 25th Air Flotilla, possessing some 63 fighters, 86 bombers and 12 seaplanes.

On May 3 Tulagi was occupied without opposition, the tiny Australian garrison having withdrawn the previous day to Vila, in the New Hebrides. This operation was carried out by forces under Rear-Admiral Kiyohide Shima, behind whom stood Rear-Admiral Aritomo Goto's main Covering Force and Rear-Admiral Kuninori Marushige's support group for the Port Moresby invasion fleet. As soon as the troops were ashore at Tulagi, Goto and Marushige withdrew, and they were soon followed by most of the transports. Late on the 3rd Rear-Admiral Frank Jack Fletcher, commanding Task Force 17 and flying his flag in *Yorktown* (19 bombers, 19 scout bombers, 13 torpedo-bombers, 20 fighters), heard of the Tulagi landing. He was then some 400 miles south-east of the Louisiade Archipelago, having spent most of the day refuelling from the oiler *Neosho* (8,000g, 1939). The second component of Task Force 17, *Lexington* (18 bombers, 18 scout bombers, 12 torpedo-bombers, 22 fighters), commanded by Rear-Admiral Aubrey W. Fitch, was about 100 miles east of Fletcher and also engaged in refuelling. The two American carriers were due to rendezvous next morning, but on learning of the Tulagi landing, Fletcher determined to attack on his own. He dispatched *Neosho,* accompanied by a destroyer as escort, to keep the rendezvous with *Lexington* and to hand orders to Fitch for the entire American force to meet him at daybreak on May 5 at a rendezvous about 300 miles south of Guadalcanal.

At 2230 Fletcher headed northwards at 24 knots and on the 4th launched three separate attack groups from a point about 100 miles south-west of Guadalcanal. The weather was dull and overcast, with a stiff south-east trade wind and frequent rain squalls, far from ideal for flying, but excellent for hiding *Yorktown* from the prying eyes of enemy reconnaissance pilots. Over Tulagi itself the weather was fine and visibility good, but there was little left for the Americans to hit. Although at the time the jubilant pilots claimed to have sunk two destroyers, four gunboats and a merchantman, to have forced a light cruiser ashore and to have severely damaged a destroyer, a seaplane tender and a merchant ship, the results of the three raids were in fact disappointing. Only three minesweepers and four landing barges were sunk, five seaplanes destroyed, the destroyer *Kikuzuki* (1,315, 1926) compelled to beach itself and a patrol craft damaged. Three of the seaplanes were destroyed by fighters, which also strafed the destroyer *Yuzuki* (1,315, 1927), killing her captain and others, but doing little damage to the ship. To achieve even this tally, the American pilots had expended 22 torpedoes, 76 1,000-lb. bombs and something like 83,000 rounds of machine-gun ammunition, and had lost three aircraft, two of them fighters which crash-landed after the attack on *Yuzuki*. Little wonder that Nimitz commented, 'The Tulagi operation was certainly disappointing in terms of ammunition expended to results obtained.'

Meanwhile, *Lexington* had met *Neosho* and her escorting destroyer at 0800 on the 4th and an hour later part of 'Mac-Arthur's Navy', the Australian cruisers *Australia* (10,000, 1928) and *Hobart* and an American destroyer, under Crace's command, joined up. For the *Lexington* group the 4th was uneventful, and at 0816 next morning Fitch's and Crace's ships met *Yorktown* at the appointed rendezvous south of Guadalcanal. The 5th also was uneventful, except that a *Yorktown* fighter on patrol shot down an enemy four-engined seaplane.

On the 4th the Port Moresby invasion force — five Navy and six Army transports, with a number of small craft and a destroyer escort — sailed from Rabaul. It was commanded by Kajioka, whose first attempt to take Wake Island had failed so

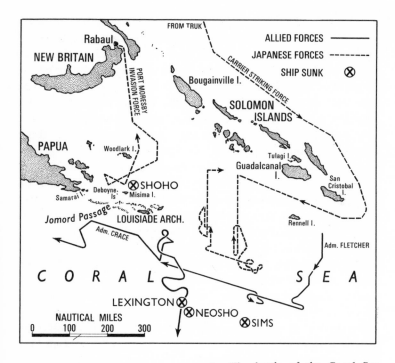

6. The battle of the Coral Sea

dismally and who was still flying his flag in the light cruiser *Yubari*. Kajioka rendezvoused with Marushige's support group off Buin, Bougainville, and by the 7th the whole force was near the Louisiade Archipelago, off the kangaroo-like tail of New Guinea, with the heavy cruisers and the light carrier *Shoho* (9,500, 1941), 12 fighters, 9 torpedo-bombers, of Goto's covering force close at hand. The transports lay on the western side of Woodlark Island and Marushige's light cruisers and gun-boats, with the seaplane carrier *Kamikawa Maru* (6,853, 1937), between Misima and Deboyne Islands, ready to pass through the Jomard Passage into the Coral Sea for the final run-in to Port Moresby.

The Japanese carrier striking force, consisting of two heavy cruisers, six destroyers, an oiler and *Zuikaku* (21 fighters, 21 bombers, 21 torpedo-bombers) and *Shokaku* (21 fighters, 20 bombers, 21 torpedo-bombers), rounded San Cristobal Island, at the southern end of the Solomons, on the 5th and two days later lay well out in the Coral Sea, to the south-east of the invasion forces. The striking force was commanded by Vice-Admiral Takeo Takagi and the carrier division by Rear-Admiral Tadaichi Hara.

Under the Allied Pacific Command set-up, naval task forces operating in the South-West Pacific area remained under the command of Nimitz, but they might be reinforced by units from the local naval forces, as had been done in this instance, and they were entitled to receive the full support of the South-West Pacific air forces. However, Brett's crews were not well trained in ship recognition and co-operation between the two forces was poor. At 1030 on the 6th four Cloncurry-based Flying Fortresses, staging through Port Moresby, bombed *Shoho* about 60 miles south of Bougainville, but their bombs fell wide and they were driven off by the carrier's fighters. Allied land-based aircraft sighted Goto's heavy cruisers at about 1200 and an hour later located the invasion fleet.

A stream of reports of enemy sightings flowed into Fletcher, but on the morning of the 6th he was still unaware that the Japanese carrier striking force was within 70 to 100 miles of him. Takagi was equally ignorant of the presence close at hand of *Yorktown* and *Lexington*. Incredibly, he had flown no search missions on the 5th or the 6th, and, although a reconnaissance plane from Rabaul at 1100 on the 6th reported Fletcher's position correctly, the report did not reach Takagi until next day. To Inouye, back in Rabaul, it seemed that the American carriers were neatly trapped between the invasion forces and his carrier striking force, and on the 6th he directed that operations should proceed that night as planned, with the invasion force and its escorts passing through the Jomard Passage the following morning.

The Kokoda Track. '*The golden stairs consisted of steps varying from 10 to 18 inches in height. Incessant rain made the track a treacherous mass of moving mud interlaced with protruding roots that reached out with hidden hands to bring the laden troops heavily to the ground*'

The Kokoda Track. '*After the first half-dozen steps, it became a matter of sheer determination forcing the body to achieve the impossible*'

The Kokoda Track. '*The New Guinea "fuzzy-wuzzies" did a magnificent job. They were overworked and overloaded, perpetually underfed. The wonder is not that so many deserted but that so many remained*'

At 1755 on the 6th Fletcher detached *Neosho* and the destroyer *Sims* (1,570, 1939), and these two vessels headed south for their next refuelling rendezvous, where Fletcher believed they would be out of harm's way. Early next morning, however, they were sighted by one of Hara's pilots, who reported them as a carrier and a cruiser. The Japanese carrier commander, accepting this report without reservation, at once ordered his planes to attack the two ships. *Sims*, hit by three 500-lb. bombs, two of which exploded in her engine-room, was split apart and sank, stern first, within a few minutes. *Neosho*, after seven direct hits and eight near misses, was left low in the water and on fire. She remained afloat until the 11th, when an American destroyer, having taken off 123 men, scuttled her. Another destroyer picked up four survivors out of 68 men who had prematurely abandoned *Neosho* on the 7th in four life rafts.

Early on the 7th Fletcher detached Crace's group—*Australia, Hobart* and the United States cruiser *Chicago* (9,300, 1930) —with its screening destroyers to close the southern exit of the Jomard Passage and attack the invasion group. Crace's five ships soon came under air attack in the same strength as that which sank *Prince of Wales* and *Repulse,* but anti-aircraft fire power and methods had improved since the opening days of the war and Crace's force successfully dodged both bombs and torpedoes. After the Japanese attack had ended, nineteen of Brett's heavy bombers from Townsville mistakenly attacked Crace's ships, but their bombs narrowly missed. During the night, word reached Crace that the Port Moresby invaders had turned back early on the previous morning.

After detaching Crace, Fletcher flew off a search mission and at 0815 a *Yorktown* plane reported two carriers and four heavy cruisers on the other side of the Louisiades, about 225 miles north-west of the American carriers. *Lexington* began launching planes at 0926 and *Yorktown* half an hour later, and by 1030 the two carriers had 93 planes airborne — 26 bombers, 27 scout bombers, 22 torpedo-bombers and 18 fighters. This force was already on its way when *Yorktown's* reconnaissance plane returned and it was learnt that a coding error had converted two heavy cruisers and two destroyers into the reported two carriers and four cruisers. The reconnaissance pilot had not sighted either the Japanese striking force or Goto's covering force, but the relatively weak support group of light cruisers and gunboats under Marushige. As luck would have it, however, the *Lexington* attack group shortly after 1100 sighted Goto's ships and attacked *Shoho,* which was hit by both bombs and torpedoes. She sank at 1135, taking 500 of her crew of 1,200 with her.

Japanese reconnaissance planes had earlier reported the positions of Fletcher's carriers and Crace's cruisers, and fearful for his transports Inouye had at 0900 ordered the invasion force not to enter Jomard Passage, but to mark time until the Allied Forces had been dealt with. As we have seen, Crace's ships were attacked but suffered no damage, but the American carriers, vulnerable while their own planes were on their strike, were not attacked. The weather worsened during the afternoon, and 12 bombers and 15 torpedo-bombers dispatched by *Shokaku* and *Zuikaku* at 1630 failed to find the American carriers in the squally weather. Picked up on radar as they were returning, they were intercepted by *Lexington* and *Yorktown* fighters and 9 of their 27 aircraft were shot down for the loss of 2 Wildcats. Lacking radar and homing devices, the remaining Japanese aircraft had difficulty in finding their own carriers, some even seeking to land on the American vessels in the belief that they were their own, and a further 11 were lost in attempting night landings. Before midnight Inouye postponed the invasion of Port Moresby for two days and ordered the invasion fleet back to Rabaul. Later, after the events of the 8th, Imperial Headquarters ordered a further postponement to July.

At 0600 on the 8th Hara sent out a search mission and 25 minutes later Fitch, who had been ordered to assume tactical command by Fletcher, ordered 18 reconnaissance planes from *Lexington* to seek the elusive Japanese carriers. Each side was now hunting the other in earnest. Hara, an hour after sending out his search planes, put an attack group of 90 aircraft into the air. Each force located the other at about the same time and their first attacks were delivered almost simultaneously. The

American attack lacked co-ordination, was less expertly delivered than the Japanese, and owing to *Zuikaku* being hidden by the overcast was concentrated on *Shokaku* alone. The torpedo-bombers, launching their slow-running torpedoes from too great a distance, scored no hits, but the bombers, 22 of which failed to find the enemy carriers in the thick weather, registered three hits on *Shokaku,* causing fires and killing 108 men and wounding 40 others. Although the fires were quickly brought under control, *Shokaku* had been so severely damaged as to be no longer operational. She was ordered to withdraw and succeeded in reaching, first, Truk and later Kure under her own power, although she very nearly capsized on the way.

In marked contrast to the Japanese carriers, *Yorktown* and *Lexington* lay in bright sunshine. The experienced and determined Japanese torpedo-bomber pilots pressed within close range before releasing their fast-running torpedoes and they attacked *Lexington* on both bows, with the result that the large carrier could not evade all the torpedoes and took two hits on the port side, which flooded three boiler rooms. Almost at the same time two bombs hit her, causing only minor damage, and a number of near misses ruptured some of her plates. Nevertheless, *Lexington* remained operational, and when her list had been corrected by shifting oil, and fires had been put out, she appeared undamaged to her returning pilots. The smaller and more manœuvrable *Yorktown,* attacked only on one bow, conned the torpedo tracks and was not hit, but took one bomb which, penetrating to the fourth deck, killed or seriously injured 66 men and started fires. However, these were soon brought under control, but on their return to their own ships the Japanese pilots reported that both American carriers had been left on fire and low in the water. The enemy concluded both had been sunk.

By 1140 the first naval battle in history in which the opposing ships never came within sight of one another was over, and both sides were withdrawing, each satisfied it was the victor. The combat effectiveness of the American carriers remained unimpaired and Fitch had 37 attack aircraft and 12 fighters fit to take the air, but Hara, forced to jettison many of the returning planes because of the crippling of *Shokaku,* had only 9 planes operational.

Suddenly at 1247 an explosion occurred deep inside *Lexington.* It was caused by a spark from a generator which had been left running and which set off an accumulation of petrol fumes. Within two hours it was followed by another violent explosion. Further smaller explosions took place and fires soon raged out of control. After about 150 wounded had been sent away in whaleboats *Lexington* was abandoned shortly after 1700. Explosions were still occurring aboard her when the destroyer *Phelps* (1,805, 1936) fired five torpedoes to send the carrier to the bottom. It was 1956 when she sank.

Yamamoto at midnight on May 8 countermanded Inouye's withdrawal orders and instructed Takagi to advance and annihilate the remaining American Forces. Takagi obeyed, but it was too late for the Japanese to catch up with *Yorktown* and her escorts, and on the 11th he was finally ordered back to Truk.

On the 10th an invasion force left Rabaul to seize Ocean and Nauru Islands, but the minelayer *Okinoshima* (4,400, 1936), flying the flag of Shima, was torpedoed and sunk by an American submarine, and when, on the 15th, the United States carriers *Enterprise* and *Hornet* were sighted 450 miles east of Tulagi, heading south at full speed, the force was hurriedly recalled to Rabaul.

The conventional view of the Battle of the Coral Sea is that it was a tactical victory for the Japanese, but a strategic victory for the Allies. If the tonnage of vessels sunk is to be the sole criterion, this verdict is correct, but the results are not to be judged simply by the fact that the Japanese lost only the light carrier *Shoho* and a few unimportant small ships against the Allied loss of *Lexington, Sims* and *Neosho.* This disregards the fact that the enemy lost substantially more aircraft and suffered twice as many casualties, and was deprived for some considerable time of the use of the severely damaged *Shokaku* and of *Zuikaku,* whose decimated air groups had to be re-formed. Taking these factors into consideration, a fairer assessment is that the Battle of the Coral Sea was a tactical draw, especially as the Japanese, when *Zuikaku* was ordered back by Yamamoto, made no attempt to take advantage of the Allied withdrawal by also turning round the transports and pressing on with the invasion of Port Moresby. Presumably the fear of land-based air attack induced Inouye to postpone the invasion attempt.

Strategically, the victory unquestionably lay with the Allies. The invasion force had been turned back, thus imposing the first check on the enemy advance and foiling the initial step of his plan to isolate Australia. The carrier-borne strikes which were to have been made against Townsville, Brisbane and other Queensland bases were prevented, and both *Shokaku* and *Zuikaku,* and their skilled and experienced air crews, had been eliminated from the forthcoming battle of Midway, in which their presence might have been decisive. These were enormous gains, even without counting the invigorating effect on American, Australian and New Zealand morale of the first reverse inflicted on the Japanese, and they were cheaply won for the loss of a single large carrier, a destroyer, a fleet oiler and a relatively small number of men and aircraft.

Yet had Inouye acted boldly and resolutely the Japanese might have garnered the strategic advantages of the battle. Crace, when he heard the invasion force had turned back, had headed for Australia and if the invasion attempt had been renewed may or may not have been able to intervene before the Japanese were ashore, although he might have prevented direct reinforcement. The inescapable conclusion is that at this period the Allied Air Forces could not alone have stopped the Japanese invasion convoy getting through to its destination. Given a little luck with overcast weather, the enemy could have landed and, since Port Moresby was inadequately defended, he must have taken this valuable objective. The record of the Allied Air Force against shipping, its failure to stop the enemy convoys reaching Buna and later Guadalcanal, and the lamentable showing of land-based aircraft at the battle of Midway, all indicate that in not immediately persisting in their attempt to capture Port Moresby the Japanese threw away one of their greatest opportunities of the Pacific war. The risks may have been great, especially from intervention by Crace, but the prize was a glittering one and even if they had failed, as events turned out, their losses would not have been as great as they were in their later overland drive against Port Moresby. But it must. be admitted that in seeing this picture so clearly today we have the advantage of hindsight: the need for boldness was not at the time so obvious to the Japanese commanders.

The Coral Sea battle had not concluded when, on May 5 (Tokyo date), Japanese Imperial Headquarters ordered Yamamoto, almost brusquely, to carry out, in co-operation with the Army, Operation 'MI', the invasion and occupation of Midway and the western Aleutians. Although the operation had been under continuous discussion for several weeks, the divergent views of the Navy and the Army, and the differences of opinion between the Combined Fleet and the Naval General Staff, had left many of the details unsettled. N-day, the Japanese equivalent of the Allied D-day,[15] for the landing on Midway was the night of June 5-6, the last night for almost a month when there would be sufficient moonlight. There was thus little time for drawing up the detailed plans and preparing men and ships for their tasks. Nagumo's carriers, which had been almost continuously at sea since Pearl Harbour, and Kondo's Second Fleet, which had been supporting the capture of the Philippines and the Netherlands East Indies, needed repair, overhaul and re-supplying. The carriers, except *Shokaku* and *Zuikaku,* sent south for the Port Moresby invasion attempt, had not returned to Japan until April 22 and 23 (Tokyo dates), and Kondo's ships, although they had reached port on the 17th, had been sent out the following day to pursue Halsey after the bombing of Tokyo. Both forces consequently had barely a month in which to refit.

However, neither the shortness of time for planning and preparation nor the result of the Coral Sea battle deterred Yamamoto, who was determined to adhere to his time-table. His object was threefold — first, to seize Midway, so that it might be incorporated in the outer defensive perimeter protecting Japan's conquests; second, to draw out the remnants of the United States Pacific Fleet and destroy them, and third, to occupy Adak, Kiska and Attu, in the western Aleutians, as a

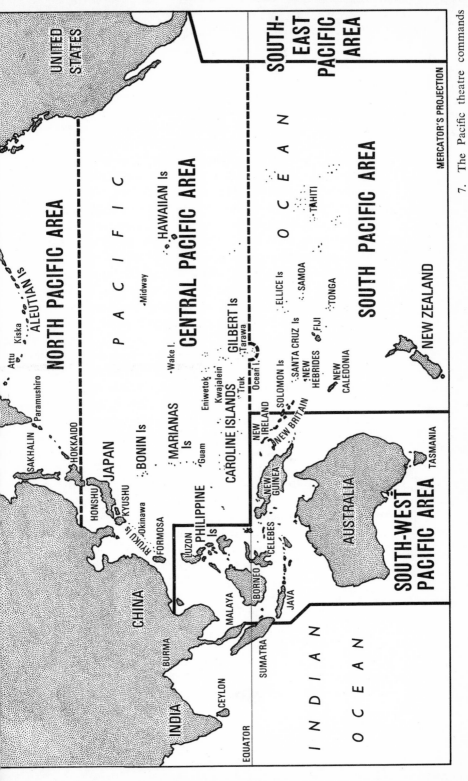

7. The Pacific theatre commands

diversion to throw the Americans off balance and to block their most direct route to Japan.

For these tasks, Yamamoto had overwhelming strength and on paper looked a certain victor. His surface forces comprised 4 fleet, 4 light and 4 seaplane carriers, of which two of the latter carried midget submarines only, 11 battleships, 13 heavy, 10 light and 1 auxiliary cruisers, 66 destroyers, 21 submarines and over 50 auxiliary vessels, including oilers and transports. His carrier-borne air strength was 407 planes, including 136 fighters, 105 dive-bombers, 126 torpedo-bombers, 24 seaplane fighters and 8 reconnaissance seaplanes. Operating from land bases at Kwajalein, Wake, Aur, Wotje and Jaluit, he had a further 178 aircraft — 72 fighters, 72 torpedo-bombers, 10 bombers and 24 flying-boats — available, but these bases were too distant from Midway for their aircraft to be used against the atoll itself.

To meet this formidable armada Nimitz had scraped together, besides the local surface defence forces of Midway and the Aleutians, 3 fleet carriers, 9 heavy and 4 light cruisers, over 30 destroyers and some 25 submarines. Aboard the carriers he had a total of 233 aircraft — 79 fighters, 56 bombers, 42 scout bombers and 56 torpedo-bombers. Outside the Aleutians, where there were 20 Catalinas and a number of Army fighters and bombers, including 13 Flying Fortresses (B-17's) and 24 Marauders (B-26's), the only shore-based air support for his ships was that on Midway itself. This gave Nimitz a somewhat miscellaneous collection of 115 additional aircraft, army and marine. There were 27 fighters, no fewer than 20 of which were obsolete Buffaloes, 19 Flying Fortresses, 4 Marauders, 27 reconnaissance bombers, a mixture of Vindicators (SB2U-3's) and Dauntlesses (SBD-2's), 6 Avenger torpedo-bombers (TBF's), making their debut in combat, and 32 Catalinas.

The Japanese were arrogantly over-confident, suffering from what they themselves came to term 'victory disease'. They were unaware that the Americans were intercepting and reading their coded orders and knew, almost as soon as they themselves, their objectives, the composition of their forces, their direction of approach and the selected date for attack. The Japanese expected to achieve surprise and believed the United States surface forces would not sortie from Pearl Harbour until after Midway had been invaded. Their operational plan was based on these two assumptions, both of which were false. Moreover, they believed that two American carriers had been sunk in the Coral Sea battle and that the two others sighted east of Tulagi on May 15[16] were probably still operating in southern waters. Thus, they believed there was a good chance that there would be no carriers with whatever forces Nimitz might bring against them. From these misconceptions sprang the fatal defects in Yamamoto's plan and the tactical errors which he and his subordinate commanders, particularly Nagumo, committed during the battle.

To furnish warning of the American fleet putting to sea, and to ascertain its strength, a force of submarines was to establish two cordon lines, one to the west and the other to the north-west of Oahu, but because of their preconceived conviction that the American fleet would not leave port until after Midway had been invaded, it was not thought necessary to have these scouting lines in position before June 1 (Hawaiian date). Two 31-ton Kawanishi Type 2 flying-boats, which had a speed of 235 knots and a range of 4,000 miles, were to fly from Wotje and, having refuelled from submarines at French Frigate Shoals, to reconnoitre Pearl Harbour in the early hours of May 31, afterwards returning direct to Wotje. During the night of March 3-4 two of these flying-boats, following the procedure just outlined, had fruitlessly bombed Oahu, and by a process of elimination the Americans had worked out how they had reached Hawaii. Steps had thereupon been taken to deny the Japanese the use of the French Frigate Shoals by stationing there the seaplane tenders *Thornton* (1,190, 1919) and *Ballard* (1,190, 1918) and by mining certain of the approaches.

The belated Japanese attempts at reconnaissance went sadly awry. When the first of the refuelling submarines arrived at the French Frigate Shoals and found the American seaplane tenders anchored there, the flying-boat operation was at first postponed and later cancelled. This not only deprived the Japanese of the information a reconnaissance of Pearl Harbour might have furnished, but it also delayed the establishment of the submarine cordon to the west of Hawaii. That to the north-west also was not established on schedule, as these submarines, due to overhaul delays, arrived on station on June 3, two days late. Yet, even if all had been in position on the 1st, as planned, they would still have been too late.

Yorktown limped into Pearl Harbour from the Coral Sea early on the afternoon of May 27, and before nightfall entered dry dock, where 1,400 men, working round-the-clock shifts, repaired her so quickly that on May 31 she was able to put to sea. *Enterprise* and *Hornet* returned from their vain rush south on the 26th. Halsey, suffering an irritating skin disease, was ordered into hospital and was relieved as task force commander under Fletcher by Rear-Admiral Raymond A. Spruance, who hitherto had commanded the force's heavy cruisers. Refuelled and resupplied, *Enterprise* and *Hornet* sailed from Pearl Harbour under his command on the 29th.

After the departure of the reconnoitring and patrolling submarines the first enemy forces to put to sea belonged to the Northern Force assigned to the Aleutians operation, the execution of which had been entrusted to the Commander in Chief of the Fifth Fleet, Vice-Admiral Boshiro Hosogaya. On May 26 (Tokyo date) the 2nd Carrier Striking Force, commanded by Rear-Admiral Kakuji Kakuta and consisting of the light carriers *Ryujo* (flagship, 8,100, 1933, 16 fighters, 21 torpedo-bombers) and *Junyo* (19,000, 1942, 24 fighters, 21 dive-bombers), 2 heavy cruisers and 3 destroyers, sailed from Ominato, in northern Honshu, and headed due east out into the Pacific. Two days later Hosogaya departed with a supply unit and the small Kiska invasion group, heading for Paramushiro, in the Kuriles, where the ships were to refuel, and a day later the larger Adak-Attu invasion group left port and set a north-easterly course direct for the Aleutians.

Nimitz, taking the risk of dividing his slender forces, a risk which but for Japanese errors might well have proved costly, had sent Rear-Admiral Robert A. Theobald with Task Force 8 to counter the enemy's Aleutians expedition. In addition to the patrol vessels and coastguard cutters of the local Aleutian defence forces, Theobald commanded 2 heavy and 3 light cruisers, 13 destroyers and 6 submarines. The local Navy and Army air forces had a strength of 156 aircraft, of which 88 were fighters, 48 bombers, including 13 Flying Fortresses and 24 Marauders, and 20 reconnaissance Catalinas.

Not appreciating the authenticity of American intelligence sources, Theobald considered that the naming of Kiska and Attu as the Japanese objectives was an enemy ruse to draw him westward while a landing to seize Dutch Harbour was made between Umnak and Cold Bay. Accordingly, he placed his main force some 400 miles due south of Kodiak, where, although well placed to defend the eastern Aleutians and Alaska, it was about 500 miles south-south-east of Kakuta's selected launching position.

In the rough seas and foggy atmosphere of the Aleutians, Kakuta slipped undetected through the picket line of small vessels and submarines watching the Pacific and Bering Sea approaches to Dutch Harbour and, thanks to the thick overcast, was unsighted by the searching planes. From a position 165 miles from Dutch Harbour he launched his first strike in the early hours of June 3. Owing to the weather the *Junyo* attack group failed to find the target, but pilots from *Ryujo,* although their only maps were charts 30 years old, arrived over Dutch Harbour to find the weather fine and a 10,000-foot cloud ceiling. They caused considerable damage to the radio station, army barracks, fuel tanks and other buildings. A second strike sent out against five destroyers sighted in Makushin Bay failed to locate its target. Having recovered his aircraft, Kakuta, about noon, began his retirement to the south-west.

Under cover of fog next day, he again made his approach undetected and at 1600 launched a second strike against Dutch Harbour. On this occasion the attack groups from both carriers found the target, where the weather was again clear. Fuel tanks were destroyed, buildings demolished or damaged, and the beached barracks ship *Northwestern* partially destroyed. During the absence of his aircraft on this strike Kakuta's carriers were at last located, but the attack on them by Army bombers was ineffective.

Meanwhile, away to the south, the main forces of both sides were on the move. Nagumo's 2nd Carrier Striking Force sailed from Hashirajima Anchorage, in the western Inland Sea, on May 27 (Tokyo date) and, passing through Bungo Strait into the Pacific, set course towards Midway. Two days later Yamamoto's main body and Kondo's covering group for the invasion force sailed from the same anchorage. The transports and their escorts, which had assembled at Saipan, sailed from there on the 28th and at the same time Rear-Admiral Takeo Kurita's close support group put out from Guam. The Japanese soon ran into bad weather, with poor visibility, and on June 2 (local date) Nagumo's carriers and their escorts, with the throb of the engines of searching American aircraft above them, were hidden in a fog so thick that visual contact between the ships was lost. At 1330, when the fleet navigator announced a change of course, Nagumo was forced to break radio silence to give the order, but although this reduced power transmission was clearly received in Yamamoto's flagship, and Nagumo later believed that it had given his position away, the signal was not picked up by the Americans. Thus, when Nagumo started his run-in to his launching position his whereabouts was still unknown to the Americans.

However, early on June 3 a patrolling Catalina sighted the transports and their escorts almost 700 miles from the atoll. They were still 570 miles out when nine Flying Fortresses bombed, but failed to score a hit. Four torpedo-armed Catalinas next attacked at 0143 on the 4th, obtaining a hit on the oiler *Akebono Maru* (10,121g, 1939), which caused only slight damage and killed or wounded 23 men.

Having reached a position 240 miles north-west of Midway, Nagumo at 0430 that morning launched the first Midway attack wave and simultaneously sent out search planes from his accompanying cruisers to ascertain if any American ships were in the vicinity. Because all concerned were convinced the American fleet was not at sea, the search was almost perfunctory and when the two planes taking the central sectors in the search pattern were delayed in take-off no attempt was made to replace them, an omission which shortly was to have disastrous results.

One of these planes was held up by engine trouble, and when this recurred after it became airborne, and foul weather was encountered, it returned without having covered the whole of its search area. The other, delayed by catapult trouble, took off 30 minutes late.

Nagumo's four carriers launched 108 planes in 15 minutes, leaving a similar number for a second strike. '*Akagi* was steaming full into the wind with speed increased, and the wind gauge showed the required velocity,' says Mitsuo Fuchida,[17] describing the take-off from his own ship. ' "Commence launching!" came the order from the bridge. Swinging a green signal lamp, the Air Officer described a big circle in the air. A Zero fighter, leading the flight of impatient war birds, revved up its engine, gathered speed along the flight deck, and rose into the air to the accompaniment of a thunderous cheer from *Akagi's* crew. Caps and hands waved wildly in the bright glare of the deck lights. The first plane was followed by eight more Zeros. Then came the dive-bombers . . . Some 4,000 metres to port, *Hiryu* was also launching planes. Thin streaks of light followed each other skyward from the floodlit deck . . . The flight deck, which moments before had been filled with a deafening din, was now silent. There were no planes, no drone of engines. Only a few deck hands ran here and there, busily stowing various pieces of gear. But the stillness was again broken by the raucous loud-speaker as it blared out the order, "Prepare second attack wave!" '

Radar and patrolling Catalinas gave the island ample warning of the attack, enabling all aircraft to be sent aloft to avoid destruction on the ground. Marine Corps fighters, pitifully few in numbers and outmatched by the superior Zero, met the attackers 30 miles out to sea, but could not get among the bombers. The anti-aircraft guns, which had been greatly strengthened in the few weeks before the attack, put up a heavy barrage, but it could not stop the raiders. By 0700 the attack was over. The Marines' command post and mess hall, the sea-plane hangar and oil tanks had been destroyed and the power-house, gasoline system, hospital and storehouses severely damaged, but the runways had not been put out of action and casualties on the ground were few. Seventeen defending fighters had been shot down. At 0700 the Japanese flight leader, Lieutenant Joichi Tomonaga, realizing that the object of destroying the American aircraft had not been achieved because they had been airborne, radioed Nagumo: 'There is need for a second attack.'

At 0530, after the departure of the enemy strike force, Nagumo's carriers had been located by search planes from Midway, and at 0603 their course, speed and position were reported, although there was an error of about 40 miles in the last. Fletcher, four minutes after receiving these details, ordered Spruance to proceed south-westward with *Enterprise* and *Hornet* to attack the enemy carriers, promising to follow as soon as he had recovered his search planes. Six Midway-based Avengers and four Marauders, armed with torpedoes and orbiting out of harm's way away from the island while it was under attack, flew off without fighter escort about 0615 and some 55 minutes later found the Japanese carriers. Four or five were shot down before they could reach a launching position, but the rest dropped their slow-running and easily dodged torpedoes, several more aircraft being brought down by anti-aircraft fire or fighters. Only one badly damaged Avenger and two Marauders, one of which crash-landed, got back to Midway.

On the off chance that his search mission might locate American surface vessels, Nagumo had kept a reserve of 93 aircraft, armed with torpedoes and bombs, ready to fly off at a moment's notice. However, no reports of American ships came in from his reconnaissance planes, so that when he received Tomonaga's report calling for a second strike, and the attack by the land-based Avengers and Marauders came in a few minutes later to confirm the flight leader's judgment, Nagumo decided to send a second attack against Midway. Many of his reserve aircraft, however, were armed with torpedoes, suitable against ships but not against land targets. He therefore ordered the flight decks cleared. This served the dual purpose of enabling him to recover the aircraft now returning from the first strike and to rearm his torpedo-bombers with bombs while they were below.

His order was being executed when, to Nagumo's dismay, the delayed cruiser search plane reported at 0728 that it had sighted 10 enemy ships about 240 miles from Midway. If this report had been received thirty minutes earlier, as it probably would have been had the plane not been delayed in its take-off, the course of the battle might have been altered. As it was, confronted with the problem of whether to strike at the ships or at Midway, Nagumo waited for 15 minutes, probably in the hope of receiving more explicit information from his search plane, before countermanding his earlier order to replace torpedoes by bombs. He now directed those planes which had not yet made the change to retain their torpedoes, but experiencing no sense of urgency he made no attempt to launch his attack aircraft, whether they carried bombs or torpedoes. At 0809, in response to a message from Nagumo, the dilatory pilot reported the American ships as five cruisers and five destroyers and about 10 minutes later added the startling information that they were 'accompanied by what appears to be a carrier'.

In between the receipt of these messages further attacks by land-based aircraft developed, lending emphasis to Tomonaga's call for a second strike at Midway. At 0755 sixteen Marine Corps Dauntless dive-bombers delivered a glide-bombing attack, the flight leader considering his pilots too inexperienced to dive-bomb, but as they came in, widely scattered, they were jumped by Zeros and half their number quickly shot down. The remainder, courageously pressing on, dropped their bombs, but all missed their target, *Hiryu*. Only eight of the dive-bombers, six badly shot up, limped back to Midway. Fifteen minutes after their attack started 15 Flying Fortresses bombed from 20,000 feet, but scored only near misses, and at 0820 11 slow Marine Corps Vindicators came in. Zeros forced these obsolete planes away from the carriers and they dropped their bombs at a battleship, without, however, obtaining a hit. By good fortune only one was shot down. In the middle of these attacks the United States submarine *Nautilus* added to the general confusion by popping up to fire a torpedo at a battleship. This missed, but the *Nautilus* survived undamaged intensive depth-charge attacks by destroyers.

The Japanese planes began returning at 0835 and within some 40 minutes all had landed. Nagumo's ships were somewhat scattered, due as much to the launching and recovery operations as to the attacks, and Nagumo decided to momentarily withdraw northwards to re-establish his proper compact steaming formation and to rearm and refuel his aircraft. He expected to launch 36 dive-bombers, 54 torpedo-bombers and 12 fighters against the American ships at 1030, but around 0920 his reconnaissance planes reported many carrier-borne aircraft approaching and it was obvious that so many could not have come from a single carrier. For the first time Nagumo and his staff realized the error of their comfortable assumption that the Americans had no carriers in the vicinity. Victory was not going to be as simple or as easy as they had imagined.

Spruance began launching his aircraft from *Enterprise* and *Hornet* at 0702. It took an hour to get the attacking force airborne, as he had decided to hit with all he had. Not counting the combat air patrol guarding the carriers, he put 20 fighters, 67 dive-bombers and 29 torpedo-bombers into the air. Fletcher, trailing Spruance, added 17 dive-bombers, 12 torpedo-bombers and 6 fighters to the strike force, holding back half his dive-bombers and a few fighters in case of any emergency arising.

Nagumo's change of course caused the 35 dive-bombers from *Hornet* and their escorting fighters to miss the Japanese carriers; for when they failed to make the expected sighting they searched toward Midway, in the opposite direction to that in which Nagumo was now headed. The American fighters, running out of fuel, had to ditch, and two of the bombers crash-landed in the lagoon at Midway when landing to refuel. The dive-bombers were to have attacked first, but in the circumstances this was now impossible. The American attackers were thrown into confusion by not locating the enemy carriers where they had expected to find them and the slower and more vulnerable torpedo-bombers went in first. The squadrons from all three United States carriers were slaughtered by the enemy fighters and the intense anti-aircraft fire.

Hornet's torpedo-bombers, which had searched northward until sighting Nagumo, pressed home their attack at low altitude.

'Beset on all sides by the deadly Zero fighters, which were doggedly attacking them in force, and faced with a seemingly impenetrable screen of cruisers and destroyers, the squadron drove in valiantly at short range,' said Captain Marc Mitscher's report on recommended awards.[18] 'Plane after plane was shot down by fighters, anti-aircraft bursts were searing faces and tearing out chunks of fuselage, and still the squadron bored in. Those who were left dropped their torpedoes at short range.' All fifteen American planes were shot down in this gallant attack and the sole survivor of the thirty pilots and crewmen was Ensign George H. Gay, who climbed out of his splashed plane before it sank and, hiding from strafing Zeros under a rubber seat cushion until nightfall, then inflated his life raft and was picked up next afternoon by a Catalina.[19]

Enterprise's torpedo-bombers were only slightly more fortunate, 10 of the 14 being shot down, and they, too, failed to score a hit. Of *Yorktown's* squadron, only 5 succeeded in launching their torpedoes, none of which hit, and 10 of the 12 planes were shot down.

'Most of the credit for this success,' says Fuchida[20], in describing these torpedo-bomber attacks, 'belonged to the brilliant interception of our fighters, whose swift and daring action was watched closely from the flagship. No less impressive was the dauntless courage shown by the American flyers, who carried out the attack despite heavy losses. Shipboard spectators of this thrilling drama watched spellbound, blissfully unaware that the worst was yet to come.'

The Japanese undoubtedly had won the first rounds. In addition to severely damaging Midway's installations, they had destroyed most of the Midway-based planes sent to attack them and all but six of the carrier-borne torpedo-bombers, and their own ships were still unscathed. But the sacrifice of the American planes was not to be in vain. The Midway-based attacks had induced Nagumo to decide to hit the atoll a second time, so that when he became aware of the presence of American surface vessels he had no attack group ready to launch immediately, and the low level torpedo-bomber attacks of the carrier groups had pulled the Japanese fighters down almost to water level.

Before they had time to regain altitude, *Enterprise* and *York-town* dive-bombers hurtled in with virtually no Zeros to oppose them.

Soryu, which had rearmed and refuelled all the planes on her flight deck and was turning into the wind preparatory to launching, was by a few minutes the first carrier attacked. Sweeping down-sun in three waves the American dive-bombers scored three hits in three minutes with 1,000-lb. bombs. These started large fires on deck and below and 20 minutes later *Soryu* was abandoned. Later a damage control party returned aboard and was trying to bring her fires under control when the *Nautilus,* which, after her earlier attack, had been following the Japanese at her best surface speed, made a periscope-depth approach and slammed three torpedoes into the burning carrier from a range of 2,700 yards. The *Nautilus* survived heavy depth-charge attacks, but *Soryu,* torn in half, sank about 1920.

The Japanese flagship, *Akagi,* took three bomb hits. The second, hitting near the amidships elevator, exploded in the hangar and detonated torpedoes, while the third exploded amid the aircraft rearming and refuelling on deck. Bombs and torpedoes, carelessly piled on deck and on the hangar floor during the changeover, first, from torpedoes to bombs and then from bombs back to torpedoes, instead of being promptly returned to their protected stores, were detonated as fires raced through the carrier.

'Looking about,' says Fuchida,[21] 'I was horrified at the destruction that had been wrought in a matter of seconds. There was a huge hole in the flight deck just behind the amidships elevator. The elevator itself, twisted like molten glass, was drooping into the hangar. Deck plates reeled upward in grotesque configurations. Planes stood tail up, belching livid flame and jet-black smoke. Reluctant tears streamed down my cheeks as I watched the fires spread, and I was terrified at the prospect of induced explosions which would surely doom the ship.'

With some difficulty Nagumo was induced to transfer his flag to a light cruiser. Efforts to bring the fires under control failed and some nine hours after she had been first hit *Akagi* was abandoned. Still burning, she was sunk before sunrise on June 5 by a torpedo from a Japanese destroyer.

Kaga took four hits. One killed everybody on the bridge, including the captain, and the others set fire to the refuelling aircraft on deck and caused explosions below. In a few seconds *Kaga* was a blazing inferno, and at 1925, after a tremendous explosion deep in her vitals, she sank.

In these fateful attacks the Americans lost 16 dive-bombers, several through shortage of fuel, and 15 or 16 fighters, but of Nagumo's carriers only *Hiryu* remained. Rear-Admiral Hiroaki Abe, commander of the carriers' support group of two battleships and two heavy cruisers, assumed tactical command of the striking force while Nagumo was in the process of transferring his flag, and he promptly dispatched two attack waves against *Yorktown*. The first — 18 dive-bombers and 6 fighters — attacked about noon, but the Wildcats exacted a heavy toll as the enemy planes came in and only eight broke through, two of which were shot down by anti-aircraft fire. The remaining six, however, made three hits, stopping *Yorktown* in the water, starting fires, knocking out her radar and communications and compelling the flooding of her magazines. Fletcher transferred his flag to a cruiser, but the damage control parties got the fires aboard the carrier under control, restarted four of her boilers and by 1340 had her doing 20 knots.

About 1430 the second *Hiryu* attack wave — 10 torpedo-bombers and 6 fighters — came in at low altitude from four different directions. They flew directly into the heavy anti-aircraft barrage and, although only four planes succeeded in launching their torpedoes at a range of 500 yards, they obtained two hits. *Yorktown*, with her rudder jammed and all power connections severed, took on an immediate list, which increased shortly to 26 degrees, and at 1500 she was abandoned. Destroyers took off her crew a few minutes before she sank.

The first attack on *Yorktown* alerted Fletcher that at least one enemy carrier was still afloat and operational. He at once dispatched a search mission, which at 1445 located *Hiryu*, two battleships, three cruisers and four destroyers. Twenty-four dive-bombers from *Enterprise,* several of which were actually refugee *Yorktown* aircraft, registered four hits on *Hiryu* at 1700, causing fires that could not be brought under control. While the carrier blazed, Flying Fortresses bombed her, but made no hits. At 0900 on June 5 *Hiryu* sank.

As the reports of the American attacks reached Yamamoto, many miles away, the Japanese Commander in Chief at last decided to bring together his widely dispersed forces. At 1220 on the 4th he ordered Kondo to join him by noon next day and told Kakuta to hurry south with the carriers *Ryujo* and *Junyo* which had attacked Dutch Harbour. Then he sped with his main force toward Nagumo, intending to deliver a night attack on the United States Fleet. However, he was too far from the scene of action and, on learning that all four of Nagumo's carriers had been lost and that the Americans probably still had at least two carriers, he decided he was not justified in risking a carrier-borne attack at dawn next day. At 0255 on the 5th he gave the order for a general retirement. Spruance, wisely declining to risk a night engagement, in which he had little to gain and might lose all, had meanwhile withdrawn eastward, but reversed course at midnight, so as to be within easy reach of Midway by dawn.

In its withdrawal, Kurita's support group, after Yamamoto had cancelled an earlier order for it to bombard Midway, sighted the United States submarine *Tambor* (1,475, 1940), which had been shadowing the Japanese ships. This was at 0342 on the 5th and in taking evasive action the heavy cruiser *Mogami* (8,500, 1935), last in the Japanese line, rammed the port quarter of *Mikuma* (8,500, 1935), the ship ahead of her. Both cruisers were damaged, *Mogami's* speed being cut to 16 knots. As a result of the *Tambor's* report a Catalina from Midway located the two cruisers soon after dawn. Flying Fortresses failed to make contact, but the cruisers and their two screening destroyers were attacked shortly after 0800 by 6 Dauntlesses and 6 Vindicators, which scored only near misses. One Vindicator, winged by anti-aircraft fire, crashed on *Mikuma's* after turret in a 'kamikaze' attack.

Early on the 6th the crippled cruisers, located by *Enterprise* reconnaissance planes, were attacked by 81 dive-bombers, 3 torpedo-bombers and 28 fighters from *Enterprise* and *Hornet*. Five hits so severely damaged *Mogami* that although she managed to make port it was two years before she rejoined the fleet. *Mikuma* was set on fire and, torn by internal explosions, she sank that night with the loss of about 1,000 of her crew.

The battle of Midway was over and had ended in an American victory, a victory which, although few realized it at the time, had sealed Japan's fate and made the loss of the war inevitable for her. Yamamoto's pursuit of too many objectives, his over confidence that he held the advantage of surprise, and his failure to concentrate his powerful forces, so as to adequately protect his carriers, be within easy supporting distance of them, and have all his forces capable of mutually supporting one another, throughout the operation, were factors contributing to the Japanese defeat. These defects in the Japanese plan were aggravated by Nagumo's tactical errors, the most serious of which were his perfunctory initial search, his drawing of his Midway strike force from all four carriers instead of holding back the planes of one or two of his carriers to attack surface vessels if the need arose and his failure to act quickly in attacking the American ships once they were reported. All Yamamoto had to show for his grandiose operation was the occupation of Attu and Kiska on June 7, paltry prizes compared with the glittering prospects before him when his armada sailed to meet its destiny. Not until after the war was Japan told that at Midway the Imperial Navy experienced the greatest defeat in its history.

NOTES AND REFERENCES

1. Ante, 74.
2. For Eisenhower's account of his interview with Marshall and subsequent developments see Eisenhower, *Crusade in Europe* (London, 1948), 19, et seq.
3. Matloff & Snell, *Strategic Planning for Coalition Warfare 1941-42*, 95.
4. Held late in December 1941.
5. Churchill, *The Hinge of Fate*, 136.
6. Post, 203, 394.
7. On this subject generally see Churchill, *Hinge of Fate*, 125, 136-46; Wigmore, *The Japanese Thrust*, 447-52, 463-5; Kirby, *India's Most Dangerous Hour*, 55 8, 103-4; Butler, *Grand Strategy*, III, 468-9; Matloff and Snell, 127-8, 130-1; Bryant, *The Turn of the Tide*, 311, n. 2.
8. See map on pages 44-45.
9. See map on page 167.
10. Post, 184-6.
11. Samuel Milner, *Victory in Papua* (Washington, 1957), 29.
12. See McCarthy, *South-West Pacific Area — First Year, Kokoda to Wau*, 45, et seq.
13. Ante, 25.

14. Potter and Nimitz, *The Great Sea War*, 213-4.
15. The Japanese did not use N-day for all operations, but changed the designation of D-day for each operation. On the other hand, the Allies permanently adopted D-day as the symbol for the starting of any operation.
16. Ante, 164.
17. Fuchida and Okumiya, *Midway: The Battle that Doomed Japan*, 151-2.
18. Mitscher's *Hornet* Action Report, Appendix, quoted by Morison, 117.
19. Gay's story will be found in *Life*, 31st August, 1942, Sidney L. James, *Torpedo Squadron 8 — as told by Ensign Gay*.
20. Fuchida and Okumiya, 176.
21. Ibid., 178.

FURTHER READING:

Again the official histories, especially Morison's *Coral Sea, Midway and Submarine Actions, May-August, 1942* (Boston, 1950), provide the fullest information on the Coral Sea and Midway battles. Potter and Nimitz, *The Great Sea War* (London, 1961) and D'Albas, *Death of a Navy* (London, 1957) may also be consulted. For the background of the build-up of Australia as a base, the military and air official histories are valuable, particularly Maurice Matloff and Edwin M. Snell, *Strategic Planning for Coalition Warfare, 1941-42* (Washington, 1953), Dudley McCarthy, *South-West Pacific—First Year, Kokoda to Wau* (Canberra, 1959), and Samuel Milner, *Victory in Papua* (Washington, 1957). The story from the Japanese point of view will be found in Ito's *The End of the Imperial Japanese Navy* (London, 1962), Fuchida and Okumiya, *Midway: The Battle that Doomed Japan* (Annapolis, 1955), and John Deane Potter, *Admiral of the Pacific: The Life of Yamamoto* (London, 1965).

seven

THE STRUGGLE
FOR NEW GUINEA

The battles of the Coral Sea and of Midway transformed the
strategic outlook in the Pacific, for with Japan's failure to
capture Port Moresby and the drastic reduction of the Imperial
Navy's air power, in skilled pilots as well as carriers, the tide
of Japanese aggression was stemmed. Henceforth the initiative
lay with the Allies, and having seized it they never relinquished it.

The immediate lesson of the Coral Sea battle, in which
nearly all participating Allied land-based aircraft were operating
at extreme range, was the need to move the Allied air forces
closer to the enemy as the first step in securing local air
supremacy over New Guinea and its approaches. This was not
simply a matter of putting aircraft into Port Moresby itself,
but involved a major programme to improve and extend existing
airfields and to develop new air bases, notably along the Cape
York Peninsula northward of Townsville and close to the south-
eastern tip of New Guinea.

Tackled vigorously by the Americans and Australians in co-operation, substantial progress had been made by May, although not until October was the work completed. New bases in the Cape York Peninsula, particularly at Mareeba, Cooktown and Coen, and the improvement of the existing fields at Horn Island and Port Moresby, where three new airfields were also built, advanced the forward bomber line by 500 miles.[1] Simultaneously, steps were taken to build up and more effectively distribute stocks of aviation fuel, which had to be imported as oil had not yet been discovered in Australia in commercial quantities.

On April 18 General MacArthur formally assumed command of the South-West Pacific area and next day announced his staff. General Marshall had pressed him to include high-ranking Australian and Dutch officers, but, determined to have a wholly American headquarters, MacArthur filled all senior positions with Americans, all but three of whom had come out of the Philippines with him. When Marshall reiterated his suggestion, MacArthur asserted that no qualified senior Australian or Dutch officers were available, although there is no evidence that he ever made any formal request to the Australian authorities for the assignment of suitable officers. A completely integrated staff, such as Eisenhower later so successfully established at Supreme Headquarters in the European theatre, could hardly have failed to give the South-West Pacific a more efficient command, but to MacArthur such a system made no appeal.

Command of the Allied naval forces went to Vice-Admiral Herbert F. Leary, U.S.N., and of the Allied air forces to General Brett. MacArthur wished also to have an American land commander, but as the bulk of the Allied land forces were Australian and both the naval and air commanders as well as MacArthur himself were Americans, Washington insisted that the appointment should go to an Australian. General Sir Thomas Blamey, who had commanded the Australian Imperial Force in the Middle East and had served in that theatre as Deputy Commander in Chief, assumed command of both the Australian and American land forces. On his return to Australia from the Middle East in March, Blamey had swiftly reorganized the Australian Army, forming two armies, two new Corps Headquarters, Northern Territory Force and New Guinea Force. He abolished the old geographical area commands, and established lines of communications area commands. On July 20 MacArthur's Headquarters and the subordinate Allied land, air and naval headquarters completed their transfer from Melbourne to Brisbane.

The build-up of forces in Australia enabled the Port Moresby garrison, which was weak, untrained, ill-armed and poorly equipped,[2] to be reinforced, although no more infantry were added until May, and provided MacArthur with a numerically strong nucleus of an offensive force. By May 14 both the 41st and 32nd United States Infantry Divisions had arrived in Australia, although both were raw and unblooded, requiring considerable training before being fit for combat. The experienced 7th Australian Division had returned from the Middle East in March and the 6th Australian Infantry Division, another battle-tested formation, would be concentrated in Australia by August, two of its brigade groups having been diverted temporarily to the garrison defending Ceylon. The Australian 1st Armoured Division, although it had not seen action and was deficient in armoured equipment, having, in May, only 142 tanks of various types, was well advanced in its training. There were also a number of independent companies — specially trained commando troops, highly skilled in jungle and guerilla warfare. The 9th Australian Division, which completed the volunteer Australian Imperial Force formations, was still in the Middle East. The total strength of the A.I.F. in Australia was slightly over 113,000, of whom 3,000 were in New Caledonia, Port Moresby and Portuguese Timor. The Australian militia, formed mainly of men who had not volunteered for service overseas, had a strength of some 265,000. There was an unjustified tendency to belittle the militia as an inferior force, but its standard was greatly raised by the infusion of experienced A.I.F. officers and N.C.O.'s and it was to prove its quality in much hard fighting. Thus, MacArthur commanded 378,000 Australian and 38,000 United States land forces.

The naval forces under Leary comprised 3 heavy cruisers — 2 Australian and 1 American — and 1 Australian and 2

American light cruisers, 15 destroyers, of which all but 4 were American, 20 modern and 11 old United States submarines, and a number of small craft. The mercantile marine, besides Australian and New Zealand coastal vessels, included 29 ships of the Dutch K.P.M. Line, which before the war had maintained a network of inter-island services in the Netherlands East Indies. These Dutch vessels, ranging in size from 500 to 6,000 tons, were invaluable for supply and amphibious operations.

The Air Force was not as strong in fact as on paper. Two American groups — one heavy and one medium bomber — were still without aircraft, and those squadrons which had been almost continuously in action since before the fall of Java were battle-weary and in need of relief. Their morale was low and their aircraft, the serviceability rate of which was poor, required replacement. On May 1 the United States fighter groups were alone at full strength, with a 50 per cent reserve. The provision of replacement and spare parts was so hedged around by red tape that delays averaging a month were frequent, while often requisitions were returned unfulfilled because they had been incorrectly made out. To front-line squadrons this was exasperating in the extreme. Ground control and facilities were generally poor, and at Port Moresby an inordinate time was required to refuel and put into the air bombers staging through for attacks on Rabaul and other targets. Insufficient attention was paid to tactics, the bombers frequently failing to fly in formation and the fighters not attacking in pairs to compensate for the inferiority of their aircraft.

American Air Force personnel stood at about 18,000. The Royal Australian Air Force had a total strength of 79,074, but several of its squadrons were stationed in other theatres, especially in Britain; about 9,000 air crew were serving in Great Britain, India, the Middle East, and elsewhere. In Australia the R.A.A.F. had 1,714 officers and 40,200 other ranks, a total of 41,914, and an additional 8,300 were being trained as air crew under the Empire Air Training Scheme. There were 350 officers and 12,500 airwomen in the Women's Australian Air Force by late 1942.

By July, the Americans, excluding 36 transport aircraft of
19 different types, had 481 planes, of which only 151 were
serviceable, and the R.A.A.F. as at August 10 had 149
serviceable aircraft out of a total of 215, excluding transport
and second-line obsolete types. Replacements were coming
forward slowly, the Americans in May and June receiving but
62 new bombers and no new fighters. Yet between April and
mid-July they lost 171 aircraft — 116 fighters and 55 bombers,
of which 53 fighters and 23 bombers were written off through
accidents.

In MacArthur's eyes nothing was right with the Air Force,
and he blamed Brett. The two men were temperamentally
incompatible and a personal antagonism existed between them,
so that they saw as little of one another as possible. MacArthur's
dislike or distrust of Brett, whether justified or not, was echoed
by his Chief of Staff, Sutherland, and probably was heightened
by the number of Australians filling senior positions on Brett's
staff. Due to the dependence of the Americans upon the
R.A.A.F. for their communications and in administrative
matters, Brett's Chief of Staff, his Directors of Intelligence, of
Defence and Communications, and his Assistant Directors of
Plans and of Operations were all Australians.

Early in July MacArthur recommended Brett's supersession
and from a list of possible commanders forwarded by Washington selected Major-General George C. Kenney. A dynamic
personality of great drive and ruthless determination, Kenney
reached Australia late in July and immediately visited New
Guinea, Townsville and other operational bases to study his
new command at first hand. Taking over from Brett on August
4, he began introducing reforms and new methods, and
from the outset made it clear to MacArthur and, more particularly, to Sutherland, that Kenney, not MacArthur's Headquarters, commanded the Allied Air Forces.[3]

Kenney reorganized the air command along MacArthur lines.
The U.S.A.A.F.I.A. and the R.A.A.F. became separate entities,
each answerable to him operationally. Most of the Australian
officers on Brett's staff were released to form the new operational Headquarters of the R.A.A.F., with the Air Vice-Marshal

W. D. Bostock as its commander, while the U.S.A.A.F.I.A. became the Fifth United States Air Force and Kenney's own staff became increasingly American in personnel. The system, which possessed flexibility and suited the peculiar problems of the theatre, worked well, although it created difficulties and ill-feeling in the chain of command of the R.A.A.F., which still had its own Chief of the Air Staff. The appointment of Brigadier-General Ennis C. Whitehead, an experienced fighter commander, as Kenney's deputy in New Guinea ensured the maximum speed and efficiency in the direction of combat operations, since Whitehead's small, mobile advanced headquarters was freed of all other responsibilities.

Immediately after the Midway victory offensive plans were evolved and quickly approved by the American Joint Chiefs of Staff. MacArthur proposed a thrust through New Guinea and the Solomons to take Rabaul and assumed, since the objectives lay within his area, that he would be in command from start to finish. Nimitz, however, insisted that Tulagi must be seized before any attack on Rabaul and objected strongly to Mac-Arthur having command, at least during the amphibious stages of the offensive. The command dispute was settled adroitly by Washington. A directive was issued on July 2 dividing operations into three stages: first, the seizure and occupation of the Santa Cruz Islands, Tulagi and adjacent positions; second, the seizure and occupation of the remainder of the Solomon Islands and of Lae, Salamaua and the north-east coast of New Guinea, and, third, the seizure and occupation of Rabaul and adjacent positions in the New Guinea-New Ireland area. The target date for phase one was originally August 1, on which date the boundary between the South-West Pacific and the South Pacific areas was to be moved to 159° East longitude, thus transferring the first phase objectives from the South-West Pacific to the South Pacific area. This placed responsibility for the first phase with Vice-Admiral Robert L. Ghormley, appointed commander of the South Pacific area by Nimitz, and for the second and third phases with MacArthur.

After the failure of the Japanese seaborne attempt against Port Moresby, fighting was restricted to the air and to small

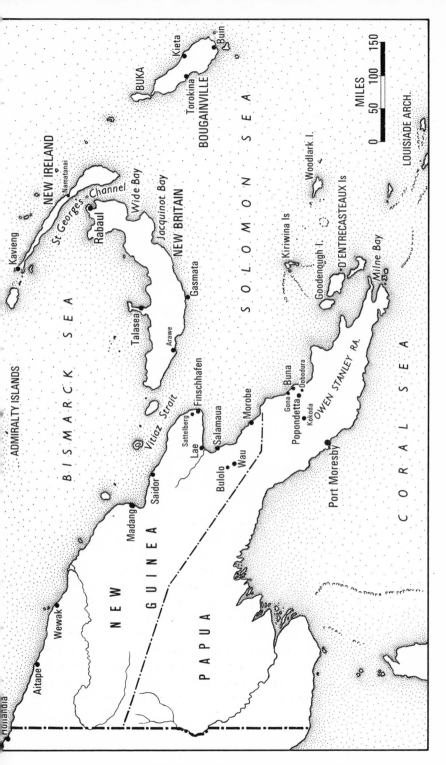

8. The Papua, New Guinea and New Britain war zones

guerilla operations in New Guinea, particularly in the Lae and Salamaua areas. The Japanese raided Darwin and made one or two small nuisance raids against Townsville. There was air fighting and bombing by both sides over New Guinea and along its sea approaches. On the night of May 31-June 1 a midget submarine attack in Sydney Harbour sank the old ferry-boat *Kuttabul,* which had been converted into a moored barracks at the naval base at Garden Island and in the early hours of June 8 a few shells were fired into a Sydney suburb, causing damage to residential buildings but no casualties. That night another submarine fired some shells into Newcastle.

The lull in large-scale activity, however, could not last. MacArthur's Headquarters foresaw that the Japanese would renew their attempt to capture Port Moresby and on June 9 indicated that the enemy was likely to land in the Buna area, on the north-east coast of Papua, from where the steep and difficult Kokoda Track ran across the razorback ridges of the Owen Stanley Mountains to Port Moresby, passing over a wide, 6,000-foot high mountain pass misleadingly named The Gap. Blamey ordered Major-General Basil Morris, commander of the New Guinea Force, to take immediate steps to defend the Kokoda Track with Australian troops. On June 24 Morris formed Maroubra Force from the 39th Australian Battalion, an untried militia unit, and the Papuan Infantry Battalion, consisting of 20 white officers and 280 natives, and entrusted this force, only a small part of which was moved up the trail, with the defence of the Kokoda Track.

Following a decision made in June, United States engineers and an Australian garrison, including the 7th Brigade, moved into the Milne Bay area, on the south-eastern tip of Papua, and by early August two R.A.A.F. fighter and one R.A.A.F. Hudson squadrons were operating from the hastily constructed airfield. A large, all-weather airfield, from which support could be given to the operations against Lae and Salamaua during the second phase of the offensive ordered by Washington's directive of July 2, was to be built on grass plains near Dobdura, 15 miles south of Buna. On July 15 G.H.Q. therefore ordered that the Buna area should be occupied about August 10-12,

a few days after the assault on Guadalcanal, D-day for which
had been put back from August 1 to 7. The commanders
charged with the Buna operation warned that the Japanese
were likely to forestall the Allies, but these warnings were
disregarded by G.H.Q., whose woeful intelligence service was
now convinced the enemy had no immediate plans for the
seizure of the Buna-Gona area. In any event, MacArthur
rejected a proposal for an immediate Allied landing on the
grounds that it could not be made in sufficient strength and
would serve only to bring Buna to the enemy's notice.

However, Japanese eyes already were fixed on the area and
plans for its occupation were well advanced. During the night
of July 21-22 the enemy landed about 1,800 combatants,
100 naval labourers and some 1,200 impressed native carriers
at Basabua, a mile and a half south of Gona and nine miles
north-west of Buna. The enemy convoy, fleetingly sighted *en
route* from Rabaul and unsuccessfully attacked by a lone
Flying Fortress and five Marauders on the afternoon of the
21st, was located off Basabua next morning by an Australian
Hudson. Bombers and fighters, encountering no air opposition,
attacked, but although 48 tons of bombs were dropped and
15,000 rounds of ammunition fired, only a landing barge was
sunk, a transport set on fire and a float plane shot down, while
enemy casualties from both bombing and strafing were light.

Colonel Yosuke Yokoyama, the engineer officer in command,
had orders from Major-General Tomitaro Horii, commander of
the South Seas Force, to reconnoitre the Kokoda Track and
ascertain if it offered a practicable route for the capture of
Port Moresby. Yokoyama's men, travelling light and largely
living off the country, pushed rapidly up the trail. The weak
Australian force of some 400 men could offer little opposition
to the Japanese, who employed their usual tactics of infiltration
and working round the flanks. By the 29th, seven days after
their landing, the Japanese firmly held Kokoda, lying in the
Yodda Valley, 1,200 feet above sea level and 50 miles inland
from Buna as the crow flies. The ease of Yokoyama's advance
induced Lieutenant-General Haruyoshi Hyakutake, who as
commander of the newly formed XVII Army, had set up his

Headquarters at Rabaul on July 24, to convert the reconnaissance into a definite attack, and he issued orders on the
28th for Horii to attack Port Moresby over the Kokoda Track
while another Japanese force, having captured the small island
of Samarai, off the south-east tip of Papua, assaulted the Allied
base from the sea. The Eleventh Air Force, commanded by
Vice-Admiral Nishizo Tsukahara, and the Eighth Fleet of Vice-
Admiral Gunichi Mikawa, which had taken over from the
Fourth Fleet, were to support the operation.

As the Japanese speeded up their preparations for the
capture of Port Moresby, they were thrown off balance by the
landings of the United States Marines on Guadalcanal and
adjacent objectives on August 7. Hyakutake decided he could
manage both fights, but the need of reinforcing Guadalcanal
left him no alternative but to postpone the two-pronged attack
on Port Moresby from August 7 to 16. The Guadalcanal
landing, which will be described in the next chapter, came as
a shock to the Japanese leaders, who had been satisfied the
Allies would be incapable of mounting a counter-offensive for
many months to come. They now received a second shock
when they belatedly discovered that the Allies had already
occupied Milne Bay. Hyakutake cancelled the Samarai operation in favour of an attack on Milne Bay, after the capture of
which his forces there were to assault Port Moresby from the
sea as Horii's troops, debouching from the Owen Stanleys,
attacked it from the landward side.

After taking Kokoda, the Japanese paused to get supplies
forward and to bring in further reinforcements. Late in July
they had landed supplies and more men, and on the 29th five
of seven Dauntless aircraft which attacked a convoy close
inshore were shot down by its escorting Zeros. The sixth Dauntless, badly damaged, was nursed into a landing at Milne Bay,
and only the seventh succeeded in returning to base at Port
Moresby. One transport, however, was sunk, but most of the
engineer unit aboard reached shore. Although one or two
convoys were turned back before reaching their destination, the
Air Force alone was incapable of preventing the Japanese
landing men and supplies, and without serious interference or

Australian troops making the precarious 3000 foot climb to Cameron's Knoll during the attack on the Japanese-held Bogadjim

Australian War Memorial

Australian troops go into the attack in New Guinea supported by a General Stuart tank

heavy casualties Horii soon commanded a force of about 10,000 combatants and 3,500 engineer and lines of communication troops.

Meanwhile, the Japanese success and the growing concern in Australia for the safety of Port Moresby were reflected in command changes on the Allied side. On August 12 all Australian and United States land forces in New Guinea were placed under the command of Major-General Sydney F. Rowell, an Australian regular who had served as Blamey's Chief of Staff in the Middle East, and who, after returning to Australia to become for a brief period Deputy Chief of the General Staff, had taken command of I Australian Corps in April. He replaced Morris, but the latter remained head of the Australia-New Guinea Administrative Unit (ANGAU). Rowell was responsible for operations on the Kokoda Track, where Brigadier S. H. W. C. Porter took over command of Maroubra Force, and at Milne Bay, where Major-General Cyril A. Clowes assumed command on the 13th. These commanders were Middle East veterans.

As far back as 1919 the formation of a naval coast-watching organization had been suggested by Captain C. J. Clare, then District Naval Officer at Fremantle, W.A., and this proposal had been gradually developed over the years by the Royal Australian Navy. At first confined to the mainland, it was later extended to New Guinea and the Solomons. At the outbreak of war in 1939 there were some 700 coast-watchers, those in the islands being equipped with tele-radios for communication. There were, however, many gaps in the coast-watching networks in the islands, and Lieutenant-Commander Eric A. Feldt, who had served in the R.A.N. during World War I and in 1923 had resigned his commission to join the New Guinea Administration, with which he became a patrol officer, was appointed to select and instruct additional coast-watchers. During the next two years he greatly extended and improved the coast-watching organization throughout the islands.

Most of the coast-watchers were civilians, but after Japan entered the war they were enlisted in the R.A.N.V.R. in an effort to prevent them being treated as spies should they be captured, and badges and rank stripes were dropped by aircraft to those who had remained behind the Japanese lines. The work demanded a bushman's instinct, an ability to withstand hardship and privation, great initiative, and outstanding moral and physical courage. No mercy was shown by the Japanese to those unfortunate enough to be captured alive, but the operational intelligence which these brave men sent back was invaluable and was an important factor in the conduct of the operations of all three Services.

It was from coast-watchers that first word was received of the Japanese movements against Milne Bay. On August 24 a coast-watcher at Porlock Harbour, south-east of Buna, reported seven large motor-driven barges moving eastward, and next day a coast-watcher at Cape Varieta, on Goodenough Island, radioed that the troops from these barges were stretching their legs and preparing a meal on the island's south-west coast. Although the Allies did not know it at the time, this force of some 350 men from Buna had been ordered to land at Taupota, on the Papuan shore of Goodenough Bay, and to march over-land to attack Gili Gili, the main Allied base near the head of Milne Bay, while a larger force, landing at Rabi, east of Gili Gili, drove along the narrow northern coastal strip against the Allied defensive position.

Alerted by the coast-watchers' messages, R.A.A.F. Kitty-hawks from Milne Bay strafed the barges as they lay drawn up on the beach, destroying all seven and thus leaving the Japanese without the means of continuing their voyage to Taupota or of returning to Buna. The immobilization of this enemy force not only removed the immediate threat of attack against Gili Gili from the landward side, but deprived the Japanese of the use of the landing barges for turning the Australians' sea flank in Milne Bay by moving troops behind the forward positions under cover of darkness.

The main Japanese force totalled about 2,700 men, with two light tanks. It was thus numerically inferior to the defenders. Clowes had under his command about 7,459 Australians and 1,365 Americans, but of this total of 8,824 only about 4,500 were infantry of the 7th and 18th Brigades. When the Japanese landed during the night of August 25-26, torrential tropical rain had been falling for a week and there was no sign of it easing. The rain and the darkness of the night misled the enemy as to his position, and his troops were put ashore at Waga Waga and Wanadala instead of at Rabi, five to seven miles farther west and closer to the main Allied base. Confused fighting, in which the advanced militia units acquitted themselves well, took place that night. Withdrawing to rest during the daytime, the enemy attacked aggressively at night, and around K.B. Mission, east of Rabi, where the well-drained plantation land was relatively firm, he effectively used his two light tanks, overrunning a veteran A.I.F. force which had been pushed forward to aid the militia.

However, the Japanese tanks bogged down once they left the plantation area, for the rain had converted the tracks into morasses into which men floundered to their knees, and on the night of August 30-31 all their attacks against the Australian infantry and American engineers dug in along the uncompleted Air Strip No. 3 failed with heavy loss. Clowes, who wisely had refused to commit all his forces while there was still the possibility of a further Japanese landing, either north or south of Gili Gili, now started a drive against the enemy along the coast. Although the Japanese had landed nearly 800 reinforcements on the night of August 29, they had seriously miscalculated Allied strength and on the 31st they began to retreat. During the night of September 5-6 most of the remaining Japanese were evacuated, and although G.H.Q. intimated that a fresh attack might be expected, none eventuated. A decisive factor in the enemy's defeat had been the strafing and bombing of his forward troops and supply dumps. From the first day of the landing the Australian fighters, despite the mist and rain, had effectively harassed the Japanese, although once or twice they had attacked their own ground forces.

On August 26, the day of the Milne Bay landing, the Japanese launched a general offensive on the Kokoda Track and despite stout Australian opposition had gained possession by September 7 of The Gap, Myola, Kagi and Efogi, the two latter villages being on the southern slopes of the mountains.

Five days later the Australians withdrew to Ioribaiwa, less than 30 air miles from Port Moresby.

At the time of the Coral Sea battle there had been only one infantry brigade in Papua. In May Blamey had sent a second militia brigade to Port Moresby, and in July and August four more brigades had arrived — the two that fought at Milne Bay and the 21st and 25th which were sent to Port Moresby. The fact that the first substantial infantry reinforcement to be sent to New Guinea was the 14th Brigade in May and no more arrived until July scarcely supports MacArthur's later claim that from the moment of his arrival in Australia he decided to defend that country in New Guinea. In fact, his directives and actions, including the establishment of his Headquarters in Melbourne until July, suggest that, like the Australians them- selves, he at first decided that Australia would have to be defended on the Australian mainland.

Back in Australia MacArthur and his staff fumed and fretted and from the events at Milne Bay and on the Kokoda Track concluded that Australian leadership in the field was inefficient and lacked enterprise and aggression. They were doubtful also of the fighting quality of the Australian troops, both militia and A.I.F. MacArthur was extremely critical of Clowes's conduct of the Milne Bay action, maintaining that the Japanese should have been vigorously hurled back into the sea immediately after they landed. Even after receiving Clowes's detailed report, which made clear the difficulty of movement in the mud and the necessity, with the Japanese having undisputed command of the sea and sending naval forces into the bay almost nightly, of holding back a substantial portion of his force against the contingency of a fresh Japanese landing either north or south of Gili Gili, MacArthur unjustly maintained his criticism.

G.H.Q.'s dissatisfaction with the slowness of the Milne Bay victory, which was also felt, though less strongly, by Blamey, influenced their views of the events on the Kokoda Track. Neither MacArthur nor his principal officers had the faintest conception of the true position. Brig.-Gen. C. A. Willoughby, MacArthur's chief intelligence officer, was convinced at the outset that the Japanese had no intention of marching overland

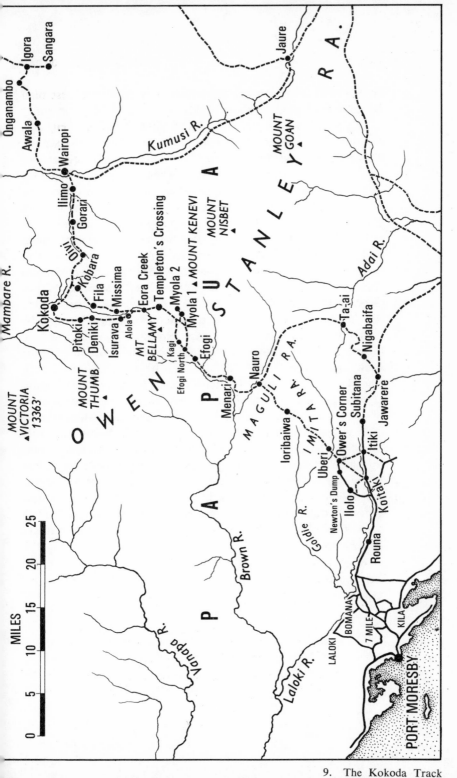

9. The Kokoda Track

on Port Moresby, but merely wanted possession of the Gona-Buna-Kokoda area for the establishment of airfields from which to raid Port Moresby and the Cape York Peninsula. He persisted in this view until the march of events proved him wrong. This preconceived opinion probably influenced his estimates of Japanese strength and he consistently underrated the Japanese forces in numbers as well as quality. Thus, MacArthur and his staff believed the Australians on the Kokoda Track were being driven back by numerically inferior enemy forces.

Nor did G.H.Q. possess any conception of the tangled mountain country in which the fighting was taking place or the tremendous supply difficulties posed by the rugged Owen Stanley Range. The suggestion of G.H.Q.'s Chief Engineer, Major-General Hugh J. Casey, as early as August 13 that points should be selected 'where the pass may be readily blocked by demolition', and that the necessary explosives should be moved forward, demonstrates how little MacArthur and his officers knew about the terrain. Doubtless, the misleading name of The Gap — and it must be remembered that no adequate maps of New Guinea were available — had conveyed the impression of a narrow trail running through a mountain pass with towering rock walls on either side. On September 6 MacArthur told Marshall that the Australians 'have proven themselves unable to match the enemy in jungle fighting. Aggressive leadership is lacking'. Three days later he belatedly realized that the Australians, instead of being in superior strength, were in fact seriously outnumbered, but not until much later did G.H.Q. come to appreciate the terrain difficulties of the New Guinea and Papuan areas.

What was the Kokoda Track like?

Colonel Kingsley Norris, Assistant Director Medical Services, 7th Australian Division, wrote in September, 1942[4]:

> Imagine an area of approximately 100 miles long. Crumple and fold this into a series of ridges, each rising higher and higher until 7,000 feet is reached, then declining in ridges to 3,000 feet. Cover this thickly with jungle, short trees and tall trees, tangled with great, entwining savage vines. Through an

oppression of this density, cut a little native track, two or three feet wide, up the ridges, over the spurs, round gorges and down across swiftly flowing, happy mountain streams. Where the track clambers up the mountain sides, cut steps — big steps, little steps, steep steps — or clear the soil from the tree roots.

Every few miles, bring the track through a small patch of sunlit kunai grass, or an old deserted native garden, and every seven or ten miles, build a group of dilapidated grass huts — as staging shelters — generally set in a foul, offensive clearing. Every now and then, leave beside the track dumps of discarded, putrefying food, occasional dead bodies and human foulings. In the morning, flicker the sunlight through the tall trees, flutter green and blue and purple and white butterflies lazily through the air, and hide birds of deep-throated song, or harsh cockatoos, in the foliage.

About midday, and through the night, pour water over the forest, so that the steps become broken, and a continual yellow stream flows downwards, and the first few level areas become pools and puddles of putrid black mud. In the high ridges above Myola, drip this water day and night over the track through a foetid forest grotesque with moss and glowing phosphorescent fungi. Such is the track which a prominent politician publicly described as "being almost impassable for motor vehicles", and such is the route for 10 days to be covered from Ilolo to Deniki.

Distances on the Kokoda Track were not to be counted in miles, but in hours of walking and clambering, sometimes on hands and knees. Centuries old, the Track, as with all native pads, followed no established principles. As Raymond Paull wrote:

It climbs the highest ridges, plunges down into the deepest ravines, and ascends the longest spurs. Between Uberi and the crest of the range, the track climbs more than 20,000 feet, although it has an altitude of 7,000 feet at its highest point. For every 1,000 feet of altitude gained, the track drops 600 feet to the foot of the next ascent.

The second day's trek along the Track from Port Moresby

began at Uberi and led up the steps known as 'The Golden
Staircase'. The historian of the 2/14th Australian Battalion[6]
wrote:

> The golden stairs consisted of steps varying from
> 10 to 18 inches in height. The front edge of
> the step was a small log held by stakes. Behind
> the log was a puddle of mud and water. Some of
> the stakes had worked loose, leaving the logs slightly
> tilted. Anyone who stood on one of those skidded
> and fell with a whack in the mud, probably banging
> his head against a tree or being hit on the head with
> his own rifle. Those who had no sticks soon acquired
> them, not only to prevent falls, but to allow the arms
> to help the legs, especially with the higher steps.
>
> After the first half-dozen steps, it became a matter
> of sheer determination forcing the body to achieve
> the impossible. It was probably the weight more than
> the climb, though the climb would have been enough
> to tire even a lightly loaded man. The rear com-
> panies, where the going is always hardest, took 12
> hours to complete the nine (barely four miles as the
> crow flies) miles. Over the first three miles the Track
> rose 1,200 feet. It then dropped 1,600 feet before
> the final climb up the Imita Range — 2,000 feet in
> the last four miles. The rear troops arrived in the
> dark, others going down to help them over the
> seemingly vertical steps of the last few hundred yards.

Another battalion historian[7] wrote of the Kokoda Track
between Myola and Eora Creek:

> Incessant rain had made the track a treacherous
> mass of moving mud interlaced with protruding roots
> that reached out hidden hands to bring the laden
> troops heavily to the ground. Vines trapped them.
> Wet boughs slapped at them. Their breath came in
> gulps. Their eyes filled with perspiration.

The Australians who scrambled and fought along this narrow
native pad carried 45-lb. packs and cumbersome rifles. Although
the jungle fighting in Malaya had shown the unsuitability of
Allied equipment for such operations and had indicated the
desirability of troops being lightly accoutred, there had not been
time to equip them more suitably.

The difficulties of the terrain were accentuated by the difficulties of the weather. The humid heat of the day was followed by the bitter chilliness of the night, and, day and night, drenching rain poured down almost without cessation. A myriad of insects plagued the troops — chiggers, mites, mosquitoes and leeches—and the incidence of tropical diseases such as malaria, dengue fever, dysentery and jungle rot was to become high. Before long, the men fighting and cursing over the Kokoda Track were wan, emaciated, gaunt, with sunken, bloodshot eyes, their perpetually wet clothes steaming in the humid midday heat, but indomitable of will and spirit, obstinately refusing to be conquered by the enemy, the terrain, the climate, or by hunger or illness.

Supplies could not be brought forward with sufficient speed or in sufficient quantity, and there was always a shortage of rations, ammunition, weapons and other essential equipment. There were never enough native carriers. The New Guinea 'fuzzy-wuzzies' did a magnificent job under appalling conditions. They were overworked and overloaded, perpetually underfed, and, with seldom a blanket for each man, were exposed to cold. The wonder is not that so many deserted but that so many remained, carrying forward supplies day after day.

The supplies taken forward by the carriers were augmented by air-drop, but supply from the air was then in its infancy. The crews were inexperienced, there were not enough suitable aircraft, and there were no parachutes. The dropping areas at Nauro, Menari and Efogi were not easy to locate and less easy to hit; many of the supplies fell into the surrounding jungle or behind the Japanese lines, so that the recovery rate was often low, and weather conditions frequently interrupted dropping operations. The contents of many sacks of dropped rations burst on impact and in the humid atmosphere quickly became contaminated. Moreover, as the Australians were pushed back they lost possession of the dropping areas.

The fighting itself was broken into a series of independent actions, fought at close quarters by hostile forces concealed from each other and from their comrades by a few yards of tropical forest. The ambush and the sniper's bullet were ever-present perils. Of a later period, àn Australian war correspondent wrote[8]:

> Jungle genius is an infinite capacity for taking pains. It is an acquired resiliency to the thousand blows man and Nature can inflict in the miasmatic stronghold of tooth and claw. It is the faculty to fight on when your head is awhirl with malaria, when your bones are cracking with dengue, when your belly is drained with dysentery, when your tongue is parched with the curse of the hard, hot kunai country, or your boots logged, your clothes soaked with sweat and ooze in the mountains of mud; when fear is in the trembling of a leaf and not mercy but murder rains from heaven; when nothing is what it seems but a trick by a cat-cunning enemy. Jungle genius is above all the power not only to conquer these terrors, but to tame them to your will and your need, and enlist them as allies, use them as artillery against your enemies.

Cut off from their comrades or from the tracks, groups of men and individuals doggedly forced their way through the jungle and climbed the spurs and ravines to rejoin their units, some after only a few days, others many weeks later. For example, Sergeant W. H. Irwin, of the 2/14th Australian Infantry Battalion, using his watch as a compass, led 22 men to safety after traversing the mountain jungle for 22 days, 19 of them without food. Many similar incidents might be recounted.

For the wounded the Kokoda Track was sheer hell. Eight men were needed to carry each bush stretcher, made of poles and vines, and as bearers in such numbers were unavailable many wounded men who should have been stretcher cases had to make their own way to the rear, with such assistance as other wounded men might be able to give. Even the sure-footed Papuans, who brought forward supplies one day and carried wounded back the next, often could not avoid spilling their stretchers, and even if this did not happen the occupants received a frightful jolting as they were carried over the treacherous Track.

A Victorian, Corporal John Metson, whose courage and self-sacrifice were an example to both Australian and American troops, refused to be placed on a stretcher or carried pick-a-back after being shot through the ankle, and, in the words of the battalion historian,[9] 'wrapped bandages around his hands and knees and crawled for three weeks, chilled, rain-soaked, mud-caked, starved, exhausted — never complaining, always encouraging', not over the Track, but through the much more difficult mountainous jungle with a party which had been cut off. With other wounded, he was eventually left at a native village until help could be obtained, but when rescuers arrived they found that Japanese had been before them and had killed the helpless men.

In the second half of September more reinforcements arrived in Papua. The 16th Brigade, which had spent only 36 days in Australia since its arrival from Ceylon, was sent to Port Moresby, where from the middle of the month the Headquarters of both the 6th and 7th Divisions were established. Thus New Guinea Force now comprised three divisions, counting the Milne Bay force as one. The only A.I.F. infantry brigades then remaining in Australia were the 19th, at Darwin, and the 17th. due to reinforce Milne Bay in October. If further reinforcements were to be sent in they would have to comprise militia brigades, of which there were now three on the island, or be drawn from the American divisions. Already, after a visit to Port Moresby by Sutherland early in September, MacArthur had decided to send American troops to the front. His first idea was that one regiment should find an alternative track by which they could place themselves astride the Kokoda Track in rear of the Japanese facing the Australians. In the upshot, the 126th and 128th Regiments were dispatched to Port Moresby from September 20 onwards, one by air, the other by sea. Thus by October New Guinea Force had approximately the same strength as Malaya Command when war broke out.

As a consequence of MacArthur's anxiety and the misconceptions of G.H.Q., the Australian Government at MacArthur's suggestion sent Blamey to take personal command at Port Moresby. He quickly clashed with Rowell, whom he relieved and sent back to Australia, probably unjustly, and appointed as new commander of the New Guinea Force Lieutenant-

General Edmund F. Herring, who since his return from the Middle East as commander of the 6th Division had been in command of the Darwin area, and later of II Corps.

The position, however, was not as desperate as it seemed. By September 17 the Australians had withdrawn from Ioribaiwa to the Imita Ridge, but the Japanese had been repulsed at Milne Bay, were facing mounting difficulties on Guadalcanal, and Horii's men on the Kokoda Track were at the end of their tether. Their long, tenuous supply line, stretching all the way back to Buna and under constant air attack, which repeatedly destroyed the bridge at Wairopi over the swift-flowing Kumusi River, had broken down completely. The stubbornness of the Australian defence after the fall of Kokoda had caused them to expend more food, ammunition and other supplies than they had anticipated and had prevented them from capturing intact any but small Allied supply dumps. Their native carriers had deserted at every opportunity and on the morning of the 17th, when they stood triumphant at Ioribaiwa, not a grain of rice was left for issuing to the starving front-line troops, whose sole subsistence for a fortnight had been barely a cup of rice daily.

Although the Allies were unaware of it, Hyakutake on August 29 had ordered Horii to switch over to the defensive on reaching the southern foothills of the Owen Stanleys. Horii selected Ioribaiwa as his best defensive position and persisted in his forward drive until the Australians had relinquished it and fallen back to the Imita Ridge. He then told his hungry and exhausted troops to dig in, but on September 18, the day after he took Ioribaiwa, came fresh instructions to prepare strong defences in the more easily supplied Buna-Gona beach-head, into which he was to withdraw after holding his positions on the Kokoda Track for as long as possible.

At Ioribaiwa, Major-General A. S. Allen, of the veteran 7th Australian Division, whose Headquarters had been established at Port Moresby since August 18, commanded the forward troops, including Brigadier K. W. Eather's 25th Brigade (from the 7th Division) and Brigadier J. E. Lloyd's 16th Brigade (from the 6th Division). A counter-offensive launched by Eather from Imita Ridge on September 28 met only token resistance. Horii had already thinned out his forward troops because his supply position was such that he could no longer expect to make a stand at Ioribaiwa. The Japanese retreated so quickly that contact was broken, and the Australians occupied Nauro, Menari, Efogi and Myola without opposition. On October 8, however, they ran into resistance in front of Templeton's Crossing. Here, at Eora Creek and in the Oivi-Gorari area, the strong Japanese rearguard fought tenaciously, displaying for the first time in this campaign that fanatical fury and determination which characterized the Japanese defence in the months ahead.

Appreciating that with every passing day the Buna-Gona defences were being strengthened, MacArthur urged speed and yet greater speed in the Australian advance. His dissatisfaction and sharp criticisms were echoed by Blamey, who urged Allen to put more troops into the attack. In his reply, Allen emphasized his supply problems and the difficulties of the terrain. On October 29, the very day the Japanese at last retreated from Eora Creek, Blamey relieved Allen and placed Major-General George A. Vasey, who had served overseas with the 6th Australian Division, in command of the 7th.

Kokoda, with its invaluable airstrip, was secured on 2nd November. A little over a week later, in a bold encircling movement, Vasey sanctioned the use of every available man, so that he was left without a reserve. But this calculated risk was worth taking. The Japanese rearguard at Oivi and Gorari was shattered with heavy losses, and its remnants, fleeing along the west bank of the Kumusi River, did not reach the coast until nearly the end of the month. There Horii and his chief of staff were drowned in trying to cross the flooded river on a raft.

The Japanese had committed some 6,000 men to the campaign along the Kokoda Track, and although their losses are not known they were certainly heavy. The Australians, who had employed three militia battalions and three A.I.F. brigades, lost 39 officers and 586 men killed between July 22 and November 16, their total casualties numbering 103 officers and 1,577 other ranks. Probably twice this number became casualties through illness.

While the Japanese were being routed on the Kokoda Track, preparations for the assault on the Buna-Gona beach-head were being vigorously pursued. MacArthur's plan was to recapture Goodenough Island and then launch a three-pronged drive on Buna, Sanananda and Gona — first, over the Kokoda Track; second, along either the Kapa Kapa-Jaure or Abau-Namudi-Jaure tracks, and last, along the coast north-westward from Milne Bay. In the event, because of the difficulties of the Kapa Kapa-Jaure Track, only one battalion of the 126th United States Regiment marched over the Owen Stanleys. The American troops, overloaded and not yet toughened into first class physical condition, suffered terribly on this gruelling trek. The advance guard started along the Track on October 6, but it was the 28th before the last of the battalion staggered into Jaure. March discipline had been extremely poor and the troops left behind them a trail of discarded raincoats, shelter tents, mosquito nets, clothing and even blankets. Following the discovery of suitable airfield sites and the provision of sufficient aircraft, the remainder of the American Forces were flown in across the Owen Stanleys.

The advance from Milne Bay, although difficult and danger-ous owing to the lack of suitable landing craft, the many uncharted reefs and exposure to enemy air attack, was success-fully accomplished. The troops marched along the coast until halted by swollen streams and glutinous swamp mud and were then ferried forward in luggers, from which they were taken ashore in native outrigger canoes, rowing boats and even canvas-sided engineer boats. By November 2 the 128th United States Regiment was at Pongani and Mendaropu, to the south-east of Buna, the 126th in the Natunga-Bofu area, south-west of Buna, and the Australians, except for those units attached to the Americans, were preparing to smash the last Japanese resistance on the Kokoda Track. MacArthur, preceded by an advanced echelon of G.H.Q., arrived at Port Moresby on the 6th to direct the assault.

The Buna-Gona beach-head was divided into two sectors by

the flooded Girua River, which served as a convenient boundary line between the 32nd United States Division on the right, east of the river, and the Australians on the left, west of the river. Part of the Japanese beach-head was covered by tangled jungle; along the coast, coconut palm groves, areas of bush scrub and patches of shoulder-high, knife-sharp kunai grass were interspersed among the innumerable mangrove, nipa and sago swamps. The climate was hot and muggy, and malaria, dengue and scrub fevers, dysentery, jungle rot, dhobi itch and other tropical ailments flourished.

The Americans, much exhausted by the trying climate, suffered greatly from illness, and they lacked jungle training and experience. Yet they were supremely confident of quickly capturing Buna. Just as over-confident were the more experienced Australians, whose task was to seize Gona and Sanananda. The truth is that no Allied commander at any level appreciated the extent and strength of the enemy defences, the size of his garrison or the fanatical fury and contempt for death of the individual Japanese soldier.

The Japanese held a narrow coastal strip 11 miles in length and varying in depth from a few hundred yards to several miles, almost every inch of which had been strongly fortified. The line ran from Gona on the Japanese right to Cape Endaiadere on their left. The fortifications, skilfully sited and carefully hidden, exploited natural obstacles to canalize the possible lines of advance. Since the water table was three feet, only shallow fire trenches could be dug, but hundreds of bunkers, massively constructed of coconut logs, had been sited on firm ground flanked by swamps. These were so well camouflaged that often they could not be identified even from a few yards. Organized in depth and mostly mutually supporting, they were so strongly built that they were impervious to air attack except from a direct hit. By sheltering in these stout bunkers during mortar and artillery bombardments, and during bombing and strafing attacks from the air, the Japanese were able to emerge and man their machine-gun nests and fire trenches as soon as the Allies attacked.

After landing about 1,000 reinforcements from a destroyer

on the night of November 17-18, the Japanese had some
6,500 troops in the beach-head, 2,500 of them facing the
Americans in the Buna area. Those who had fought over the
Kokoda Track or had been stationed in the Buna area for any
length of time were tired and emaciated and a great number
were suffering from tropical diseases. Nevertheless, a considerable proportion of the defenders were fresh, experienced and
well-equipped troops.

Willoughby originally assessed the Japanese strength at about
4,000, but by November 14 concluded their numbers did not
exceed 2,000. The Australian command estimated the enemy
at between 1,500 and 2,000, while the Headquarters of the
32nd United States Division considered there was not above a
battalion in the Buna area. Moreover, the American divisional
commander, Major-General Edwin F. Harding, and his staff
believed the Japanese command had no intention of seriously
defending Buna, but would fight only a delaying rearguard
action.

The Allies began to close in on the beach-head on November
16, but as soon as they came up against the forward
Japanese position their attacks were halted. Both east and west
of the Girua River the assault bogged down with heavy losses.
In this grim initial fighting, in appalling conditions of terrain
and weather, the green American troops reacted much as had
the Australian militia units in the first shock of combat along
the Kokoda Track. Kenney wrote[10]:

> Stories of inaction and even cowardice of our
> troops were filtering back. The officers didn't know
> their jobs. The commanders were too far to the rear.
> Instead of fighting, there seemed to be an idea that
> if they waited long enough the Japs would starve to
> death or quit. We were bringing back planeloads of
> shell-shocked and sick boys every day. The number
> of men who had actually been wounded was small . . .
> The troops just did not go. They acted scared to
> death of Jap snipers. There were cases of men throw-
> ing away their machine-guns and running in panic.
> Their officers didn't seem to know what to do.

MacArthur decided to relieve Harding, and urgently called

to Port Moresby Lieutenant-General Robert L. Eichelberger, who had taken up duty as Commander of I United States Corps. 'I'm putting you in command at Buna,' MacArthur told him.[11] 'Relieve Harding. I am sending you in, Bob, and I want you to remove all officers who won't fight. Relieve regimental and battalion commanders; if necessary, put sergeants in charge of battalions and corporals in charge of companies — anyone who will fight.'

The 32nd Division, like the Australian militia battalions, was unprepared for the miseries and terrors of jungle warfare, and in both forces some of the officers and men failed. Nearly a decade later Eichelberger wrote[12]:

> Actually, this long after, I'm inclined to believe that the men were more frightened by the jungle than by the Japanese. It was the terror of the new and unknown. There is nothing pleasant about sinking into a foul-smelling bog up to your knees. There is nothing pleasant about lying in a slit trench half submerged, while a tropical rain turns it into a river. Jungle noises were strange to Americans — and in the moist hot darkness the rustling of small animals in the bush was easily misinterpreted as the stealthy approach of the enemy.

Just as the Australian militiamen became splendid fighters with experience, so also did the men of the 32nd United States Division. The Buna-Gona beach-head was as hard a task-master as the Kokoda Track, and the lessons of both were learnt the hard way, but they were lessons which were never forgotten by those who survived.

Eichelberger did what MacArthur had told him to do. He relieved those officers he considered had failed, and he pushed the assault forward resolutely. But progress was slow and costly. All-out assaults achieved little, and the only tactics which brought results were probing attacks designed to locate the positions of the Japanese defenders. Each bunker and pillbox had to be winkled out one by one. Slowly, inexorably, in hard, bitter fighting, the Australians and Americans, fighting side by side for the first time in one of the cruellest campaigns of the Pacific War, pushed the Japanese back against the sea. Even when they were cornered and hopeless, the Japanese fought savagely, launching suicidal counter-attacks and preferring death to surrender. Starvation aided the Allies. Towards the end the Japanese supply position was so desperate they ate anything edible they could find.

The end did not come until January, 1943. Buna Mission finally fell on the 2nd and Sanananda village on the 18th. In each sector the mopping-up of isolated pockets of resistance followed. At Buna, where 1,390 Japanese dead were counted, only 50 prisoners were taken, most of them Korean or Chinese coolies. Not more than 200 or 300 Japanese escaped from the Buna area, mostly by swimming, to join their comrades around Sanananda. In all, the Japanese probably lost about 13,000 killed out of the total of, roughly, 20,000 who were committed to the battle, including the attack on Milne Bay and along the Kokoda Track. In the beach-head fighting the Japanese suffered about 12,000 killed or died of wounds or illness.

Two Australian divisions and one American had been employed in the actual fighting from July onwards. They comprised seven Australian brigades and four American regiments. Until December New Guinea Force was the largest body of European troops the Japanese had encountered in this war. And in New Guinea for the first time they met battle-hardened veterans, and these had soon gained a tactical mastery over them that would be decisively confirmed in the next phase in New Guinea. Total Australian and American battle casualties between July 22 1942 and January 22 1943 were 8,546, of whom 3,095 were killed and 5,451 wounded. The Australians had 5,698 battle casualties, including 2,037 killed in action or died of wounds, while the Americans' casualties totalled 2,848, of whom 787 were killed in action or died of wounds. These figures are for the ground forces alone, and do not include the very heavy toll from malaria and other infectious disease.

NOTES AND REFERENCES

1. See map on pages 282-283.
2. On its disabilities see Raymond Paull, *Retreat from Kokoda*, 12-3, 22-3.
3. George C. Kenney, *General Kenney Reports: A Personal History of the Pacific War*, passim, particularly 29-30, 33, 35-6, 39, 42-3.
4. Quoted by Raymond Paull, 34-5.
5. Raymond Paull, 35.

6. W. B. Russell, *The 2/14th Battalion*, 124-5.
7. Malcolm Uren, *A Thousand Men at War: The Story of the 2/16th Battalion, A.I.F.*, 124.
8. Allan Dawes, *Soldier Superb*, 9.
9. Russell, 150.
10. George C. Kenney, 154, 157.
11. Robert L. Eichelberger, *Jungle Road to Tokyo*, 42.
12. Ibid., 47-8.

FURTHER READING:

Of the official histories, both Dudley McCarthy's *South-West Pacific Area — First Year, Kokoda to Wau* (Canberra, 1959) and Samuel Milner's *Victory in Papua* (Washington, 1957) give very full accounts of the New Guinea campaign, and they should be supplemented by the official United States and Australian histories of the air war. Several unit histories, such as W. B. Russell's *The 2/14th Battalion* (Sydney, 1948) and Malcolm Uren's *A Thousand Men at War: The Story of the 2/16th Battalion, A.I.F.* (London, 1959), throw much light on the campaign and are especially useful in giving a closer view of the men who fought over the Kokoda Track. Raymond Paull's *Retreat from Kokoda* (London, 1958), Lieutenant-General Robert L. Eichelberger's *Jungle Road to Tokyo* (London, 1951) and George C. Kenney's *General Kenney Reports* (New York, 1949) present individual points of view.

eight

GUADALCANAL:
FIRST ALLIED OFFENSIVE

The Allies launched their first offensive in the Pacific on the morning of August 7 1942 exactly eight months after Pearl Harbour.

Major-General Alexander A. Vandegrift's reinforced 1st United States Marine Division, whose first echelon reached New Zealand on June 14 and its second on July 11, had left the United States not expecting to go into action before 1943, but as its elements arrived at their destination their ships were quickly unloaded and then reloaded, this time ready for immediate combat. On July 1 the reinforced 1st Marines of the 2nd Division sailed from California in five combat-loaded ships under escort of carrier *Wasp* (14,700, 1939), recalled from the Mediterranean. The entire force — a total of 82 ships — rendezvoused at a point in mid-ocean some 400 miles south of the Fijis on July 26. The landings were rehearsed, under conditions which were scarcely realistic, at Koro Island, in the Fiji group, before the force sailed for Guadalcanal on the 31st.

Operation 'Watchtower' was hurriedly planned and hurriedly executed, and because it was carried out with such meagre resources, the troops dubbed it 'Operation Shoestring'. Admiral Ghormley conferred with MacArthur in Australia on July 7, and next day they jointly recommended postponement of the operation until both the South Pacific and the South-West Pacific areas could be substantially strengthened. That, of course, would have been the prudent course, but in war victory goes more often to the bold than to the cautious, and on the 10th the Joint Chiefs of Staff rejected the appeal and ordered the attack to proceed.

Little data about the Solomons was available. As with New Guinea, there were neither adequate maps nor modern charts, and the planners relied mainly upon topographical information collected from Australians and New Zealanders who had resided in the Solomons over the years. Some was good, some bad, and all inadequate for effective military planning, so the expedition took along a number of its informants as guides.

Thinly populated and undeveloped, with a humid, exhausting climate and a rainfall which was tropically heavy even during the so-called dry season from April to October, Guadalcanal was 90 miles long and averaged about 25 miles in width. Its mountainous backbone, running the length of the island, was heavily forested, and the narrow coastal belt, which in the central section of its northern coast, between Aola Bay and the Matanikau River, broadened into a flat, grassy plain, and was split by deep, swift rivers and creeks, many of which became stagnant pools at their mouths because of sand bars and silting. Coconut plantations and patches of high kunai grass were interspersed along the beach fronts, while inland there was the thick jungle. Seen from the air the island stood out brilliantly green from the surrounding limpid blue waters, and approached from the sea the warm air was fragrant with the smell of tropical flowers. But Guadalcanal was no island paradise. It was unhealthy, a fertile breeding ground for tropical diseases.

Sealark Channel, narrow and reef-strewn, its southern arm known as Lengo Channel, separates Guadalcanal from the Nggela group of islands to the north — Florida, Olevuga and

Buena Vista, with Tulagi, which has a fine harbour, and the twin islands of Tanambogo and Gavutu, linked by a 300-yard causeway, lying with other small islets close to the southern shore of Florida Island. Indispensable Strait, named for an almost forgotten British frigate, lies athwart the southern exit of Sealark Channel, between south-eastern Guadalcanal and the island of Malaita. At the northern end rises the hump of symmetrically round Savo Island, rather closer to Guadalcanal than to Florida. In the desperate weeks following the Allied landings, because of the number of ships to find a last resting-place on its bottom, Savo Sound came to be known as Iron-bottom Sound. The island-strewn waters to the north-west, lapping the shores of Choiseul and Santa Isabel on the one side and of Vella Lavella, Kolombangara and New Georgia on the other, were called The Slot.

Admiral Fletcher, fresh from the battles of the Coral Sea and of Midway, was in overall command of the expeditionary force, with Rear-Admiral Leigh Noyes as his Air Support Group Commander. The United States carrier force comprised *Saratoga* (in which Fletcher flew his flag), *Wasp* and *Enterprise,* the new battleship *North Carolina,* five heavy and one light cruisers, sixteen destroyers and three oilers. The Amphibious Force was commanded by Rear-Admiral Richmond Kelly Turner, described by Morison as a man 'whose grizzled head, beetling black brows, tireless energy and ferocious language were to become almost legendary in the Pacific.'[1] Eight cruisers, three of them Australian, and nine destroyers under Rear-Admiral V. A. C. Crutchley, R.N., escorted the transports. The expedition had between 470 and 480 landing-craft, the majority without ramps, and an early type of amphibian tractor, un-armoured and mounting two machine-guns, which was making its first appearance in combat. All land-based aircraft in the South Pacific came under the command of Rear-Admiral John S. McCain.

Ghormley, whose directive gave him no control over the task force commanders except in circumstances of emergency, estimated originally that some 3,100 Japanese were in the Guadalcanal-Tulagi area. This figure was about the actual

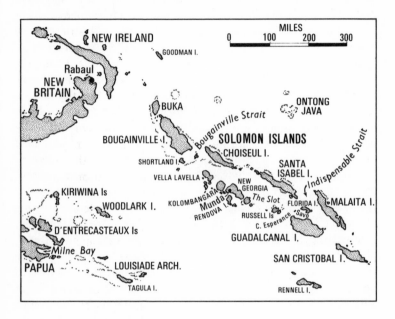

10. The Allied campaign in the Solomon Islands

number there when the marines landed. Other commanders over-estimated Japanese strength. Turner put the number at more than 7,000 — 1,850 on Tulagi and rather more than 5,200 on Guadalcanal — and Vandegrift's first estimate, arrived at after consultation with MacArthur's Headquarters, was 8,400.

The Expeditionary Force, moving under an overcast and shrouded by frequent rain squalls, was not detected by the enemy as it approached Guadalcanal from the west. It sighted Savo Island at 0200 on August 7. Forty minutes later the transports split into two groups, the smaller passing north of

Savo and heading for Tulagi, the larger entering Savo Sound between Savo Island and Cape Esperance and steering for its disembarkation area off shore, about midway between Lunga and Koli Points. When the fire support groups began bombarding Guadalcanal and Tulagi within a few minutes of one another, around 0615, the Japanese were taken by surprise.

Bombing and strafing attacks by the aircraft from the carriers, which lay in open water 75 miles south of Guadalcanal, followed the naval bombardments. The Tulagi landing met no resistance on the beaches, and the north-western half of the two-mile-long island was quickly secured. In the afternoon, however, the marines ran into strong opposition from Japanese holed up in caves, dugouts and tunnels on high ground close to the island's north-eastern tip. The naval shells and aerial bombs, as was so often to happen in the future, had done little harm to the enemy or his defences at this spot. The Japanese, refusing to surrender, fought stoutly to the death. They repeatedly charged the American perimeter during the night and on each occasion were repulsed. Not until 1500 on the 8th was resistance on Tulagi finally crushed, with the loss to the marines of 36 killed and 44 wounded. Except for three Japanese who surrendered and about 40 who escaped to Florida by swimming, the enemy garrison was wiped out, about 200 being killed.

On Gavutu the Japanese took toll of the invaders as they approached the beaches and continued fighting from caves, dugouts and slit trenches on the island's single hill until the afternoon of the 8th. The first assault on Tanambogo failed when the naval bombardment started a fire that silhouetted the attackers just as they came in to land in the early evening. A second attack on the 8th, spearheaded by two light tanks, eliminated all resistance by nightfall. On these two islands the marines' casualties were 108 dead or missing and 140 wounded, but they killed about 500 Japanese. The adjacent islands of Mbangai, Makambo and Kokomtambu were occupied without opposition.

On Guadalcanal's northern shore the landing on Red Beach, between the Tenaru and Tenavatu Rivers, about three miles east of Lunga Point, began an hour after the landing on Tulagi

and was unopposed. The beach-head was secured to a depth
of 600 yards and the troops began to move inland. The objective for the first day's attack was Mount Austen, a dominating
series of ridges 1,514 feet high, but in the absence of reliable
maps the planners had obtained their topographical details from
former residents and when the marines got ashore it was found
that Mount Austen, lying six miles south-west of Lunga Point,
was further inland than had been supposed and was separated
from the shore by trackless jungle. Obviously it could not be
quickly seized. The direction of the attack was therefore
changed, and the objectives for the 8th became the partly constructed airfield east of the Lunga River and, west of the river,
Kukum village, the main Japanese encampment. Both were
seized before nightfall against light and sporadic resistance.
The Japanese at the airfield, most of whom were construction
workers, retreated without attempting to destroy the installations.

Although the landings took the enemy by surprise, his
immediate reaction was prompt. His bombers and fighters came
over twice on the 7th, but adequate warning of their approach
came from coast-watchers at their posts along the Solomons,
and all ships were under way, with carrier-borne fighters over-
head, when the raiders arrived. Dive-bombers scored a hit on
the destroyer *Mugford* (1,500, 1938), killing 22 men, but
otherwise the warships and transports escaped damage. Air
losses were almost even, the Americans claiming 14 bombers
and 2 fighters for the loss of 11 fighters and a dive-bomber.
On the 8th there came another air raid, warning of which was
given by a coast-watcher on Bougainville. One enemy aircraft
crashed on the transport *George F. Elliot,* which was set on
fire and became a total loss. The destroyer *Jarvis* (1,500, 1937)
was badly damaged. She later sailed, unescorted, for Noumea
and Sydney, but disappeared, being sunk *en route* by enemy
aircraft with the loss of all her crew. The Americans claimed
17 enemy planes shot down in the attacks on the 8th, while
they lost a further 10 of their carrier-borne aircraft.

At Rabaul Vice-Admiral Mikawa, the aggressive-minded
commander of the Eighth Fleet, hastily embarked troops in

six transports in an attempt to reinforce the Guadalcanal garrison. But when one transport was sunk by American submarine *S-38* (850, 1923), with the loss of 342 men, 14 miles west of Cape St George at midnight on the 8th, the other five were recalled to Rabaul.

However, Mikawa, hoisting his flag in the heavy cruiser *Chokai* (9,850, 1932), led six other cruisers and his only available destroyer towards Guadalcanal. As it left St George Channel about 2000 on the 7th, this squadron was sighted and reported by *S-38* and next morning was picked up by an Australian Hudson about 30 miles north-east of Kieta at 1026. The Hudson pilot identified Mikawa's ships as three cruisers, three destroyers and two seaplane tenders or gunboats. Because of radio failure, he was unable to report until he returned to Milne Bay at 1242. The American statement that the pilot did not return to base until late afternoon and then had a meal before making his report[2] is untrue. For some reason the report was delayed and did not reach Turner and Crutchley until after 1800, and the mistaken identification of two of the vessels as seaplane tenders caused the Allied commanders, and also MacArthur's Headquarters, to conclude that the Japanese intended mooring the tenders at Rekata Bay, on the north-western coast of Santa Isabel Island, or at Shortland Island, preparatory to launching air attacks next morning. Neither Turner nor Crutchley, in view of the pilot's report, expected a surface attack down The Slot, and through basing their plans on what they considered the enemy's probable intention, rather than the various courses open to him, they allowed themselves to be surprised.

Having lost *Lexington* in the Coral Sea battle and *Yorktown* at Midway, Fletcher had a healthy respect for the enemy's torpedo-bombers and was determined not to expose his carriers to their attacks for longer than was absolutely necessary. At the rehearsal conference in the Fiji group he had announced that the carriers would remain on station for no longer than two days. Turner, knowing that the transports could not be unloaded in under four days and that without air cover they would be unable to remain off Guadalcanal, had protested vehemently but unsuccessfully.

Late on the afternoon of the 8th Fletcher decided to implement his previously announced decision. Despite his earlier warning Turner and Vandegrift were appalled at Fletcher's caution. There was no indication that Japanese pilots had discovered the position of the American carrier force, which still had ample fuel and, despite its loss of 21 fighters, had one more Wildcat than the three United States carriers had aboard at the beginning of the battle of Midway. But Fletcher was adamant and that evening he retired.

By August 9 Turner had landed 10,900 troops on Guadalcanal and 6,075 on Tulagi, with only about 1,000 men remaining to be taken ashore from the transports. The landing of supplies, however, had broken down.

The air raids on the 7th interrupted unloading for about three hours, and because so many of the landing-craft lacked movable bow ramps the actual work of unloading proved more time-consuming than had been anticipated. Yet, although the work was behind schedule, conditions on the beach were chaotic. It was cluttered with unsorted supplies, and at 2330 that night unloading was suspended until 1000 next morning. The beach simply could not be cleared quickly enough, the planners having underestimated the number of men required to keep the supplies moving steadily inland. On the evening of the 8th, when Fletcher announced his withdrawal, less than half the food and only four days' supply of ammunition out of 10 had been landed. In addition, much essential equipment, including earthmoving machinery for the construction of the airfield, was still afloat. It was clear that if the transports now had to retire the marines might find themselves in a dangerous plight.

As night fell on the 8th, Crutchley's cruisers and destroyers took up their positions. With Turner's approval, he had divided his force into three — the Southern, consisting of the cruisers *Australia, Canberra* and *Chicago* and the destroyers *Patterson* (1,500, 1938) and *Bagley* (1,500, 1938), to block the entrance into the Sound between Savo Island and Cape Esperance; the Northern, comprising the heavy cruisers *Vincennes* (9,400,

1936), *Astoria* (9,950, 1933) and *Quincy* (9,375, 1935), attended by the destroyers *Helm* (1,500, 1938) and *Wilson* (1,500, 1939), to watch the entrance between Savo and Florida, and the Eastern, formed by the light cruisers *San Juan* (6,000, 1942) and *Hobart,* with the destroyers *Monssen* (1,630, 1940) and *Buchanan* (2,100, 1942), to guard the Indispensable Strait end of Sealark Channel, where submarines rather than surface forces represented the most likely danger. The destroyers *Blue* (1,500, 1937) and *Ralph Talbot* (1,500, 1938) patrolled a line west of Savo to give early warning of the approach of any surface forces, but their radar was an early type and there was a gap of no less than 20 miles between them when they were at the opposite ends of their patrol line.

Turner asked McCain for an additional reconnaissance over The Slot because he feared the South Pacific and South-West Pacific Air Forces, who divided responsibility for reconnaissance, might fail to cover the entire area. At it happened, bad weather prevented this search mission being carried out, but it was very late when this became known to Turner. Even had he known earlier it is unlikely it would have induced him to take any action.

At 2032 on the 8th, Turner, concerned with Fletcher's premature withdrawal, urgently summoned Crutchley and Vandegrift to a conference aboard his flagship, lying off Red Beach. The peremptory nature of Turner's order caused Crutchley to haul *Australia* out of line and head for the beach area, as there did not seem sufficient time to make the trip in a small boat. He ordered Captain Howard D. Bode (*Chicago*) to take command of the Southern Force, but expecting Crutchley back before midnight Bode kept *Chicago* at the stern of the line and did not, as officer in tactical command, take station ahead of *Canberra*. Whether it would have made any difference to the night's events if he had taken his proper station is doubtful. Turner's summons was as fateful as it was unnecessary. He had no need of Crutchley's advice as to his proper course now that Fletcher was leaving, and by calling him to the conference he deprived the Southern Force of one of its cruisers and the whole force of its leader.

As Mikawa approached Guadalcanal at about 25 knots the float-planes of his cruisers reconnoitred Savo Sound and reported on the number and disposition of the Allied surface forces. On the evening of the 8th, he again catapulted these planes, this time with orders to drop flares to illuminate his unsuspecting victims. At 0054 *Chokai,* leading the Japanese ships in line ahead, sighted *Blue* on the starboard bow, stern on. Mikawa reduced speed to 12 knots, so that the phosphorescent wakes of his ships would not show up so prominently, but *Blue's* lookouts presumably were all staring ahead and the Japanese ships passed astern undetected.

Less than an hour later, at 0136, with Savo to port, the Japanese sighted *Canberra* and *Chicago,* and Mikawa ordered his captains to fire torpedoes independently. Seven minutes later, when their torpedoes were already speeding on their way, Mikawa's ships were seen by *Patterson,* which promptly broadcast the radio alarm: 'Warning! Warning! Strange ships entering harbour!' Almost simultaneously the Japanese float-planes dropped brilliant flares and *Chokai, Aoba* (7,100, 1927) and *Furutaka* (7,100, 1926) opened fire at *Canberra* with their main and secondary batteries at ranges varying from 4,500 to 9,000 yards. Because of static, *Patterson's* warning was not heard by all the American vessels, most of which had seen or picked up on radar the enemy planes and, in the absence of a general alarm, had concluded they must be friendly. After an exhausting day all the cruiser captains, with the exception of Captain F. E. Getting, R.A.N., who was still on the bridge of *Canberra,* were sleeping in their emergency cabins and, rushing on deck when suddenly awakened, were confused, with their subordinates unable to give them any clear picture of events. The majority at first concluded either Japanese submarines or aircraft had made a sudden appearance.

There was no confusion among the Japanese. Their crews, well trained in night fighting, went about their work methodically and coolly, and their tactics were superb and their gunnery accurate. Searchlights illuminated the Allied vessels and held them in their beams until the first shells and torpedoes tore home, causing fires which dispensed with the need for further illumination. The Japanese salvoes hit almost at once. *Canberra,* whose captain was mortally wounded at the outset of the battle, was struck by twenty-four shells within about a minute. She was able to fire only two torpedoes and a few shells from her 4-inch secondary armament, and, stopped in the water and listing ten degrees to starboard, she was blazing almost from stem to stern. *Chicago* was more fortunate, but a torpedo blew off part of her bow. In six minutes the action against the Southern Force was over, but neither Bode nor anybody else thought to warn the Northern Force or to tell Turner or Crutchley what was happening.

Mikawa turned to pass north of Savo Island, but his ships executed the movement raggedly, so that they were split into two groups — an eastern composed of *Chokai, Aoba, Kako* (7,100, 1926) and *Kinugasa* (7,100, 1927), and a western formed by *Yubari* (2,890, 1923), *Tenryu* (3,230, 1919) and *Furutaka.* This accident enabled Mikawa to take the Northern Force between two lines of fire, one of his columns passing ahead and the other behind the American ships.

The action east and north of Savo opened at 0148, when *Chokai* fired four torpedoes. Of the American cruisers, *Quincy,* although she suffered severely from the crossfire, returned the heaviest fire of any Allied ship that night. But the Japanese left her a blazing wreck and at 0235 she capsized and sank. *Astoria,* hit by shell after shell at a range of between 5,000 and 6,000 yards, was soon burning fiercely. *Vincennes,* last to be attacked, was so heavily hit that she capsized and sank at 0250, only a quarter of an hour after *Quincy.* In all cases, the first enemy shells struck amidships, where fabric-covered float-planes, aviation fuel, and oil were concentrated, virtually unprotected, on the well decks of the cruisers. This inflammable material was quickly set alight, so that the leaping flames silhouetted each ship for the enemy.

At 0220 Mikawa gave the order for withdrawal. He briefly debated whether to strike at the transports, but rejected the idea because his force was in disarray and would take time to reform, so that, with dawn near, he would be within easy reach of air attack. His prudent decision undoubtedly was correct, since he did not know of Fletcher's retirement, but had he acted more boldly he would probably have destroyed most, if not all, the transports off Guadalcanal and Tulagi and at the very outset might have won the battle for the island.

A valiant attempt was made to save *Canberra,* but she had to be sunk by a friendly torpedo at about 0800, while *Astoria,* after a magazine explosion, sank at 1215. Several of the destroyers had suffered damage and casualties, but none was sunk. The Allies lost 1,023 officers and men killed or died of wounds and 709 wounded, of whom 84 killed and 55 wounded were from *Canberra,* including one American ensign. The heaviest casualties were in the Northern Force cruisers, which might have been so easily warned by the Southern Force, *Quincy* having 370 killed, *Vincennes* 332 and *Astoria* 215. The Japanese casualties totalled 58 men killed and 53 wounded. Only a few shells struck their ships, which suffered no serious damage. However, as four of the Japanese ships were returning to Kavieng, in New Ireland, on the 10th the small, elderly American submarine *S-44* (850, 1923) torpedoed the cruiser *Kako,* which sank within five minutes.

The Battle of Savo Island was the worst defeat ever suffered by a predominantly American force in a surface action. In the anger of the moment the surviving cruiser captains were transferred to less onerous and less responsible posts and Fletcher was dropped as a carrier task force commander. However, following an inquiry by Admiral Arthur J. Hepburn, a former Commander in Chief of the United States Navy, it was decided that blame was so evenly distributed that action against any individual officer was unjustified. King expressly exonerated Turner and Crutchley, but it would seem that each contributed to the disaster.[3]

Preoccupied with the battle for New Guinea and thrown off balance by the unexpectedness of the Allied offensive in the Solomons, the Japanese Army reacted to the Guadalcanal landing more slowly and less aggressively than the Japanese Navy. Its intelligence underestimated American strength, which was thought at first not to greatly exceed 1,000. When the XVII Army at Rabaul assumed control of operations, General

Hyakutake dribbled in reinforcements, partly because of New Guinea commitments, partly because sufficient troops were not immediately available and partly because of a shortage of transports, but primarily because he concluded the Americans were not in any great strength and would be easily defeated. This miscalculation, leading to a policy of too little too late, was to cost the Japanese dearly.

The battle for Guadalcanal was a struggle for possession of the airfield, around which the marines established a defensive perimeter 10,000 yards from east to west and less than 5,000 yards from north to south. Construction of this field, which lay in the Lunga area and which the Americans named Henderson for a Marine Corps hero of the Battle of Midway, had been begun by the Japanese in July. The Americans improved and lengthened it, and on August 20, less than a fortnight after the landing, the 1st Marine Corps squadrons flew in, to be quickly joined by Navy and Army aircraft. Henderson Field from then on was under constant air attack by day and frequent naval bombardment by night, and its pilots were called upon continuously to meet enemy bombing raids, to attack Japanese ships, to defend Allied convoys and to support the ground forces. In these circumstances, and hampered by lack of spare parts and inadequate maintenance facilities, the attrition rate among aircraft was high. Only with great difficulty were sufficient fighters and bombers kept operational. Allied supply resources were taxed to the full, since all aviation material and equipment, including fuel in drums, had to be landed across the beaches. A similar supply problem existed at Espiritu Santo, in the New Hebrides, where an airfield was hacked out of coconut grove and jungle to ensure heavy bomber support for the Guadalcanal operation and where the first Flying Fortress landed on July 20.

Guadalcanal, consequently, was primarily a battle of supply, with each side seeking to build up its own strength while preventing the other from bringing in men and supplies. Once aircraft began operating from Henderson Field the paradoxical position arose that while the Allies exercised control over the waters of Savo Sound during daylight hours control passed at

Above, the grisly aftermath of
a beach assault by American
marines. Right, marines wade
ashore in comparative safety
after the first assault troops
have destroyed Japanese
defences

Australian soldiers watch as a tank attacks Japanese pillboxes at Buna before troops move in on them

night to the Japanese Navy. American reinforcements came in during the day, Japanese at night. The enemy's destroyer-transports ran down The Slot and entered the Sound with such regularity that the Americans aptly dubbed them the 'Tokyo Express'. They landed their cargoes both east and west of the perimeter and before withdrawing generally shelled Henderson Field. Their deliveries were supplemented by landing-barges and small boats, which crept down the coast at night and holed up in rivers and creeks by day.

Both sides suffered losses in their attempts at reinforcement. The destroyer *Blue,* her stern sliced off by a torpedo from the destroyer *Kawakaze* (1,368, 1937), was scuttled off Tulagi on August 23; fast transport *Colhoun* (1,060, 1918) was sunk in the same area by air attack seven days later with the loss of 51 men, and in the early hours of September 5 Japanese destroyers sent the small American destroyer-transports *Little* (1,060, 1918) and *Gregory* (1,060, 1917), which had been ferrying troops and supplies from. Tulagi to Guadalcanal, to join the other ships at the bottom of Savo Sound. On August 24, in the carrier battle of the Eastern Solomons, *Ryujo* was sunk by an attack group from *Saratoga* and the seaplane carrier *Chitose* (9,000, 1938) damaged, the Americans having *Enterprise* damaged and 74 men aboard her killed. On the morning of August 25 land-based aircraft damaged the cruiser *Jintsu* (5,195, 1925) and set fire to the armed merchantman *Kinryu Maru* (9,309g, 1938), and Flying Fortresses from Espiritu Santo, scoring one of their rare successes at sea, sank the destroyer *Mutsuki* (1,315, 1926) and damaged another destroyer. These successes were followed later by the sinking of the destroyer *Asagiri* (1,700, 1930) and the damaging of two other destroyers by Henderson-based aircraft, which were successful in preventing a Japanese landing east of the perimeter.

However, both the Americans and the Japanese brought in men and supplies. On August 18 Colonel Kiyono Ichiki landed with about 1,000 men at Taivu Point, east of the perimeter. Convinced of Japanese invincibility and perhaps misled by his superiors' estimate of American strength, Ichiki did not wait for his second echelon to arrive, but on the night of August

20-21 rashly attacked across the Ilu River. He suffered such a bloody repulse, losing nearly 800 men killed in less than 24 hours, that he committed *hara-kiri*.

Undeterred by this premature and suicidal assault, the Japanese redoubled their reinforcement efforts, and between August 29 and September 11 the 'Tokyo Express' landed 6,000 men east of the perimeter. This force included Ichiki's second echelon and was commanded by the veteran, Major-General Kiyotake Kawaguchi, who refused to be tempted into an engagement when the marines raided Tasimboko, near Taivu Point, in an effort to dislocate the coming attack.

After nightfall on September 13 Kawaguchi's men determinedly, if unskilfully, attacked the perimeter, advancing from the south against the low ridge, which their blood that night was to baptize Bloody Ridge, along which the American line lay. They forced the marines back to the last knoll in front of Henderson Field, and during the night launched assault after assault in the face of sustained artillery, mortar, machine-gun and rifle fire, but the marines held firm and the Japanese ranks were shattered. When dawn broke, Kawaguchi's exhausted troops turned and fled, harried by aircraft from Henderson Field. There seems little doubt that had he possessed artillery support Kawaguchi would have broken through to the airfield, although, perhaps, not in sufficient strength to withstand American counter-attacks or to gain the time needed for him to be reinforced. Of the 2,000 men who attacked Bloody Ridge about 1,100 were killed or wounded, the Japanese admitting the loss of 633 killed in action and 505 wounded. The American loss was under 150 — 31 killed, 9 missing and 103 wounded.

This second failure compelled Japanese Imperial Headquarters to belatedly recognize that it could not maintain two offensives successfully, and it therefore decided to concentrate upon the recapture of Guadalcanal while standing on the defensive in Papua. The Americans' tails were up, if only temporarily. By September 18 their supply position had so improved that combat troops, who had been on two meals daily since the withdrawal of the transports on August 9, were restored to full rations. Vandegrift decided to follow up his victory by striking across the Matanikau River at the village of Kokumbona, west of the perimeter, to which Kawaguchi's surviving troops had withdrawn in a difficult, week-long march round the southern slopes of Mount Austen. This raid, however, was hastily planned and poorly executed, and the marines, one of whose battalions was surrounded and only cut its way out under cover of a barrage from a destroyer, were fortunate to extricate themselves with the loss of but 60 killed and 100 wounded.

A second and more ambitious operation in the same area between October 7 and 9 was more successful. It trapped a considerable enemy force, on whom heavy casualties were inflicted, but failed in its objective of establishing a line west of the perimeter which would place Henderson Field beyond the range of newly landed Japanese artillery.

Meanwhile, Japanese submarines were active and successful. In a single afternoon, two submarines, *I-19* (1,950, 1941) and *I-15* (1,950, 1940), slammed three torpedoes into *Wasp*, which had to be sunk when fires aboard her could not be brought under control, put *Saratoga* out of action for three months, sent *North Carolina* limping to Pearl Harbour with a 32-foot underwater gash in her hull, and so damaged a destroyer, *O'Brien* (1,570, 1939), that, despite patching at Espiritu Santo and Noumea, she broke in half and sank off Samoa when bound for a West Coast shipyard.

At the beginning of October, as the marines ashore were being hard hit by malaria, there came clear indications that events were mounting to a crisis and that at last the Japanese were developing an all-out offensive to recapture Guadalcanal. Deciphered enemy messages were corroborated by reports from coast-watchers and reconnaissance aircraft, which observed shipping concentrations in the Shortland Islands and increased air activity at Rabaul and other airfields as additional aircraft were brought into the area. The 'Tokyo Express', running more regularly than ever despite interference from aircraft based on Henderson Field, was landing as many as 900 men a night, and Japanese strength on Guadalcanal, which at the time of

228 THE WAR WITH JAPAN

Kawaguchi's assault on Bloody Ridge had been little more than half that of the Americans, was increasing rapidly.

Ghormley acted quickly and aggressively to the new threat, but prompt and vigorous as was his reaction it was not sufficient to save him his command. He risked the carrier *Hornet* in a strike against the shipping in the Shortlands, but two attacks in poor weather on October 5 failed to score and merely caused the Japanese to disperse their ships. He also sent Rear-Admiral Norman Scott, with four cruisers and five destroyers, to derail the 'Tokyo Express', but this force blundered into a Japanese bombardment group of three heavy cruisers — *Aoba, Kinugasa* and *Furutaka* — and two destroyers which had come down The Slot under cover of a heavy air raid launched against Henderson Field on the afternoon of October 11. Scott, who for three weeks had given his force rigorous training in night action, was off Cape Esperance, covering the passage between Savo Island and the Cape, at 2330. As the Americans were reversing course from north-east to south-west by the somewhat complicated manœuvre known as column movement the light cruiser, *Helena,* equipped with the latest radar, reported enemy ships nearly 16 miles to the north-east, headed for the Sound. Thus, by sheer luck, aided by the inexcusable laxity of the Japanese commanders, who in their over-confidence were not keeping a proper look-out, Scott achieved the classic manœuvre of crossing the T. Due to ambiguities in the American signal book, his gunners opened fire before he intended them to, but they began hitting their targets at once.

In the Battle of Cape Esperance the Americans, who at the time elatedly claimed four cruisers and four destroyers sunk, sent the cruiser *Furutaka* and the destroyer *Fubuki* (1,700, 1928) to the bottom and so heavily damaged *Aoba* that she had to go to Japan for repairs. Admiral Goto, the Japanese commander, was mortally wounded early in the action, and was succeeded in command by Captain K. Kijima, who was relieved by Mikawa on his return to port. The American heavy cruisers escaped lightly, but the light cruiser *Boise* was heavily damaged and had to be sent to Philadelphia for repair, and Scott's van destroyers, caught between the opposing cruisers, were battered by both sides. *Duncan* (1,700, 1942), heavily hit and gutted by fire, sank six miles north of Savo Island, and *Farenholt,* holed by two American shells, was saved only by her crew listing her nine degrees to starboard so as to bring the holes above sea level. Although favoured by luck, Scott deserved victory because he had issued clear pre-battle orders and maintained control over his ships once the action began.

Air attacks early on the 12th failed to inflict further damage on the retreating Japanese ships, but during the day Henderson Field pilots accounted for the destroyers *Murakumo* (1,700, 1929) and *Natsugumo* (1,500, 1938), belonging to the 'Tokyo Express'. With other vessels, they had landed men, stores and heavy artillery near Kokumbona, and on their way out of the Sound had fished from the water Japanese survivors from *Furutaka* and *Fubuki*. This delay enabled Henderson Field dive-bombers to attack them before they got out of range.

On the 13th an American convoy discharged without loss 3,000 men and supplies of the United States Americal Division, which had been garrisoning New Caledonia. However, the Battle of Cape Esperance had neither destroyed the enemy's determination nor suppressed his aggressiveness. Twice that day his aircraft heavily and accurately bombed Henderson Field, which was also for the first time brought under fire by Japanese heavy artillery, and that night two Japanese battleships deluged the airfield with 14-inch shells in a 90-minute bombardment. Next day two further heavy air raids added to the chaos and destruction, so that by nightfall less than half Henderson's aircraft were operational and little aviation fuel remained. No respite was given the Americans during the night of the 14th-15th. While the 'Tokyo Express' was bringing in some 4,500 troops, Japanese 8-inch cruisers bombarded Henderson Field. The Japanese were so certain they had put the airfield out of action that their ships continued unloading next day off Tassafaronga Point.

Henderson, however, still had a sting left. Its airmen, like the marines, were exhausted from lack of sleep, from the daily air raids and the nightly bombardments, and many suffered from malnutrition and malaria, but they could still fly, even if their operational aircraft were few. Using their last few gallons of fuel, they strafed and bombed the transports, despite the latter's guard of destroyers and fighters. Flying Fortresses from Espiritu Santo lent weight but not always accuracy to the attack, which was maintained by marine and army transport planes flying in aviation fuel throughout the day. These magnificent but desperate efforts enabled the Japanese convoy to be kept under almost continuous air attack. Three large transports were forced to beach, each becoming a total loss, the troops suffered casualties as they landed, and the enemy air force was further whittled down. The Allied attack was so heavy and pressed with such determination that at 1600 the remaining enemy ships withdrew. That night there was another intensive bombardment by enemy 8-inch cruisers.

The mounting Japanese assault, presaging another bitter land battle, depressed American morale. Life for the marines, hourly expecting attack, was almost unbearable. The humid climate, draining all energy, did nothing to restore nerves near breaking-point. 'This is the hottest place we have hit so far,' wrote James J. Fahey, a seaman, of Tulagi Harbour,[4] 'you could fry eggs on the steel deck, there is no air in here, you never stop sweating. It is impossible to sleep below in the compartments as the heat is suffocating.' Life was ghastly for all, and there wasn't much to choose between life aboard ship and life in the jungle ashore.

In Pearl Harbour and Washington, where the horrors of Guadalcanal were remote, it seemed that Guadalcanal was about to be lost. On October 15 Nimitz decided that 'the critical situation requires a more aggressive commander,' and three days later Halsey, who was about to again take command of a carrier group, after recovering from dermatitis, suddenly found himself elevated to Commander in Chief of the South Pacific. With meagre resources and restricted command powers, performing everything at speed, Ghormley had done as good a job as possible and hardly deserved to be relieved of command. Yet his supersession was justified. At this juncture the South Pacific needed as its commander a forceful personality possessed of the gift of inspiring the officers and men of all three services.

There were differences regarding tactics between Turner and Vandegrift, the former advocating a more aggressive defence by offensive measures, the latter insisting on concentration upon the defence of the perimeter,[5] and Ghormley had been unable to reconcile their views. 'Bull' Halsey was the dynamic type of commander the situation required. At the same time, at the insistence of Roosevelt, steps were taken to increase the strength of Halsey's new command in ships, aircraft and men. Against similar measures in the European and Mediterranean theatres these efforts may appear small, but to the 'shoestring' Pacific a task group around a new battleship, *Indiana* (35,000, 1942), a rejuvenated and repaired carrier, *Enterprise,* another 24 large submarines, an additional 50 Army fighters, some 24 extra Flying Fortresses and the 25th United States Division, released from garrison duties in Hawaii, were far from contemptible reinforcements.

The Japanese air raids and naval bombardments were a prelude to attack. The reinforcement programme by mid-October had brought Japanese strength on the island to approximately 1,000 men fewer than the Americans — 22,000 against 23,000 in round figures.[6] Hyakutake was so confident of recapturing Henderson Field that Yamamoto sent a powerful force of carriers, battleships and cruisers under Vice-Admiral Nobutake Kondo to hover north of Guadalcanal, ready to annihilate American naval forces and convoys and to fly in aircraft once the Rising Sun fluttered over the airfield. However, the cumbersome Japanese plan, calling for a wide enveloping movement against Vandegrift's left, east of Bloody Ridge, and careful co-ordination of this main assault with subsidiary thrusts against his right on the Matanikau River from both west and south, defeated itself. It had been drafted by Hyakutake's own staff, whose lack of knowledge of the terrain caused them to set the troops an impossible task.

Lieutenant-General Masao Maruyama's enveloping force was divided into two wings, the right under Kawaguchi, whose protests against the plan so angered his superiors that he was replaced by Colonel Toshinari Shoji before battle was joined, and the left under Major-General Yumio Nasu. The force numbered about 5,600 infantrymen and several hundred artillerymen and engineers. Cutting a narrow, one-man track with axe, machete and saw as they advanced, the enemy made a slow, gruelling march of 15 miles through the jungle south of Mount Austen. Every infantryman, in addition to his normal combat equipment, carried a shell, and the mountain guns, mortars and machine-guns had to be manhandled along the swampy track and hauled by ropes up the cliffs. Since all supplies had to be carried by hand, the force was placed from the outset on half rations. It wriggled slowly forward, deluged by tropical rain, in a long single file strung out for miles. Gradually guns and mortars were abandoned, so that when the force at last attacked it was supported by machine-guns only.

Maruyama's advance was so slow that on three successive days the attack was postponed 24 hours, which, along with the difficulties of communication, made control and co-ordination of the separate attacks impossible. The attackers, although screened by the jungle, were detected in their approach, enabling the Americans to reinforce the threatened points. When the Japanese finally attacked at 0030 on October 25, Shoji's eastern wing lost its way in the blackness of the rainy night and took no part in the action. The infantrymen of the left wing, with stubborn courage, attacked again and again, but were repulsed, and the repeated assaults on both wings next night also failed. Courage alone could not triumph over the prepared defences of the marines and soldiers, who enjoyed all the advantages of effective artillery and mortar support.

The piecemeal attacks against Vandegrift's right were no more successful, although Colonel Akinosuka Oka's men, attacking northward, broke through at one point, only to be thrown off the ridge they had captured by a hasty counter-attack by headquarters personnel, bandsmen, special weapons troops and a marine platoon.

Hyakutake's grandiose plan, impossible of execution in the terrain, had collapsed like a pack of cards. He had failed to fulfil his repeated assurances to Yamamoto that the airfield would be his in a matter of hours, and he had lost over 2,000 men killed against total American casualties of less than a tenth of that figure.

Meanwhile, the opposing naval forces, milling around in the waters north and east of Guadalcanal, had been playing games of blind man's buff and hide-and-seek without much result. Before dawn on the 26th, however, Halsey, back at Noumea, sent out the Nelsonian order, 'Attack, repeat attack', and a few hours later the rival search planes almost simultaneously located their opponent's carriers.

The Americans drew first blood in the carrier battle of the Santa Cruz Islands, their search planes ripping a 50-foot hole in the flight deck of *Zuiho* when her aircraft were aloft, but the Japanese were first to get their main strikes into the air. As they sped towards the other's carriers the rival air fleets passed one another and a dozen Zekes peeled off from their formation to knock down three fighters and three torpedo-bombers from *Enterprise*, losing three of their own planes.

As the Japanese attackers came in, *Enterprise* was hidden by a rain squall and the weight of the attack fell on *Hornet*. The American fighters, poorly positioned by fighter direction, were too low and too close in for effective interception, and the Japanese pilots, despite intense anti-aircraft fire, scored several bomb and two torpedo hits on the carrier, while two crippled planes crashed aboard in suicide dives, the bombs of one detonating as the aircraft burst through the flight deck. The 10-minute attack, which was over by 0920, left the carrier dead in the water and on fire.

Forty minutes later came the turn of *Enterprise,* but the Japanese dive-bombers and torpedo-bombers, having become separated during flight, failed to deliver a co-ordinated bomb and torpedo attack, and only two bombs hit home. Three torpedoes intended for *Enterprise* struck the cruiser *Portland* (9,800, 1933), but all three failed to explode — a rare circumstance with the usually deadly Japanese warheads. One torpedo-bomber, in a suicide dive, crashed the destroyer *Smith* (1,480, 1936), setting her ablaze forward, but the fires were extinguished and she remained operational. As the attack against *Enterprise* came in the Japanese submarine *I-21* (1,950,

1941) slammed a torpedo into the destroyer *Porter* (1,850, 1935), which became a raging inferno and had to be sunk. Another air strike soon after 1100 failed to hit *Enterprise,* but got bombs home on the battleship *South Dakota* and the anti-aircraft cruiser *San Juan.*

The American strikes were less successful in finding carrier targets. Several waves missed them and attacked battleships or cruisers, one of which, *Chikuma,* was severely damaged, although she limped home. However, *Hornet's* leading wave of 15 dive-bombers found *Shokaku* and the still smoking *Zuiho* at 0930, and shattered the former's flight deck and hangars. Although she made good her retreat, as also did *Zuiho,* *Shokaku* was out of the war for nine months.

In the afternoon small Japanese strikes, coming in separately, again found *Hornet.* The tow was hurriedly cast off and the carrier, now lying dead in the water, was an easy target even for a mere handful of planes. A torpedo and two bomb hits sealed her fate. She was abandoned, but although torpedoed and shelled by American destroyers, remained obstinately afloat until enemy destroyers sent her to the bottom with three torpedoes at 0135 on the 27th.

Both sides now retired, the Americans dodging torpedoes from submarines during their withdrawal. Tactical victory rested with the Japanese, but their mounting losses of aircraft and skilled pilots in the long run more than outweighed the American surface losses; for while the latter could be replaced Japan already was experiencing difficulty in making good the attrition of her aircraft and pilots.

With the collapse of Hyakutake's offensive, Vandegrift, determined to allow the enemy no respite, once again attacked toward Kokumbona, but, as in October, abandoned the operation in the face of yet another threat of a Japanese offensive. However, he put an enemy force which had landed at Koli Point, east of the perimeter, to flight with the loss of 450 killed and would have annihilated it but for a gap in the American lines, through which the Japanese survivors escaped. They were harried in their retreat south of Mount Austen by a Raider battalion, which covered 150 miles in a 30-day march and killed over 400 of the enemy for a loss of 17 men killed.

The 'Tokyo Express' was working overtime to build up Japanese strength, but the reinforcements ordered to the South Pacific by Roosevelt were also arriving. In fact, a large American convoy was first into Savo Sound on November 11 and, weathering successfully a vicious air onslaught, only retired when air reconnaissance indicated the approach of an enemy surface force. On the evening of November 12, having escorted his transports to safety, Rear-Admiral Daniel J. Callaghan returned to the Sound with five cruisers and eight destroyers, but issued no battle orders and distributed no intelligence reports to his subordinates. Vice-Admiral Hiroaki Abe, whose mission was to bombard Henderson Field, had two battleships, their magazines filled with bombardment instead of armour-piercing shells, a solitary light cruiser and fourteen destroyers, all without radar. Although Abe did not anticipate a surface action, he was aware American cruisers and destroyers were close to Guadalcanal.

At 0141 the opposing forces sighted one another head on, and a scrambling, confused mêlée developed at short range, with both sides firing alike on friend and foe. In this furious, 30-minute brawl two Japanese destroyers were sunk and the ancient battleship *Hiei,* hit by over 50 shells, was left disabled north of Savo Island, where Allied aircraft attacked her after daylight until she went down. The American destroyers *Cushing* (1,465, 1935), *Laffey* (1,700, 1941), *Barton* (1,700, 1942) and *Monssen* joined the sunken ships of Ironbottom Sound, as also did the cruiser *Atlanta* (6,000, 1941), which was so severely damaged she had to be abandoned and sunk. Another American cruiser and destroyer were seriously damaged, but not fatally, and the cruiser *Juneau* (6,000, 1941) was torpedoed and sunk by the submarine *I-26* (1,950, 1941) during the American withdrawal to Noumea, only 10 of her crew of 700 surviving. American casualties, which included two admirals, Callaghan and Scott, were much heavier than the Japanese.

Although Henderson Field had been saved from a 14-inch bombardment, it was a costly American defeat, which would have been even costlier had Abe's battleships had armour-piercing shells. As it was, most of his shells, while they did a good deal of damage to the superstructures of the American ships, bounced off their armour and failed to penetrate below deck. Nor did the battle save Henderson Field from being bombarded on the night of the 13th-14th, when two heavy cruisers fired 8-inch shells for 40 minutes, destroying a bomber and 17 fighters and damaging another 32 fighters.

These Japanese bombardments had been planned to cover an ambitious reinforcement attempt by eleven transports and a similar number of destroyers under Rear-Admiral Raizo Tanaka, who sailed from the Shortlands at nightfall on the 12th. However, the force had prudently returned to port early next morning. Tanaka soon set sail again, seeking to land his 10,000 to 13,500 troops on Guadalcanal after sunset on the 14th. As he made his way down The Slot that morning, Mikawa's Support Group, probably quite involuntarily, decoyed the Allied airmen away from the transports. Mikawa lost the cruiser *Kinugasa* and had other ships damaged, including two heavy cruisers. But before midday Marine, Navy and Army aircraft were hitting the transports. These planes came from Henderson Field, where some carrier bombers had landed to strengthen Guadalcanal's air power, from Espiritu Santo, the Flying Fortress base, and from the carrier *Enterprise,* lying to the south-west of Guadalcanal. By nightfall Tanaka had lost seven transports, the troops on some of which had been taken aboard his destroyers before they went down. Despite these losses, Tanaka pressed on resolutely, intending to land men and supplies that night as Kondo's force, composed of a battleship, 2 heavy and 2 light cruisers and 9 destroyers, bombarded Henderson Field.

Waiting for Kondo in the Sound, however, was Admiral Willis Augustus Lee, with two battleships and four destroyers, and at 2317 he opened fire on the approaching Japanese. An intense, close range gun battle saw Lee's destroyers savagely battered and was followed by an equally close range duel between the battleships. At 0025 Kondo, frustrated in his bombardment attempt, gave the order to retire. As soon as the rival heavy ships disappeared the persistent Tanaka beached his transports and resumed unloading. With the first streaks of daylight all four vessels were bombed and shelled and quickly set on fire or ripped apart. These attacks were made by aircraft, shore batteries and the lone destroyer *Meade* (1,700, 1942) and prevented the enemy destroyers disembarking the troops they had picked up the previous day. Statistics of the number of Japanese soldiers landed are conflicting, the enemy stating they got only 2,000 ashore, but other sources putting the figure at 4,000 and a mere five out of the 10,000 tons of ammunition, food and other supplies the ships carried. Some 3,000 of the troops were drowned or killed.[7] The destruction of the remaining transports was some compensation for Lee's loss of the destroyers *Walke* (1,570, 1939), *Preston* (1,480, 1936) and *Benham* (1,500, 1938), and the extensive damage which sent *South Dakota* back to the United States for repair and refitting. Kondo was forced to scuttle the battleship *Kirishima* and the destroyer *Ayanami* (1,700, 1930), both heavily damaged by gunfire.

The three-day naval battle of Guadalcanal was decisive. The Japanese now knew that their last chance of recapturing Guadalcanal had gone and that they could hope to do no more than delay for as long as possible the American drive. On December 9 Vandegrift handed over command to Major-General Alexander M. Patch, whose Americal Division had relieved the exhausted marines. By early January, when Allied ground, air and naval strength on Guadalcanal totalled some 50,000 men, large-scale offensive operations were launched, and although these were not pushed forward with sufficient speed to annihilate the entire Japanese force, the 'Tokyo Express' was running in reverse by the first days of February. In all, these hard-worked destroyers evacuated about 12,000 Army and 1,000 Navy troops.

The first Allied offensive in the Pacific had cost the United States Army and Marine Forces some 1,600 men killed in action and 4,245 wounded, with more than 10,000 victims of malnutrition and tropical illnesses. The enemy, of whom about 36,000 fought on Guadalcanal, lost 14,800 killed or missing, 9,000 dead of disease and 1,000 taken prisoners. To these figures have to be added air and naval personnel losses, which cannot be accurately assessed. The confident Japanese had been thoroughly thrashed, but the real gains of the Guadalcanal campaign, as of the campaign in Papua, were, first, the great upsurge in Allied morale and, second, the heavy losses Japan had suffered in aircraft and pilots, the full harvest of which was to be garnered months later as Japanese air strength degenerated into impotency.

NOTES AND REFERENCES

1. Morison, *The Struggle for Guadalcanal*, 14.
2. Ibid., 25. The Australian official air history makes no mention of these sightings, and the second volume of the official naval history, covering the period of the Guadalcanal operation, has yet to be published. However, the General Editor, Mr Gavin Long, supplied a copy of the relevant portion of the naval history and the account in the text is based on this. The American statement is in Morison, 25.
3. Morison, 62-3, summarizes Hepburn's conclusions. Cf. Newcomb, *Savo*, 228 sq.
4. James J. Fahey, *Pacific War Diary, 1942-1945* (Boston, 1963), 25.
5. Potter and Nimitz, *The Great Sea War*, 264.
6. Ibid., 263.
7. Morison, op. cit., 282; Miller, *Guadalcanal: The First Offensive*, 188; Potter and Nimitz, 266.

FURTHER READING:

The fullest account of Guadalcanal is, of course, the official Army history — *Guadalcanal: The First Offensive* (Washington, 1949). Morison's volume, *The Struggle for Guadalcanal, August, 1942-February, 1943,* is eminently readable and invaluable for the naval actions. *The Great Sea War,* mentioned previously, is excellent for a summarized version of the campaign. Richard F. Newcomb's *Savo: The Incredible Naval Debacle off Guadalcanal* (Sydney, 1963) is a full-length study of the battle of Savo Island, popularly written. John L. Zimmerman's *The Guadalcanal Campaign,* the official Marine Corps monograph of the campaign, can be recommended and its maps are excellent. Many participants in the campaign have written books about it, of which Brigadier-General Samuel B. Griffith II *The Battle for Guadalcanal* (New York, 1963); Robert Leckie, *Challenge for the Pacific* (London, 1966); Gen. Alexander A. Vandegrift and Robert B. Asprey, *Once a Marine, the Memoirs of General A. A. Vandegrift* (New York, 1964); Herbert L. Merillat's *The Island* (Boston, 1944); Frank Hough's *The Island War* (Philadelphia, 1947) and John A. De Chant's *Devilbirds* (New York, 1947) are recommended.

nine

TWO-PRONGED ALLIED DRIVE

In the first months of 1943 the character of the war was everywhere changing. In Europe and the Middle East as well as in the Pacific the initiative was being wrested from the Axis powers and Allied plans were maturing for offensives which ultimately were to lead to victory. The first impact of the massive industrial capacity of the United States and of her untapped reservoir of manpower was exerting itself and re-shaping the scope and size of Allied operations.

A few months earlier, when Allied shipping losses were high in the battle of the Atlantic, when Russian armies were reeling back as the Germans drove across the Don, threatening Iraq and Persia, when Tobruk had fallen and the British been driven back to the gates of Egypt, when the Japanese had completed their widespread conquests with ease and swiftness, the pros-pects of ultimate Allied victory had appeared bleak and remote. By early 1943 all the gloomy clouds had not rolled away, but they had lightened and the first rays of hope were gleaming steadily, if still faintly.

Slowly the U-boat campaign in the Atlantic was being mastered. Shipping losses, and, equally vital, the number of new ships being launched, were at more acceptable levels. In the Middle East the Battle of El Alamein opened on October 23 and by November 4 the enemy was in headlong retreat. Four days later Allied armies in the Torch operation landed in North Africa. On February 23 the Kasserine Pass, in Tunisia, through which the enemy had broken five days earlier, was recaptured, and a month later General Montgomery's Eighth Army smashed through the Mareth Line to resume its race to link up with the Allied forces in Tunisia. On January 16, presaging a mounting air assault on Germany, Berlin was raided for the first time since November 7 1941 and in Russia, where the Soviet forces had surprised the Germans by suddenly going over to the offensive in November, the final resistance of the German Sixth Army at Stalingrad ended in January and the investment of Leningrad was broken in the same month.

Throughout 1942 the Central Pacific Area, in contrast to the South-West and South Pacific Areas, was quiescent. So meagre were Allied resources in the Pacific theatre that when the demands of the Guadalcanal and Papuan campaigns had been satisfied little was left for the Central Pacific. Apart from planning for an advance across the Pacific in 1943 by way of the Gilbert, Marshall and Mariana Islands, Admiral Nimitz was compelled by sheer lack of means to limit his activities to raids on Japanese island bases by air and light naval forces and to submarine attacks on Japan's naval and merchant shipping.

The submarine campaign in the Pacific, even in the crowded waters of the South-West Pacific and on the supply lines to Guadalcanal, fell far short of expectations. From the day of Pearl Harbour to the last day of 1942 Allied submarines sank only 139½ Japanese merchantmen totalling 590,165 tons gross, all but about 2 per cent by American submarines. This was an average of only 45,397 tons a month. On the other hand, enemy submarines during the twelve months of 1942 sank 1,160 Allied and neutral ships of a gross tonnage of 6,266,215, a monthly average of 522,184 tons gross.[1] Lack of combat experience and the excessive caution of submarine skippers, defects in the depth control and exploders of American torpedoes, faulty dispositions, the employment of insufficiently aggressive tactics, and the absence of radar — all these were factors which contributed to the Allied failure. There were some highly successful patrols and combat missions by individual submarines, but the overall results against naval as well as merchant shipping tonnage were disappointing. Far too many torpedoes missed their targets or, when they hit, proved duds. Some of the defects were remedied during 1942. The installation of radar, both air and surface search, improved greatly the efficiency and effectiveness of American submarines, but defective torpedoes continued to plague the crews until the last half of the year.

On January 19 1943 Rear-Admiral Robert H. English, commanding the United States submarines in the Pacific, was killed in an air crash at San Francisco. He was succeeded by Rear-Admiral Charles A. Lockwood, who, with headquarters at Fremantle, had been submarine commander of the South-West Pacific. Lockwood at once moved the United States submarine base forward from Pearl Harbour to Midway Island, thus saving submarines 2,400 miles of travel on each patrol, and improved morale by relieving seagoing crews of responsibility for their boats when in port and instituting improved recuperation facilities. These measures and the technical improvements, coupled with more aggressive dispositions and tactics, were to make the submarine campaign in the Pacific an important factor in Japan's defeat.

Only in Burma was there a set-back on land. There Wavell's campaign in the Arakan for the recapture of Akyab foundered on the obstinate Japanese defence of Donbaik, on the coast ten miles from the tip of Mayu Peninsula, and at Rathedaung, on the opposite side of the precipitous and jungled Mayu Range. Repeated attacks against both places failed with heavy losses, largely because of unimaginative leadership and, after the initial repulses, flagging morale. Wavell, promoted to Field Marshal on January 1, persisted too long in demanding the capture of Donbaik by frontal assault, and shares responsibility with his subordinate commanders for the failure. The defeat was the more astonishing because the British and Indians from the outset enjoyed overwhelming numerical superiority, a preponderance of artillery and a monopoly of armour.

The original plan was to retake Akyab by an advance down the Mayu Peninsula in co-operation with an amphibious landing. Circumstances forced the abandonment of this plan. Wavell, having sent an infantry division and the 7th Armoured Brigade to the Middle East because of the German threat to Iraq and Persia, was short of trained troops, and political difficulties, culminating in the civil disobedience campaign led by Mahatma Gandhi, had interrupted and delayed training. More important, landing craft had been retained longer than expected for the Madagascar operations. He was therefore forced to substitute an attack down the peninsula with a short-range seaborne operation against Akyab from the peninsula itself, an operation which had to be carried out during the short, dry season between November and May.

The Eastern Army, composed of British and Indian troops under Lieutenant-General N. M. S. Irwin, failed to move boldly or swiftly. The Japanese were thus given time in which to augment their small forces and to dig in at Donbaik and Rathedaung, where they constructed heavy bunker defences similar to, and as difficult to reduce as, those at Buna and Gona. Complacently believing the jungle of the mountain range was impenetrable, so that envelopment from the land side was impossible, the British subordinate commanders confined their attacks against Donbaik to set-piece frontal assaults, the plan for each successive attack being almost identical with those that had preceded it. Nor was any attempt made to outflank the Japanese defensive position by a seaborne attack in its rear. A request for Valentine tanks resulted in only eight being sent, although Slim and the tank force commander argued strongly against sending so few. They were overruled and this attack, like its predecessors, failed lamentably. One of the unsolved mysteries of this campaign is why its planning and execution was not left with XV Corps Headquarters, commanded by Slim.

Lieutenant-General Takishi Koga's 55th Division was ordered by General Iida, XV Army Commander, to hold Rathedaung, Laungchaung and Donbaik. It did so with brilliant success, but the aggressive Koga saw that the British dispersion — they had advanced along the sea coast and astride the Mayu River on the other side of the range, with a flanking detachment further east of the river in the Kaladan Valley — invited defeat in detail. He won Iida to his way of thinking and, using his comparatively small forces with great boldness and speed, soundly defeated his opponents. He cleared the Kaladan Valley between March 7 and 19, driving the British twelve miles back to Zedidaung. This retreat exposed the left flank of the forces on the Mayu Peninsula. Wasting no time, Koga crossed the river at night, struck the flank of the brigade at Rathedaung and rolled it up. The brigade disintegrated, losing practically all its equipment, and its scattered remnants struggled back in small, disorganized parties. Koga then crossed the mountain range, which the British had accepted as impassable, and struck behind another brigade, scattered it and overran its headquarters.

The British and Indians in this mismanaged offensive lost 2,500 men killed, missing and wounded. They gained neither strategic nor tactical advantage and not one mile of ground. With no results to show for its efforts and with two brigades having ceased to exist as fighting formations, the Army's morale, not surprisingly, was low. The men, British and Indian, had lost confidence in themselves as well as in their leaders.

The campaign had been a costly defeat, but fortunately for all concerned attention was diverted from the Arakan fiasco by the first raid deep behind the Japanese lines by Brigadier Orde Charles Wingate's Chindits. The Chindits (their name was taken from their emblem, the Chinthe, a mythological beast, half lion and half eagle, carved on Buddhist temples throughout Burma) covered from 1,000 to 1,500 miles in their incursion into upper Burma between mid-February and early May. Supplied from the air, and split into a number of individual columns, divided into two main groups, the 3,000 men traversed jungle and mountain and crossed both the Chindwin and Irrawaddy Rivers.

The romantic nature of their guerilla operations, with their immense demands upon courage and endurance, and the bold, imaginative conception of such a long-range penetration behind enemy lines in inhospitable country, captured the world's fancy. The colourful reports of the Chindits' exploits excluded from the pages of the press the dismal news of the failure in the Arakan.

Wingate was one of the most arresting and remarkable military leaders to come out of World War II. He was something of a mystic, a non-conformist with original and unorthodox military views, arrogant and egotistical, violently antagonistic to all who disagreed with him, and constantly in conflict with the military hierarchy, which he flayed with bitter scorn. A legend in his own lifetime, he is today still a controversial figure whose military achievements in Burma are not easily evaluated. Of him, Slim wrote[2]:

> Wingate was a strange, excitable, moody creature, but he had fire in him. He could ignite other men. When he so fiercely advocated some project of his own, you might catch his enthusiasm or you might see palpable flaws in his arguments; you might be angry at his arrogance or outraged at so obvious a belief in the end, his end, justifying any means; but you could not be indifferent. You could not fail to be stimulated either to thought, protest, or action by his sombre vehemence and his unrelenting persistence.

Ambitious, eccentric, with a streak of ruthlessness and prone to attacks of melancholia, a man who might be garrulous one moment and grimly silent the next, Wingate possessed an astonishing gift of leadership. He had been summoned to India by Wavell, under whom he had served in Palestine and Abyssinia. Wavell, always an advocate of unorthodox methods and a fine judge of character, able to appreciate and deal with difficult subordinates, approved Wingate's plans and gave him the means with which to test his theories.

The 77th Indian Infantry Brigade, as the Long Range Penetration Groups were formally styled for security reasons, received rigorous training resembling that of the Japanese Army.

Wingate's biographer, Christopher Sykes[3], described it in these terms:

> The rule was merciless severity throughout: to make men able to bear privation and fatigue up to the very limit of human endurance, and far beyond what men thought they could endure. The men had to outdo our earliest ancestors in power of survival; if they collapsed under the stress of heat in long marches with full loads they were revived with no more comforting equipment than the shade of trees and makeshift fans; when the monsoon broke they were forced to continue the exercises in mud and incessant rain with no allowance for rising rivers and unpassable grounds; they had to carry out heavy tasks on light rations; they had to ignore thirst; they had to learn to bear midges and mosquitoes and leeches by will rather than protection; and they were virtually forbidden to go sick.

The original plan was for the Chindits to make their deep penetration in conjunction with a limited Anglo-Indian offensive from Assam against the Chindwin towns of Sittaung and Kalewa and a drive by Stilwell's Chinese armies from the north and north-east against Myitkyina, Bhamo and Lashio, with the object of opening the land route to China. In the event, neither offensive took place, but Wingate persuaded Wavell to allow the Chindits to enter upper Burma simply as guerillas.

Wingate's elaborate deception measures to mislead the Japanese were brilliantly successful. For some time the enemy believed only small reconnaissance parties were operating and did not realize that a sizable Anglo-Indian force was being maintained behind their lines by air. The Chindits crossed the Chindwin and on the Mandalay-Myitkyina railway blew bridges, cut the line in numerous places and blocked it by dynamiting a gorge. The Irrawaddy was next crossed, but the Japanese, now thoroughly alarmed and extremely active, herded the Chindits into a triangular area of waterless and trackless forest east of the Irrawaddy and between that river and the Shweli River. The Japanese forces at the base of the triangle, well served by

tracks and motorable roads, were able to move swiftly from
point to point, and by vigorously patrolling the Irrawaddy they
prevented the Chindits recrossing the river as a cohesive fighting
force. Wingate's raiders were worn out by their exertions and
privations, and on March 24 he gave the order for the
columns to be broken down into dispersal groups, each of which
was to make its way back to India as best it could. Forced to
abandon most of their equipment and animals, and harried by
strong Japanese patrols and ambushes, about 2,100 Chindits
eventually returned to India out of the 3,000 who had set out.

Wingate had little enough to show for his first expedition.
The Japanese suffered only light casualties and quickly repaired
the damage to the railway. On the other hand, the Chindits
lost almost a third of their strength and their entire equipment,
and of those who returned some 600 were so incapacitated
through their hardships and privations on the expedition that
they had to be invalided out of the services. Apart from experience in supply dropping from the air, the sole gain from the
expedition was psychological. Wingate's bold incursion was of
value in restoring morale, and, as Slim wrote later, its propaganda value was exploited to the full.

Those who had always condemned his theories as heretical
and impracticable proclaimed the raid a failure. Slim, whose
view perhaps represents the orthodox post-war military opinion,
asserts that it had no immediate effect on Japanese dispositions
or plans, and that if anything was learnt of air supply or jungle
fighting it was a costly schooling. He considers the raid was
justified on psychological grounds, however, and says it was
worthwhile because to the troops in India it 'seemed the first
ripple showing the turning of the tide'.[4]

Major-General S. Woodburn Kirby, the official British
military historian of the war against Japan, believes the evidence
proves that the Chindit raid radically altered Japanese strategy.
Late in December, 1942, the Japanese had decided to stand
on the defensive in Burma in 1943. The Chindit operation
changed this decision. The Japanese leaders, fearing a repetition
of the raid on a large scale and in conjunction with a major
offensive, decided to adopt an offensive-defensive policy instead

of a purely defensive one — 'a decision,' as Kirby points out, 'which was eventually to lead them to disaster.'[5] He sees this change in Japanese military thinking, with its adoption of a new policy in Burma, as the outstanding outcome of the raid. With the historical perspective which we now possess, Kirby's view is certainly correct.

Although his incursion achieved this, there is no evidence to suggest that Wingate foresaw or consciously intended such a result. It seems entirely fortuitous, an unexpected but welcome by-product. Yet his persistent and ardent advocacy of long-range penetration may have been based on a realization that such operations could force an enemy to take strategic decisions which no other means would induce him to attempt. Admittedly, the six reasons he gave for continuing the operation when it became clear the accompanying offensives could not take place give no hint of such a doctrine, but it is not impossible that Wingate felt a vague intuition that such a possibility was inherent in this method of warfare. If we knew the answer beyond all doubt, it would be easier to evaluate Wingate's military stature and especially Churchill's rather extravagant claim, made in a speech in the House of Commons, that he 'was a man of genius who might well have become also a man of destiny'.

At the ten-day Casablanca Conference, which began on January 14 1943 the policy of first defeating Germany was reaffirmed as the cardinal principle of Allied strategy. The decision disappointed the advocates of stronger action in the Pacific, of whom the most vehement was Admiral King. Using questionable figures, he urged that 30 per cent of Allied military power should be deployed in the Pacific — double what he estimated was then being employed.

Roosevelt and Churchill, accepting the compromise plan hammered out by the Combined Chiefs of Staff in their game of strategic give-and-take, refused to do more than affirm that adequate forces — a vague term they made no attempt to define — should be maintained in the Pacific, so as to keep pressure on Japan and retain the newly won initiative. They ordered that after the capture of Rabaul, about which they were far more optimistic than the Pacific commanders, Central Pacific forces were to advance west through the Gilberts, Marshalls and Marianas, that the British were to recapture Burma with the help of American ships and landing-craft, that aid to China, now solely dependent on the tenuous air supply route over the Himalayan 'hump' from Assam to Yunnan, be increased, that the Aleutians be secured, and that after Germany's defeat a full-scale offensive be launched against Japan. Of the decisions relating to the European and Mediterranean theatres, the most fateful for the Pacific was that to begin a combined bomber offensive against Germany by the middle of the year.

The Pacific naval and military leaders at the time were unanimous only in their dislike of the Casablanca decisions. Each, having hoped through reorientation of overall global strategy to substantially strengthen his own forces, was unenthusiastic over the results of the conference. Between Nimitz and MacArthur there was a sharp cleavage of opinion, first, as to whether island-hopping through the South-West Pacific or the Central Pacific represented the best strategic approach to Japan and, second, whether the Army or the Navy should be in overall command of Pacific operations. Command rivalry, which the Joint Chiefs of Staff had earlier neatly side-stepped by their convenient alteration of theatre boundaries, persisted and was reflected in the attitude of their subordinates.

On March 28 the results of the Pacific Military Conference at Washington, which had not been attended by Nimitz, MacArthur or Halsey, but to which all three had sent their chiefs of staff and other key officers to expound their plans, were crystallized in a new directive from the Joint Chiefs of Staff. This settled the command problem by placing MacArthur in strategic command of the South-West and South Pacific areas, with Halsey retaining tactical control in the latter area subject to MacArthur's general directives. Nimitz, retaining undisputed control of the Central Pacific area, was to allocate ships and aircraft, for the different operations, as he saw fit.

In the absence of a properly integrated unified command for the entire Pacific on the Eisenhower model in the European theatre, this probably was as satisfactory a solution of the command system as could have been devised. At least, it mollified the touchy 'prima donnas' among the American top commanders and got them working together with reasonable goodwill.

The tasks allocated to MacArthur or Halsey by the directive were to establish airfields on Kiriwina and Woodlark Islands, lying in the Solomon Sea to the north-east of the D'Entrecasteaux Islands; to capture the Lae-Salamaua-Finschhafen-Madang area and occupy Western New Guinea, and to seize and occupy the Solomon Islands, including the southern portion of Bougainville. Revamping his earlier proposals, MacArthur issued his operational plan for the South-West and South Pacific areas on April 26, after a meeting with Halsey. It was a plan which provided for mutually supporting drives along two lines of approach, finally converging on Rabaul, and it took heed of most eventualities. Only its timing was over-optimistic. It envisaged the successful conclusion of the operations in eight months from the occupation of Kiriwina and Woodlark Islands.

MacArthur, who had always resented placing American land forces under Australian command, now decided that the attack on New Britain should be made by an army under entirely American command. In effect, he renamed Lieutenant-General Walter Krueger's Sixth Army, established in Australia in February, Alamo Force, and gave it the status of an independent task force. This had the effect of removing most American ground forces from the operational control of Blamey, the Allied land commander. The Australian commander was left in command, under MacArthur's G.H.Q., of New Guinea Force and the other land forces. Alamo Force was primarily an American outfit, and the New Guinea Force, while containing American elements, was essentially Australian. MacArthur's arrangements, although they created some subordinate command problems, were eminently sensible, and he was quite right to create two distinct commands — one for the New Guinea mainland and the other for the New Britain operations — under his own control.

During the fighting in Papua the small Australian Kanga

Force, continually harassed by shortage of supplies, had been conducting successful guerilla operations in the Wau-Salamaua-Lae area to the north. Kanga Force's work was tremendously important, demanding initiative, courage and bushcraft, and the force's achievements, though less known, were similar to and more successful than those of Wingate's Chindits.

Having received strong reinforcements, the Japanese late in January launched a drive from Mubo to capture Wau, with its airfield. The Allies, however, had warning of the impending attack, and on January 14 General Kenney's transport fleet began flying in the veteran 17th Australian Brigade. This was an illustration of how command of the air conferred great mobility and flexibility on the Allies, but weather conditions over New Guinea always made reinforcement and supply by air a chancy business. It was so on this occasion. The clouds closed down on the Owen Stanleys, and on several days few planes got through, so that as the Japanese advanced, Allied strength at Wau built up slowly.

In fact, if the enemy had not enmeshed himself in difficulties of his own making he might have captured Wau before Australian strength had been built up sufficiently to defend it successfully. By electing to cut their way forward along a disused and forgotten track, the Japanese gained a measure of surprise, but they lost the most precious asset in war-time. Even so, it was touch-and-go for the Australians. On January 29, when the enemy was pressing his attack on the airfield, 60 aircraft brought in 814 troops and next day the transport aircraft landed some 25-pounder guns. This timely reinforcement enabled the Australians to gain the upper hand, and by the end of February the starving Japanese, probably having lost over 1,200 men killed, had been driven back to Mubo.

The repulse before Wau spurred the Japanese commanders at Rabaul to further reinforce the garrisons of Lae and Salamaua. Soon after midnight on March 1 8 destroyers, 7 transports and a special service vessel left Rabaul. The convoy was quickly detected and virtually the entire Allied air strength was concentrated against it. Overcast weather protected it from the heavy bombers during the daylight hours of the 1st, but as it sailed within range of medium and light bombers it was bombed and strafed unceasingly. MacArthur's Headquarters, which believed the convoy comprised 12 transports, 3 cruisers and 7 destroyers, claimed its total destruction, but post-war analysis of enemy records proves that it never exceeded sixteen vessels and that four destroyers and slightly under 6,000 men survived. The destruction of twelve ships and over 3,000 men in the Battle of the Bismarck Sea, however, was a great success for the Allied air forces and ensured that the Japanese would not again use large ships to bring in reinforcements or supplies.

Six weeks later the South Pacific air forces were to score an even more remarkable success. Through their ability to read the Japanese naval code, the Americans learned the exact time on April 18 when Yamamoto, his chief of staff and other officers were due to arrive on a visit by air to Buin. Eighteen Lightnings (P-38's), at the extreme limit of their range, ambushed the two Japanese planes about thirty-five miles north-west of Kahili, the airfield near Buin, just as their escort of six Zeros was about to leave. Both Japanese transport aircraft were shot down, that containing Yamamoto crashing into the jungle and the other, in which was his chief of staff, falling into the sea. Yamamoto was killed, but his seriously injured chief of staff survived. Yamamoto's death had a depressing effect upon the spirits of the Japanese armed services; for he was outstandingly the greatest and most respected Japanese navy officer since Togo, who had led the Imperial Navy to victory in the war against Russia at the opening of the century. Yamamoto's successor as Commander in Chief of the Combined Fleet was Admiral Mineichi Koga.

Apart from incessant air activity, Kanga Force's smashing of the Japanese offensive against Wau, and aggressive patrol skirmishing in New Guinea, there was a lull in active operations in both the South-West and South Pacific areas, as the Allies organized for their twin offensives and the Japanese regrouped their forces and brought up reinforcements to replace their severe losses. The lull lasted until toward the end of June. The gathering of the Allied Forces and the constant movement of supplies to forward bases presented the Japanese with opportunities to disrupt Allied preparations by strong blows from the air, but they were in no state to avail themselves of these opportunities. Apart from the inability of Japanese commanders to grasp the fundamental principles of the proper use of air power, there was a failure to secure effective co-ordination of the efforts of the Army and Navy air forces and both had been seriously weakened by the heavy losses of skilled pilots and experienced air crews. Although their pilots had always made extravagant claims as to the results they achieved, the Japanese High Command must now have realized not only that it was incapable of wresting air superiority from the Allies but that its air forces were being shot down at an alarming rate.

At the beginning of March, early in April, in the middle of May and again in June the Japanese delivered some heavy bombing raids, but for the most part they were directed at widely separated targets. These sporadic efforts, which were never sustained for more than a few days, caused relatively little damage, and even if Allied claims of the enemy raiders shot down were exaggerated, Japanese losses in air combat and from anti-aircraft fire were rarely less than double or treble Allied losses. Such a rate of attrition in trained crews and aircraft could not be sustained for long. It was at this critical period, when their standards were falling away rapidly, that the enemy air forces were called upon to meet resolute, well-trained Allied pilots flying aircraft of better performance, in far greater numbers and more ably directed, than in the earlier campaigning. While Allied air power was expanding, and methodically developing new techniques of strategic bombing and tactical co-operation with ground forces, Japanese air power, which over Pearl Harbour, in the Philippines and over Malaya had surprised the world, was already headed for eclipse, as its impotence in the face of the Allies' offensive preparations abundantly proved.

After postponements caused by the difficulty of assembling troops, ships, aircraft, equipment and supplies, and in completing vital installations, such as airfields and improved port facilities, June 30 was selected as D-day for both the South-West Pacific and South Pacific areas. On the night of the

29th-30th, when the invasion forces were sailing forward to battle, the conditions in each area were dark, wet and stormy, with heavy seas and a high wind.

In the South-West Pacific three forces were on the move. The first two were to occupy Woodlark and Kiriwina Islands respectively, and the third to put ashore at Nassau Bay, south of Salamaua, a United States Army force under Colonel Archibald R. MacKechnie, commander of the 162nd Infantry Regiment. Neither Woodlark nor Kiriwina had been occupied by the Japanese. This was fortunate; for although advance parties had gone in ahead of the main bodies, inadequate reconnaissance, faulty planning and a four hours' delay in arrival resulted in some of the landing-craft at Kiriwina hanging up on the encircling coral reef or, the tide being out, on sandbanks off the beaches. Casualties in the crowded landing-craft might have been heavy had there been resistance. Airfield construction work began immediately and very soon fighters were operating from a 5,000-foot long, coral-surfaced runway on each island.

The purpose of the Nassau Bay landing was twofold — first, to establish a sea line of communications for the supply of the Australian brigades advancing on Salamaua from the Wau area and hitherto air supplied, thus partly relieving Kenney's air force of its supply dropping missions, and, second, to strengthen the diversionary attack on Salamaua in the hope that the Japanese would divert troops to its defence from Lae, MacArthur's real objective. The MacKechnie Force was to secure the bridge-head and then link up with the Australians inland, and advance on their right.

The landing did not go smoothly.[6] The Australian patrol detailed to set up leading lights reached the beach five minutes late after an exhausting march through thick jungle, and on that dark night the pinpoints of light were not visible sufficiently far to sea. The leading vessels overshot their objective and on turning back threw the small flotilla of landing-craft into confusion. However, despite the difficulty in finding the beaches and the fact that the vessels bunched together on one beach, almost 800 men were landed. Only one landing-craft was able

to make a second trip, as the rest broached in the heavy surf,
and the one which retracted met a similar fate when it came in
for its second landing. The men received a ducking, their
radios were put out of action and a good deal of equipment was
lost. The third wave, either because it could not locate the
beaches or saw what had happened to the landing-craft of the
first two waves, did not land.

It took some time to organize the inexperienced Americans
and to get them off the beach, but the garrison of about 100
Japanese had fled into the jungle without manning its beach
defences and, except for a few patrol skirmishes in the afternoon, there was no fighting. At night the Americans withdrew
to their beach perimeter, but, as was so often the case with
untried troops, whatever their nationality, they were jittery in
the unfamiliar surroundings of the jungle. When a few Japanese
attempted to infiltrate their positions they imagined they were
under heavy attack, and in the indiscriminate firing during the
night, eighteen Americans were killed and twenty-seven
wounded — most, if not all, it is to be feared, by American
bullets.

While the MacKechnie Force eventually moved inland to
take up its position alongside the Australians, another battalion
of the 162nd United States Infantry, having assembled at Nassau
Bay, moved forward under Major Archibald B. Roosevelt to
Tambu Bay, immediately south of Salamaua, where it established itself on July 18. Known as the Coane Force, after
Brig.-Gen. R. W. Coane, commanding the artillery of the 41st
United States Division, its task was to open a new supply base,
establish a position for artillery and assist in the capture of
the dominating Mount Tambu. Roosevelt, however, refused to
admit he was under Australian command and insisted that he
took his orders only from Coane. This was typical of difficulties
which sometimes occurred between the Australians and subordinate American commanders and which caused friction and
confusion. Herring had resumed command of New Guinea
Force on May 23 and had placed Major-General S. G.
Savige, commander of the 3rd Australian Division, in tactical
command of the drive for Salamaua. Commonsense, tact and

firmness usually settled these command problems, but they would have been better solved had the question of command been clearly laid down at the outset instead of often being left deliberately vague.

The going in New Guinea was always slow and tough. Frontal assaults on vital knolls and ridges occupied by the entrenched Japanese, even when supported by artillery fire and air strikes, were costly and futile. It was difficult to establish observation posts for the direction of artillery fire in this blind country, while when air support was called in pilots found it difficult to locate terrain features and not infrequently bombed and strafed Allied positions as well as those of the enemy. The only way to dislodge the tenacious Japanese was to encircle their positions and cut their supply routes. This catch-as-catch-can patrolling and ambushing along the jungle tracks demanded coolness, aggressiveness, and great physical endurance. Heavy tropical rain turned the sodden jungle tracks into muddied quagmires and turned rivers and creeks into swollen torrents, slowing down all movement. The Americans had now to learn in the bitter school of experience the hard lessons which the Australians had already assimilated.

Under General Imamura, whose Eighth Area Army had been established at Rabaul in January, Lieutenant-General Hatago Adachi's XVIII Army was responsible for the defence of New Guinea. He was determined to hold Salamaua, but he had no means of reinforcing it except by taking troops from Lae as MacArthur had hoped he would. He sent all but about 2,000 of his 11,000 troops in the Lae-Salamaua area to defend Salamaua against the Australian and American advance. During July and August the 3rd Australian Division and the 162nd American Regiment, in a series of hard-fought engagements, thrust north towards Salamaua along the coast and through the tangled mountain country south of the Francisco River. By August 19 the Japanese in their strong defensive positions round Mount Tambu had been encircled and they made a long and skilfully executed withdrawal to the last high ground surrounding Salamaua. Soon after this the 5th Australian Division relieved the 3rd. The big offensive against Lae opened on

September 4 and on the 6th Adachi decided to give up Salamaua in order to reinforce Lae. Australian troops entered
Salamaua at 1430 on September 11 and the Americans next
day.

Meanwhile, after an eleven-minute bombardment by five
destroyers, Major-General G. F. Wootten's 9th Australian
Division landed on beaches near the Buso and Bulu Rivers,
eighteen miles east of Lae. There was no opposition on the
ground, the landing taking the Japanese by surprise, and
attempts by the Japanese air forces to break up the invasion
failed. On the 5th, in the first tactical landing of Allied paratroopers in the South-West Pacific, the 503rd United States
Parachute Infantry Regiment was dropped at Nadzab, in the
Markham River Valley. MacArthur and Kenney, each in a
Flying Fortress, watched the American paratroopers jump. The
ninety-six transport planes (C-47's) had flown over the Owen
Stanleys and rendezvoused with bombers, fighters and weather
planes over Marilinan, more than 300 aircraft from eight
different air bases participating in the operation. In the afternoon Australian artillerymen of the 2/4th Field Regiment,
volunteers who had undergone a quick course of instruction
under American 'jump masters', but some of whom had never
made a parachute landing, joined the American paratroopers
in Nadzab. As the landing was unopposed on the ground,
however, their 25-pounders were not needed. Three Americans,
whose parachutes failed to open, were killed and another thirty-
three injured; only one Australian gunner was hurt.

On the 7th Kenney's transport aircraft began flying the 7th
Australian Division, commanded by Major-General G. A.
Vasey, into Nadzab. As the men were being taken to the airfield
for emplaning, a bomb-laden Liberator taking off from Jack-
son Field at Port Moresby crashed in the early morning
darkness and hit five of the trucks carrying the Australians.
In this disaster 15 Australian infantrymen and all 11 members
of the bomber's crew were killed, another 44 infantrymen died
of their injuries, bringing the total death roll to 70, and another
92 men of the 7th Division were injured. Apart from this
mishap and the fact that on three successive days aircraft were

Australian War Memorial

Above, an Australian outpost in New Guinea from which raids were made into enemy-held territory. Below, Australian troops hurriedly dismantle a tent near Shaggy Ridge as their position comes under Japanese fire

Australian War Memorial

United States Navy

An American warship bombarding Japanese-held Makin Atoll prior to a marine invasion

unable to get through to Nadzab, delaying the drive on Lae, the transfer of the 7th Division to the Markham Valley went smoothly.

Adachi had been out-manœuvred in the battle for Salamaua and Lae, and the latter now fell easily into Allied hands. The 9th Australian Division, driving against Lae along the coast from its landing place, was briefly held up by the swiftly flowing, rain-swollen Busu River, which was divided into three channels. It might have crossed unopposed but for vexatious delays in getting bridging material forward. The Japanese, however, had not the strength to withstand the determined Australian attack, and on September 16 the 7th Division, advancing down the Markham Valley, entered Lae. Its leading elements were first strafed and bombed by American aircraft and then shelled by the 9th Division's artillery, fortunately with only one casualty, before word could be spread that Lae had been captured. Although MacArthur's communique — they were never over modest in their claims — optimistically asserted that four Japanese divisions, with an original strength of 20,000 men, had been encircled, the main body of the Japanese garrison escaped, retreating over the high mountains by little known and little used tracks. Many stragglers were shot down by pursuing Australian patrols, and others, whose numbers will never be known, died of wounds or illness, cold or starvation.

The fighting for Salamaua and Lae, from April onwards, cost the Australians over 500 killed or missing and nearly 1,300 wounded, while the American ground forces between June 29 and September 11 had 81 killed and 396 wounded. Against total Allied ground casualties of around 2,300, the Japanese casualties between April and August totalled about 8,100, including 2,722 killed, and at Salamaua and Lae their casualties amounted to probably another 2,200 men, apart from those who died in the retreat over the mountains.

There was no lull in operations after the capture of Lae. Both the Allies and the Japanese wanted to gain control of the Markham River and Ramu River Valleys, which, running from south-east to north-west, separated the Huon Peninsula from the rest of New Guinea. The Australians won the race. On

September 19 the 2/6th Australian Independent Company, audaciously moving forward without support after being flown in, captured Kaiapit, in the Markham Valley, in a bold and dashing attack. Additional troops and engineers were flown in, and on October 4 the 7th Division took Dumpu, in the Ramu River Valley. The Allies promptly set about building airfields in both areas, while the Japanese, beaten to the punch, cancelled their projected moves into the river valleys.

On September 22 Rear-Admiral Daniel E. Barbey's little Seventh Amphibious Fleet put the 9th Australian Division's 20th Brigade group ashore near the mouth of the Song River, six miles north of Finschhafen, after an eleven-minute bombardment by five destroyers and a strafing attack by aircraft. In the darkness the four assaulting companies, much intermingled, were landed to the left and right of the intended place. This saved them from heavier casualties, since the beach on which they were to have landed was more strongly held by the enemy, who occupied a number of log and earth defences. The landingcraft had been instructed not to fire, but, fortunately, disobeyed orders and their fire helped the Australians clear the jungle fringes of the beach. By nightfall the first day's objectives had all been secured.

As it retired, the Amphibious Fleet was sharply attacked by thirty or forty fighters. Barbey's ships, however, were under an air umbrella which the Japanese pilots did not suspect or see until it was too late, and the defending fighters claimed 10 bombers and 29 fighters shot down for the loss of 3 Lightnings, while the Fleet's anti-aircraft gunners claimed a further 9 torpedo-bombers.

On the 23rd the Australian advance towards Finschhafen began. It made steady progress, meeting no resistance, until the Bumi River was reached. Here the Japanese were strongly entrenched on the southern bank, and while mortars were brought up to support the Australians at the river's mouth other units turned westward, painfully pushing through the dense vegetation to the crest of a rocky ridge. This force was reinforced next morning and in the afternoon, having forded the river, which was up to their waists, under fire, the Australians established a bridge-head on the south bank.

While these operations were proceeding the Japanese Air Force was active, bombing the Australian beach-head and artillery. The need for cutting a jeep road to enable supplies to be brought forward delayed the Australian attack, but on the 26th there was heavy fighting as the bridge-head was enlarged. The Australians, after stumbling downhill, had to pull themselves 200 feet up a precipitous slope in the face of Japanese fire and grenades. The enlargement of the bridge-head and the gaining of the high ground gave the Australians dominance over the main Japanese positions, but did not break the dour Japanese defence. Not until October 2, after further stiff fighting, was Finschhafen village and harbour captured and contact made with the 22nd Australian Battalion, which had been pushing up the coast towards Finschhafen from Lae, where the Allies were busily establishing a major base for further offensive operations.

The Australians at Finschhafen, however, were very much out on a limb. Before their landing Adachi had set Lieutenant-General Shigeru Katagiri's 20th Division in motion to reinforce Finschhafen, but as it could not be transported to Finschhafen by sea because of the threat posed by the Allied air and naval forces it was compelled to make an overland march of 200 miles. It was at Gali, 100 miles away, when the Australians landed and was not due to reach Finschhafen until October 25. When news of the landing reached him, Katagiri speeded up his march. Meanwhile, the Japanese commander at Finschhafen, Major-General Eizo Yamada, had concentrated his remaining troops at Sattelberg, a dominating peak, 3,400 feet high, six miles west of the Australian landing beaches, and here Katagiri and part of his division arrived on the 10th. Stretched out along the coast, too few in numbers, the Australians were vulnerable. Pleas for reinforcements were at first rejected by MacArthur's Headquarters, which failed to realize the strength of the enemy forces or the critical situation of the Australians, but additional troops were brought in eventually in time.

On the 15th Katagiri's order for a counter-attack was found on the body of a Japanese officer, and this enabled the Australians to get ready. They easily repulsed a seaborne assault launched in the early hours of the 17th after a heavy bombing raid on Finschhafen. The attackers had lost about half their strength when, on the 15th, PT boats had sunk four of their troop-laden barges. From Sattelberg the Japanese attacked stubbornly throughout the 17th and 18th, splitting the Australians into two groups, on either side of a creek, but failing by a narrow margin to reach the sea. Disorganized by the obstinate defence and their heavy losses, the Japanese were compelled to pause and for three days they made no major move. This halt gave time for reinforcements to be hurriedly brought in, along with a troop of tanks, beginning on the night of the 19th-20th. The crisis was now over, although the Japanese continued to attack, but before the end of October, with Allied strength continuing to build up and their own supply position becoming difficult, the Japanese were thrown on the defensive. On November 17 the Australians opened their attack on Sattelberg, but in that difficult country, although heavy infantry tanks were used, it was tough going against the enemy's determined resistance.

Although it was not fully realized at the time, the capture of Pabu, a wooded knoll astride the Gusika-Wareo road, was the turning-point in the assault on Sattelberg. The Japanese counter-attacked desperately and repeatedly from all sides in an effort to recapture Pabu, but the Australians, suffering heavy losses, held firm for seven days. The capture and retention of Pabu severed the main supply route of the Japanese to Wareo and Sattelberg, and despite the rugged country and stubborn Japanese resistance, the Australians by the 23rd had begun to encircle the Sattelberg positions and next day gained a precarious toehold on the heights. Next morning, the 25th, Sattelberg was found abandoned.

For several months prior to the fighting for Salamaua, Lae and Finschhafen, Allied operations had also been proceeding in the South Pacific. Halsey's plan for New Georgia provided for the simultaneous seizure of Segi Point, Wickham Anchorage, Viru Harbour and Rendova Island, preparatory to assaults against Munda and Vila. In the event, however, Segi Point had to be taken ahead of schedule. It was here that New Georgia's principal coast-watcher, Donald G. Kennedy, a New Zealander, had his hideout and on June 20, reporting that the Japanese were moving toward him, he asked for assistance. Without hesitation, Halsey sent a party of Marine Raiders to Segi Point, where they arrived, ahead of the enemy, early on the 21st. They were reinforced next day and by July 11 American Seabees, those ubiquitous naval construction units who proved so indispensable in the Pacific War, had a fighter staging strip ready for use.

At Wickham Anchorage early on the 30th the first waves landed on the wrong beach and a number of landing-craft broached in the surf, but there was no opposition on the shore and by nightfall, after some jungle skirmishing, the Anchorage was firmly in American hands. Marine Raiders from Segi Point, being delayed in their twelve-mile march over difficult country, were not in position to cover the landing at Viru Harbour when the attackers arrived and at midday the ships went on to Segi Point. By nightfall, however, the overland advance had secured the harbour and next day Viru itself was occupied.

The capture of Segi Point, Wickham Anchorage and Viru Harbour protected the lines of communication of the main body, which landed successfully at Renard Entrance, at the northern end of Rendova Island. Here it was to build up its strength and supplies before crossing the Roviana Lagoon to assault Munda, on New Georgia. Enemy reaction to the landing was slow. Hyakutake, whose XVII Army was still responsible for the defence of the Solomons chain, was thrown off balance by the reports of simultaneous landings at Nassau Bay and Rendova, and, like his subordinates at Munda, was confused by the Rendova landing. The Japanese had expected a frontal assault on Munda and they at first thought the Rendova landing was a feint. Expecting the transports to suddenly head toward Munda, their mainland batteries held their fire, and it was only after the bulk of the Americans had landed that they began shelling the ships. The transports were at once hidden by a smoke screen, while the destroyers started counter-battery shelling.

The Japanese airfields within easy reach of Rendova had been heavily hit by the Allies in their pre-invasion bombing, and the effectiveness of these tactics was now shown by the slowness with which the enemy air force took up the fight. It was 1100 before the first fighter sweep came over and 1500 before the first bombers arrived. The Allied air umbrella gave short shrift to these raiders, but one torpedo hit Turner's flag-ship, the transport *McCawley* (7,712g, 1928), which that night, being mistaken for a crippled Japanese vessel, was put to the bottom by friendly PT boats, fortunately, without loss of life. The enemy air attacks did little harm until July 2, when, bad weather having closed the Allied bases, bombers and fighters swept in over the beach-head with only anti-aircraft fire to oppose them. They started fires in fuel dumps and caused damage to supplies and equipment. American casualties from this raid were 30 killed and 200 wounded. That night the beach-head was bombarded by a light cruiser and nine destroyers, but there were no casualties and little damage.

It was on the 2nd that the Americans crossed to New Georgia. The Southern Landing Group landed at Zanana, east of Munda, and began to build up its strength for the arduous advance through the jungle — rugged terrain interspersed with swamps — which separated Zanana from Munda. The same day Major-General Noboru Sasaki, commander of the South-Eastern Detachment, took command of the 10,000 Army and Navy troops defending New Georgia. Imamura had already agreed to reinforce Sasaki with 4,000 troops of the XVII Army, but two days later he refused to find a further 11,000 men for the defence of New Georgia. Had he agreed, and if these reinforce-ments had arrived, the Americans might well have suffered a bloody and disastrous repulse before Munda.

Perhaps unwisely, Turner had decided to send in a lightly equipped landing force by way of Kula Gulf, between the north-western shore of New Georgia and the circular Kolom-bangara Island. Although with no heavier weapons than mortars and machine-guns, the Northern Landing Force was to take

Rice Anchorage and Bairoko Harbour, thus preventing reinforcements from Vila reaching Munda and severing the
Japanese escape routes against the time when the enemy would
be driven from Munda by the Southern Landing Force. In the
early hours of July 5 the 7 destroyer-transports, escorted by
3 light cruisers and 9 destroyers under Rear-Admiral Walden
L. Ainsworth, entered the Gulf. Almost at the same time three
Japanese destroyers, carrying the first echelon of the 4,000
army reinforcements Imamura had directed should be sent to
Munda, slipped into the Gulf. Each force was unaware of the
other's presence.

The Japanese destroyers were alerted when Ainsworth bombarded first Vila and then Bairoko Harbour, and less than 15
minutes later the Americans picked up two of the enemy ships
on radar. The Japanese ships, having landed some 850 troops,
immediately fled after firing torpedoes at long range towards
the invasion fleet. One of these sank the destroyer *Strong*
(2,100, 1942) with the loss of 46 lives, but the 2,600 men of
Colonel Harry B. Liversedge's force were put ashore with no
more opposition than some ineffective shelling by shore batteries.

As Ainsworth retired down The Slot he received word that
the Japanese were preparing a second reinforcement effort, and
although his destroyers had no fuel to spare he turned about
and headed back to Kula Gulf, where he arrived about midnight
on the 5th-6th. The Japanese were already within the Gulf
with ten destroyers, seven of them loaded with troops. They
were detected by American radar at 0140, seven minutes before
the Japanese first became aware of the presence of the American
ships. Ten minutes later, at 0157, the American ships opened
fire, the Japanese destroyers almost simultaneously launching
torpedoes.

The battle lasted little over thirty minutes, with brief clashes
between rival destroyers long after the main action had ended.
Ainsworth lost the veteran light cruiser *Helena*, struck by three
torpedoes, the first of which sliced off her bow and a quarter
of her length. Although the American cruisers fired some 2,500
rounds from their 6-inch guns, only the destroyer *Niitzuki*
(2,701, 1942) was sunk, although other enemy destroyers were

damaged. Some 300 men went down with the *Niitzuki,* including the Japanese commander, Rear-Admiral Teruo Akiyama.
The Japanese transports unloaded their men and supplies at
Vila, but one, the *Nagatsuki* (1,315, 1926), ran aground at
Bambari Harbour, five miles north of Vila, and could not be
got off. Allied bombers set her on fire later in the day and she
was destroyed when her magazines blew up.

Ainsworth's next tangle with the Tokyo Express was in the
Battle of Kolombangara in the early hours of July 13. He
had 3 light cruisers and 10 destroyers against Rear-Admiral
Shunji Izaki's light cruiser *Jintsu,* 5 destroyers and 4 troop-
laden destroyer transports. The Americans had the advantage
of radar and the help of a 'Black Cat', a Catalina (PBY)
equipped for night spotting, and they knew about the enemy's
reinforcement effort. Yet the Japanese were aware of Ainsworth's approach and, in fact, plotted his course for an hour
before the action opened with both sides firing torpedoes
almost simultaneously at 0108.

Izaki, who had replaced Tanaka, relegated to the beach
because of his outspokenness, lost *Jintsu* when she was overwhelmed by 6-inch gunfire directed on to her by the 'Black Cat'.
Within a few minutes of the battle opening she lay dead in the
water, and, after two torpedoes slammed into her, broke in two.
There were few survivors, Izaki and 482 officers and men going
down with her. The New Zealand cruiser *Leander* (7,270,
1933), which had replaced *Helena* and was a sister ship of
Achilles and *Ajax,* conquerors of the German pocket battleship
Admiral Graf Spee, was the only ship of Ainsworth's hit by the
enemy's opening salvo of torpedoes. She had a 30-foot hole
blown in her port side amidships and five compartments flooded,
giving her a 10 degree list to port.

The Japanese destroyers retired, but having reloaded their
torpedo tubes they crept back and around 0200 fired another
torpedo salvo at the American ships. These damaged Ainsworth's two remaining cruisers, each of which had her bows
crumpled, and blew up the destroyer *Gwin's* engine-room. She
had to be scuttled after a gallant attempt to save her, with 62
of her crew lost. Under a large air umbrella the three crippled

cruisers reached Tulagi late on the afternoon of the 13th. It was November before the two American cruisers, *Honolulu* and *St Louis,* were in action again, while *Leander* spent more than a year under repair at Boston. Although Ainsworth sank *Jintsu* and forced the enemy destroyers to retire, the Japanese had succeeded in their mission, the transports unloading 1,200 troops on the west coast of Kolombangara.

Ashore the battle was not going well. The Northern Landing Group overcame enemy resistance at Enogai Point and blocked the Munda-Bairoko track, but it failed to seriously interfere with the flow of reinforcements through Bairoko to Munda and it failed to storm Bairoko. In a determined attack on the 20th it seized a ridge only 300 yards from the shore of Bairoko Harbour, but without artillery or air support it was unable to consolidate its gains and heavy mortar fire eventually forced Liversedge's men off the ridge. Against Munda, the Southern Landing Group's attack from the Barike River, south-west of Zanana, was slow to get going. The river was in flood and the ground in its immediate area jungle-clad and swampy. The untested American troops found the unfamiliar surroundings too much for them. The attack was launched on the 9th, but quickly stalled under heavy bombing and a bombardment by destroyers and mortars. The 172nd Regiment, although more than three hours late in starting, gained 1,100 yards by nightfall, but on its right the 169th Regiment hardly moved. One of its battalions succeeded in advancing 100 yards west of the Barike, but its other two battalions were still east of the river when night fell. Referring to the happenings in the 169th's sector on the night before the attack, the American official historian wrote[7]:

> When the Japanese made their presence known to the three battalions, or when the Americans thought there were Japanese within their bivouacs, there was a great deal of confusion, shooting and stabbing. Some men knifed each other. Men threw grenades blindly in the dark. Some of the grenades hit trees, bounced back, and exploded among the Americans. Some soldiers fired round after round to little avail. In the morning no trace remained of Japanese dead

or wounded. But there were American casualties; some had been stabbed to death, some wounded by knives. Many suffered grenade fragment wounds, and 50 per cent of these were caused by fragments from American grenades. These were the men who had been harassed by Japanese nocturnal tactics on the two preceding nights, and there now appeared the first large number of cases diagnosed as neuroses. The regiment was to suffer 700 by July 31.

Despite this initial setback, the attack at last got under way, but made slow progress against an enemy dug in on the high ground. As in New Guinea, the rugged terrain proved to be as formidable as the enemy. Supplying the forward troops was an added difficulty. Every requirement had to be landed on the beaches at Zanana and then carried over the muddied jungle trails to the front line. As there were no native carriers, the task of bringing forward ammunition and rations, and of carrying back wounded, fell upon the troops, reducing the number of combat troops who could be put into the fighting. It was here that the diversion of the Northern Group was felt, for the presence of the men of this force would have strengthened the Southern Group's attack. The problem was eased when a new beach was captured at Laiana, two miles south-east of Munda airfield, by an overland attack, and on the 14th troops and supplies began to land there. There was still a long carry forward to the troops attacking the high ground, but it was at least 5,000 yards shorter than the route from Zanana.

The Americans' early troubles had revealed some weaknesses in command, and a number of subordinate commanders were superseded. Major-General Oscar W. Griswold, commanding the XIV United States Corps and the Guadalcanal base, assumed command of the New Georgia Occupation Force. The same day Nimitz recalled Turner to Hawaii to take command of the Amphibious Force for the forthcoming Central Pacific advance. His post was taken over by Rear-Admiral Theodore S. Wilkinson, while Halsey informally appointed Lieutenant-General Millard F. Harmon, the commanding general of the United States Army Forces in the South Pacific, as his deputy, a post previously held by Wilkinson.

With the aid of light tanks and flame-throwers, the latter having their first extensive use in the Pacific, the Americans, launching a two-division attack on July 25, made slow progress at first, but then gathered momentum. Despite extensive enemy fortifications — in one place 74 log and coral pillboxes were encountered on a 600-yard front — by August 1 the attackers had driven the enemy completely from the ridges. However, a Japanese force well out on the American right flank had not been detected and when it counter-attacked it drove into the rear areas, causing much consternation and confusion and cutting off the 148th Regiment from its left-hand neighbour. The encircled Americans, after heavy fighting, broke through, and the Japanese withdrew, Munda falling on the 5th. By the 14th the airfield was in use, and on the 25th, Bairoko Harbour was occupied without battle.

Meanwhile, the Battle of Vella Gulf had been fought. As with the earlier naval actions, this clash on the night of August 6-7 arose out of an attempt by the 'Tokyo Express' at reinforcement, this time of Kolombangara. When Wilkinson learned of the Japanese move he had no cruisers available, so he sent six destroyers under Commander Frederick Moosbrugger to Vella Gulf. Expecting to meet only PT boats, the Japanese were not as alert as usual, and the first they knew of the Allied vessels came when torpedoes hit two of their four destroyers. Three of their vessels were carrying 900 soldiers for the garrison at Kolombangara, and all three ships were torpedoed in the first few minutes of the action and later became the targets for American gunfire. The destroyer *Kawakaze* went down a few minutes before midnight, and the destroyers *Arashi* (2,033, 1940) and *Hagikaze* (2,033, 1940) soon after midnight, taking with them some 1,500 soldiers and sailors. The fourth Japanese destroyer made good her escape.

Halsey now decided to by-pass Kolombangara, which was believed to have a garrison of 10,000 men and was likely to prove difficult to capture without heavy losses. He therefore leap-frogged forward to Vella Lavella, north-westernmost island of the group. Although less than 100 miles from the Japanese bases on the Shortlands and Bougainville, it was occupied by only a few stragglers, mainly survivors from the Battle of Vella Gulf. Preceded by an advance party, the Americans landed at Barakoma, on Vella Lavella, on August 15, meeting no resist-ance on the ground. A month later a Japanese barge base at Horaniu, on the north-eastern end of Vella Lavella, was captured, and the 3rd New Zealand Division was then called in to mop up the Japanese survivors and to garrison the island. Vella Lavella was taken at small cost, for there was no real fighting on the ground, although it was constantly bombed and strafed by aircraft flying from nearby Japanese airfields.

Arundel Island, at the head of Kula Gulf, was invaded on August 27. Survivors from Munda and Bairoko had taken refuge on Arundel and had been heavily reinforced from Kolom-bangara. The Japanese fought tenaciously, and the Americans had to bring in reinforcements before the island was captured on September 21.

The enemy had already decided there was no purpose in clinging to Kolombangara, and its evacuation began on the night of September 28-29. By the night of October 2-3 the Japanese had evacuated about 9,400 men, and on the night of the 6th-7th the few men left on Vella Lavella were picked up under cover of an action between nine Japanese and six American destroyers. In the Battle of Vella Lavella the Japanese lost one destroyer, but sank one American destroyer and damaged two others. In all, rather under 600 men were rescued by the Japanese from Vella Lavella. American losses in the capture of New Georgia had totalled 1,098 killed, 23 missing and 3,873 wounded.

Having lost Salamaua, Lae and Finschhafen in New Guinea, the Japanese had now been pushed out of New Georgia, and it was clear to their leaders that new offensives against their defensive perimeter were being prepared.

NOTES AND REFERENCES

1. Theodore Roscoe, *U.S. Submarine Operations in World War II* (Annapolis, 1954), 524; S. W. Roskill, *The War at Sea* (London, 1956), II, 485.
2. Slim, *Defeat into Victory*, 162.
3. Christopher Sykes, *Orde Wingate* (London, 1959), 373.
4. Slim, 162-3.
5. S. Woodburn Kirby, *The War Against Japan*, II, 329: *India's Most Dangerous Hour* (London, 1958), 329.
6. Compare the accounts of the night's events in John Miller, *Cartwheel: The Reduction of Rabaul*, 66, and David Dexter, *The New Guinea Offensives*, 98-9.
7. Miller, 112-3.

FURTHER READING:

The official histories give the fullest accounts of the New Guinea and New Georgia operations. The United States military history is John Miller's *Cartwheel: The Reduction of Rabaul* (Washington, 1959) and the Australian, David Dexter's *The New Guinea Offensives* (Canberra, 1961). The best account so far published on the naval operations is *Breaking the Bismarcks Barrier, 22nd July, 1942-1st May, 1944* (Boston, 1950), the sixth volume in Samuel Eliot Morison's tangy history of United States naval operations in World War II. S. D. Waters, *The Royal New Zealand Navy* (Wellington, 1956), has an account of H.M.N.Z.S. *Leander's* part at the Battle of Kolombangara. The air side is fully covered by the American and Australian air histories, to which reference has been made in previous reading lists. Malcolm Uren's *A Thousand Men at War* (Melbourne, 1959) covers the Markham and Ramu Valley operations in New Guinea, and other unit histories recommended are R. P. Serle's *The Second Twenty-Fourth* (Brisbane, 1963) and Rupert Charlott's *The Unofficial History of the 29th/46th Australian Infantry Battalion, A.I.F.* (Melbourne, 1952). Peter Ryan's *Fear Drive My Feet* (Sydney, 1959) provides good general reading.

ten

ISLAND-HOPPING
THE CENTRAL PACIFIC

While operations in the South Pacific and South-West Pacific areas were of vital importance to the defeat of the Japanese, the fighting in the Aleutians was without influence on the war's outcome. For the Japanese, possession of these islands was a liability rather than an advantage and for the Americans no sound military reason dictated the decision to recapture the Aleutians. Sentiment alone prompted it, a wish to free American territory of the Japanese invaders, no matter how wasteful in men, ships and resources such a patriotic gesture might prove. The United States leaders no more contemplated invading Japan by this short but difficult and navigationally hazardous route than the Japanese proposed using it to attack Alaska.

After the Japanese occupation at the time of Midway fighting in the Aleutians was restricted to harassing air, surface and underwater raids against one another's positions and supply lines. The success of these attacks was repeatedly limited or defeated by foul weather. On August 30 1942 United States forces, seeking more favourably sited airfields, moved into Adak and on January 12 1943 into Amchitka. For their part, the Japanese, after temporarily withdrawing from Attu after the American move into Adak, reoccupied it in October.

On January 4 Admiral Theobald was relieved by Rear-Admiral Thomas C. Kinkaid, who brought with him as commander of his strike force of cruisers and destroyers Rear-Admiral Charles H. McMorris. The latter soon tangled with Vice-Admiral Boshiro Hosogaya, who early in March pushed a convoy into Attu from Paramushiro, in the Kuriles, over 1,000 miles away to the east. When he tried to repeat his success later in the month he ran into McMorris. Although superior in strength, Hosogaya failed to defeat the Americans or to get his convoy through. On March 26, in a three hours chase of the American ships known as the Battle of Komandorskis, Hosogaya threw away his advantage of speed by zigzagging to bring the forward and after turrets of his ships to bear, enabling McMorris to escape with damage only to cruiser *Salt Lake City* (9,100, 1929), freshly repaired after the Battle of Cape Esperance. Hosogaya's faulty tactics and lack of resolution cost him what should have been a decisive victory and on his return to base he lost his command.

Boldly by-passing nearer Kiska, Kinkaid on May 11 invaded Attu, whose garrison of about 2,600 men was less than half that of Kiska. The 7th United States Division landed without opposition at Holtz and Massacre Bays, respectively on the island's north and south coasts. The preliminary air strike and naval bombardment, the latter carried out at too great a range, failed to destroy or severely damage the Japanese defences, and as soon as the Americans pushed inland they came under heavy machine-gun and artillery fire. The bewildered 7th Division, ill-led, badly trained and having its first experience of combat, went to pieces, showing no dash or initiative. The divisional commander was superseded and more troops were landed, but not until 11,000 men, including the entire reserve, were ashore was any progress made. The defenders sold their lives dearly, as on the 29th, when over 1,000 Japanese penetrated a gap in the American line, and their banzai charge over-

ran two command posts. Although 500 Japanese committed
suicide by blowing themselves up with grenades, other futile
attacks followed, and it was the end of the month before
Japanese resistance was crushed. The capture of Attu cost the
Americans 600 killed, 1,200 wounded and, because of unsuitable footwear and clothing, 1,500 ill from the Aleutian cold.
Except for 28 Japanese taken prisoners, the entire garrison
was killed or committed *hara-kiri*.

Attu was a costly lesson from which the Americans determined to benefit. They took no chances when they invaded
Kiska in company with a force of Canadians on August 13.
For six weeks, whenever the uncertain weather allowed, the
Japanese defences and installations were pounded from the air
and bombarded by battleships, cruisers and destroyers. Everything was to be pulverized into rubble. The invasion force,
crushingly superior, comprised 29,000 American and 5,300
Canadian troops adequately equipped with Arctic gear and
clothing, and backed by nearly 100 warships. The landing was
faultlessly executed, but not a Japanese was left on Kiska.
They had escaped under the unseeing eyes of the Americans.

In May and June 820 men had been evacuated by I-class
submarines, but the loss of seven of the thirteen submarines
employed and the slowness of the process caused the abandonment of the underwater for a surface evacuation. Late in
July Rear-Admiral Shofuku Kimura, in one of the most brilliant
withdrawals of the war, lifted 5,183 men in two cruisers and
six destroyers, which he loaded in 55 minutes. Kimura was
aided principally by fog but also by the Battle of the Pips, in
which American surface ships, misled by a Catalina's mistaken
report of a Japanese reinforcement group of seven ships and
then by what they believed they saw on their own radar screens,
fought a night action with a phantom fleet that existed only in
their imagination. During the battle the American ships fired
518 rounds of 15-inch and 487 rounds of 8-inch shell and
hit nothing more lethal than the waves.

In the three weeks between the Japanese evacuation and the
American invasion Kiska was constantly strafed, bombed,
bombarded and photographed. Yet nobody, apparently, even

United States Marine Corps

Marines land at Tarawa amid the rubble of trees and buildings levelled by the naval gunfire

Marines pinned down on Tarawa by enemy fire. The capture of Tarawa was achieved at great cost with over 1000 marines killed

United States Marine Corps

Marines carrying rocket equipment and shells up to the front lines

Above, Torokina airstrip, right, on Bougainville Island used by fighters to give air cover to the Empress Augusta Bay beach-head and later for sweeps over Rabaul. Below, New Zealand troops loading landing craft in preparation for their attack on Green Islands

suspected that the Japanese already had left, destroying most of what they could not carry away with them. The failure to detect the evacuation was one of the strangest episodes of the war in the Pacific.

Meanwhile, Admiral Nimitz and his subordinate commanders were creating a fleet the like of which had never before been seen. It was unique in the long history of naval warfare, a fleet, built around the strength of its air component, that carried its own supply, repair and maintenance facilities along with it and was thus largely independent of distant rearward bases. It could keep the seas for weeks at a time, even when engaged in large-scale operations.

New warships, fresh from the fitting-out berths of United States shipyards, came forward steadily. They included tne first of the new *Essex* class of carriers, 32-knot, 27,000-ton vessels, as well as of the equally fast 11,000-ton *Independence* class of light carriers and smaller, slower escort carriers. What may conveniently be called the Fifth Fleet from the outset, although not so named officially until 1944, was commanded by Admiral Spruance, and soon comprised 6 heavy, 5 light and 8 escort carriers, 5 new and 7 old battleships, 9 heavy and 5 light cruisers, 56 destroyers, 29 transport and cargo ships, and numerous landing and beaching craft.

The carriers, with their supporting battleships, cruisers and destroyers, were split into a number of Fast Carrier Task Force groups, each of which normally was built around two heavy and two light carriers. These came under the command of Rear-Admiral Charles A. Pownall. The Fifth Amphibious Fleet, commanded by Admiral Turner, was split into several task forces as operations dictated, and V Amphibious Corps, comprising army and marine land forces, was commanded by Major-General Holland M. Smith, whose violent outbursts when things went wrong gained him the nickname of 'Howling Mad' Smith. The Fifth Fleet had its own land-based air force, consisting of army, navy and marine corps squadrons, under Rear-Admiral John H. Hoover, and behind it stood the Seventh Army Air Force, the main striking power of which comprised 90 Mitchell (B-24) heavy bombers.

The fleet was highly mobile and extremely flexible in its organization. The American genius for organization was nowhere better exemplified during the Pacific war than in the manner in which the Fifth Fleet was maintained forward. Service squadrons, finding a temporary home in an atoll lagoon or some other protected anchorage, moved forward with the fleet, and by means of its tenders, repair ships and floating dry-docks kept the combatant ships operational. Only ships so heavily damaged as to need major repairs in established shipyards needed to return to rearward permanent bases. Underway mobile replacement groups—relieving one another as each in turn was emptied—refuelled, rearmed and resupplied the fleet close to its operational area.

Originally Nimitz planned to move first against the Marshalls. As a preliminary move the Americans advanced into the Ellice Islands and established a bomber base and anchorage at Funafuti Atoll, 700 miles from Tarawa, in the Gilberts, but when resources had to be diverted to the battle for Guadalcanal the development of the Ellice Islands for offensive purposes was neglected. In mid-June 1943, however, it was decided that the Marshalls were too tough a nut to crack initially and the opening assault was switched to the Gilbert Group. Again, a necessary preliminary was the development of the Ellice Islands. In July bomber strips were built on Nukufetau and Nanumea, in the Upper Ellices and in September a fighter strip was laid down on Baker Island, 480 miles to the east of the Gilberts. The latter group served as outpost positions to the Marshalls.

More than a year earlier, on the night of August 16-17 1942 some 220 marines of the 2nd Raider Battalion under Lieutenant-Colonel Evans F. Carlson, carried to their destination in the United States submarines *Nautilus* and *Argonaut* (2,710, 1927), had raided Makin Atoll, in the Gilberts. At a cost of thirty marines killed and missing, the raid inflicted some casualties on the small Japanese garrison and damaged local installations, but its strategical consequences, which the American command did not foresee, proved costly. The raid induced the Japanese to considerably strengthen their positions in the

Gilberts. Within a month they had occupied Tarawa and Apamama (also known as Abemama) and had begun to strengthen the defences of Makin. They continued to build up garrisons, particularly that on Tarawa, where strong defences were constructed. Thus, when the decision to move into the Gilberts was taken the Americans found the defences more formidable than they would have been had there been no Carlson raid.

Nimitz planned to take Apamama, Tarawa and Makin, lying in that order from south to north. With the object of training his new task groups and confusing the Japanese as to where the blow would finally fall, he raided Makin, Tarawa, Marcus and Wake Islands. As a result the Japanese pulled back their air units from the Gilberts, except for a few reconnaissance aircraft. This relieved pressure on the Ellice Islands at a time when preparations for the offensive were being completed.

While Nimitz and his staff were getting ready for the drive across the Central Pacific, Halsey's South Pacific forces moved against Bougainville. Knowing that the Allies were preparing another offensive in the South Pacific, Admiral Koga early in October decided to reinforce Rabaul with the aircraft of the Third Fleet, but a false alarm that the United States Pacific Fleet was to sortie from Pearl Harbour delayed the transfer. However, by November 1 the air groups of the carriers *Zuikaku, Shokaku* and *Zuiho,* totalling 173 fighters and bombers and 192 pilots and crewmen, had reached Rabaul. Throughout October the base and neighbouring airfields had been under constant attack from the air. These heavy and widespread raids by the air forces of the South Pacific and South-West Pacific commands were designed to confuse the Japanese as to the Allies' next objective and to neutralize the airfields from which they might strike at the invasion fleets.

Because the Allied move into Bougainville was for the sole purpose of securing forward airfields from which fighters and light bombers might participate in the aerial bombardment of Rabaul, Halsey decided to by-pass the heavily defended southern part of Bougainville. The Japanese had some 60,000 troops on Bougainville and in the nearby Shortlands, most of whom were stationed around Kahili in the south and Buka and Bonis in the north. In central Bougainville, in the Empress Augusta Bay area on the island's west coast, there were only between 2,000 and 3,000 Japanese scattered over a considerable area, and it was here that Halsey determined to make his main landing. His decision made sound strategical and tactical sense. Resistance promised to be so light that the men and their supplies could be landed quickly and the transports withdrawn before strong air attacks developed. Moreover, the rugged mountains and swampy country surrounding the area and cutting it off from the rest of Bougainville would make it difficult for the Japanese to move large forces quickly, so that there was every chance strong counter-attacks would not start until the Allies had established a strongly defended perimeter covering the sites of the new airfields.

The campaign for Bougainville was launched with the seizure of the Treasury Islands by the 8th Brigade group of the 3rd New Zealand Division on October 27, a landing in which LCI's converted into gunboats were used for the first time in the Pacific. Simultaneously, as a diversion, 725 United States marines began a seven-day raid on Choiseul. On the night of October 31-November 1 Buka and Bonis were bombarded and later raided by carrier-borne aircraft, and before dawn the Shortlands were also bombarded. Under cover of these diversionary raids the landing was made at Cape Torokina, in Empress Augusta Bay, at dawn on November 1. The 300 Japanese in the immediate vicinity offered merely token resistance and by nightfall, when the transports put to sea, 14,000 troops and 6,000 tons of supplies were ashore. Twenty-four dogs, mostly Doberman pinschers, were for the first time used for pointing snipers in the jungle.

Rear-Admiral Sentaro Omori, hoping to destroy the invasion fleet, which he wrongly believed to be still off the beaches, brought down from Rabaul a force of 2 heavy and 2 light cruisers and 6 destroyers, but was intercepted west of Empress Augusta Bay by Rear-Admiral Aaron S. Merrill's task force of 4 light cruisers and 8 destroyers. Merrill planned to exploit his radar advantage by first launching his two destroyer divisions in torpedo attacks, opening fire with his cruisers only after the torpedoes began to hit. Captain Arleigh Burke's division actually launched its torpedoes, but at that moment the Japanese ships unexpectedly altered course, and Merrill, realizing the torpedoes would now miss, opened fire. The confused, high-speed action which followed was notable for the number of collisions—two on the Japanese side and one between American ships. Omori lost the light cruiser *Sendai,* sunk because of the jamming of its rudder, and the destroyer *Hatsukaze* (2,033, 1939), and Merrill the destroyer *Foote* (2,100, 1943), whose stern was sliced off by a torpedo. American casualties, totalling 19 killed and 26 wounded, were much lighter than those of the Japanese; 320 were lost in *Sendai* and there were no survivors from *Hatsukaze.* Omori, who showed little skill and less resolution, was relieved of command on his return to base—a fate common to defeated Japanese naval commanders.

On the 2nd, in an effort to prevent air interference with the beachhead, Rabaul and other Japanese airfields were heavily bombed and strafed. At the time MacArthur's G.H.Q. claimed that this raid on Rabaul destroyed 85 aircraft and sank or damaged 114,000 tons of shipping. Even after the war, when the capture of Japanese documents made possible a proper assessment of results, Kenney wrote that 'never in the long history of warfare had so much destruction been wrought upon the forces of a belligerent nation so swiftly and at so little cost' as in this raid of the 2nd.[1] This was absurd. Much damage was done to Rabaul, many aircraft were destroyed and much shipping was sunk or damaged during the numerous raids, but the destruction and damage were a great deal less than was claimed at the time. In the raid of the 2nd, for example, the Japanese lost only twenty aircraft and not much over 5,000 tons of shipping sunk or damaged.

The claims of Japanese pilots were equally fantastic. With them, landing craft and other small vessels were magnified into battleships, carriers or cruisers, and these almost invariably were claimed to have been sunk or left smoking and stationary in the water, only waiting to be engulfed by the waves. Allied

air losses were always wildly over-stated. Thus, in the raid of
the 2nd, the first in which the aircraft from carriers assisted
the defending fighters, the Japanese claimed to have shot down
22 Allied bombers and 79 fighters. Actual losses were 9
bombers and 10 fighters.

The attacks to neutralize Rabaul continued. After Omori's
failure, Vice-Admiral Takeo Kurita was sent south from Truk
with a stronger and better balanced cruiser-destroyer force.
He reached Rabaul safely with 8 cruisers, 7 of them heavy, 4
destroyers and a fleet train, and the presence of this force
at Rabaul, when all Halsey had were Merrill's few light cruisers
and destroyers, posed a serious threat to the security of the
beachhead at Empress Augusta Bay. Despite the risks involved
in using carriers in close proximity to hostile air bases, Halsey
unhesitatingly struck at Kurita with Admiral Frederick C.
Sherman's *Saratoga-Princeton* carrier group, which he had
borrowed from Nimitz and which had bombed Buka and
Bonis on the morning of D-Day. On the 5th Sherman launched
45 bombers and 52 fighters from a position 230 miles south-
east of Rabaul, and although they sank no ship their bombs
and torpedoes damaged 5 or 6 cruisers (one so seriously
that it was unable to leave Rabaul and 4 so extensively that
they had to be sent to Japan for repair) and 2 destroyers.

Another carrier-borne raid hit Rabaul on November 11.
Sherman launched his planes from a position near Green
Island, north-north-west of Bougainville, and those of Rear-
Admiral Alfred E. Montgomery's carrier group, also borrowed
from the Fifth Fleet, took off from *Essex* (33,100, 1942),
Bunker Hill (27,100, 1943) and *Independence* (11,000, 1943)
when they were 60 miles south-east of Rabaul. However,
Kurita had fled back to Truk because, after Sherman's raid
on the 5th, Koga was not prepared to risk basing his cruisers
at Rabaul. Sherman made his escape undetected. Montgomery
was strongly attacked from the air, but escaped with slight
damage and shot down about 35 Japanese planes.

The aerial pounding of Rabaul was decisive. Koga, after
further raids on the 11th, ordered what were left of his carrier
aircraft to pull out also, and they did so next day. They had

lost 121 of their 173 aircraft and 86 of the 192 men sent forward, while in the same period the 11th Air Fleet had lost about 70 planes. With the withdrawal of the cruisers and carrier aircraft, Rabaul ceased to be an offensive threat, and henceforth it remained no more than a powerful defensive position. More important still, Koga's losses in cruisers, carrier aircraft and trained pilots immobilized the Combined Fleet, which dared not stir out of Truk to combat the threat to the Gilberts.

The Americans were now so strong at sea and in the air that they could afford to disregard the principle of concentration and advance from three directions at once—across the Central Pacific, up the Solomons and through New Guinea—and this despite the fact that the Japanese, possessing the interior lines, could concentrate more quickly against each threat. As it was, each campaign, by absorbing Japanese forces and resources, simplified the tasks of the others and speeded up the progress of all three.

The Japanese command at Rabaul foresaw the possibility of an allied landing at Empress Augusta Bay, but the local commander, whose headquarters was at Kahili, was convinced that the main landing would be in the south, or on Choiseul or the Shortlands, or, less likely, in the north, against Buka and Bonis. He clung tenaciously to this belief even after the Allied landing, dispatching only small forces toward Cape Torokina in the belief that the landing here was either a subsidiary or diversionary one. Not until toward the end of December, when the Allied perimeter had been firmly established and the airfields were in use, did he appreciate that the main Allied effort was being made at Empress Augusta Bay.

On November 7 four destroyers landed 475 Japanese soldiers on the left of the beachhead undetected, but their attack failed and they were quickly eliminated, mainly by artillery fire. Along the tracks inland there were small attacks and a good deal of skirmishing, but within a fortnight 34,000 men and 23,000 tons of supplies had been landed, a fighter and bomber strip had been completed, and the perimeter pushed out to enclose an area of twenty-two square miles. There were constant Japanese air raids, which sometimes caused considerable damage, but the Japanese command still committed only small land forces against the beachhead. On the night of November 24-25 the Japanese attempted to reinforce Buka, but the three destroyer-transports and their two escorting destroyers were intercepted by Burke and in the battle of Cape St George he sank the two escorts and one of the laden transports and drove the other two back to Rabaul. On the 25th the Americans captured Hellzapoppin Ridge, where the Japanese had succeeded in emplacing artillery to bring the beachhead under fire. This 300-foot long ridge, steep and narrow crested, which had defied every effort to take it, was finally captured in a co-ordinated air, artillery and infantry attack. By then the Allies had four airfields operational only 220 miles from Rabaul, and three of them were suitable for heavy bombers.

Major-General Roy S. Geiger, who had relieved Vandegrift on November 9, the latter having been ordered to Washington to become commandant of the Marine Corps, was himself relieved on December 12 by Major-General Oscar W. Griswold, and the Americal Division was brought in to replace the 3rd Marine Division, which Halsey wanted to use for the attack on Kavieng. One of Griswold's most picturesque and efficient units was the 1st Battalion of the Fiji Infantry Regiment, whose 800 men, mostly Fijians of military bearing and powerful physique who were skilled jungle scouts, watched the Japanese movements on the east coast from forward jungle positions supplied by air.

D-day for the capture of the Gilberts was November 20. Makin lay only 190 miles from Mili, the nearest Japanese base in the Marshalls, and so that the fleet might be quickly released and not become the target for damaging air attacks, Nimitz ordered the 27th Infantry Division to overrun the atoll in a single day. The main island, Butaritari, was lightly held and fortified. Its garrison of 800 included construction troops, Korean labourers and seaplane ground crews, with 284 naval landing troops commanded by a junior lieutenant. Major-General Ralph C. Smith's 6,500 assault troops, after a naval bombardment and air strike, landed against light opposition, but the inadequately trained 27th Division, in combat for the first time, was unequal to the task and made slow progress. Not until the 23rd, at a cost of 64 men killed and 152 wounded, did it capture Makin. Except for one soldier and 104 construction troops and labourers taken prisoners, the entire garrison was killed. A turret explosion in the battleship *Mississippi* (33,400, 1917) during the pre-landing bombardment killed 43 men and wounded 19, and when the escort carrier *Liscombe Bay* (7,800, 1943) was torpedoed by a Japanese submarine on the 24th her stored aerial bombs were exploded by the blast and nearly 650 of her crew of 900 were killed.

At Tarawa the target was two-mile long Betio Island, which was nowhere more than 10 feet in height. It was garrisoned by 4,800 men, including 2,600 well trained naval infantry, 1,000 construction troops and 1,200 Korean labourers, under Rear-Admiral Meichi Shibasaki, who had taken command in August. A coral reef, barely submerged at low tide, completely surrounded Betio, and this natural obstacle was reinforced by anti-vehicle and anti-personnel mines, by a double-apron barbed wire fence 50 to 100 yards from the shore, and by concrete tetrahedrons and coral and metal obstacles, the purpose of which was to impede the movements of landing craft and to force them into lanes covered by artillery and other weapons ashore. On the landing beaches a four-foot high retaining wall of stout coconut logs provided positions for machine-guns and anti-boat weapons. Beyond this log barrier lay emplacements for coast, anti-aircraft, anti-tank and anti-boat guns, heavy and light machine-gun nests, and steel reinforced concrete blockhouses, bomb-proof shelters, trenches and foxholes.

As at Guadalcanal, the hydrographic information available was scanty and inaccurate and in the main had been gathered from former residents. The existence of the encircling coral reef was known, but there was little reliable data as to the depth of water on it. The selected D-Day was at the period of neap, or low, tides, but the consensus of opinion was that there would be five feet of water over the reef at the time when the ordinary landing craft were scheduled to arrive on the beaches, and this was twelve inches more than was required. However, a

11. The islands in the Central Pacific campaign

New Zealand army officer, Major F. L. G. Holland, who had lived on Bairiki, the island adjacent to Betio, for 15 years, disagreed. He stated that the neap tide would provide not over three feet of water on the reef, even at extreme high tide, and he forecast the possibility of a low 'dodging' tide on D-day—an irregular neap tide, ebbing and flowing at unpredictable intervals and maintaining a constant level for hours on end. Despite Holland's warning—at a staff meeting during the rehearsals for the landing he bluntly said he 'never dreamed that anyone would try to land on the neap tide'[2]—it was decided not to postpone D-day, but so seriously was the warning regarded that the assaulting marines were instructed what to do should the water on the reef be insufficient to permit their landing craft to reach the shore.

A total of 125 amphibian tractors (amtracs) were available for the assault. Fifty of these, shipped direct from the United States, were of a new type, mounting machine-guns and partially armoured, but the rest were veterans from Guadalcanal, where they had been employed in supply operations only. In these, machine-guns had been fitted forward and an attempt made to armour them by riveting on boiler plates. This was the first time amtracs were to be used tactically, and after a small number had been placed in reserve for later use in landing supplies, there were only enough to lift the first three waves of the assault battalions.

Battleships and cruisers began a 75-minute bombardment of Betio at 0620, firing at ranges between 2,000 and 15,000 yards, and followed this with 45 minutes of neutralization fire, designed to prevent the garrison manning the beach defences. When the assaulting troops were still several hundred yards out aircraft strafed the beaches. Various factors, principally the headwind and choppy sea, delayed the amtracs and the assault waves landed 15 to 20 minutes after the last strafing attacks. Nevertheless they got ashore with comparatively light losses, thanks to the covering fire of destroyers and minesweepers inside the lagoon. Their fire, which peppered the beach fringes until the amtracs were almost ashore, caused the defenders to bunch in two main groups, leaving the extreme right and left centre of the beachhead only lightly defended, and this proved the key to the success of the assault.

Many of the amtracs were hit and destroyed and when the assault was over only 35 remained operational. Nowhere was there more than three feet of water on the reef and in places the depth was merely a few inches. Only the amtracs were able to negotiate the reef. The landing craft bringing in the remaining waves of the landing teams grounded, and the marines had to wade 500 or 600 yards to shore under murderous machine-gun and rifle fire. One observer estimated that the low water tide increased casualties by 50 per cent, and certainly the fourth, fifth and sixth waves suffered far heavier casualties in getting ashore than had the first three waves.

By nightfall on the 20th the Americans held two narrow and shallow beachheads, the smaller to a depth of about 150 yards, the larger running inland for double that distance. Elsewhere they were pinned down on the beaches, huddled for the most part in the shelter of the four-foot beach wall. About 5,000 marines, including nearly all the reserves, had reached land, but at least a third of them were casualties. A few tanks and some light artillery managed to get ashore, but when conventional landing craft were unable to cross the reef the assault lost momentum after the landing of the first three waves. As night fell the invaders were desperately situated, but two factors saved them—first, the inability of Shibasaki, because of the destruction of the Japanese communication network during the naval bombardment, to organize a co-ordinated counter-attack, and, second, the failure of the Japanese air force, because of its losses at Rabaul, to deliver strong raids against the beachhead and the shipping on which the marines were dependent. There were no counter-attacks, not even local ones, on the 20th or during that night, and in the daylight hours only one large-scale air raid, directed at shipping, took place. In this raid the light carrier *Independence* was so damaged that she had to withdraw to Funafuti, but no other vessel was seriously damaged. The raids of the next few days, small in number and each carried out by few aircraft, were wholly ineffective.

The critical position ashore on the 20th resulted in regimental and divisional reserves being committed at once, and next morning the last battalion of the corps reserve was brought ashore. Naval gunfire and carrier-based air strikes, growing in accuracy, and the landing of supporting artillery on the afternoon of the 21st on Bairiki Island, helped the marines expand their bridgeheads. The entire western shore was brought under control and the marines penetrated to the southern shore. There were no counter-attacks on the 21st or during that night, and on the 22nd the Americans began mopping up pockets of resistance, Shibasaki being among those killed. Tanks, flamethrowers and charges of TNT, the latter mostly placed in position by hand, were used to clear shelters and pillboxes whose doomed defenders refused to surrender. By nightfall the Japanese remnants had been squeezed into the western end of the island, where they launched three desperate counter-attacks during the night. Each was beaten back with heavy loss and on the afternoon of the 23rd all organized resistance ended.

On the 25th a battalion of marines embarked at Tarawa for Apamama, 76 miles to the south, where they found the island had been captured the previous day by a reconnaissance company landed from the submarine *Nautilus* on the 21st. All twenty-three Japanese on the atoll were dead, most having committed *hara-kiri* rather than surrender.

The marines at Tarawa lost 1,090 officers and other ranks killed, died of wounds or missing and 2,311 wounded. These heavy losses appalled the American public, and it was little consolation that 4,690 Japanese—the entire garrison except for 17 Japanese and 129 Korean labourers taken prisoners—had died. Unquestionably, it was a mistake to have assaulted Tarawa when the tide was unsuitable. The excessive casualties were due to the marines of the later waves having to wade ashore and to the failure of the naval bombardment and air strikes, which were not executed with sufficient deliberation, to destroy the stout defences. The assault, however, could not have been delivered earlier than November 20 because even that target date was only just met, and the alternative to accepting an unfavourable tide period was postponement of the attack. This would have meant a month's delay, since the first favourable date when the high tide coincided with the most suitable time tactically for an assault was on December 27.

However, it is a facile argument to insist that by giving the Japanese another month in which to prepare their defences in the Gilberts and the Marshalls the capture of the latter would have cost heavier casualties. This contention cannot be advanced as an argument against postponement. As the air assault on Japanese bases would have continued throughout that month it is doubtful if the Japanese could have done much to strengthen their defences or to reinforce their garrisons, and they would still not have foreseen where the Americans would strike. Moreover, those historians who argue that delay would have been dangerous and more costly fail to mention that a postponement would have given the Americans additional time for training and rehearsal, and in a month needed items of equipment might have reached the front-line.

Holland Smith alone among the military leaders claimed after the war that Tarawa was a costly blunder. He asserted that as Tarawa had no particular strategic value it should have been by-passed, with the Americans moving straight into the Marshalls.[3] Guided by hindsight, this view possibly is correct, but at the time nobody appreciated how heavily Japan's air power had been hit in the South Pacific and South-West Pacific operations against Rabaul or that the Combined Fleet would not give battle for the retention of the Marshalls. Nor was the weakness of the defences of the Marshalls realized; for it was still believed that these had been heavily fortified before the war. Considering the knowledge available at the time, the Gilberts were strategically valuable, because only there could fighter and bomber bases be established to support fully the move into the Marshalls. The Gilberts were, in fact, spring-boards for the further advance westward.

When the wisdom of the Tarawa operation is under question, it is well to remember that it was probably inevitable that the first atoll assault in the Central Pacific, no matter when or where it took place, should lead to heavy casualties. The capture of a tiny atoll was a different operation altogether from the seizure of an island by Halsey's or MacArthur's forces. An atoll gave little room for manoeuvre while the islands—such as Guadalcanal and Bougainville—were mostly of considerable extent. The technique of amphibious landings on atolls was still little understood and it needed the hard stimulus of practical experience before perfection could be attained. Tarawa revealed many faults, deficiencies and misconceptions. If its capture was wasteful of lives, it certainly saved many lives later, not because the Japanese were denied an additional month in which to prepare, but because the lessons of Tarawa were assimilated quickly and applied immediately, effecting enormous improvements in administration, organization and tactics, which reduced casualties. In spite of the blunder of going ashore when the tide was unfavourable and the loss of perhaps twice the number of lives that should have been lost, the conclusion is inevitable that Tarawa was worthwhile strategically and tactically.

Planning for the next jump forward, the capture of the Marshalls, was in hand before the Gilberts had been secured. The original intention was to assault simultaneously Maloelap, Wotje and Kwajalein atolls, possession of all three of which was considered necessary to secure the victory Nimitz sought. However, the lesson drawn by Holland Smith from the fighting for Tarawa was that the American forces were not yet sufficiently strong to undertake three major assaults simultaneously. He proposed therefore that Maloelap and Wotje be taken first and that Kwajalein, the Japanese headquarters, be attacked after the first two had been secured. Spruance and Turner supported his recommendation, but Nimitz, with great boldness and sure strategical sense, suggested that Maloelap and Wotje be by-passed and that the assault be carried straight into the heart of the Marshalls by attacking Kwajalein alone. His subordinates, with the memory of the difficulties and casualties of Tarawa still fresh in their minds, protested vigorously against such a course. Nimitz, however, remained adamant. He divined that a move against Kwajalein would surprise the Japanese even more than it had surprised his subordinates and

Marines in action in the Pacific islands. Right, 'flushing out' Japanese snipers from a cleverly concealed pillbox. Below, a marine charges into the attack past a wounded soldier receiving first aid

Marines aboard landing craft head towards Saipan Island and some of the bitterest fighting in the Pacific war

American ships launch rockets against the Japanese on Peleliu Island. The Japanese were so well entrenched on this island that initial sea and air bombardments made less impression than usual

that this atoll was likely to be the least well prepared both in the size of its garrison and the strength of its prepared defences. Events proved Nimitz right. The Japanese expected the Americans to move against Mili, Jaluit or Wotje and possibly Maloelap, but not against Kwajalein. They therefore gave preference to the defence of the outer atolls, neglecting to reinforce or strengthen Kwajalein itself.

Nimitz, realizing the need for speed, moved quickly. Early in January 1944 the campaign for the capture of the Marshalls opened. Rear-Admiral Hoover's land-based aircraft, flying from the Ellice Islands and the newly-built airfields in the Gilberts, began continuous raids on Jaluit and Mili so as to neutralize these bases. At the end of the month, on the 29th, an expanded Fast Carrier Task Force under the command of the redoubtable Rear-Admiral Marc A. Mitscher, the greatest carrier task force commander of the war, raided Kwajalein with such effect that in this single raid every Japanese plane on the atoll was destroyed. That night, to prevent aircraft being ferried in under cover of darkness from Eniwetok, the navy bombarded the airfields on Kwajalein, and on the 30th Mitscher's aircraft struck at the aircraft banked up at Eniwetok and hit Kwajalein's defences. Escort carriers of the attack forces dispatched their aircraft to help Mitscher's and the warships began bombarding the defences.

The attackers were divided into two groups. The Northern Attack Force, under Rear-Admiral Richard L. Conolly—'Close in Conolly'—fresh from amphibious experience in the Mediterranean, was to capture Roi and Namur, twin islands linked by a causeway, at the northern end of the atoll. The objective of Turner's Southern Attack Force was Kwajalein Island, in the south-eastern corner of the lagoon. In preliminary operations on the 31st both forces were to seize small islets close to their objectives so that artillery might be landed on them to support the major assaults.

In the south, where the assault on Kwajalein was to be made by the 7th Division, which had been blooded in the capture of Attu, the preliminary operations were carried out smoothly and efficiently. The story in the north was different. Here the assaulting troops, belonging to the 4th Marine Division, had not previously been in combat, their hastily recruited amtrac drivers were undisciplined and, like the crews of the landing craft, inexperienced. Moreover, relations between the marines and naval personnel, especially between the amtrac drivers and the tank-landing-ship crews, were far from cordial, and if the discord was a good deal less than has been claimed, it was nonetheless sufficient to seriously interfere with co-operation between the two services. The landing of artillery on the islets was botched. Some amtracs had to make as many as three journeys from ship to shore, and when these were finished many of the men were exhausted, and there was no opportunity to rest before the assault preparations began. Some of the invaluable amtracs ran out of fuel or were rendered unserviceable. The muddle and confusion in the Northern Attack Force was so great as to gravely jeopardize the assault landings on February 1.

In these circumstances it is not surprising the attack on Roi and Namur on the 1st was slow to get under way. The pre-invasion bombardment, carried out, as one of the lessons learnt at Tarawa, with deliberation so as to destroy rather than neutralize, proved effective, knocking out most of the Japanese fixed defences and killing more than half the defending garrison. But the assaulting troops reached the departure line late and, preceded by the improvised shallow draught gunboats which had been given their first trial at the Treasury Islands, hit the beaches more than two hours behind schedule. When the first waves were dispatched shoreward at Namur almost 40 per cent of the assaulting troops had not yet reached the departure line. Fortunately for the Americans there was no opposition on the beaches. At Roi, in spite of the choppiness of the lagoon waters and numerous collisions between amtracs, the marines landed in good order and, pushing rapidly inland, captured the island by nightfall. The piecemeal, disordered landings on Namur flaked out quickly, the assault losing momentum because of the late arrival of a great part of the force.

On Namur the marines progressed slowly as they pushed

inland over the wilderness of rubble from the bombardment and air strikes. In the process of reducing by-passed pillboxes and blockhouses infantry-engineer demolition squads exploded stored Japanese ammunition. The first explosion, followed within thirty minutes by two violent but smaller blasts, showered a wide area with fragments of all kinds, blanketed the island under a thick cloud of smoke, and killed many Americans and Japanese. The regimental commander estimated that one of his battalions incurred half its casualties in this series of explosions. However, progress was more rapid on the 2nd and by early afternoon the island had been captured.

At Kwajalein, where the one beach suitable for an assault lay at the western end and was but 500 yards wide, the landing was made on time. Here, in contrast to Roi-Namur, the seas were smooth and in twelve minutes 1,200 troops were ashore and by nightfall no fewer than 11,000. Since the attackers had to drive the full length of the island, the advance was made throughout on a narrow front, with no room for manoeuvre, so that a handful of Japanese were able to slow the rate of advance. Moreover, the soldiers moved forward more deliberately than did the marines on Roi-Namur, preferring to mop up pockets of resistance as they went rather than by-pass them. Aided by naval gunfire, supported from artillery on the nearby islands and bombing and strafing planes, they pushed the Japanese slowly into the island's northern tip. By the afternoon of the 4th all effective resistance on Kwajalein Island had ceased and the entire atoll was in American hands.

Two hundred and sixty-five miles away to the south-east, undefended Majuro Atoll, in the charge of a single Japanese naval warrant officer, was occupied on January 31. Its seizure provide the Americans with an advanced naval base advantageously situated on the eastern rim of the Marshalls.

The capture of Kwajalein was effected comparatively cheaply. At Roi and Namur the marines lost 196 killed and about 550 wounded, and on Kwajalein Island the 7th Division had 177 killed and about 1,000 wounded—a total of 1,923 casualties, less than two-thirds the total incurred in taking Tarawa. Few Japanese survived. At Roi and Namur 51 Japanese and

40 Koreans were taken prisoners; at Kwajalein 49 and 125. Over 8,300 men, a mere fraction of them trained combatant troops, were killed—over 3,500 at Namur and Roi and 4,800 on Kwajalein and its adjacent islets.

Wisely, Nimitz decided to complete the conquest of the Marshalls without delay. He was already ahead of schedule and he did not propose to give the Japanese leaders time to recover their equilibrium. The quicker he put more pressure on them the cheaper would be his victories and the swifter his progress across the Central Pacific. The fact that the capture of Kwajalein had not required the committal of the corps reserve meant that he had troops immediately available for the invasion of Eniwetok, largest of the western Marshalls, with a lagoon relatively free of coral heads and spacious and deep enough to accommodate the entire Pacific Fleet. Its capture would give the Fifth Fleet an excellent forward base for another leap westward and would prevent the Japanese ferrying aircraft into Wake Island or into Maloelap, Wotje, Mili and Jaluit, the by-passed atolls in the Marshalls.

With the fall of Kwajalein, Koga withdrew the Combined Fleet to the Palaus, leaving behind at Eniwetok, to bolster the local naval defences, 2 light cruisers and 8 destroyers. The Japanese were making desperate efforts to make good their air crew losses, but the skilled pilots and experienced air crews who had been sacrificed in the Coral Sea and Midway battles and in the defence of Rabaul were irreplaceable. The training of their successors was inadequate. So urgently needed were pilots and crewmen that they had to be dispatched from Japan to the front-line bases with but enough training to have a reasonable chance of successfully flying to their destination.

On February 17 and 18 Mitscher's strong carrier task force bombarded Truk heavily, and at the same time battleships, cruisers and destroyers swept the adjacent waters in pursuit of shipping. This two-day raid revealed that 'Fortress Truk's' claim to invincibility was as hollow as had been Singapore's. Rather belatedly, the belief that before the war Japan had strongly fortified her mandated islands was found to be a myth. Truk's defences were a great deal less formidable than had been imagined. Striking first at Truk's air strength and then at shipping, the two-day raid destroyed about 200 aircraft and some 200,000 tons of shipping. During this attack the first carrier-based night strike against shipping in the history of the United States Navy was delivered. When the last American planes left Truk on the 18th, Koga's 2 light cruisers and 4 of his 8 destroyers had been sunk, as well as 3 auxiliary cruisers, 2 submarine tenders, a number of smaller naval vessels, 5 tankers and 17 cargo ships. American losses were light. The carrier *Intrepid* (33,100, 1943), hit by a night-flying torpedo plane and knocked out for several months with the loss of 11 killed and 17 injured, was the only major American vessel severely damaged. Thirteen bombers and 12 fighters were lost and 29 pilots and crewmen killed or missing.

On the 23rd Mitscher hit Guam, Tinian and Saipan, adding another 150 aircraft, newly arrived from Japan, to his bag and, more important, securing excellent photographs of airfields and beaches against the day when the Central Pacific drive would move into the Marianas.

Against Eniwetok the tactics which had been successful at Kwajalein were employed. The islands of Engebi, Parry and Eniwetok were prepared for assault by aerial bombing, naval gunfire and artillery bombardment. With a superiority of only two to one, the assault troops could not take all three islands simultaneously. On February 18 the 22nd Marines landed on Engebi Island against light opposition and six hours later had captured the island. Eniwetok, assaulted the same day by units of the 7th Division, proved more difficult. Instead of the stout blockhouses and pillboxes built above ground level which had been encountered at Tarawa and Kwajalein, the defences consisted mainly of invisible, well camouflaged foxholes and trenches. These were not destroyed by the bombardment and at Eniwetok, unlike Engebi and Parry, artillery support from neighbouring islets was lacking. The assaulting troops met heavy machine-gun, mortar, grenade and rifle fire on the beaches, and as they pressed inland they had to beat off strong counter-attacks launched under cover of mortar barrages. A marine landing team had to go to the assistance of the two battalions of the 27th Infantry Division before, after three days' fighting, Eniwetok was captured. Parry Island, like Engebi, was taken in a single day on the 22nd.

Eniwetok's capture was effected for the loss of 262 Americans killed, 77 missing and 757 wounded. As elsewhere, the Japanese garrison died almost to a man, only 66 Japanese and Koreans being taken prisoners.

The Central Pacific drive was the main Allied effort and with the taking of the Gilberts and the Marshalls the threat of invasion was already casting its shadow over Japan, although the Allied forces were still many hundreds of miles from the Japanese mainland. The Fifth Fleet had made tremendous strides in the techniques of amphibious warfare between Tarawa and Eniwetok, and with the conquest of the Marshalls it had become a superbly efficient organization. The Allies had come a long way from those early days in 1942 when all was crumbling before the onslaught of the Japanese hordes. First in the South-West Pacific, then in the South Pacific and now in the Central Pacific the myth of Japanese invincibility had been unmasked. The Japanese were courageous fighters, but courage alone could not win the war for them.

NOTES AND REFERENCES

1. George C. Kenney, *General Kenney Reports*, 319-21.
2. James R. Stockman, *The Battle for Tarawa*, 4, n. 12.
3. Holland M. Smith, *Coral and Brass*, 111-2.

FURTHER READING:

The United States Army official history is Philip A. Crowl and Edmund G. Love, *Seizure of the Gilberts and Marshalls* (Washington, 1955), and should be read in conjunction with S. E. Morison's *Aleutians, Gilberts and Marshalls, June 1942- April 1944* (Chicago, 1952) and the official history of the United States Army Air Forces in World War II—vol. iv: *The Pacific, Guadalcanal to Saipan*—mentioned in previous reading lists. The Australian official histories and Potter and Nimitz, *The Great Sea War*, details of which appear in earlier reading lists, should also be consulted. Among other books may be mentioned Holland M. Smith, *Coral and Brass* (New York 1949), James R. Stockman, *The Battle for Tarawa* (Washington, 1947), the official monograph of the United States Marine Corps, Peter A. Isely and Philip A. Crowl, *The United States Marines and Amphibious War* (Princeton, 1951), Robert D. Heinl, *The Marshalls: Increasing the Tempo* (Washington, 1954) and Henry I. Shaw and Douglas T. Kane, *History of the United States Marine Corps Operations in World War II*, vol. ii: *Isolation of Rabaul* (Washington, 1963). Two popular accounts are Fletcher Pratt's *The Marines' War* (New York, 1948) and Robert Sherrod's *Tarawa: The Story of a Battle* (New York, 1944). John Miller's *Cartwheel: The Reduction of Rabaul* (Washington, 1959) and John N. Rentz, *Bougainville and the Northern Solomons* (Washington, 1948) cover the South Pacific area operations, particularly Bougainville.

eleven

TOWARDS THE PHILIPPINES

Admiral Halsey's drive up the Solomons and General Mac-Arthur's campaign in New Guinea were launched to pave the way for the storming of Rabaul, centre of the spider-web of Japanese defences. At the time it seemed that Rabaul would have to be captured, no matter what the cost in lives, ships and aircraft. Aloof from the anxieties of the day-to-day direction of operations, the Washington planners were the first to sense that the capture of Rabaul might not be necessary. This feeling quickly hardened into conviction as events and plans moved forward and by August 1943, when President Roosevelt and Mr Churchill met for the Quadrant Conference at Quebec, the United States Chiefs of Staff had agreed to by-pass Rabaul. Their views being accepted by the Combined Chiefs of Staff, the Quadrant Conference, in confirming that the principal offensive against Japan was to be by way of the Central Pacific, directed that Rabaul should be by-passed and that MacArthur, seizing Manus in the Admiralty Islands and Kavieng in New Ireland, should advance along the north coast of New Guinea to the Vogelkop Peninsula of Dutch New Guinea.

MacArthur was unenthusiastic about these decisions. Despite earlier rebuffs, he still clung to his belief that the main Allied effort should be made in the South-West Pacific. What most troubled MacArthur was that his forces had been given no mission beyond the Vogelkop Peninsula. This seemed to indicate he was to be pushed on to the sidelines, and it heightened his opposition to the doctrine that strategically, logistically and tactically the shorter and more direct Central Pacific route represented the best approach to Japan. Not surprisingly, his immediate reaction was to insist that Rabaul should be captured and again urge that the main Allied effort should be made under his command and in his theatre of operations. Both proposals were rejected, but astute General Marshall, aware that to some extent MacArthur's arguments were influenced by his vanity and personal ambition, directed him to plan to advance from the Vogelkop Peninsula into Mindanao for the reconquest of the Philippines.

This tactful instruction considerably mollified MacArthur. He saw in it the promise of an opportunity to fulfil his 'I shall return' promise to the Filipinos. Probably he had seen earlier that Rabaul could be by-passed and he now agreed to this, but his conviction that the main thrust should be along the New Guinea-Philippines axis remained unshaken. As late as February 1944 he sent General Sutherland to Washington to again urge adoption of his plan.

While higher strategy was being debated, the Japanese in the South-West Pacific were under relentless pressure. Allied PT boats carried on an unceasing and successful campaign against Japanese supply lines, sinking numerous loaded barges as they crept southwards, thus depriving front-line troops of needed ammunition, food and medical supplies. Everywhere in forward areas the Japanese were half starved and suffering from illness as they were called upon to meet Allied offensive thrusts. Their courage and tenacity remained unbroken, but victory long since had slipped from their grasp.

Having captured Sattelberg, the Australians in the New Guinea coastal area were confronted by naturally strong defensive positions in tangled country. Clearing the Gusika-

Wareo area of Japanese was slow, heart-breaking work. It began with the re-opening of contact with the force isolated on Pabu. Aided by three tanks, Gusika, on the coast, was captured on November 29, and while another Australian force pushed westward along the Wareo track from Pabu, a third force advanced from Sattelberg down the Song valley, forced a crossing of the river and against heavy resistance occupied Kuanko on December 1. The Japanese fought stoutly and not until the 8th were the Australians able to enter Wareo, which had been abandoned.

Although weary from months of continuous and difficult campaigning under conditions of unimaginable hardship, the Australians resolutely pursued the Japanese, now in full retreat. Their ill-equipped rearguard fought courageously, but the Australian advance was slowed more by the difficulties of supply and terrain. On January 15 the Australians reached Sio. Here the 5th Australian Division took over the pursuit from the 9th, but monsoonal conditions along the coast slowed the advance.

Inland vigorous Australian patrolling, including several deep penetrations lasting from seven to ten days, prevented Japanese incursions into the Ramu and Markham Valleys. Early in December a Japanese attack in the Kesawai area was defeated, and by the end of the month the Australians in the Finis-terres had gained a lodgment on dominating Shaggy Ridge, narrow, razor-backed and mist-veiled, 5,000 feet high, the outpost of the main Japanese positions on Kankiryo Ridge.

On December 15 the 112th United States Cavalry Regiment, meeting light opposition, seized Pilelo Island and the Arawe Peninsula, at the southern end of New Britain, but its attempt to cut the Japanese escape route at Umtingalu, to the north-east, was repulsed when twelve of its fifteen rubber boats were sunk and the weaponless survivors had to be rescued by small boats and taken to the main landing beach at Arawe. On the 26th the 1st United States Marine Division landed at Cape Gloucester, in south-west New Britain, where drenching rain, swampy ground and thick jungle proved more formidable obstacles to progress than the half-hearted Japanese defence. By the 29th, however, the airfield was in American hands.

Neither Arawe nor Cape Gloucester were worth their cost of over 300 killed and more than 1,100 wounded. They were not developed as major airfields, nor did Arawe become a PT base. The decision to by-pass Rabaul had rendered both landings unnecessary, and the Allies could have effectively controlled Dampier and Vitiaz Straits without their capture. As events were to prove, it would have been more profitable to have moved into Saidor earlier and in greater strength.

The Saidor landing took place on January 2 1944, when a regimental combat team of the 32nd United States Division went ashore without difficulty. Brigadier-General Clarence A. Martin appealed for reinforcements, so that he might push inland to cut off the retreating Japanese, retiring before the Australians advancing from the Finschhafen-Sattelberg area by way of Sio, 65 air miles from Saidor. But higher authority restricted his mission to cutting the coastal route. Nonetheless, in their frightful retreat over the inland tracks the Japanese lost heavily. Many were killed by the pursuing Australians, but the heaviest toll was taken by starvation, disease and exhaustion, thousands dying in the inhospitable jungle and on the steep mountain slopes. Of some 12,600 Japanese who had fought in the Sattelberg area probably not more than 4,300 staggered into Madang weeks later.

American patrols from Saidor linked up with the Australians near the Yaut River, fourteen miles south-east of Saidor, on February 10. The 7th Australian Division, having overrun the strong Japanese defensive positions in the Finisterres and broken out of the Ramu Valley, made contact with the Americans at Kul, 35 miles north-west of Saidor, on March 21 and captured Bogadjim, on Astrolabe Bay, on April 13. With a small American patrol, the Australians entered Madang, which the Japanese had evacuated, on April 24.

Throughout this period the air forces of the South-West Pacific and South Pacific areas continued their neutralization of Rabaul. At first their efforts to pound the Japanese base were repeatedly foiled by the clouds which habitually built up

over Rabaul in the afternoons, but once the Bougainville airfields were completed Rabaul could be attacked in the mor-
nings, before the clouds obscured the target. This systematic
aerial bombardment, coupled with the pressure exerted on the
Japanese by the Central Pacific drive, rendered Rabaul impotent. After the November disasters the Japanese burrowed
underground and by January their headquarters and other
installations were so deep beneath the coral that they were
impervious to air attack. Neither the harbour nor the airfields
could go underground, however, and they were attacked to such
good purpose that by January ships were no longer using
Rabaul and by mid-February the airfields were bereft of aircraft.

With the Central Pacific drive well under way, there was need
early in 1944 for future plans to be determined. The two offensives were converging and it was essential that they should be
closely co-ordinated. Moreover, MacArthur and Halsey were
dependent for carrier support upon Nimitz and if they wished
to borrow carrier task forces their operations had to be timed so
they would fit into the Central Pacific timetable. The Joint
Chiefs of Staff rejected MacArthur's plea for unity of command,
vested in himself, over the forces of the South-West Pacific and
South Pacific when they advanced into the Bismarck Archipelago preparatory to invading the Philippines, but ordered
Nimitz to attach more warships and assault shipping to Mac-
Arthur's and Halsey's forces. He was told also to provide fleet
support and cover, under his direct command, for the projected
invasions of Manus and Kavieng. Halsey, Nimitz, Kenney and
Sutherland separately visited Washington for strategic discussions, either before or after a meeting of the senior leaders
at Pearl Harbour on January 27.

The decisions reached were never implemented as originally
planned. Events telescoped so rapidly that the pace of the war
began to outstrip planning, but as a consequence of the visits
of Pacific commanders to Washington (with the exception of
MacArthur) and the strategical discussions which took place
the planners in Washington knew the problems and divergent

views of the different commanders charged with the conduct of actual operations.

On February 15 Major-General H. E. Barrowclough's 3rd New Zealand Division, with American specialist troops attached, seized the Green Islands, 37 miles north-east of Buka. By the 20th the small Japanese garrison had been killed. Here a PT boat base was opened and before the end of March fighters and light bombers were flying from its new airfields to attack Kavieng, previously within range only of heavy bombers from Bougainville.

The invasion of the Admiralties, 200 miles north-east of New Guinea, followed. Because his airmen could see few signs of any Japanese—they noted particularly the absence of washing hanging out to dry—and were not being fired at, Kenney concluded Los Negros and Manus were lightly held and Mac-Arthur agreed to his suggestion of a reconnaissance in force, although his own Intelligence chief, General Willoughby, estimated the Japanese garrison at about 4,000. What the Allied leaders did not know was that the Japanese commander, Colonel Yoshio Ezaki, had ordered his troops not to fire on Allied aircraft or to move about in daytime, hoping thus to conceal his defence positions. Through this misunderstanding, the invasion of the Admiralties was mounted ahead of schedule.

On February 29, with MacArthur and Kinkaid watching from the bridge of the cruiser *Phoenix* (9,700, 1938), 1,000 men under Brigadier-General William C. Chase, with an A.N.G.A.U. detachment of Australians, landed at the south end of Hyane Harbour, on the east side of Los Negros. Bad weather prevented more than token air support, but a naval bombardment aided the troops and by 1250, although fired on from both points at the harbour entrance, they were all ashore. The Japanese, who had expected any landing to be by way of the front door, Seeadler Harbour, were taken by surprise, and Momote airfield, overgrown with weeds and littered with the debris of smashed aircraft, was quickly occupied. Landing at 1600, MacArthur ordered Chase to remain on the island, holding the airfield at all cost.

The decision to turn the reconnaissance into an invasion was a bold one, but Ezaki, probably expecting a further landing and handicapped by a lack of small boats in which to transfer troops from Manus to Los Negros, reacted slowly. During the first two nights ashore only small attacks and attempts at infiltration troubled the Americans, and when stronger attacks were launched on the night of the 3rd-4th they were unco-ordinated and unskilfully delivered, so that they were easily repulsed. Reinforcements having been brought in, the Americans on the 6th seized Salami Plantation, on Seeadler Harbour, where three days later further troops were landed. The same day Australian Kittyhawks landed on Momote airfield.

With Negros firmly held, the Americans turned to the neighbouring island of Manus, where a landing was made on the 15th at Lugos Mission. Two days later the airstrip was taken and on the 18th Lorengau village was occupied. By the end of the month mopping-up had been completed and, except for the seizure of a few outlying islands early in April, the Admiralties had changed hands. A great strategic prize, they became a fighter and bomber base, with runways on outlying islands for carrier aircraft, in future operations. At Seeadler Harbour, a superb deep water port, one of the largest naval bases in the Pacific was constructed. Here the Third, Fifth and Seventh Fleets were all serviced. The cost had been small. American losses were 326 killed, 4 missing and 1,189 wounded. Probably 4,380 Japanese, 3,280 of whom were buried by the Americans, were killed, and 75 prisoners were taken.

While the Allies were capturing the Admiralty Islands, the long-awaited Japanese counter-offensive to recapture Empress Augusta Bay was delivered. Shortage of landing craft prevented General Hyakutake combining an overland advance with an amphibious assault, but he used barges to ferry artillery and other heavy equipment to the vicinity of Cape Torokina, where it was laboriously manhandled inland over the steep hills. The Japanese had the advantage of the higher ground, which gave them good observation of the entire American perimeter and enabled them to bring artillery fire to bear on all parts of the beachhead. They had estimated the Allied strength at about 30,000, of whom they thought about 10,000 were Allied ground crews. This was a serious under-estimate, since it cut the Allied strength by half.

With only between 15,000 and 19,000 men forward, Hyakutake had little prospect of driving the Allies into the sea, and he threw away such advantages as he had by loose security, which allowed the Americans to capture documents detailing the Japanese plans and disclosing their artillery positions. Hyakutake divided his force into three groups, each of which attacked a different sector of the perimeter. The attack, opening on March 8, lasted sixteen days, but without air support and with inadequate artillery the attackers scored only local successes, and eventually, the Americans with the aid of tanks, bazookas and flame-throwers, drove them from the ground they had captured. On the 27th the Japanese XVII Army, having lost over 5,000 men killed as against 263 Americans, was ordered to retreat.

While the fighting on Bougainville and in the Admiralties was in progress Allied strategy was revised. Early in March, MacArthur, confident of the outcome of the Admiralty invasion, suggested that he at once capture Kavieng and move straight into Hollandia, in Dutch New Guinea. Since the latter objective was beyond the range of his most westerly-based fighters, his plan was feasible only if Nimitz could lend him carrier support. On the 12th, therefore, the Joint Chiefs of Staff issued a new directive. This reaffirmed the principle of advancing in both the Central Pacific and the South-West Pacific, and ordered the cancellation of the assault on Kavieng, which neither Halsey nor Nimitz favoured. In its place MacArthur was to take Emirau Island, north-west of Kavieng and midway between it and Manus, and, neutralizing Rabaul and Kavieng with minimum forces and by-passing Wewak and Hansa Bay, he was to seize Hollandia, and be ready to invade the Philippines on November 15. For his part, Nimitz, beginning in mid-June, was to seize Saipan, Tinian and Guam in the Marianas. Furthermore, in mid-September, he was to secure bases in the Palaus, in time to cover MacArthur's movement into the Philippines.

The seizure of Emirau Island presented no difficulties. There were no Japanese there and it was occupied on March 20, only eight days after the issue of the directive from the Joint Chiefs of Staff. Considering that it was the largest amphibious operation yet undertaken in the South-West Pacific, involving the movement of some 80,000 men and the employment of over 110 vessels, including landing craft, the Hollandia operation was staged with equal speed. Knowledge of the area was scanty and an attempt to rectify this ended disastrously when a party of veteran Australian and New Guinea scouts, landed in the area by an American submarine, were betrayed to the Japanese by natives. They were killed or dispersed, a few living miserably in the jungle until they came into the Allied lines after the landing. One New Guinea soldier walked 125 miles to Aitape, in Australian New Guinea, where a landing was made as part of the Hollandia operation so as to afford air support for Hollandia after the departure of the carrier task forces.

The landings at Aitape and Hollandia were made simultaneously on April 22. Aitape was secured with little difficulty and within 48 hours the captured airfield was ready for occupation by Australian Kittyhawks. At Hollandia, where estimates of Japanese strength ranged from 9,000 to 14,000 General Eichelberger landed his I United States Corps simultaneously at Humboldt Bay and, 25 miles to the west, at Tanahmerah Bay. Between them lay the short range of the 7,000-foot high Cyclops Mountains, with the Japanese airfields on the Lake Sentani Plain south of the mountains. The untried 24th United States Division was to make the main effort from Tanahmerah Bay, but when the troops got ashore unopposed except for scattered rifle fire it was found that the main landing beach was small and fringed by swamps, while at the secondary beach a coral reef prevented landing craft beaching except at high tide. Not only was the landing of supplies difficult, but congestion on the beach quickly became acute, especially as the road inland to the Lake Sentani Plain, which Allied planners had believed to be a motor road in reasonable condition, proved to be a mere track, winding across the hills in a series of hairpin bends and with slopes in places as steep as 60 degrees. In these circumstances the main effort was transferred to Humboldt Bay.

However, the 24th Division met little resistance. Elaborate deception measures had been taken to suggest that the next Allied objectives were Hansa Bay and Wewak. Both were bombed and shelled, PT boats were active in patrolling the coast, submarines launched empty rubber boats to suggest that reconnaissance parties were ashore and dummy parachutists were dropped. Whether or not these measures were successful, the Japanese defences at Tanahmerah Bay were found unfinished and unmanned, and although heavy rain turned the inland track into a quagmire, the 24th Division, using at one stage 3,500 combat troops to hand carry supplies forward and arranging air drops from eastern New Guinea when the weather permitted, struggled across the hills to capture the Hollandia airfield on the 26th. It was a fine achievement for a green division. The same day, after an amphibious crossing of Lake Sentani, the 41st Division occupied the Cyclops and Sentani airfields, and that afternoon linked hands with the 24th Division. Surprise had also been secured at Humboldt Bay, where enemy resistance had been less than had been anticipated.

The Japanese at Hollandia, mostly air force and service personnel, had no stomach for a fight and they fled into the jungle, to be harassed by American patrols. This was another frightful Japanese retreat. Their nearest base was at Sarmi, 145 miles to the west-north-west, and of some 7,200 men who set out to reach it all but about 1,000 died of starvation or disease on the way. Another 3,300 had been killed by the Americans, who captured the unusually large total of 611 prisoners. American casualties from the day of the landings to June 6, by which date no Japanese were left in the area, totalled 124 killed, 28 missing and 1,057 wounded.

There was no Japanese naval reaction and little air reaction to the Hollandia operations. The carriers of Mitscher's Task Force 58 hit the Palaus on March 30 and 31 and raided other islands in the western Carolines, including Yap, Ulithi, Ngulu and Woleai. These raids forced the Combined Fleet to relinquish the Palaus as an advanced base, so that Koga was in no position to intervene when the Hollandia landings took place. Mitscher's carrier planes claimed to have destroyed about 150 aircraft in the air or on the ground and to have sunk two destroyers, four escort vessels and about 104,000 tons of merchant and naval shipping. Allied air raids on the Hollandia fields between March 30 and April 3 had destroyed or damaged 300 Japanese aircraft, mainly on the ground, a loss which could not be made good. The result was that only a few Japanese planes attempted to raid the Hollandia beach-heads and most of these were successfully intercepted. An indication of the destruction which might have been wrought on the congested beaches if the Japanese had been able to mount strong attacks was provided by a solitary night-flying plane. At Humboldt Bay one of its bombs, hitting a Japanese ammunition dump, started a series of fires which destroyed about 60 per cent of the ammunition and rations then on the beach—the equivalent of eleven LST loads.

With the landings at Hollandia and Aitape about 180,000 Japanese troops and 20,000 civilian workers had been by-passed, and to all intents and purposes they were out of the war for the duration. No supplies could reach them except by submarine. Rabaul and Kavieng, although still defensively strong, were incapable of further offensive action. The XVIII Japanese Army at Wewak, commanded by General Adachi, launched a counter-offensive against Aitape, with about 20,000 of his 50,000 troops, but they were short of weapons, ammunition, essential equipment and food, and, as Adachi realistically realized even before the attack, his supply problems had doomed his counter-offensive even as his troops got into position. His attack on the night of July 10-11 broke through the first American line along the Driniumor River but then stalled, and when the Americans launched an offensive on the 31st Adachi had already decided to retreat. Between April 22 and August 25 the Japanese lost perhaps 9,000 men killed, almost half the force Adachi had employed forward in his attack. In the same period 98 Japanese were taken prisoners and the Allies lost 440 killed, 10 missing and 2,550 wounded.

Under the impetus of the Allied offensives, the Japanese

brought forward reinforcements and effected changes in their command structure. All Japanese army units in the Central Pacific islands were placed under XXXI Army, whose commander, Major-General Hideyoshi Obata, established his headquarters on Guam. He was answerable directly to the headquarters of the Combined Fleet. The defence of the Palaus became the responsibility of the Second Area Army, which assumed command of rear echelons and other forces previously belonging to the Eighth Area Army. Lieutenant-General Sadae Inoue, commanding the 14th Division, was appointed Palau Sector Group commander. Because the Eighth Area Army and XVII Army had been isolated, command of the XVIII Army and 4th Air Army was transferred to Second Area Army, which thus became responsible for the Japanese bases at Hansa Bay, Wewak, Aitape and Hollandia. At the same time control of the Second Area Army passed from Imperial General Headquarters to the Southern Army, whose commander, still Count Terauchi, had his headquarters at Singapore. The headquarters of Second Area Army were located at Manado, in the Celebes, where it controlled the II, XVIII and XIX Armies—about 170,000 troops, of whom 50,000, forming the II Army, were in western New Guinea and the Halmahera area and another 50,000, belonging to the XIX Army, in the Netherlands East Indies. In the Philippines the total Japanese strength was around 100,000, of whom about 45,000 were combat troops of the XIV Army. The XXXI Army in the Central Pacific totalled about 60,000 men, half of whom were in the Palaus.

In bringing reinforcements forward the Japanese suffered heavy losses. United States submarines, now armed with more dependable torpedoes and their crews more experienced, were taking an increasingly heavy toll of Japanese shipping. Japanese shipping lanes were now restricted to the Western Pacific, and the ability to read the Japanese naval codes placed priceless information in Allied hands regarding the departure and routes of convoys. In the last four months of 1943 American submarines sank 147 Japanese ships of 651,235 gross tons. The figures rose to 179 ships and 798,947 gross tons for the first four months of 1944 and to 219 and 1,018,736 for May to August inclusive.

In February a fast convoy carrying troops from Korea to reinforce Saipan and Guam was intercepted by the submarine *Trout* (1,475, 1940), which sank a transport containing 4,124 soldiers, more than half of whom were drowned, before she herself was sunk by depth charges. In March the light cruiser *Tatsuta* and two merchantmen in a convoy carrying reinforcements to the Marianas were sunk by *Sandlance* (1,525, 1943), and early in April one of seven transports bound for the Marianas and Truk was sunk. The convoy carrying the bulk of the Japanese 35th Division from Shanghai to the Vogelkop Peninsula and western New Guinea lost four of its transports and thousands of the soldiers were drowned. The convoy taking the 43rd Division to the Marianas also lost heavily, although the remnants of the division reached their destination in May. Early in June a convoy carrying 7,200 men to reinforce Saipan lost five of its seven transports and freighters to United States submarines, and although the escorts picked up most of the soldiers they were landed at Saipan without their weapons and tanks. The sinking of transports returning empty after having delivered their troops also placed a heavy strain on the Japanese transport service and dislocated timetables for the reinforcement of the scattered garrisons.

MacArthur's next leap forward was to Wakde Island, 130 miles north-west of Hollandia, which was defended by about 800 men. Occupation of Wakde, with its airfield, would afford air support for MacArthur's next forward move to Biak, the large island in the mouth of Geelvink Bay, 190 miles north-west of Wakde. Wakde lay only two miles off the New Guinea shore, and to ensure artillery support for its assault and to prevent it being shelled by the Japanese after its capture the American regimental combat team assigned to the attack landed on the mainland on May 17. There was no opposition. A beach-head at Arare was quickly developed and the same day Insoemanai Island, 3,500 yards off shore, was occupied. Artillery fire was then opened on Wakde from Arare and Insoemanai, and next day Wakde was invaded. The island was cleared in two days and on the 21st the first aircraft landed. Japanese casualties in these operations were over 800 killed against an Allied loss of 43 killed and 139 wounded. Four Japanese were taken prisoners. A drive on the mainland towards Sarmi continued until the beginning of September, when Allied casualties had risen to over 400 killed and 15,000 wounded, with 3,870 Japanese killed and 51 captured.

The invasion of Biak followed on May 27. The Hurricane Task Force was comprised of the remainder of the 41st United States Division—it had provided a regimental combat team for Wakde—under the divisional commander, Major-General Horace H. Fuller. It was believed that Biak was lightly held and Fuller expected to take the island quickly, but the Japanese garrison in actual fact totalled over 11,000 men, of whom about 4,000 were trained combat troops. Lieutenant-General Takuzo Numata, chief of staff to the Second Area Army commander, Lieutenant-General Korechika Anami, was on a visit to Biak and assumed command of the defence from the garrison commander, Colonel Nasyiki Kuzume, only relinquishing it when he left the island on June 15.

Biak's three airfields on the south-east shore were needed to support the Central Pacific drive into the Marianas and the further advance up the New Guinea coast. Nimitz had scheduled the invasion of Saipan for June 15 and MacArthur and Kenney wanted bombers operating from Biak by that date. Speed, then, was required in the conquest of Biak.

However, the island proved more difficult to capture than anyone had anticipated. American estimates of the strength of its garrison and defences were sadly astray. Its coral terrain of tangled ridges, steep terraces and deep caves provided naturally strong defensive positions, which the Japanese had skilfully strengthened. These prepared positions lay to the north and west of Mokmer Drome. The first American attack got to within 200 yards of the airfield, but the attackers were then driven back. Reinforcements had to be summoned. By June 8 Mokmer had been seized, but as it was still under heavy fire from the dominating ridges and caves it could neither be repaired nor used.

The entire operation was now running behind schedule. In the next few days little progress was made and Fuller demanded further reinforcements. On the 1st he had occupied Owi and Mios Woendi islands, belonging to the Paidado group off the south-east corner of Biak, but although artillery had been moved into both islands to support the infantry on Biak the attacks against the ridges failed. A fighter strip was begun on Owi and two fighter squadrons flew in on the 21st.

Late in March, when Mitscher's carriers had been sighted heading towards the Palaus for their three-day strikes against that group and the western Carolines, Koga, convinced he must at all cost hold the line of the Marianas, Palaus and western New Guinea, had ordered forward all available aircraft and had directed the fleet to sortie. With his staff, he had then left by air to set up new headquarters at Davao, in Mindanao, but two of the aircraft, including Koga's, crashed when they ran into bad weather. The commander-in-chief of the Combined Fleet was killed. He was succeeded by Admiral Soemu Toyoda, who was ordered by the Naval General Staff to actively seek a decision at sea instead of continuing Koga's purely defensive strategy. He therefore issued orders for Operation *A-GO*, which called for Fleet action in the western Carolines and the use of land-based aircraft to offset Japan's inferiority in ships and aircraft, especially in carriers. The basic conception was to lure the United States Pacific Fleet into a combat area where land-based aircraft could join in attacking it. Toyoda organized a First Mobile Fleet along the lines of Mitscher's carrier task force and placed it under the command of a veteran, Vice-Admiral Jisaburo Ozawa. The plan was based on Toyoda's belief that the Allies intended to pursue only the New Guinea-Philippines axis of advance and that Mitscher's carrier forces would continue to support MacArthur's advance. When the Biak landing was made he realized that as an Allied bomber base within convenient range of the proposed combat area it menaced the successful carrying out of Operation *A-GO*.

Toyoda's reaction therefore was prompt and decisive. He ordered Biak to be reinforced and held and he rushed aircraft from Japan and the Central Pacific to western New Guinea and

Halmahera. This increase in air strength led to raids on Wakde in which 60 Allied aircraft were destroyed, but the onslaught was short-lived, as the unacclimatized air crews quickly fell victims to malaria and jungle fever. The *KON* operation, as the Japanese styled the attempt to reinforce Biak, failed. The first attempt, however, very nearly resulted in disaster to the Allies; for if the Japanese convoy and its escorts had pushed on they would have reached Biak and found no surface forces to oppose them. Not only would the reinforcements have been landed, but the naval force would almost certainly have destroyed the shipping off shore and have created havoc by bombarding the beachhead. An unknown Japanese reconnaissance pilot saved the Allies. He reported Allied naval forces at Biak, including carriers, when in actual fact there was nothing larger than a destroyer, and this caused the Japanese convoy to turn back.

Other attempts were equally unsuccessful, although over about four weeks the Japanese managed to reinforce Biak with some 1,200 men. These were brought in mostly by barge and were used piecemeal as they arrived, so that except to prolong the stubborn defence they did not have much influence on the course of the fighting. On balance, the *KON* operation was costly to the Japanese. It lost them a number of ships sunk, including several barges loaded with troops whose loss could be ill spared.

While these reinforcement efforts were going on the Americans were making little or no progress on Biak. General Krueger, whose Alamo headquarters directed all western New Guinea operations, was dissatisfied. He felt the divisional commander was not pressing the attack sufficiently or dealing ruthlessly enough with the lack of aggressive leadership at battalion and company level, and with MacArthur's approval General Eichelberger took over command on Biak on June 15, the day on which G.H.Q. had expected bombers to be flying from Biak in support of the Saipan invasion. It was intended that Fuller should retain command of his 41st Division, under Eichelberger, but Fuller asked to be relieved of command of the division and requested a posting outside MacArthur's area. This was agreed to.

After the war Eichelberger wrote of Biak[1]: 'Nastier terrain could hardly have been found. Behind the first ridge there were not only caves and the raw upjutting coral cliffs, but also deep ravines and tangled jungle ... As yet we did not definitely know the locations of the major caves which hid the main enemy forces and some of their mortar and mountain batteries. The caves obviously had connecting corridors and exits which permitted the Japanese, literally, to disappear from the face of the earth and to re-appear at will in our midst.'

MacArthur's headquarters had reported optimistically on June 1 that enemy opposition was collapsing and on the 3rd that mopping-up was proceeding. The facts, as we have seen, were very different. Almost no progress had been made and fighting against unyielding resistance was proving costly. The reduction of the caves by flame-throwers, ignited petrol and charges of TNT was a slow and difficult process. In many cases the only way was to seal the entrances and exits, leaving the Japanese within to die of suffocation or starvation. Not until mid-August were the last pockets of Japanese resistance eliminated, and by then the Americans had lost over 400 men killed and more than 2,000 wounded. Japanese losses were 4,700 killed and 220 captured. Kuzume committed *hara-kiri* when he realized the end was near.

The basis of Toyoda's Operation *A-GO* was destroyed when the Central Pacific forces invaded Saipan on June 15. This move took the Japanese commander-in-chief by surprise. Not anticipating further attacks in the Central Pacific, he had denuded his island bases in this area of aircraft so as to reinforce western New Guinea. It is not known exactly how many aircraft were transferred, but estimates range from one-third to one-half the planes which were available in the Central Pacific. Despite his misinterpretation of Allied intentions, Toyoda decided there was still a chance that he could lure the United States Pacific Fleet into a combat area where it could be heavily hit by land-based aircraft and the aircraft of Ozawa's carriers.

The Japanese had about 540 land-based aircraft available, but most were at southward bases and only some 170 were located in the Marianas. By June 15, on Toyoda's orders, the

First Mobile Fleet was in the Philippine Sea, having been hastily recalled from its abortive efforts to reinforce Biak. Its presence and location were reported by patrolling American submarines. In contrast to the success of the United States submarines, the Japanese underwater craft, of which at least twenty-five were scouting or on patrol, furnished Toyoda and Ozawa with practically no information of American movements and failed to sink or damage a single ship. Against these negative results, their losses were extremely heavy, with no fewer than seventeen Japanese submarines sunk.

Admiral Spruance, in command of the Fifth Fleet, had more ships and aircraft than Ozawa. He had 15 carriers and light carriers against 9, 7 battleships against 5, 8 heavy cruisers against 11, 13 light cruisers against 2, and 69 destroyers opposed to a mere 28. The disparity in carrier aircraft was even more marked—956 (475 fighters, 232 dive-bombers, 184 torpedo-bombers) against 473 (222 fighters, 113 dive-bombers, 95 torpedo-bombers). His battleships and cruisers carried 65 float-planes whereas Ozawa's fleet was equipped with only 43.[2] Most important of all, the American carrier pilots were fully trained and thoroughly experienced, but most of Ozawa's aviators were green and inadequately trained. He had only a small leavening of experienced pilots, the few survivors of the squadrons which had dominated the sea skies on the outbreak of war.

Ozawa hoped that land-based aircraft at Guam, Rota and Yap would somewhat redress the balance in his favour and that his numerical disadvantage would be further offset by his carrier-aircraft using these bases for rearming and refuelling. The local air base commanders seem not to have informed him of their severe aircraft losses in the relentless Allied raids. The odds were decidedly against him, but Ozawa was a capable carrier admiral, resolute in action.

His searches were more successful than the American. On the afternoon of the 18th Mitscher's planes failed to locate the Japanese, but Ozawa's found the Americans and Rear-Admiral Sueo Obayashi, commanding Ozawa's van carrier division, late in the afternoon decided to launch a 67-plane strike. He already had some of his aircraft aloft when he received an order from Ozawa announcing that strikes would be launched next day, and he thereupon recalled his aircraft and cancelled the operation. It was perhaps a fateful decision; for had the strike been launched it might well have taken the Americans by surprise and perhaps have gained for Ozawa an initial victory.

During the night Ozawa's scouts successfully shadowed Mitscher's force, but the early American searches on the 19th terminated 40 to 50 miles short of the Japanese van. There was a good deal of air combat over Guam, where American fighters patrolled to prevent Japanese land-based aircraft getting into the air. The first Japanese strike was launched by Obayashi at 0830 and was followed by three further strikes. American fighter interception and anti-aircraft fire were extremely good and the Japanese raids achieved nothing, only one ship being hit in the first raid. The inexperience of the Japanese pilots was obvious. They broke formation as soon as attacked by fighters, failed to co-ordinate their attacks and did not press them home.

Heavy losses were suffered in all but the third strike, and that escaped lightly only because part of the strike force failed to find the target. In the first strike the Japanese lost 42 of 69 planes, in the second 97 out of 128, in the third 7 out of 47 and in the fourth 72 out of 82. Nineteen of the aircraft which took part in this raid landed at Guam, but as the airfield there had been bombed and was under attack at the time most of the Japanese pilots crashed on landing and all 19 aircraft were badly damaged.

Ozawa had deliberately exploited his advantage in range. His aircraft were capable of carrying out strikes at a greater distance than the Americans and he had launched his planes from just beyond the range of the American aircraft. In any case, Mitscher had failed to locate the opposing carriers and he launched no strikes on the 19th. For this Spruance was partly responsible. He had two missions—to protect the Saipan landing and to strike at the Japanese Fleet. He feared that Ozawa might lure him away from Saipan and then strike the beachhead and the shipping there, and for this reason he preferred the Japanese to come to him. These tactics paid off in the heavy toll taken of Japanese planes, and in the long run the destruction of Japanese aircraft and air crews was probably more important than the sinking of their carriers.

The only Japanese carriers sunk on the 19th fell to the torpedoes of United States submarines. *Albacore* (1,525, 1942) hit the big new carrier *Taiho* (29,300, 1943), but a second torpedo was prevented from hitting when a bomber pilot, observing it heading for the carrier, crashed on it and exploded it in a suicide dive. *Taiho* sank when she was ripped apart by a terrific explosion caused by petrol and oil fumes released throughout the ship by the torpedo hit. About 1,600 of her crew were lost. *Cavalla* (1,525, 1944) torpedoed the veteran *Shokaku*, which went down when one of her bombs exploded and shattered her.

Although Mitscher had suitable night-flying aircraft he sent out no searches during the night of the 19th-20th and the Japanese carriers were not located until an afternoon search on the 20th. Ozawa, having transferred his flag from the doomed *Taiho* to a cruiser, at 1300 on the 20th shifted to *Zuikaku*, whose more satisfactory communications brought him the unwelcome news that he had lost 330 aircraft the previous day and now had only 100 planes remaining operational. From the reports of his aviators, however, he believed several American carriers had been sunk and a large number of hostile aircraft shot down. He therefore did not retreat. Mitscher, although the location of the Japanese fleet meant that his aircraft would be operating at extreme range and the late hour would necessitate night recovery operations, put in a strike. The carrier *Hiyo* (24,140, 1941) was sunk, two tankers hit, both being scuttled during the night, and the carriers *Zuikaku* and *Chiyoda* damaged, although each made port. Ozawa managed to get 75 of his remaining planes into the air before the attack, and of these 65 were destroyed, reducing his operational aircraft to only 35.

American losses were also heavy. Many aircraft had to be ditched through lack of fuel or crashed in attempting hazardous night landings. Mitscher, boldly risking submarine attack, lit up the carriers for the returning pilots, and cruisers and destroyers searched the seas with searchlights in an effort to find and rescue aviators forced to ditch. In the actual attack on Ozawa's fleet 20 aircraft had been shot down by fighters or anti-aircraft fire, and a further 80 fell into the sea or crashed, although all but 16 pilots and 33 crewmen were rescued. Ozawa's total losses were 426 aircraft and about 445 carrier crewmen against an American loss of 130 aircraft and 76 air-crew. The Japanese lost at least another 50 planes on Guam and 66 more were shot down on the 24th by an American strike force on its way to pound Iwo Jima and Chichi Jima. No American ships had been sunk, but Tokyo, after first claiming to have sunk eleven United States carriers and destroyed a large number of aircraft, later scaled down its claim to five carriers and at least one battleship.

In the landing on Saipan on June 15, 8,000 assault troops were put ashore at eight beaches along a four-mile front at Charan Kanoa in 20 minutes, and by evening the Americans had no fewer than 20,000 men ashore. The naval and air bombardment, in which rocket-firing aircraft participated for the first time in the Pacific, had left many of the skilfully sited, well camouflaged Japanese positions intact, and artillery, mortar and machine-gun fire on the reef and beaches was heavy from the time the fourth assault wave came ashore. Lieutenant-General Yoshitsugu Saito launched strong counter-attacks on that and the following night, but although those on the night of the 16th-17th were supported by 44 tanks they were repulsed with heavy loss. By the 17th the beachhead was secure, but the first Japanese air attacks, which were to continue, came in that night, sinking or damaging some ships and landing craft. On the 22nd Aslito airfield, which the Americans renamed Isely, received its first fighters, making interception of Japanese raids easier.

Attempts by the Japanese to land reinforcements from Tinian, Guam and Truk came to nought, and an amphibious counter-attack on the 18th was defeated, most of their loaded barges being sunk. Despite these successes there was much hard fighting ahead. The rugged terrain and limestone caves provided naturally strong defensive positions, and although, after the defeat of Ozawa's fleet, Saito could not hope to hold Saipan he was determined to make its capture costly for his opponents. On the night of July 6-7 he staged a massive banzai attack. It met some success, breaking into the American positions, but was finally halted. The Americans had 400 men killed in this attack, but the Japanese lost 4,300. Even this costly onslaught did not end Japanese resistance. Not until August 10 was the island secured, and mopping up of individual Japanese and small parties continued until the war's end.

The capture of Saipan saw some of the bitterest fighting of the Pacific war. More than 67,000 troops were employed in taking it, and of these 3,426 were killed and 13,099 wounded. The Americans killed 23,811 Japanese and many more were entombed in the caves or perished in the jungle. Saito and Admiral Nagumo, who had commanded the Pearl Harbour Striking Force at the beginning of the war, both committed suicide on Saipan. The number of prisoners totalled 1,780, of whom 921 were Japanese and 838 Koreans, and 14,560 civilians, of whom 10,258 were Japanese, were interned, although many men, women and children committed suicide rather than surrender.

Nearby Tinian, doomed once Saipan fell, was invaded on July 24, after it had been softened up by air and naval bombardment. The landing, made over two short beaches on the north-west shore opposite Ushi Point airfield, was supported by artillery on Saipan. Preloaded trucks and vehicles were ferried across the five-mile channel between Saipan and Tinian and, using special landing ramps to get off the beaches, greatly eased the supply problem and beach congestion. For the first time napalm was used against the Japanese. It was first dropped from the air on the 22nd, but until the right mixture of napalm powder with gasoline or oil had been worked out it was not particularly effective.

Tinian was secured by August 1, but, as at Saipan, mopping up continued for several months and many Japanese were entombed in caves at the island's south end. The capture of Tinian and the mopping-up operations during the next three months cost the Americans 427 men killed and 1,941 wounded, while probably some 8,000 Japanese were killed or committed suicide and 252 surrendered.

Three days before the landing on Tinian, General Geiger's III Amphibious Corps, comprising the 3rd Marine Division and 1st Provisional Marine Brigade, and the 77th Infantry Division, invaded Guam, where the Japanese had a garrison of around 19,000 men. The Guam landing was notable, first, because the pre-landing air and naval bombardment was the most prolonged yet delivered in the Pacific and, second, the underwater obstacles were the most formidable so far encountered. The unexpected stubbornness of the Japanese defence of Saipan, which caused D-day for Guam to be postponed from June 18 to July 21, partly accounted for the prolonged air and naval softening-up, but Japanese defences were still strong when the Americans landed.

The landings were made at Asan in the north and Agat Bay in the south. Both had serious disadvantages. The Asan beaches were faced by a semi-circle of hills, the Agat overlooked by high cliffs. Losses to Rear-Admiral Conolly's force on the beaches were heavy, but the resistance was strongest at Agat. Here accurate artillery and mortar fire was brought down on the reef and beaches from the high ground. Many amtracs and LTV's were put out of action. At Asan the Japanese counter-attacked at daybreak on the 22nd, but were beaten back. A heavier counter-attack, carefully prepared and skilfully executed, was delivered on the 25th. This developed into the decisive battle for Guam and the Japanese assaults were defeated with heavy loss after fierce fighting. They then retreated to the northern end of the island for a last stand in the rugged ground of Mount Santa Rosa, on the eastern shore, five miles south of Pati Point.

By August 12 Guam was secured, but many Japanese remained at large and the mopping up of guerillas continued until the end of the war. The island's reconquest cost the Americans 1,290 men killed, 145 missing and 5,648 wounded. Almost 18,000 Japanese were killed and 1,250 captured, of whom 8,500 were killed or taken prisoners after August 10.

These operations in the Marianas were supported by Mitscher's carrier aircraft and Kenney's land-based aircraft of the Allied air forces in the South-West Pacific. The delay in taking Biak meant that Wakde had to serve as the principal base for Kenney's Australian and American squadrons, but it successfully fulfilled this role. Even with the capture of Biak more airfields were still needed to support MacArthur's New Guinea operations and his movement into the Philippines.

MacArthur therefore decided to invade Noemfoor Island, midway between Biak and the Japanese base of Manokwari, at the north-east tip of the Vogelkop Peninsula. The Cyclone Task Force of 8,000 men landed on Noemfoor on July 2. The pre-assault naval bombardment was the heaviest yet delivered by South-West Pacific forces, but there was no opposition on the beaches. On the 3rd and 4th the assault troops were reinforced by the 503rd United States Parachute Regiment, who were dropped on Kamiri Drome instead of being brought forward by sea. The Japanese on Noemfoor did not exceed 2,000 men, of whom less than half were combat infantry, and although mopping up continued until the end of August the airfield area was secured in the first day's operations. American losses, including casualties during the mopping up, were 63 killed, 3 missing and 343 wounded. About 1,730 Japanese were killed and 186 captured.

MacArthur's next objective was the Vogelkop Peninsula. He decided to by-pass Manokwari, which, as the principal Japanese base and the location of their headquarters, was likely to be strongly held. His original plan was to seize Sorong, a Japanese troop and supply base on a small island off the peninsula's north-west shore, and Waigeo Island, 60 miles north-west of Sorong. However, this plan was cancelled in favour of capturing Mar and Sansapor, two mainland villages 70 miles north-east of Sorong and 60 miles east of Waigeo. The landing at Mar was made on July 30, six weeks earlier than originally planned. To secure surprise there was no pre-assault air or naval bombardment and the assaulting forces were under strict radio silence until they got ashore. These measures succeeded and there was no opposition. Widespread attacks on Manokwari, Sorong and airfields in the Halmahera-Ceram-Ambon area prevented Japanese air interference. On the 31st troops moved to Cape Sansapor without resistance, and by August 17 the first air strip was operational.

The New Guinea operations were making good progress. As his next objective MacArthur had the choice of Halmahera or Morotai. As the former island was believed to be garrisoned by 30,000 men, including at least 11,000 combat effectives, he decided its capture might prove costly and resolved to take Morotai Island, which the Japanese had neglected. They had started to construct an airfield there, but had abandoned it and G.H.Q. believed that there were only about 500 men on the island—Formosans commanded by Japanese officers. Employing the same tactics used to secure surprise at Mar and Sansapor the 31st Division and a regimental combat team of the 32nd Division landed in overwhelming strength on September 15, meeting no opposition on the beaches. This force of 28,000 combatants and 40,200 service personnel, principally engineer units charged with responsibility for airfield construction, encountered more trouble from natural obstacles than from the defenders. Clay and mud on the reef, as well as coral heads, held up many vehicles, and the men had to wade ashore in water from three to five feet deep. The landings were made on beaches north and south of the top of the Gila Peninsula, on the western side, but easier beaches were soon found, and by the 16th landing craft were dropping their ramps at high tide on to the beach at Pitoe Bay, on the opposite side of the peninsula.

A perimeter was rapidly established around the airfields in the south-west of the island, and while patrols hunted down scattered Japanese parties, the engineers set to work to lengthen and strengthen the strips. Allied fighters were operating from Morotai by the 29th, and bombers by October 4. The cost of taking Morotai had been light—30 Americans killed, 1 missing and 85 wounded. The Japanese lost 104 killed and 13 captured.

When the move to Morotai was planned, MacArthur intended next to take the Talaud Islands, between Morotai and

United States Marine Corps

The marines took Peleliu Island, but at great cost. The action was scheduled to last four days; in fact it went on for over two months and cost the Americans some 1792 dead and the Japanese 11,000

The recapture of Borneo. Above, Australian troops come ashore during the attack on Labuan Island. Below, machine-gunners fire on Japanese positions in Balikpapan. The assault on Balikpapan was the largest amphibious operation carried out by Australian troops during the war

Mindanao, and to then move into the Philippines by way of Mindanao. D-day for Mindanao he had scheduled as November 15. In the Central Pacific, where Nimitz launched his attack on the Palaus on the same day as MacArthur's forces invaded Morotai, it was planned to take Yap and Ulithi early in October. These were required to provide air and naval bases in the western Carolines so as to further neutralize by-passed Truk and to provide cover for MacArthur's assault on the Philippines. However, when Japanese air strength in the Philippines was found to be weaker than had been expected, Halsey suggested that Yap be by-passed and only Ulithi taken. This change of plan was approved. It released additional troops and amphibious equipment to MacArthur, who, with the approval of Nimitz and the Joint Chiefs of Staff, decided he could now move directly to Leyte instead of starting the reconquest of the Philippines in Mindanao. He therefore cancelled operations against both the Talaud Islands and Mindanao and set October 20 as the target date for the invasion of Leyte.

Halsey's assault on the three largest islands of the southern Palaus—Peleliu, Angaur and Ngesebus—began on September 15 with the assault on Peleliu, the most southerly island within the reefs surrounding the Palaus. The energetic and determined Lieutenant-General Sadae Inoue had seen that Peleliu was strongly fortified and well defended. Colonel Kunio Nakagawa had about 10,500 men, of whom 6,000 were combat troops, for the defence of Peleliu. Over 1,000 mines had been laid in the sea approaches, the first time they had been encountered in such numbers, and elaborate off-shore obstacles had been constructed. These were covered by specially sited artillery and machine-guns. Although Inoue had given orders for the assault to be defeated on the beaches, prepared defences had been prudently constructed inland in case the beach defences were overrun. On the ridges of Peleliu, whose terrain closely resembled and was as difficult as that of Biak, bunkers, pillboxes and machine-gun nests had been built.

The III Amphibious Corps had a strength of 49,500, of whom 24,300 were marines and 19,800 army troops. Major-General Wilham H. Rupertus, commander of the 1st Marine

Division, expected to take Peleliu in four days. His division, landing on the south-west shore, opposite the airfield, found that the preliminary air and naval bombardment had been less effective than had been expected and had left many of the Japanese beach defences unscathed. Artillery fire on the beaches was heavy and accurate and knocked out many amphibians. However, Nakagawa failed to hold the beaches and when his D-day counter-attacks were beaten back he withdrew to the ridges and high ground north of the airfield. As the Americans pushed farther inland, resistance stiffened appreciably.

Immobilized by a broken ankle, Rupertus had to rely on the reports of his subordinates, whose over-optimism led him to believe all was well. He therefore did not ask for all or part of the 81st Division to be sent in, probably feeling the marines had Peleliu in hand and preferring that its capture should be essentially a marine affair. General Geiger, III Amphibious Corps Commander, therefore allowed the 81st Division to land on Angaur on the 17th. It met light opposition, confined mainly to mortar fire and scattered small arms fire. A feint landing off the western shore may have caused the island commander, Major Ushio Goto, to hesitate about committing the bulk of his 1,400 men to counter-attack the landing on the north-east coast, and when he finally discovered no other landing was to be made the Americans were already firmly ashore.

Goto now withdrew into the north-west hills, where he had constructed bunkers and pillboxes in the jagged coral. His night counter-attacks were repulsed. Southern Angaur was cleared by the 21st, but Goto's men were not overrun in their prepared positions in the north-west until October 21.

Long before then, however, the island was sufficiently secured for Geiger to transfer troops to help the marines on Peleliu, where little progress had been made and severe casualties incurred. On September 23 the 321st Regimental Combat team reached Peleliu from Angaur and began relieving the battered 1st Marines. Even with the assistance of air bombing and strafing, naval and artillery shelling and tanks, the reduction of the Japanese defences was only slowly achieved and at heavy cost. The Umurbrogol Pocket, last centre of Japanese resistance, was not finally eliminated until November 26, a sufficient commentary on Rupertus's optimistic belief that he would clear the island in four days. Ngesebus and Kongauru Islands, lying off the northern tip of Peleliu, had been seized on September 28, so that artillery, mortar and automatic fire might be brought to bear on the Japanese on Amiangal Mountain, in northern Peleliu. These defences in caves and on the mountain's broken slopes had been finally overrun on October 2. Ulithi had been taken on September 22, no opposition being met.

The capture of the Palaus was one of the bloodiest operations yet undertaken. The Americans had 1,792 men killed or missing and 8,011 wounded, the majority on Peleliu. Of the 13,600 Japanese who died in defence of the Palaus, some 11,000 died on Peleliu. Prisoners captured numbered only 400, mostly Koreans and Okinawans.

The tragedy of the Palaus was that the Americans had no need to take them. They could have been and should have been by-passed. As early as mid-June Halsey had correctly suggested this course, but the views of MacArthur, Nimitz and the Joint Chiefs of Staff, believing that the Philippines could not be invaded without the Palaus being in Allied hands, prevailed. As events proved, they were not as useful as had been anticipated, and in view of the weakness of Japanese air and the success of carrier and land-based planes in neutralizing Japanese air bases, they posed no serious threat to the flanks of the Allies moving into the Philippines.

NOTES AND REFERENCES

1. Robert L. Eichelberger, *Jungle Road to Tokyo* (London, 1951), 154-5.
2. I have taken these comparisons from Samuel Eliot Morison, *New Guinea and the Marianas* (English edition, 1953), 233.

FURTHER READING:

Two volumes in the official history of the United States Army in World War II—*Campaign in the Marianas*, by Philip A. Crowl (Washington 1960) and *The Approach to the Philippines,* by Robert Ross Smith (Washington, 1953)—give the best accounts of the events described in this chapter. They

require to be supplemented by the volume in the official history
of the U.S. Army Air Forces mentioned in the preceding
reading list and by Morison's *New Guinea and the Marianas,
March 1944-August 1944* (English edition, 1953) and *Leyte,
June 1944-January 1945* (English edition, 1958), the first
part of which deals with the Palaus. Several Marine Corps
monographs, the maps in which are excellent, are readable and
detailed—*Saipan: The Beginning of the End,* by Carl W.
Hoffman (Washington, 1950), *The Recapture of Guam,* by
O. R. Lodge (1954), *The Seizure of Tinian,* by Carl W. Hoffman (1951) and *The Assault on Peleliu,* by Frank O. Hough
(1950). Smith's *Coral and Brass,* Eichelberger's *The Jungle
Road to Tokyo,* both mentioned in previous reading lists,
Marine at War, by Russell Davis (Boston, 1961), *Coral Comes
High,* by George P. Hunt (New York, 1946), and *On to West-
ward: War in the Central Pacific,* by Robert Sherrod (New
York, 1945) contain first-hand accounts of various phases of
the operations.

twelve

THE FORGOTTEN ARMIES

In contrast with the bustling activity of the Pacific, the Burma and China theatres throughout 1943 remained quiescent. There was much air activity as the Allies increased the number and weight of their attacks and developed the air lift to China, but on land, after the Arakan disaster and the withdrawal of the Chindits, there was no large-scale fighting. The monsoon season saw little more than skirmishing and patrol clashes. Occasionally these led to hand-to-hand fighting in the Chin Hills, where the Japanese had much the better of it, in the malarious Kabaw Valley beyond Imphal or in the extensively flooded no man's land separating the forces in Arakan.

Behind the front lines, however, there was feverish activity. Operation after operation was suggested, planned and finally cancelled, often in favour of some new venture. Meanwhile, the work of expanding and training the Indian Army, of raising its morale from the slough into which it had fallen, of building up and bringing forward supplies, and of extending and improving roads and railways was pressed forward.

To the Americans, who possessed little knowledge of the difficult administrative, political and economic problems and did not understand how starved for essential supplies were the 'Forgotten Armies', it seemed that the British and Indians did not want to fight. Among the United States Chiefs of Staff in Washington this view stemmed largely from General Stilwell's reports. This curiously difficult and complex personality believed the British commanders were not offensive-minded and were exaggerating their difficulties, and in his usual blunt fashion he said so. Yet, unjust and erroneous as were his strictures, they contained some substance.

Mr Churchill was angered by what he considered the lack of energy and drive in India. He was better informed than Stilwell as to the problems of his senior commanders. After the disasters their armies had suffered, the military leaders were understandably cautious, and sometimes were intimidated by their difficulties. Nor were they all receptive to new ideas, as Wingate's fight against conservative thinking proved. The command machinery in India was rendered inefficient by personal jealousies, by the sanctity of seniority and by antagonism between British and Indian officers.

Before his appointment in June 1943 to succeed the Marquis of Linlithgow as Viceroy of India, General Wavell rejected an Australian suggestion that Australian officers should be seconded to instruct and train his troops in the art of jungle fighting and that British and Indian officers should learn this branch of their trade by serving with Australian forces in New Guinea. Fortunately, the offer was repeated and accepted after General Auchinleck succeeded Wavell as Commander-in-Chief on June 18. A number of Australian officers served in India while officers from India served with Australian units in New Guinea. This, of course, was a matter of minor importance, but is significant as a small pointer to the lack of forward thinking within the Indian command.

The problems of China and Burma were not lessened by clashes of personality among senior commanders or simplified by the vigorous advocacy of their divergent views by the individualists who helped frame South-East Asian strategy. All agreed it was vital to hammer the Japanese, but each wanted to do the hammering in his own way, with his own forces and in the place of his own choice. Inevitably, this led to misunderstandings and misinterpretations.

Appalled at the high proportion of 'teeth' to 'tail' in the Indian Army and dismayed at the absence of energetic and aggressive leadership, Churchill characteristically advocated an invasion of Sumatra or at least of the Andaman Islands, primarily in order to open a route to the Chinese coast by way of the South China Sea but also as the prelude to the reconquest of the Netherland East Indies and Malaya. Generalissimo Chiang Kai-shek flatly rejected all operations that did not directly support his own armies or that reduced the flow of supplies to China, which he demanded should be stepped up from under 4,000 to 10,000 tons a month. General Chennault wanted everything else subordinated to the build-up of his air forces in China, believing that by concentrating upon Japanese shipping their attacks could be made decisive. Brigadier Wingate urged that large resources in men, weapons, equipment and aircraft should be funnelled into his long-range penetration groups. Stilwell, insistent upon the opening of land communications with China by the construction of the Ledo Road, felt the key to victory lay in the formation of thirty additional Chinese divisions, all to be fully equipped and trained by the Americans.

In addition to the internal differences of opinion within the ranks of each ally, as exemplified in the conflict between the 'air' and 'land' policies of Chennault and Stilwell and between the unorthodox thinking of Wingate and the conservativeness of most British generals, there was a fundamental difference of outlook between the British and the Americans. For the latter, the reconquest of upper Burma was merely a means to an end, necessary only because it would enable the restoration of land communications with China. Once the Japanese had been ejected from upper Burma the new Ledo Road could be linked with the old Burma Road by way of Myitkyina and supplies poured over it into China. On the other hand, to the British, who had less faith in Chiang Kai-shek and the Chinese armies than the Americans, the reconquest of Burma meant the liberation of British territory overrun by the enemy, as the defeat of the Japanese in the Aleutians had meant to the Americans the liberation of American territory. The British wanted to reconquer the whole of Burma, believing that this would be a major defeat for the Japanese and that by retaking Rangoon the best route for supplying China, the Burma Road, would be reopened.

President Roosevelt's entanglement with the Chinese, whose cause he had vigorously espoused long before Pearl Harbour, meant that politically he could not afford to abandon Chiang Kai-shek. In any case, the Americans and British were unanimous on the need for keeping China in the war, and with misguided optimism the Casablanca Conference in January 1943 endorsed a proposal for a large-scale counter-offensive at the end of the monsoon in November for the reconquest of Burma. By the time the Trident Conference assembled in Washington in May it was clear this ambitious project was impracticable. Priority was therefore given to increasing the air lift to China and, as the first stage in the re-establishment of land communications with China, to launching a limited offensive from Assam into northern Burma in conjunction with an advance by Chinese forces from Yunnan. Minor amphibious operations for the capture of Akyab and Ramree Island were sanctioned.

Wingate was summoned to London on the eve of Churchill's departure for the Quadrant Conference at Quebec in August. He so fired Churchill's imagination that the Prime Minister took him to Quebec. There his passionate but balanced advocacy before the Combined Chiefs of Staff of long-range penetration so impressed the Americans that they decided immediately to form their own unit to train with the Chindits. There was now general belief in the practicability and value of long-range penetration. The conference directed that during the dry weather of 1943-44 the capture of northern Burma should be undertaken with the object of re-opening land communications with China and securing the air route. Planning for future amphibious operations was to continue, but they were not to be launched until 1944 and, except for the capture of Akyab and Ramree, the objectives were to be selected at a later date.

In the interval between the Trident and Quadrant Conferences discussions took place regarding the establishment of a Supreme Command for South-East Asia, responsible for the conduct of active operations within the area and independent of the Commander-in-Chief, India. The Americans advocated the North African system, under which General Eisenhower was directly responsible to the Combined Chiefs of Staff, but the British preferred it to be modelled on the MacArthur pattern, with the Combined Chiefs of Staff dictating strategic policy and the British Chiefs of Staff directing operational policy. The British won their point, and on August 25, the day after the Quadrant Conference ended, Admiral Lord Louis Mountbatten's appointment as Supreme Commander, South-East Asia Command—SEAC—was officially announced.

At the time Mountbatten was serving as Chief of Britain's Combined Operations, and because of his youth, energy and known aggressiveness his appointment delighted the Americans. They believed he would bring a fresh and invigorating influence to bear on operations in Burma and China. Stilwell became Deputy Supreme Commander, but retained the posts he already held—those of Commander-in-Chief of United States air and ground forces in South-East Asia, Commander-in-Chief of the Chinese army in Burma, and Chief of Staff to Chiang Kai-shek. His multitudinous and often conflicting responsibilities created numerous difficulties in the smooth working of SEAC and tended to cause the Americans to by-pass the Supreme Commander. Mainly because of Mountbatten's tact, however, the new command, despite its inherent defects, worked satisfactorily.

Mountbatten arrived at Delhi early in October, but SEAC did not formally come into being until midnight on November 15-16. A month earlier, on October 15, Eastern Army was abolished, a Fourteenth Army, commanded by Sir William Slim, being formed to take over its operational tasks. It was made responsible to SEAC through 11th Army Group, commanded by Sir George Giffard, who thus became Mountbatten's land commander. It was unfortunate that Stilwell and Giffard were temperamentally incompatible; personal antipathy caused the American to flatly refuse to serve under the Englishman. Mountbatten solved the impasse by inducing Stilwell to agree to serve under Slim, a compromise which worked happily and effectively. Naval commander of SEAC was Admiral Sir James Somerville, Commander-in-Chief of Britain's Eastern Fleet, and Air Chief Marshal Sir Richard Peirse became the air Commander-in-Chief. The command staff was an integrated Anglo-American one.

Earlier the Japanese also reorganized their command in Burma. On March 27 Burma Area Headquarters was formed under Lieutenant-General Masakazu Kawabe to control Lieutenant-General Renya Mutaguchi's XV Army and the divisions assigned to the defence of central and northern Burma and Arakan. Between June and September Lieutenant-General K. Sato's 31st Division reached Burma to reinforce the XV Army. Its communications had been improved by the completion, after a year's work, of the infamous Burma Railway— the 250-mile long, single line, metre-gauge railway built by British, Australian, Dutch and American prisoners of war and thousands of impressed coolies, all of whom were underfed, brutally treated and mercilessly driven. A fifth of the prisoners of war engaged on this project died of starvation, brutality or disease, and among the unfortunate coolies the death roll was even higher. When it began operating in November 1943 the railway increased the capacity of the Japanese lines of communication.

In July 1943 Subhas Chandra Bose, one-time President of the Congress Party of India, established a provisional Government of Free India at Singapore and appointed himself Commander-in-Chief of the Indian National Army. He urged the Japanese to invade India from Burma. It is doubtful if his representations had any effect. The Japanese command in Burma, alarmed by the operations of the Chindits in their first campaign, had already decided that an offensive policy was preferable to a strictly defensive one, and eventually Imperial General Headquarters approved the change. On August 15

Mutaguchi was ordered by Tokyo to begin planning the offensive towards Imphal he had proposed. Further changes in the Burma Command were now made. The XXVIII Army (2nd, 54th and 55th Divisions) under Lieutenant-General Seizo Sakurai was created to control the Arakan front; the north, where the Japanese faced Stilwell's Chinese armies, was placed under XXXIII Army (18th and 56th Divisions), while XV Army (15th, 31st and 33rd Divisions and the 7,000-strong 1st Indian National Army Division) became responsible solely for the Chindwin front, where the offensive was to take place.

Wingate, promoted to major-general by the War Office at his own insistence and without reference to India, returned to his command on September 16. The following month the American long-range penetration unit, later known as Merrill's Marauders, arrived to train with the Chindits. Wingate's position was impregnable, and within reason he could expect to receive everything he demanded. At first he encountered dilatoriness and even obstruction, but as his enhanced prestige became more widely known his difficulties disappeared. He had the blessing of the Americans and the wholehearted support of Churchill, who, breaking all canons of military command, had authorized him in emergency to communicate direct. The United States air chief, General Arnold, had assigned No. 1 Air Commando, commanded jointly by Colonels Philip Cochran and John Alison and comprising bombers, fighters and transport aircraft, to co-operate exclusively with the Chindits. This unit, whose equipment included gliders, was not, as Slim ungraciously claimed[1], a private air force controlled by Wingate. Its joint commanders were answerable to the United States Army Air Forces, of which No. 1 Air Commando, although serving with the Chindits, continued as an integral part.

In November 1943 the Sextant Conference opened at Cairo and was attended by Mountbatten, Stilwell, Chennault and the Chinese Generalissimo, who would not give a firm undertaking to launch an offensive from Yunnan. Before the conference concluded there were discussions at Tehran with Stalin, as a result of which the Allies agreed that in May 1944 Anglo-American forces would invade Europe. In return, the Russians

THE WAR WITH JAPAN

undertook to wage war on Japan immediately after Germany was defeated. This agreement meant that landing craft previously earmarked for amphibious operations in South-East Asia had now to be returned to Europe, and that Fourteenth Army already, in the words of its commander, 'the Cinderella of all British armies', dropped even lower on the priority list for essential equipment and supplies.

In outlining the tasks of SEAC, the Sextant Conference reaffirmed the policy of building up the American and Chinese air forces and the Chinese Army, ordered a very long range bomber force to be established at Calcutta, with an advanced base at Chengtu, for the bombing of targets on and near the Japanese mainland, and sanctioned limited offensives by the British in upper Burma and Arakan in the spring of 1944. All major amphibious operations were postponed until after the monsoon, and it was stipulated that if the limited offensives were continued in the autumn it must be with the forces available.

Mountbatten gave effect to these decisions in a directive he issued on January 15 1944. In this he ordered Stilwell's American and Chinese forces on the northern front to advance against Mogaung and Myitkyina by way of Shaduzup, IV Corps (Lieutenant-General G. A. P. Scoones), on the central front, to drive towards the Chindwin from Imphal, in co-operation with the Chindits operating against the Japanese communications, and XV Corps (Lieutenant-General A. F. P. Christison) to advance overland in Arakan with the ultimate object of recapturing Akyab. The first two of these three limited offensives were to be undertaken whether cr not the vacillating Chiang Kai-shek ordered his armies to attack from Yunnan.

By the end of 1943 the British in Arakan had closed up to the main Japanese positions east of the Mayu range, and under cover of active patrolling began in January to complete their preparations for the coming offensive. The Japanese, however, beat them to the punch. On the night of February 3-4 their main spearhead under Major-General Tohutaro Sakurai, infantry commander of the 55th Divisional group, infiltrated through the widely separated British posts undetected, except for its rearguard, and began a wide enveloping movement to isolate and destroy the 7th Indian Division.

Sakurai attacked boldly and resolutely, with an almost contemptuous disregard of his parlous supply position and his long and tenuous lines of communication. The parties replenishing his ammunition and food had either to infiltrate the by-passed British forward positions or move around them by a difficult, long and circuitous route.

The strength and direction of the Japanese attack surprised the British. Having occupied Taung Bazar, a small village to the north-east of the British positions, Sakurai's columns moved farther westward before turning southwards to strike in behind the British left. On the 5th, when Sakurai was making good progress, a smaller Japanese spearhead struck northwards from beyond the British right, infiltrating behind the 7th Division in an effort to link hands with Sakurai in the vicinity of Sinzweya. Next day Sakurai overran the headquarters of the 7th Division a mile to the north-east of Sinzweya, but the divisional commander and most of his staff eluded the Japanese and made their way back to Sinzweya in small groups. After nightfall on the 6th the Japanese seized Ngakyedauk Pass, thus cutting the road across the mountains and separating the 7th Division east of the range from the 5th Indian Division on the west.

On the morning of the 7th the position seemed critical, but the new tactics of Fourteenth Army paid off. Slim had ordered any unit surrounded or by-passed not to withdraw, but to stand firm within its defensive area, employing a floater force outside its perimeter to attack the assaulting enemy in flank or rear. His troops were well trained in these tactics, and, borrowing a leaf from Wingate's notebook, he had set up an organization to supply these encircled forces from the air. For a few days enemy air interference forced the transport aircraft to drop supplies at night, but with the disappearance of the Japanese fighters, which had been transferred to the central front for the coming offensive against Imphal, daylight drops again became possible.

As British reserves hurried forward, a fierce battle developed for possession of Ngakyedauk Pass, while all Japanese efforts to capture Sinzweya, where a large British ammunition dump was set on fire by Japanese shelling, were repulsed. The Japanese had relied upon capturing British supply dumps, and when none fell into their hands they were left acutely short of food, ammunition, petrol and other essentials. Their supply gamble was their undoing, and when the British recaptured the Pass on the 23rd, Sakurai ordered a general withdrawal. Sakurai's troops, who had suffered heavy losses, were starving and almost exhausted. His offensive, which had forestalled their own preliminary attacks by a day, cost the British and Indians 3,506 casualties, slightly under half of which were incurred by the 7th Division.

In the Kaladan Valley to the east the 81st West African Division began an advance on February 29, but quickly found itself in difficulty and eventually was driven from the entire valley. But this setback did not interfere with the British plans for an offensive, and on March 9 the 7th Division captured Buthidaung and on the 12th the 5th Division took Razabil. These two divisions were now relieved, but heavy fighting continued for Point 551, overlooking the final stretch of the Maungdaw-Buthidaung road, and it was not finally wrested from the Japanese until the night of May 3-4, when the Japanese holding it were thinned out to provide men for a fruitless attempt on the 5th and 6th to recapture Buthidaung. The British had never intended to hold Buthidaung during the monsoon and on the 7th they evacuated the town. As the monsoon came both sides began to pull out.

For the first time British and Indians had defeated a determined Japanese offensive and successfully carried through their own attack. They had gained an excellent jumping-off place for resuming the offensive once the monsoon season ended. The coastal port of Maungdaw, the range to the east and the road from Maungdaw to Buthidaung as far as Point 551 were all firmly in their hands, and they had proved that with their new tactics they were more than a match for the Japanese.

On the northern front Stilwell took personal command of the United States and Chinese forces on December 21 1943. His action in thus adding the duties of a corps commander to his other and more important responsibilities has been much criticized, since it took him from Chiang Kai-shek's side and isolated him from SEAC, of which he was deputy Supreme Commander. Nevertheless, his decision was wise. It was essential that the Chinese should be induced to fight and that they should be victorious, and only Stilwell had the drive and power of leadership to ensure this. Even with his presence it was the beginning of February before the leisurely moving 22nd and 38th Chinese Divisions were in position for the first phase of their offensive.

Merrill's Marauders and the Chinese cleared Maingkwan and secured control of the Hukawng Valley, thus clearing the way for the Ledo Road to be pushed through to Maingkwan, where it was to connect with the all-weather road running to Myitkyina by way of Mogaung. However, these operations had taken much longer than Stilwell had anticipated and with the monsoon only two months away he seemed to have but a slender chance of taking Myitkyina before the rains made movement impossible. Without a word to his superiors, Stilwell prepared in great secrecy for a dash to Myitkyina, which he hoped to seize by a *coup de main.*

On the central front, where the forces were approximately equal, it was obvious before the end of January that the Japanese were preparing to attack. The British were widely scattered and their long lines of communication were vulnerable, but Scoones, Slim and Giffard were confident they could smash the Japanese offensive when it came. The British planned to withdraw their forces to the Imphal plain and to there launch a counter-offensive at a suitable moment and on ground of their own choosing. The tactics which were soon to prove so successful in Arakan were to be employed also on this front.

At Quadrant, Wingate had proposed the use of three long-range penetration groups on the Japanese lines of communication in the Indaw area in conjunction with offensives on the northern front and from Yunnan. On his return to India his fertile imagination devised a new technique for the Chindits. He proposed that they should operate from well sited bases defended by conventional units. Each was to be located in a naturally strong defensive position, difficult of access, and so placed that the defended area covered a landing strip outside, not inside, the base. The tactics to be employed in defending these bases apparently on Slim's suggestion, were those initiated by Fourteenth Army, with a floater column operating outside the perimeter. It was basic to Wingate's stronghold theory that it should be defended by a conventional unit with conventional weapons. Wingate, however, was not given sufficient conventional units and he was compelled to use some of his own men for garrison duties.

The 16th Long Range Penetration Brigade commanded by Brigadier Bernard Fergusson, was the first to move out. On February 5 its leading elements left Tagap, on the Ledo Road, on a 360-mile march into Burma. When it reached the Chindwin on the 28th, establishing a bridge-head across the river next day without meeting opposition, it was already ten days behind schedule. By March 5 the entire brigade was east of the river and headed for Indaw.

Back at Lalaghat, a fair-weather airfield south-west of Imphal, the 77th L.R.P. Brigade, commanded by Brigadier J. M. Calvert, was assembling that day preparatory to being flown in behind the Japanese lines. Slim and Wingate were there to watch the first fly-in of Chindits, and as they waited for zero hour, with the Dakotas and gliders preparing for take-off, a speeding jeep, its progress marked by a cloud of dust, reached the airfield. It carried photographs taken that morning of the three selected stronghold sites in the Indaw area. These revealed that while Broadway, 35 miles east-north-east of Indaw, and Chowringhee, a similar distance east of Indaw, were free of obstructions, Piccadilly, 40 miles north-east of Indaw, was obstructed for its full length by tree trunks laid in rows. An anxious debate followed, but it was decided to proceed with the fly-in. Long after it was learned that Piccadilly had not been obstructed by the Japanese, but by Burmese tree fellers who, as was their normal custom, had dragged felled teak logs into the open to dry.

The take-off of 77th Brigade began an hour behind schedule.

The advance guard, landing safely, made a flare path and set up ground control and radio-telephone communications. When all was ready at Broadway, the Dakotas, each towing two gliders, began to leave Lalaghat, but some of the nylon tow ropes parted soon after take-off, causing four gliders to make forced landings. Other gliders, having been overloaded or improperly stowed, became unstable or proved too heavy for the Dakotas to clear the mountains, and had to be cast off to crash land behind the Japanese lines. At Broadway thick grass concealed deep ruts in the ground and these caused gliders to crash in landing. Before the debris could be removed other gliders came into land with disastrous results. The Dakotas and gliders already airborne were recalled. Wingate and his staff, not knowing the reason for the signal from Broadway, concluded the brigade had been ambushed.

Sixty-two gliders were dispatched from Lalaghat on the night of March 5-6. Of these, eight were recalled, eight crash-landed within the Allied lines, and eleven came down in enemy-held territory. The remaining 35 reached Broadway and all but three were wrecked or damaged in landing. In the circumstances, casualties at Broadway were not excessive, thirty men being killed and a similar number injured. Four hundred men, with sufficient mechanical equipment for the construction of an air strip, had been landed. The strip was completed on the 6th and that night 62 Dakotas, of which only two were slightly damaged in landing, flew in 900 men, 100 animals and 20 tons of stores. Under cover of darkness on the three following nights the rest of the 77th Brigade and the stronghold garrison were flown in.

At Chowringhee the advance party landed on the night of the 6th-7th and the fly-in of the 111th L.R.P. Brigade, commanded by Brigadier W. D. A. Lentaigne, began, but Wingate decided to abandon Chowringhee because of the danger of air attack and the brigade's other two battalions were flown into Broadway on the night of the 10th-11th.

In seven nights 9,000 men, 1,350 animals, 250 tons of stores, and a Bofors and a 25-pounder battery had been landed behind the Japanese. The Japanese had expected airborne operations, but at first they believed only small forces were involved. By the 12th, however, Kawabe knew that substantial forces had landed. He ordered a special force to be formed to deal with the invaders, but it was the end of the month before the whole of this force had concentrated at Indaw.

On the 15th the 77th Brigade blocked the Mandalay-Myitkyina railway near Henu, north of Mawlu, and formed a new stronghold which, from the number of supply parachutes draping the trees, soon came to be dubbed White City. Local Japanese forces attacked immediately, but were driven off. They quickly resumed the attacks with tank, artillery and mortar support. In savage hand-to-hand fighting over seven days the 77th Brigade, aided by heavy air strikes, resisted successfully all Japanese efforts to overrun White City. When the Japanese at last withdrew they had lost over 700 men killed.

On the night of March 23-24 the 14th L.R.P. Brigade, under the command of Brigadier T. Brodie, began its fly-in to Aberdeen, a stronghold 27 miles north-west of Indaw, established by the 16th Brigade in its march against that centre. On the 24th Wingate visited Broadway, White City and Aberdeen and in the afternoon he returned to Imphal. That evening he set off from Imphal to visit Lalaghat, but his Mitchell (B-25) bomber never reached its destination, and its scattered remains were eventually seen from the air on the western slopes of the Bishenpur hills. It had crashed and burst into flames, killing Wingate and the other eight men aboard.

The death of Wingate deprived the Chindits of their forceful and imaginative leader and of continued and influential support. Lentaigne, who succeeded Wingate, was not able to ensure the continued supremacy of Wingate's ideas. To suggest, as the official British historian, Lieutenant-General S. Woodburn Kirby has done[2], that Wingate may have died at a propitious moment for his own reputation is an unwarranted assumption. It may be that even had he lived the campaign of the L.R.P. Brigades would still have failed, and that before his death he himself had sown the seeds of their failure.

After Wingate's death the Chindits were compelled to perform tasks for which they were not equipped. Stilwell, in particular, demanded more of them than they were capable of giving and Lentaigne's protests were in vain. Wingate's theories were constantly evolving and developing, and what appear to have been errors of judgment in the few days immediately before his death may not have proved mistakes or may have been rectified. He was so secretive in his planning that we do not know exactly what he intended to do or how he proposed to achieve results, and we cannot be certain that he would have been more successful than Lentaigne. All we can be certain of is that any chance of success the Chindits had was lost when Wingate died.

The Japanese correctly divined Wingate's objective. Fergusson had pleaded with him for time to rest his weary brigade after its long march from Tagap, but Wingate refused to delay the attack. It failed, the Japanese already having reinforced Indaw strongly, and the 16th Brigade was forced to withdraw from the area. What is inexplicable, rendering it difficult to decide what might have happened had Wingate lived, is his diversion of the 111th Brigade to a task other than to assist Fergusson and his failure to advise Fergusson of that decision.

On the northern front, Stilwell's *coup de main* against Myitkyina failed narrowly. On May 17, surprising the Japanese, he seized Myitkyina airfield, into which he flew, within 36 hours, a regiment of the Chinese 30th Division, engineers, a light anti-aircraft battery and eight United States fighters. The garrison of the town itself, however, defied every effort to dislodge it, and Myitkyina remained in Japanese hands. Stilwell called for help and the Chindits, whose primary tasks had always been to assist Stilwell's attack and to create a favourable opportunity for an offensive from Yunnan, were ordered north and placed under his command. He directed them to take defended villages, but although with great gallantry they twice broke into the Japanese positions at Waingmaw, on May 30 and June 2, they could not hold their gains. They then moved farther north and twice attacked Maingna unsuccessfully. Very fatigued, without adequate weapons and short of food and ammunition, they suffered such heavy losses in these attacks that they could do no more than harass the Japanese and eventually had to be evacuated.

Clearly, when it came to directing Wingate's Special Force, the otherwise unorthodox Stilwell was far too orthodox in his tactical thinking. He used them for tasks for which they were not equipped, and when they failed Stilwell considered they had not fought aggressively and had disregarded his orders. There was some truth in the second charge, but his orders were not always capable of fulfilment by such lightly equipped forces. Calvert's 77th Brigade and the 114th Chinese Regiment took Mogaung by June 26, using flamethrowers in place of the artillery they did not possess, but by then the brigade had lost nearly half its strength and had only 300 men fit for action. When Stilwell asked that the Chindits be removed from his command because of their disobedience of his orders, Slim had to smooth matters over, and eventually the entire Special Force was withdrawn.

The garrison of Myitkyina rose to 3,000 by June 6 and it fought so stubbornly that the town did not fall until August 3. Its siege cost the Allies 5,383 casualties and 1,168 sick. From the beginning of the year to August 19 the Chinese battle casualties on the northern front totalled 13,618 and the Americans 1,327. Heavy as was this price the Japanese had been thoroughly whipped.

While these events were taking place the Japanese launched an offensive in China. As Stilwell had forecast when opposing Chennault's advocacy of air action alone, the Japanese, as soon as the American air force became a nuisance, launched an attack directed at the Allied airfields in south-east China. On April 17 the Japanese China Expeditionary Force crossed the Yellow River, seized the southern portion of the Pekin-Hankow railway and occupied Loyang. They met little resistance and their drive, as it swept relentlessly onward, created alarm and despondency among the Allies, especially among the Americans. Liuyang was captured on June 14 and Changsha occupied on the 18th. Unlike the defenders of Changsha, the X Chinese Army, aided by United States air forces, fought well and stubbornly at Hengyang, which did not fall until August 8. Using

Chengtu, American long-range bombers launched raids against the Japanese mainland on June 16 and July 7. These raids, in the first of which 68 and in the second only 18 bombers participated, inflicted little damage, but attacks on targets outside Japan proper were more successful and rewarding.

This offensive was the indirect cause of Stilwell's recall. It created political difficulties between Roosevelt and Chiang Kai-shek, who claimed that Stilwell had lost his confidence and on September 28 demanded his recall. As Chiang refused to accept any compromise, Roosevelt eventually agreed and on October 27 Stilwell left India for the United States. Lieutenant-General Albert C. Wedemeyer replaced Stilwell as Chief of Staff to the Generalissimo, and the China-Burma-India theatre was divided into two, Wedemeyer taking command of the China portion and Lieutenant-General Daniel I. Sultan assuming command of the India-Burma portion under SEAC. The Japanese offensive, after being temporarily halted by administrative difficulties and slowed down by rain and the need for mopping up by-passed Chinese troops, achieved its objective before the end of 1944, overrunning the Allied airfields in the Kwangsi and Hunan provinces.

On May 10 the Chinese Eleventh and Twentieth Army Groups, totalling over 70,000 men, began an offensive on the Yunnan front. They crossed the Salween unopposed, but moved forward very slowly and, having little artillery, failed to take Lungling. It was September before they broke into the walled city of Tengchung. Given strong artillery and air support, the Chinese at the end of October again attacked Lungling, which the Japanese, threatened with envelopment, evacuated on November 3. The Chinese did not immediately follow up their victory and, when they did at last move, their advance towards Mangshih and Wanting was a leisurely affair, with lengthy pauses.

All these operations were of minor importance compared with the battle on the IV Corps front, where the Japanese drive against Imphal and Kohima proved the decisive battle for Burma. As had happened in Arakan, the strength and direction of the Japanese attack surprised the British and only the quick transfer of reserves to the central front by air retrieved the position.

The 33rd Japanese Division began the offensive on the night of March 9-10, when, with the object of attracting British reserves to its front, it began advancing along the roads leading towards Imphal from the south-west and south-east. A week later, on the night of the 15th-16th, the 31st and 15th Japanese Divisions crossed the Chindwin and drove forward, the 31st to close in on Kohima from north, east and south and the 15th advancing towards the Imphal Road from south of Ukhrul.

The British did not at first realize that the Japanese offensive had begun. When they belatedly became aware that the Japanese were on the move the 17th Indian Division, on the British right, was already encircled and its line of withdrawal to Imphal cut. Thus, at the outset the British plan, which had provided for a timely withdrawal to the Imphal plain for the organization of a counter-offensive, was imperilled. Local reserves had to be employed to extricate the 17th Division, a task which was facilitated by a spirited defence that held up, between the 19th and 26th, the advances of the 15th Division and the left column of the 31st. The Japanese failure to crash through quickly in the centre delayed the cutting of the Imphal Road until the 29th, gave the British time in which to begin flying in reinforcements from Arakan, and enabled the withdrawal to the plain to be executed.

However, the Japanese attack against Kohima developed more quickly and in greater strength than had been thought possible, and at this 4,700-foot mountain pass, the ancient invasion route to north-east India, the position was soon critical. The outnumbered British were sorely pressed. The fighting along the Kohima Ridge was as bitter and desperate as anywhere in the Pacific. Under constant assault, acutely short of water—the Japanese had cut the water mains from the reservoir—and with rations and ammunition running low, the British were compressed into the confined space of Garrison Hill. A Japanese breakthrough seemed imminent, threatening to overrun the base at Dimapur, whose defences had been neglected and only now were being hurriedly improvised. 'I had badly underestimated the Japanese capacity for long range infiltration and for their readiness to accept odds in a gamble on supply', wrote Slim, after the war.[3] 'We were not prepared for so heavy a thrust; Kohima, with its scratch garrison, and Dimapur, with no garrison at all, were in deadly peril.'

However, the peril was averted, although not without some anxious moments and at heavy cost. The dogged defence of Kohima, tactical errors by the Japanese commanders, the diversion of transport aircraft from the China air lift to the urgent task of flying reinforcements from Arakan to the Assam front and Japanese supply difficulties combined to prevent the breakthrough. With the road cut north of Imphal, XXXIII Corps was brought in from India, where it had been training in amphibious operations, and its commander, Lieutenant-General M. G. N. Stopford, assumed control of the Kohima-Dimapur operations. The first elements of his 5th British Division began to arrive in the area on April 2 and the crisis soon passed. The siege of the Kohima garrison, assailed from south, north and east, was raised when tanks and infantry broke through from Dimapur to reinforce the exhausted British and Indians.

The Japanese offensive against Imphal and Kohima was halted by April 21. Heavy fighting, in which tactically important features often changed hands several times, continued, but the British position had been immeasurably strengthened. By June 30 12,550 reinforcements and nearly 19,000 tons of supplies had reached Imphal and the supply position had been greatly improved by the evacuation of 13,000 sick and 43,000 non-combatants, enabling the restoration of full rations. Even after their attacks had been halted the Japanese refused to admit defeat, and there was heavy fighting over ground made muddy and slippery by torrential rain. By May 13 the Japanese hold on scorched and scarred Kohima Ridge had been broken, and the men of Lieutenant-General K. Sato's 31st Division were either in full flight or being blasted to death in their dugouts and bunkers. On the Imphal plain that day IV Corps attacked the 33rd Japanese Division, whose commander had been superseded, and when the Japanese themselves attacked a few days later each side cut the other's communications. Delivered with great *élan*, the Japanese attack overran a British brigade's administrative area and lapped the headquarters of the 17th Indian Division, but after seven days fierce fighting the Japanese were thrown back and on May 29 they began withdrawing into the hills. To the north the 5th British Division began an offensive which by the night of June 22 had reopened the Imphal Road.

A few days later, after storms and heavy rain had imposed a delay, the Fourteenth Army began an encircling attack on Ukhrul, in an attempt to sever Japanese communications with the Chindwin. The Japanese, aided by the weather, which converted creeks into swollen torrents and roads and tracks into muddied quagmires, fought grimly to hold Ukhrul, but by July 8 organized resistance had been smashed and next day Kawabe ordered a general retreat. The pursuit was pressed despite the monsoon. A large part of the badly mauled 15th and 31st Japanese Divisions escaped their pursuers only to die of starvation or disease, and by early October, with bridge-heads across the Chindwin, the Fourteenth Army was ready to launch an offensive for the reconquest of the remainder of Burma as soon as the monsoon ended.

The prolonged and hard-fought battle of Imphal-Kohima, as Slim has said[4], had swayed 'back and forth through great stretches of wild country; one day its focal point was a hill named on no map, the next a miserable, unpronounceable village 100 miles away. Columns, brigades, divisions marched and counter-marched, met in bloody clashes, and reeled apart, weaving a confused pattern hard to unravel.' From this confused fighting a decisive victory had been gained by the British and Indian forces. The Japanese XV Army lost almost half its strength, no less than 30,502 men being killed, or dead of wounds or illness. Many of its remaining 30,775 men were wounded or suffering from malnutrition. British and Indian casualties totalled 16,700, of which almost a quarter had been incurred in the fighting at Kohima.

As in Burma and the Pacific generally, the war in Europe underwent a transformation during 1944. In June the Allies opened a Second Front by invading Normandy and later they also invaded southern France. Before the year was out General Eisenhower's armies were on the upper Rhine, and in the east Russia was sweeping victoriously forward, already having reached Warsaw. The Mediterranean had been cleared and the Allies in Italy were moving towards the Po. Germany's defeat was being sealed on three fronts as surely as Japan was being hammered into ultimate capitulation in the Pacific.

NOTES AND REFERENCES

1. Sir William Slim, *Defeat into Victory*, 217.
2. S. Woodburn Kirby, *The War Against Japan*, III, 223.
3. Slim, 305.
4. Ibid., 296.

FURTHER READING:

The official histories of the campaigns in Burma and China are: British, S. Woodburn Kirby, *The War Against Japan*, III (London, 1961) and IV (1965); Indian, S. N. Prasad, K. D. Bhargava and P. N. Khera, *The Reconquest of Burma*, 2 vols, (Calcutta, 1958 & 1959), and N. N. Madaw, *The Arakan Operations 1942-1945* (Calcutta, 1954); United States, Charles F. Romanus and Riley Sunderland, *Stilwell's Mission to China* (Washington, 1953), Stilwell's *Command Problems* (1956) and *Time Runs Out in CBI* (1959). These cover the entire period of the war. For air operations, Denis Richards and Hilary St. G. Saunders, *Royal Air Force 1939-1945* 3 vols (London, 1953-54) and W. F. Craven and J. L. Tate, *The Army Air Forces in World War II*, V: *The Pacific, Matterhorn to Nagasaki, June 1944 to August 1945* (Chicago 1953) should be consulted. In the field of more popular reading there is a wide choice of volumes of varied quality, but the following can be recommended: *The Campaign in Burma:* Prepared for South-East Asia Command by the Central Office of Information (London, 1946); Christopher Sykes, *Orde Wingate* (London, 1959); Sir William Slim, *Defeat into Victory* (London, 1956); Lieutenant-General Sir Geoffrey Evans and Antony Brett-James, *Imphal A Flower on Lofty Heights* (London, 1965); John Masters, *The Road Past Mandalay: A Personal Narrative* (London, 1961); Lieutenant-General Sir Geoffrey Evans, *The Johnnies* (London 1964); Arthur Campbell, *The Siege: A*

Story from Kohima (London, 1955); Michael Calvert, *Prisoners of Hope* (London, 1952); Charlton Ogburn, *The Marauders* (London, 1960); and E. B. Stanley Clarke and A. T. Tillott, *From Kent to Kohima, being the History of the 4th Battalion, The Queen's Own Royal West Kent Regiment (T.A.) 1939-1947* (Aldershot 1951).

thirteen

FINAL DRIVE TO VICTORY

The invasion of the Philippines, running two montns ahead of schedule, was preceded by a widespread and intensive air campaign to reduce the Japanese air defences. In raids which began early in September 1944 and continued almost without interruption, land- and carrier-based aircraft destroyed hundreds of Japanese planes in the air or on the ground, although the destruction and damage were less than thought at the time. Japanese shipping was also successfully attacked and, in addition to warships and small craft, 105 merchant ships were sunk in Philippine waters by air, surface and underwater attack and another 20 sizeable cargo ships in the Ryukyus, thus dislocating the Japanese programme for the reinforcement of the Philippines.

Allied losses were light, but off Formosa the cruisers *Canberra* (13,600, 1943), the first vessel in the United States Navy ever to bear the name of a foreign city, and *Houston* (10,000, 1943) were torpedoed on October 13 and 14 respectively. Both ships remained afloat. Japanese pilots claimed the annihilation of the United States Third Fleet (which, as mentioned, was the designation of the Fifth Fleet when commanded by Admiral Halsey while Admiral Spruance was ashore planning the next operation) by sinking or seriously damaging 57 American warships, including 19 of Admiral McCain's carriers. Halsey decided in view of this exaggerated claim to use the stricken cruisers as bait to lure out the Japanese. A force was sent out to dispatch what the Japanese believed were the crippled remnants of the American fleet, but it hurriedly retired when reconnaissance aircraft located Halsey's task forces lurking in the wings for an opportunity to strike.

As the largest convoy ever seen in Pacific waters—totalling 701 vessels of all sizes—voyaged toward Leyte, American Rangers seized three islands at the entrance to Leyte Gulf without opposition. These were Saluan, where it was hoped, in vain, that vital mine charts reputedly located in a lighthouse would be found, and Dinagat and Humonhon, on both of which navigation lights were to be set up to guide the invasion armada into the Gulf. Saluan and Dinagat were taken on October 17 and Humonhon next day. These operations and minesweeping, which, beginning on the 17th, destroyed 227 mines before the assault went in on the 20th, denied surprise to the invaders. Lieutenant-General Krueger's 200,000-strong Sixth Army, comprising X Corps from the South-West Pacific and XXIV Corps from the South Pacific, went ashore on beaches some fourteen miles apart on Leyte's east coast.

Fourteenth Area Army, responsible under Southern Army for the defence of the Philippines, had some 387,000 troops distributed throughout the islands and had been commanded since mid-September by General Yamashita, the conqueror of Malaya and Singapore. His predecessor, Lieutenant-General Shigenori Kuroda, a realist who had not hesitated to tell his superiors that Japanese air power was negligible, had been relieved for paying too much attention to golf and his personal affairs. Yamashita, uncertain until the last moment as to where the Allied blow would fall, had only some 22,000 troops on Leyte, where the main combatant unit was Lieutenant-General Shiro Makino's 16th Division.

Beginning with the defence of Peleliu, Imperial General
Headquarters had reversed its earlier tactical doctrine of
annihilation on the beaches in favour of defence in depth
inland, and this policy was pursued on Leyte. The Americans
thus encountered little resistance as they came ashore. In the
north Major-General Franklin C. Sibert's X Corps landed
across beaches immediately south of Tacloban, on the shores
of San Pedro Bay, and quickly captured Tacloban airfield, on
Cataisan Peninsula. They also took Hill 522, on the American
left flank, where pillboxes, tunnels and seven-feet deep communication trenches were largely unmanned. In the south,
XXIV Corps, commanded by Major-General John R. Hodge,
came ashore between San Jose in the north and the Daguitan
River in the south, and meeting sporadic artillery and mortar
fire and marshy terrain, made rather slower progress, failing to
take Dulag airfield before nightfall. Some 55 miles further
south Panaon Strait was secured without opposition, thus
ensuring safe passage for naval vessels through it into the
Camotes Sea. American casualties of 49 killed, 6 missing and
192 wounded sufficiently revealed the weakness of the defence
of the beaches.

Japanese reaction to the invasion of Leyte was immediate.
Tokyo decided the decisive battle for the Philippines should
be fought at Leyte. Yamashita began pouring in reinforcements,
heavy air attacks began on the 24th and continued in considerable strength for four days, meeting heavy loss and proving
largely ineffective, and, alerted by Admiral Toyoda on the 18th,
the scattered forces of the Japanese Navy began converging on
Leyte Gulf.

Toyoda's plan was to lure the Third Fleet northwards by
exposing Vice-Admiral Ozawa's Main Force and to then move
in and shatter the transports off the invasion beaches. Ozawa
had 1 fleet, 3 light and 2 converted battleship carriers, escorted
by 3 light cruisers and 8 destroyers. So heavy had been naval
air losses in trained pilots that he had no aircraft aboard the
converted carriers and only 116 planes, 80 of them Zeke
fighters, spread through the other four carriers. The 1st and
2nd Diversion Attack Forces, the former composed of 2 new

and 5 old battleships, 11 heavy and 2 light cruisers and 19 destroyers, and the latter of 2 heavy cruisers and 1 light and 9 destroyers, were to slip through San Bernardino and Surigao Straits to attack the American invasion fleet.

Ozawa sailed from Kure and Beppu Bay on the 20th. The two divisions rendezvoused and then passed into the Pacific, undetected because the American submarines on watch had dispersed to seek and destroy merchant ships. That same day the 1st Diversion Attack Force reached Brunei Bay, in northwest Borneo. Its main body, under Vice-Admiral Takeo Kurita, was to head for San Bernardino Strait, and a detachment, under Vice-Admiral Shoji Nishimura, for Surigao Strait, where it was to be supported by Vice-Admiral Kiyohide Shima's 2nd Diversion Attack Force. The latter was scheduled to leave the Pescadores on the 21st. The plan was a good one, but for success the different forces had to be in the right place at the right time, a task which required careful co-ordination and excellent radio communications. There was no margin for error.

As the Japanese steamed on their different courses, the Americans drew first blood. The submarines *Dace* (1,525, 1943) and *Darter* (1,525, 1943) on the 23rd torpedoed and sank heavy cruisers *Atago* (9,850, 1930), Kurita's flagship, and *Maya* (9,850, 1930), and heavily damaged a third, *Takao* (9,850, 1930), which limped back to Brunei under escort of two destroyers. Next day carrier aircraft, having slightly damaged an old battleship and a destroyer of Nishimura's command, delivered five strikes at Kurita. The super-battleship *Musashi* (62,315, 1943), hit by 19 torpedoes and 17 bombs, capsized with the loss of 1,100 men, half her complement, and the heavy cruiser *Myoko* (10,000, 1927) was so severely damaged she had to turn back. Several other ships were hit.

Kurita was without air cover. Every available plane on Luzon had been sent to attack Rear-Admiral Frederick C. Sherman's Task Group Three, which had been located by a reconnaissance plane. Japanese losses in this attack were heavy, but Sherman's only casualty was the light carrier *Princeton* (11,000, 1943). Set on fire by a bomb, *Princeton* was shattered when six torpedoes loaded on aircraft exploded simultaneously and caused fires which could not be brought under control. On reaching her torpedo stowage, the flames set off a tremendous explosion that killed over 200 of the crew of light cruiser *Birmingham* (10,000, 1943), which at that time was alongside helping to fight the fires. Sherman was also attacked by Ozawa, who was endeavouring to draw attention to his force, but the Japanese lost all but about 20 of their 76 attacking aircraft without inflicting damage.

In the afternoon the Americans sighted Ozawa's Main Force and Halsey at once swallowed the bait which Toyoda had dropped so temptingly in front of him. Gathering his task forces together, he sped north, intent upon sinking the Japanese carriers. San Bernardino Strait was now left unguarded. Assuming that the Third Fleet would watch it, Admiral Kinkaid had moved the entire Seventh Fleet Bombardment and Fire Support Group of 6 old battleships, 4 heavy and 4 light cruisers, and 21 destroyers under Rear-Admiral J. B. Oldendorf, to guard Surigao Strait.

Around 2300 on the 24th Nishimura approached the southern exit of the strait. He already knew by radio that Kurita, delayed by the carrier-borne air attacks, would be unable to rendezvous with him within Leyte Gulf at 0430 next morning, as had been planned. In fact, he knew Kurita could not hope to be off the beachhead until 1100. Spoiling for a fight and determined to carry through his attack orders, the aggressive Nishimura was undeterred by this timing mishap— and sailed into a deadly trap.

He entered the southern part of Surigao Strait in bright moonlight, but was left in pitch dark when the moon set soon after midnight. The first of 39 American PT boats patrolling the strait picked up the Japanese ships on radar at 2236 and four-teen minutes later made visual contact. From then until 0213 successive waves of PT boats delivered torpedo attacks, but scored no hits and were driven off by fire from Nishimura's secondary batteries. An uneventful interval of 90 minutes followed before the Japanese were called upon to meet a succession of determined torpedo attacks by destroyers, which then retired under cover of smoke as the Japanese ships fired on them. In these attacks two Japanese destroyers were sunk, the battleship *Fuso* (29,330, 1914) was hit and later blew up, a third destroyer was put out of action and hits were scored on other ships, including several on the battleship *Yamashiro* (29,330, 1915), Nishimura's flagship. The last American destroyers to attack found themselves under fire from friend and foe alike as Oldendorf's battleships and cruisers, at the strait's northern entrance, opened fire on the remnants of the Japanese force. One American destroyer, taking some 19 hits, was stopped in the water with the loss of 34 of her crew killed and 94 wounded, but was towed clear by another American destroyer which lashed herself to the crippled ship.

The gun duel began at about 0351, when Nishimura's force had been whittled down to a battleship, a heavy cruiser and a destroyer. Nearly 300 rounds of 14- and 16-inch and over 4,000 rounds of 6- and 8-inch projectiles splashed about the three Japanese survivors in the first eighteen minutes after the American heavy ships opened fire. *Yamashiro* began to sink and finally capsized at 0419, the Japanese admiral going down with his ship, and only a handful of her crew being picked up. The heavy cruiser *Mogami* soon retired southward with destroyer *Shigure,* the former fiercely ablaze but the latter almost unscathed.

Shima's force, 40 miles behind Nishimura, came under torpedo attack from PT boats as it approached the southern end of Surigao Strait at about 0315. Within 10 minutes the light cruiser *Abukuma* (5,170, 1923) sheered out of line when slowed to 10 knots by a torpedo which crashed into her port side. Shima's two heavy cruisers and four destroyers continued northwards, passing the two halves of *Fuso*, which they took to be the remains of Nishimura's two battleships. Visibility was poor owing to the heavy smoke made by the American destroyers in escaping after their torpedo attacks, and, ignorant of Nishimura's fate, but fearing the worst, Shima decided about 0425 to retire from the strait. As his ships withdrew, the heavy cruiser *Nachi* (10,000, 1927) collided with the blazing *Mogami. Nachi's* stern was badly damaged and her speed reduced to 18 knots, but *Mogami's* damage control parties had

United States Navy

American battleships and cruisers move into position to bombard Luzon before the landing

A captured suicide or kamikaze plane similar to the ones that sank or damaged many allied ships in the Pacific towards the end of the war

Australian War Memorial

Meat strips on its ...ship...

worked to such good effect that she was able to fall in with Shima's column. *Shigure,* despite her steering engine being out of order, was also able to join.

The American cruisers and destroyers were slow to take up the pursuit, and although PT boats delivered some torpedo attacks they scored no hits and Shima's ships escaped. The destroyer *Asagumo* (1,961, 1937), whose bow had been sheered off when struck by a torpedo in one of the earlier destroyer attacks, was sunk by gunfire. She fought until the last, firing her final salvo from her after turret—the forward one already was awash—as she sank at 0721. The pursuit by surface vessels was called off shortly afterwards, but aircraft from escort carriers soon after 0900 brought the still blazing *Mogami* to a stop. A destroyer took off her crew and she was then sent to the bottom by a friendly torpedo. On the 27th, south-west of Negros, Army Air Force bombers sank damaged *Abukuma,* but *Nachi* reached Manila, where carrier aircraft sank her on November 4. *Shigure,* sole survivor of Nishimura's force, made Brunei Bay on October 27, and *Ashigara* (10,000, 1928) got safely into Bacuit Bay, Palawan. Shima's four destroyers, with no more than minor damage, also escaped.

While Nishimura and Shima were heading to disaster in Surigao Strait, Kurita was passing through unguarded San Bernardino Strait and out into the Pacific. He was steaming down the coast of Samar toward Leyte Gulf when he intercepted a wireless message from Nishimura announcing the attack in Surigao Strait. Later Kurita took in Shima's discreet if ambiguous message to Toyoda: 'This force has concluded its attack and is retiring from the battle area to plan subsequent action.' Soon after sunrise Kurita sighted first the masts and then the hulls of carriers and their escorts and wrongly deduced they belonged to Halsey's Third Fleet task forces. Actually they were the northernmost group of Rear-Admiral Thomas L. Sprague's Seventh Fleet escort carrier units, Halsey being now well away to the north in pursuit of Ozawa.

Instead of bringing his superior fire power and speed to bear by forming line of battle, Kurita ordered a general attack and in a good deal of confusion the Japanese ships opened fire at 0658 at a range of 30,000 yards. Rear-Admiral Clifton A. F. Sprague, commanding 'Taffy 3'—each task unit was known by its voice radio call sign—promptly turned away to open the range, made smoke, began launching from his carriers every plane that was operational and called loudly in plain language, for help. 'Taffy 2' (Rear-Admiral Felix B. Stump), to the south, and 'Taffy 1' (Rear-Admiral Thomas L. Sprague), southernmost of the task units, 120 miles away, immediately took steps to dispatch aircraft to Clifton Sprague's assistance. Tacloban airfield was made available for re-arming and re-fuelling aircraft. Clifton Sprague also ordered his screen of 3 destroyers and 4 destroyer escorts to launch torpedo attacks and to help hide his carriers from the Japanese gunners by making smoke.

The running battle lasted for two hours and a half. The air attacks (with pilots making dummy runs when they had fired their bombs or torpedoes or expended their ammunition) and the destroyer attacks compelled the Japanese to take constant evasive action. This not only spoiled the aim of their gunners, but slowed down the pursuit of the escort carriers, and thus deprived Kurita of his great advantage in speed—24 or 25 knots to 18. He was unable to round up his victims and his shooting was poor. When the escort carriers emerged from rain squalls which had veiled them, Kurita refused to cut the corner because he was determined to retain the windward gauge so that the carriers could not turn into the wind to launch further aircraft, although actually all they had were already airborne. He thus threw away a priceless opportunity to get among the thin-hulled vessels and blast them out of the water at short range. Furthermore, by turning north to avoid tor-pedoes, his flagship fell so far behind in the chase that Kurita lost tactical control of the battle and did not know exactly what was happening.

The air attacks did most of the damage to the Japanese, but the American destroyers pressed home their torpedo attacks and it was a torpedo from the destroyer *Johnston* (2,100, 1944) that put the heavy cruiser *Kumano* (8,500, 1936) out of action. Kurita, with 4 battleships, 6 heavy and 2 light cruisers, and 11 destroyers, should have sunk all Clifton Sprague's carriers, each of which had only a single 5-inch gun with which to oppose the 14-, 16- and 18-inch guns of the Japanese heavy ships. Soon after 0900 Kurita gave the order to turn away, just when it seemed that 2 of his heavy cruisers, with 2 battleships following them, were about to finish off what remained of 'Taffy 3'.

For three hours, as he collected his ships and restored them to some semblance of cohesion and order, Kurita debated whether to continue into the gulf and attack the amphibious shipping off the beaches. During this time he received reports of plain language orders passing between the Americans and, shortly after 1000, a radio report to Toyoda from Commander Nishino, captain of *Shigure*: 'All ships except *Shigure* went down under gunfire and torpedo attack'. This message, read in conjunction with the Americans' plain language requests and orders, seemed to indicate the presence of powerful forces in the vicinity and thus, taking counsel of his own fears, Kurita at 1236 ordered a withdrawal. The Japanese thus missed the opportunity of delivering a disastrous blow at the Leyte invasion shipping.

In the action off Samar the Americans lost the escort carrier *Gambier Bay* (7,800, 1943), which capsized and sank after a pounding from Japanese gunfire, the destroyers *Hoel* (2,100, 1943) and *Johnston* and the destroyer escort *Samuel B. Roberts* (1,350, 1944). Including aviators from the escort carriers and Task Group 38.1, casualties were 1,130 killed or missing and 913 wounded. The Japanese lost three heavy cruisers—*Chokai, Chikuma* and *Suzuya* (8,500, 1934)—but the damaged *Kumano* made Dasol Bay, where she was sunk in shallow water by carrier aircraft on November 25.

Halsey, as we have seen, had gone north in search of Ozawa. He had three of his four fast carrier task groups under Mitscher, and it was the latter who had tactical command in the carrier battle off Cape Engano. His scouts located Ozawa's force early on the morning of October 25 and his first strike of 180 aircraft took off at 0600. Two other strikes took off before noon and a further two during the afternoon. The Japanese had only about a dozen fighters with which to defend their ships and these were quickly shot down during the first strike, but their anti-aircraft fire, at least at the beginning of the battle, was intense and accurate.

Considering how overwhelming the odds were in their favour the results achieved by the American airmen were disappointing. Their day-long strikes, each made with 180 to 200 aircraft, sank only the heavy carrier *Zuikaku*, the last of the carriers which had raided Pearl Harbour and veteran of all the Pacific carrier battles except Midway, the light carriers *Chitose* and *Zuiho* and a destroyer. Another light carrier, *Chiyoda*, which had been set on fire and stopped during the second American strike, was sunk by a pursuing cruiser-destroyer force under Rear-Admiral Laurance T. DuBose, which in a running fight after dark with three destroyers sank one of them. The light cruiser *Tama* (5,100, 1920), damaged and slowed down by air attack, was sunk by a submarine as she limped away after the battle. Ozawa's two converted battleship-carriers and eight of his eleven escorts made good their escape and returned to Japan.

Halsey, when Ozawa was located, formed a surface task force, which included all his battleships, and set off in pursuit, with the object of disposing of any vessels crippled by Mitscher's air strikes and to engage and destroy those vessels remaining undamaged. As he sped towards the Japanese he received a stream of messages regarding the actions in Surigao Strait and off Samar, including a message in plain language from Kinkaid calling for air strikes and support by fast battleships, one of the messages which played an important part in Kurita's ultimate decision not to press forward to the beaches off Leyte. There was also a message from Nimitz which, because portion of its end padding—all ciphered messages were buried in padding to make deciphering more difficult—had been included, appeared to be an insulting reprimand. Under the prodding of these messages, the angry Halsey at about 1100 turned south. He was then only a little over 40 miles from Ozawa's damaged carriers. It was a fatal mistake. He threw away all chance of a surface action with Ozawa's remnants and was too late to catch Kurita, who had much more than a head start. Only the destroyer *Nowake* (2,033, 1940) had not passed through San Bernardino Strait and she was quickly sunk—a paltry reward for much hard steaming.

Although the battle of Leyte Gulf was a resounding Allied victory, achieved by forces which were predominantly American, and deprived Japan finally of all prospect of a naval victory, Toyoda's plan nearly succeeded. Halsey's failure to leave part of Third Fleet to guard San Bernardino Strait and Kinkaid's failure to send out an adequate search to reconnoitre it and locate Kurita combined to present the Japanese with a great opportunity. Kurita, however, failed to grasp it. His handling of his fleet in action was tactically unsound and his timidity when he had re-formed it prevented him from retrieving the position. If Nishimura and Kurita had been in one another's places the story might have been a very different one.

In its attempt to support the navy's plan to smash the amphibious shipping off Leyte, the Japanese Air Force formed the first unit of the Kamikaze Special Attack Corps. It came into being at Clark Field, on Luzon, on October 20 and was sponsored by Vice-Admiral Takijiro Ohnishi, who had taken command of the 1st Air Fleet only three days earlier. The first unit drew its volunteer pilots from 201 Air Group and was commanded by Lieutenant Yukio Seki. The corps was named Kamikaze—'Divine Wind'—from the typhoon which reputedly saved Japan from Mongol invasion in the late 13th century by scattering the invasion armada of Kublai Khan. The initial plan was for suicide pilots to crash their bomb-laden Zekes on hostile warships or land installations, concentrating at sea, however, on American carriers.

The first Kamikaze attack was delivered on the Australian cruiser *Australia* off the Leyte beaches soon after first light on October 21. The bomber crashed on the cruiser's bridge killing 20 of her crew, including her captain, and wounding 54, among whom was Commodore John A. Collins. So damaged was the cruiser that she was forced to withdraw under escort to Manus.[1] Missions were flown by Kamikaze pilots later that day and on succeeding days, but the Japanese lacked reconnaissance aircraft and the overcast weather did not favour them, with the result that Allied targets were not located or could not be attacked. On the 25th Kamikaze aircraft found Thomas Sprague's 'Taffy 1' as his escort carriers were launching planes to aid Clifton Sprague in his battle with Kurita. *Santee* (11,400, 1942) and *Suwannee* (11,400, 1942) were both hit. Fires were started on *Santee,* fortunately without exploding eight 1,000-lb. bombs she was carrying, and within five minutes of the fires being extinguished she was hit by a torpedo from an undetected Japanese submarine. In neither case was the damage fatal, and within about two hours both carriers resumed flight operations.

Further north, after Kurita had broken off his action, five Kamikaze planes, coming in at a very low altitude, caught Clifton Sprague's carriers as they were recovering aircraft. The approach of the Japanese was not detected and their attack took the Americans by surprise, everything happening so quickly that the American fighters aloft had no time in which to . intervene. Twenty minutes after this initial attack a second and stronger Kamikaze attack took place. In these attacks one bomb-laden Zeke crashed through the flight deck of *St. Lo* (7,800, 1943) and burst into flames below, causing seven explosions among the stored bombs and torpedoes. Ablaze from stem to stern, *St. Lo* went down in minutes. *Kitkun Bay* (7,800, 1943), *White Plains* (7,800, 1943) and *Kalinin Bay* (7,800, 1943) were damaged and suffered casualties when suicide pilots either crashed or near-missed them, two actually crashing on *Kalinin Bay.*

These attacks heralded a new phase in air fighting in the Pacific. Suicidal attacks by bomb-laden aircraft became commonplace, caused heavy casualties, and sank or damaged many ships. Incomplete statistics suggest that over 34 warships were sunk and over 300 damaged by Kamikaze attacks. The majority of these were American, but Australian, British and other Allied ships fell victims to the Kamikaze pilots. When the British Pacific Fleet began operating with the Americans most of its fleet carriers were crashed at one time or another by suicide pilots. Casualties in the United States Navy alone from this form of attack probably exceeded 4,400 killed and 5,400 wounded.

However, before the war's end the Kamikaze menace had been largely mastered. The first suicide pilots were volunteers anxious to sacrifice their lives for their country and their Emperor, and they performed their duty determinedly and faced death unflinchingly, but as the supply of volunteers dwindled and pilots had to be coerced into embarking on suicide missions more and more of them returned to base without having attacked, claiming failure to locate their targets. The Allies developed improved techniques for meeting attacks, and in the face of new tactics Kamikaze pilots found it increasingly difficult to crash their selected victims. The Special Attack groups had no opportunity to improve their own tactics and techniques. Because those who undertook such missions did not return to relate why they had succeeded or failed, the Japanese could build up no body of combat information to enable improvements to be effected.

Ohnishi, the originator of Kamikaze, committed *hara-kiri* before dawn on August 16 1945, the day after Japan's decision to surrender was publicly announced. 'I wish to express my deep appreciation to the souls of the brave special attackers,' he wrote, in a farewell message. 'They fought and died valiantly with faith in our ultimate victory. In death I wish to atone for my part in the failure to achieve that victory and I apologize to the souls of these dead fliers and their bereaved families.'

While the battle of Leyte Gulf was being fought and the first Kamikaze attacks were being delivered, the American invaders extended their hold on Leyte. Resistance became heavier as they pushed inland, but by November 2 both the north and south sections of Leyte Valley were firmly held. The weather at first caused heat exhaustion among the soldiers, but the heat soon gave way to almost continuous rain as the wet season set in. In November, when a typhoon swept over the area, the rainfall for the month was 23.5 inches. This made movement over the poor-quality roads and mired tracks, the deep swamps and flooded rice paddies arduous, difficult and sometimes impossible, and also delayed the construction of airfields. The

Fifth Air Force could not deploy adequate forces forward, and despite great efforts by the engineers and a display of much ingenuity, such as the pumping of coral from the ocean bed a mile through pipes to the Tacloban airfield, where it was used as a base for the strips, improvements came slowly.

The difficulties of weather and terrain prolonged the fighting on Leyte by delaying the American plans and allowing the Japanese to bring in substantial reinforcements. Although many of their ships were sunk, severely damaged or prevented from completing their unloading, the Japanese brought in through the port of Ormoc, on the west coast, some 45,000 troops and over 10,000 tons of *matériel*.

At the beginning of November, with the capture of Carigara, the Americans were ready to push into the Ormoc Valley in a drive to capture Ormoc. Lieutenant-General Sosaku Suzuki, commander of the XXXV Army, rushed reinforcements northward, and at Breakneck Ridge, covering the highway, the fighting assumed the familiar Pacific pattern—a bitter battle for precipitous ridges and steep knolls, honeycombed with defences and rendered treacherously slippery by the rain. Artillery, mortars, machine-guns, flamethrowers, bazookas, tanks—all had to be called into use to overcome the stubborn resistance of the 1st Japanese Division, which although lacking recent combat experience was one of the best equipped Japanese formations and fought courageously and intelligently.

By noon on November 12 the Americans had captured the crest of the ridge, and next day a hastily-mounted amphibious landing, aided by Filipino guerillas, captured 900-foot Kilay Ridge, its elaborate defences unoccupied, a few thousand yards behind the Japanese front line and commanding the road from Ormoc. Heavy fighting continued in this area until December 14. By then Japanese attempts to cross the central mountains to fall on the American rear in the Leyte Valley had failed, a co-ordinated ground and airborne attack against the Burauen airfields in southern Leyte Valley, although isolating Fifth Air Force headquarters for five days, had miscarried, and the Americans had made great progress at the southern end of Ormoc Valley. Here XXIV Corps troops had pushed across the mountains to the west coast. On November 9 the 26th Japanese Division had landed at Ormoc, but Allied air power had prevented the ships from completely unloading and the division had little artillery or equipment and few rations. Only one of its battalions landed its machine-guns. Rushed south, the division failed to dislodge the weak American force holding a perimeter on aptly named Shoestring Ridge and after fierce fighting, and with reinforcements reaching the Americans, was itself driven slowly back northwards. Then the 77th Division, in a completely successful amphibious landing that surprised the Japanese, came ashore at Deposito, just south of Ormoc, and the remnants of the 26th Division, trapped between two American forces, were compelled to withdraw into the mountains. On the 10th Ormoc, lying under a pall of heavy smoke, was captured, being cleared street by street and house by house. There was further hard fighting before the X and XXIV Corps linked hands north of Ormoc on December 22 to finally secure the entire Ormoc Valley.

Only a few hundred men of the XXXV Army escaped from Leyte to neighbouring islands. Suzuki himself was killed when the vessel in which he was fleeing was bombed in mid-April. The Japanese remnants, most half-starved, fled into the mountains of north-western Leyte, but they were denied the use of the small port of Palompon, on the north-west coast, by its capture in an unopposed amphibious landing on Christmas Day.

MacArthur thereupon declared organized resistance on Leyte at an end, but mopping up operations continued into May. The Sixth Army's capture of Leyte cost 3,504 killed, 89 missing and 11,991 wounded and it took far longer than MacArthur's or Krueger's headquarters had anticipated. No reliable figures are available for Japanese losses. Apparently about 800 were taken prisoners, but estimates of the dead vary from over 80,000, an Allied estimate, to nearly 50,000, a Japanese estimate which includes personnel of all three services.

Before the conclusion of the Leyte operations, to ensure adequate air cover for the invasion of Luzon, MacArthur's forces moved against Mindoro, which was known to be only lightly held by the Japanese. On December 13, as the invasion force made its approach, it came under Kamikaze attack, and a Val dive-bomber (Aichi), armed with two bombs, crashed on the cruiser *Nashville* (9,700, 1938), flagship of Rear-Admiral Arthur D. Struble, commander of the Attack Force. The flag bridge, combat information centre and communications office were wrecked, and fires caused ready ammunition to explode. A total of 133 officers and men were killed or died of wounds and 190 were wounded. The landing went in at San Jose, in south-western Mindoro on the 15th and met no opposition, but the Kamikaze attacks continued, especially against the resupply convoys, until the suicide pilots were directed against the vast armada advancing for the invasion of Luzon.

On December 17 Halsey's Task Force 38, which, covering the landing, had pounded the Luzon airfields whenever the uncertain weather allowed, began refuelling until worsening weather caused the hoses to be cast off. Next day an unsuspected typhoon whirled in on the fleet, bringing wind velocities of over 100 knots and mountainous seas. Three destroyers, having waited too long to reballast their partly empty tanks with sea water, capsized and sank; a number of other vessels were damaged, several being fortunate to survive; over 180 aircraft were lost overboard or destroyed, and nearly 800 officers and men died.

The assault on Luzon was scheduled for January 9 1945, when Krueger's Sixth Army was to come across the Lingayen Gulf beaches, as the Japanese had done a little over three years before. Except for Mindoro, the Luzon landings by Sixth Army differed from all the amphibious operations in the South-West, South and Central Pacific areas in that for the first time the immense amphibious fleet became the target of heavy Kamikaze attacks. These were more successful than the more orthodox tactics which had been employed against the invasion fleets in other amphibious landings, but although they took heavy toll of shipping and caused heavy casualties they did not stop the invasion or even dislocate its time-table.

Oldendorf's Assault Group—a total of 164 vessels including

63 minesweepers—passed through Surigao Strait into the Sulu Sea and thence by way of Mindoro Strait to Lingayen Gulf. On January 3 the first Kamikaze attack came in, and between then and the 13th Oldendorf and the amphibious forces which followed in his wake were under Kamikaze attack almost daily. In the first attack the escort carrier *Ommaney Bay* (7,800, 1944), hit by a Kamikaze carrying two bombs, was set on fire, had to be abandoned with 93 of her crew killed and missing and 65 wounded, and then sunk by a friendly torpedo. Although she survived and remained in action, refusing an offer of relief, the Royal Australian Navy's heavy cruiser *Australia* was the unluckiest Kamikaze victim. Between the 6th and 9th no fewer than five planes crashed her, two of them on the same day. Her casualties were 44 killed and 72 wounded and she was extensively damaged, but remarkable work by her damage control parties kept her in action, and she was fortunate that the last three crashes caused no casualties.

Following Third Fleet air strikes against Formosa on the 4th and 5th, which prevented aircraft being ferried into Luzon, and heavy raids on the Luzon fields on the 6th and 7th by Third Fleet, escort carrier and army planes, the intensity of the Kamikaze attacks died down. After the 7th there were no concerted attacks, but individual pilots came in from time to time. In all, on Oldendorf's and the amphibious fleets, between January 3 and 13 four vessels were sunk and 54 hit, of which 26 suffered damage ranging from moderate to serious. More than 738 Allied officers and men were killed and over 1,300 wounded.

On the 9th the assault troops landed on beaches higher up Lingayen Gulf—between Alacan, north of San Fabian, on the left, and Lingayen on the right—than those across which the Japanese had stormed in 1941. Except for some light shelling there was no opposition and by nightfall the troops were three miles inland. That night about 70 wooden power boats entered the gulf in an effort to attach explosives to the sides of Allied ships, but most were sunk or driven off and only one small ship was sunk and six damaged.

Against his better judgment, Yamashita had fought the

decisive battle for the Philippines on Leyte. Forces, equipment and supplies he needed for Luzon's defence had been funnelled by Terauchi's orders into the holocaust of Leyte and could not be replaced. Yamashita had nearly 275,000 men—about 125,000 more than the total estimated by General Willoughby, MacArthur's intelligence officer—but in numbers, equipment and quality, and with only token air support, they could only delay MacArthur's crushing offensive. Accordingly, Yamashita decided to make no attempt to hold the central Luzon plain or Manila, but to concentrate his forces in three mountainous strongholds with the object of pinning down as many United States divisions as possible for as long as possible. A garrison of 16,000 navy and 5,000 army troops in Manila was to fight a delaying action for the capital.

The most important of Yamashita's three strongholds was the Shobu redoubt, in the mountains east and north-east of Lingayen Gulf, with the fertile Cagayan Valley upon which the Japanese had to depend for much of their food. Here Yamashita, with his headquarters in the summer capital of Baguio, took personal command of some 152,000 of the best troops in Luzon. He intended reinforcing this group with the 105th Division from southern Luzon, but the first elements of this division were only tardily moving north when invasion came. In the second stronghold, the hilly country west of the central plain, dominating Clark Field, with its complex of airfields, stood Major-General Rikichi Tsukada's Kembu group, about 30,000 strong. The third, the Shimbu, redoubt lay in southern Luzon, where Lieutenant-General Shizuo Yokoyama's 80,000 men, a quarter of them naval troops, were concentrated in the mountains east and north-east of Manila. The lateness of the Japanese decision to abandon Leyte—it was not reached until mid-December—and the unexpected speed with which the invasion was mounted, coupled with the inadequacies of Luzon's transport facilities and the harassing tactics of the numerous guerillas, prevented Yamashita from adequately stockpiling food, ammunition and other supplies in the redoubts.

Once ashore, Sixth Army found itself fighting a war which was strange to it and for which it had not been trained. Instead of the fetid jungle it was confronted with open country, with highways and roads in place of muddied jungle trails, with blown bridges, mines and road blocks instead of cunning ambushes and steep defended ridges. Under these conditions supply services broke down, engineers and trucks were too few, and there was a serious shortage of bridging *matériel*. Except at two beaches in the I Corps sector, unsuspected sandbanks caused landing craft to ground some distance off shore. LCVPs could not get closer than 20 to 30 yards, while LSTs found themselves 100 yards from their beaches. In many cases three-pontoon causeways had to be constructed and sometimes even these fell short. Unloading with beach congestion fell behind schedule, and as the troops had pushed inland farther and faster than had been expected it took longer to deliver what had been landed to the front-lines.

These factors slowed the drive southward towards Manila of Lieutenant-General Griswold's XIV Corps, on the American right, even though the early rehabilitation of the Manila railway helped solve the supply problem. On the American left, Major-General Innis P. Swift's I Corps pushed forward against the weakly-held forward defences of the Shobu redoubt, but occasionally encountering determined resistance Swift became conscious that he was confronted with a much larger and stronger force than MacArthur believed existed. Griswold's fear of a large-scale counter-attack against the left flank and rear of XIV Corps if the latter pushed too rapidly ahead of I Corps, also helped slow the advance southwards.

MacArthur, anxious for the safety of prisoners of war and civilian internees in Manila and perhaps eager to enter Manila on his—and, incidentally, also Krueger's—birthday on January 26, prodded the commanders ashore for speed and still more speed. He himself was under pressure from Nimitz, who was anxious for long-range bombers to be deployed on Clark Field as a necessary preliminary to the invasions of Iwo Jima and Okinawa by the Central Pacific forces. Taking some risks with its exposed left flank, XIV Corps, which had secured bridge-heads across the Aaro River on the 17th, speeded up its advance southwards and by the 29th had reached San Fernando. There had been some stiff fighting with the Kembu group, and Clark Field was not securely in American hands until February 1.

Events now began to crowd in on one another as MacArthur implemented plans to speed up the conquest of Luzon. On January 29, 30,000 men of Major-General C. P. Hall's XI Corps, belonging to General Eichelberger's Eighth Army, landed on the beaches of San Felipe, San Narciso and San Antonio, on the coast 45 miles across the continuation of the Zambales Mountains from San Fernando. The area was already under guerilla control and the troops landed without preliminary air or naval bombardment and without meeting resistance. By February 5, pushing east from Subic Bay, they had joined hands with XIV Corps, sealing off the Bataan Peninsula. From the Zambales beaches on January 30 a small force was ferried across to seize Grande Island, near the mouth of Subic Bay, and next day 11th Airborne Division (Major-General J. M. Swing) landed on beaches on Nasugbu Bay to seize Nasugbu, western terminus of the road network running to Manila. These 8,000 men began their advance on Manila from the south-west, but met strong resistance and were unable to capture Nichols Field until February 12.

Before this XIV Corps had really got moving. Late on February 3 tanks of 1st Cavalry Division, rushing the Nova-liches bridge over the Bulacan River on the outskirts of Manila before it could be demolished by the Japanese, liberated 3,700 emaciated prisoners at Santo Tomas and a further 3,767 at the University of Manila. Next day 37th Division pushed into Manila from the north-west, freeing more than 1,000 prisoners of war in Bilibid prison. Although Yamashita had decided not to fight in Manila, Vice-Admiral Denshichi Okochi had ordered Rear-Admiral Sanji Iwabachi, commander of the 31st Naval Base Force, to defend it to the last and this he did. The capital had to be cleared almost yard by yard, and when on March 4 it was finally in American hands the capital, including the ancient Intramuros, was a mass of rubble. The Japanese garrison died almost to a man.

Before the fall of Manila operations for the reduction of

Corregidor and the other island forts, and the securing of Manila Bay, began. On February 15 American troops, transported from Subic Bay and covered by a bombardment support group under Commodore H. B. Farncomb, flying his flag in H.M.A.S. *Shropshire* (9,830, 1929), landed at Mariveles Bay on Bataan Peninsula. Willoughby had estimated that the Japanese had a considerable force in Bataan and feared Bataan might become the scene of a final stand similar to that made by the Americans in 1942. Actually the Japanese had only about 1,400 men instead of the 6,000 estimated and Bataan was simply a mopping-up operation. On the other hand, Corregidor was more strongly held than the Americans estimated. Willoughby thought there were only 850 Japanese on the island and the assault was planned on this basis, but it turned out the garrison numbered 5,000. Corregidor was brought under constant air and naval bombardment from January 21 and at 0830 on February 16 paratroops were dropped on two small areas on Topside. A second descent took place at 1240. These parachute attacks took the Japanese by surprise, but the dropping areas were small, and jump casualties were high, particularly in the first drop, many men falling into the sea or drifting over the high cliff edges. In all, 2,050 men floated down on the 16th and jump casualties, which had run as high as 25 per cent in the first drop, averaged 14 per cent for the two—approximately 280 men. In the first drop the island's commander, Captain Akira Itagaki, was killed when an observation post was captured, and through his death the defence lost much of its spirit and cohesion. An amphibious landing began in a cove on the island's south side at 1030 on the 16th, and by the 26th most of the island had been cleared. The Japanese had to be dug out or sealed in, as they fought to the last from caves and tunnels. The capture of Corregidor cost the Americans, in addition to jump casualties, 225 killed or missing and 405 wounded. A total of 4,500 Japanese dead were counted and it was estimated another 700 died escaping or were buried alive in caves. The tally of prisoners was only 20. MacArthur ceremonially returned to Corregidor on March

2. The other islands were then cleared, the last being occupied on April 16.

The work of clearing Manila Bay of mines and wrecks proved long, difficult and arduous, but the first Allied ship was able to enter the harbour on March 15. Over 500 mines had to be exploded and several hundred wrecks demolished or raised and removed. Wharves had to be repaired or rebuilt, approach roads constructed and cranes and other facilities provided. Commodore William A. Sullivan, who had cleared Mediterranean and European ports, including Naples and Cherbourg, considered Manila the worst salvage job he had been called upon to tackle.

The task of mopping up Yamashita's three redoubts, begun by the Sixth Army and turned over to the Eighth on June 30, had not been completed when the war ended. Yamashita, despite the capture of Baguio on April 27, fought determinedly and skilfully. By the end of June his men were holed up in the high mountains and had only nuisance value, but when the war ended he had 50,500 men to surrender. The Shimbu group surrendered 6,300, and in the Kembu group there were around 1,500 at the war's end. On Luzon 205,535 Japanese were killed or died as a result of military operations and 9,050 prisoners were taken. A further 50,260 were killed or died in defending the Central and Southern Philippines, excluding Leyte and Samar, with 2,695 being taken prisoners and 52,910 surrendering at the end of the war. Thus, exclusive of Leyte and Samar, the defence of the Philippines cost the Japanese 255,795 killed or dead and 11,745 taken prisoners, and on Japan's final defeat 114,011 surrendered. Nor were United States casualties light. American ground forces of the Sixth and Eighth Armies lost 10,380 killed and 36,550 wounded— 8,310 killed and 29,560 wounded on Luzon and 2,070 killed and 6,990 wounded in liberating the Central and Southern Philippines, excluding Leyte and Samar.

These operations in the Central and Southern Philippines, which began with a landing on Palawan on February 28, involved 38 landings between then and mid-April. Some of them were small affairs, carried out on tiny islands where there were few Japanese or which were unoccupied. Others involved heavy fighting against unyielding Japanese forces of considerable strength. Landings were made on Zamboanga Peninsula, Mindanao, on March 10, on south Panay on the 18th, on Cebu on the 29th, on Negros on the 29th, and on Jolo, in the Sulu Archipelago, on April 10. Deprived of air and naval support, the Japanese garrisons were doomed and their destruction, almost everywhere achieved with guerilla assistance, was merely a matter of time.

While the mopping-up in the Philippines was being carried out, the drive towards Japan by the Central Pacific forces under Nimitz, recently created a full admiral, was resumed. The delay in capturing Leyte had dislocated MacArthur's time-table, forcing him to postpone the invasion of Luzon from December 20 to January 9. As a result he could not release the Third Fleet until toward the end of January, and Nimitz, in turn, was compelled to postpone his next two assaults—that on Iwo Jima from January 20 to February 19 and that on Okinawa from March 1 to April 1. Halsey, having made an incursion into the South China Sea, where unfavourable weather reduced the effectiveness of his strikes against air and shipping targets, did not return to Ulithi until January 25. In accordance with the principle of alternating command he then handed over to Spruance and Third Fleet once again became Fifth Fleet.

Bombing of the Tokyo area from Saipan by Superfortresses (B-29s) began in November 1944, the first raid taking place on the 24th. The 3000-mile round trip cut bomb loads from ten to a mere three tons per aircraft. Also, the unescorted bombers were exposed to fighter attack, and with no intermediate landing-ground available on the return trip, those crippled by anti-aircraft fire or fighter attack or developing mechanical failures had no alternative, when they could not make base, but to ditch in the sea. Fighter opposition en route came mainly from airfields in the Bonin and Volcano Islands, midway between Saipan and Japan, which also alerted Tokyo to the approach of the bombers. The results of the raids were not only disappointing, but they provoked retaliation. Intermittent raids against the Saipan airfields by aircraft staged through Iwo Jima had by January 2 destroyed 11 Super-fortresses, seriously damaged 6 and caused minor damage to 35.

The disadvantages of bombing mainland Japan from Saipan had naturally been foreseen and in October, when the Joint Chiefs of Staff had ordered MacArthur to invade Luzon, they had directed Nimitz to seize one or more positions in both the Bonin-Volcano Islands and the Ryukyus. The Bonin Islands, the southern group of which was called the Volcano Islands, were mostly tiny volcanic cones and only Chichi Jima and Iwo Jima could be used as bomber bases. The latter, lying 660 miles south of Tokyo and 625 miles north of Saipan, was selected as the more suitable. Therefore it was made the first objective. In the Ryukyus, running for 600 miles from Honshu, southernmost of the Japanese home islands, to Formosa, there were five or six roomy islands, but since the need here was for an air and naval base which could be used if Japan had to be invaded the choice fell on Okinawa, which possessed a good harbour. It was made Nimitz' second target.

Iwo Jima, central island of the Volcano group, was only four miles and a half long and two and a half wide. It presented naturally strong defensive positions. In its south-western tip stood the extinct volcano of Mount Suribachi, 550 feet high and dominating the only suitable landing beaches on both the island's east and west coasts. At the opposite end of the island, in its north-eastern corner, were low, jagged hills, composed almost entirely of lava. Having correctly deduced that the Americans would soon move to seize Iwo Jima, the Japanese had strongly reinforced its garrison and the island's able commander, Lieutenant-General Tadamichi Kuribayashi, had elaborately fortified it. He had constructed more than 400 pill-boxes and blockhouses, mutually supporting and connected by a maze of tunnels, some of which had as many as five levels. Deep caves, none less than thirty feet underground, provided living and sleeping quarters for the garrison and, when the island was under air or naval bombardment, served as safe shelters. The pillboxes and bunkers, in contrast to the defences of other Pacific positions captured by the Americans and

Australians, were not built of coconut logs and earth but of concrete, and the coast defence guns were protected by concrete four to six feet thick. Artillery, mortars and machine-guns had been skilfully sited, and everywhere the defences had been art-fully camouflaged. The navy had built beach defences, which Kuribayashi's troops manned, so that at Iwo Jima the Japanese combined the two techniques of defence on the beaches and in depth inland.

Through air reconnaissance and photography the Ameri-cans had watched the defences grow. They knew Iwo Jima was being heavily reinforced with troops and *matériel*, and by air, surface and underwater action they did what they could to interfere with the flow of men and supplies. Chichi Jima was frequently bombed; for the absence of a harbour at Iwo Jima necessitated the Japanese landing men and supplies on Chichi Jima and transhipping them to Iwo Jima in small craft under cover of darkness. About 1,500 men intended to reinforce Kuribayashi's garrison were killed *en route* to the island, but when the Americans invaded he had 21,000 well-trained combat troops, a third of which were naval men and their morale was high. Although they knew Iwo Jima was being energetically strengthened and that the postponement of the assault gave the Japanese more time for improving the defences, the Americans did not realize just how formidable these had become. They expected to take the island in four days.

On February 16 and 17 the Fast Carrier Task Force, once again commanded by Mitscher, who had relieved McCain when Spruance relieved Halsey, raided the Tokyo area. It struck at airfields and factories, but, handicapped by bad weather, achieved only meagre results. The Fifth Fleet then sped back to provide cover for the invasion fleet and to lend support to Rear-Admiral William H. P. Blandy's Support Force, which on the 16th had opened the pre-landing bombardment.

Iwo Jima had already been under unremitting attack for many weeks. Early in December the Seventh Air Force, which had been keeping by-passed islands such as Truk, Ponape, Wotje, Marcus and Wake neutralized, had been ordered to con-centrate on Iwo Jima, and on the 8th it attacked with 62

Superfortresses and 102 Mitchells in co-ordination with a 70-minute bombardment by three heavy cruisers and six destroyers. Thereafter it was raided at least once daily and during the first fortnight of February was brought under day and night attack. It had also been a target for naval bombardment. When Blandy's force closed the island on February 16 Iwo Jima already had been deluged by 6,800 tons of bombs, 203 rounds of 16-inch, 6,472 rounds of 8-inch and 15,251 rounds of 5-inch projectiles, all within ten weeks. Heavy as had been the scale of attack it had never kept the airfields inoperational for more than a few hours at a time, and it had not stopped but merely delayed the reinforcement of the island's garrison and the elaboration of its defences. When the pre-landing air and naval bombardment concluded Iwo Jima had received the heaviest pounding of any island in the Pacific.

The 16th was overcast, with intermittent rain, and the deliberate bombardment did little damage. Next day visibility was much improved and results were correspondingly better. When the underwater demolition teams went in under the protection of small craft the Japanese evidently believed the invasion was starting, and batteries and machine-guns opened up, revealing their positions for the first time. The existence of these defences, especially of some coastal batteries, had not been suspected by the Americans, and although the small craft suffered severely the premature disclosure of the existence of the defences, by giving the Americans an opportunity to destroy them, saved many lives on D-day. To eliminate as many as possible, heavy fire was brought down on the 18th in the immediate vicinity of all known beach defences and on blockhouses, pillboxes and battery positions further inland.

On the 19th the pre-assault bombardment began at 0640, stopped briefly at 0800 to allow an air strike with bombs, rockets and napalm charges, and then concluded with half-an-hour's rapid neutralization firing. As the bombardment stopped, carrier aircraft swept in to give the beaches a seven-minute strafing, and they were followed by a dozen new, 160-foot long Landing Support Craft, Large (LST(L)), firing salvoes of 120 4.5-inch rockets and 40-mm. 20-mm. and 50-calibre

machine-guns. As they withdrew, the first assault waves landed
at 0900. Many amtracs bogged down in the soft volcanic ash
and cinders, which also slowed infantrymen from a run to a
walk. For some time enemy fire was not heavy, but within 20
or 30 minutes the beaches were under a withering fire, predominantly from mortars.

The landing on Iwo Jima was made by Major-General
Harry Schmidt's V Amphibious Corps, comprising the 3rd,
4th and 5th Marine Divisions, with Lieutenant-General Holland
M. Smith as commander of all troops. The 4th Division on the
right and the 5th on the left went ashore on the east coast beaches
running north-eastwards from the base of Mount Suribachi.
Progress was slow as the assault troops literally crawled up the
beaches and over the first lava terraces. Tanks were able to
lend little assistance, many being put out of action by anti-tank
fire or land mines or being bogged down in the soft ash, and
flamethrower teams were found more effective in blowing up
pillboxes and sealing off the entrances to caves and tunnels.
Thirty thousand men were landed that day and by nightfall,
when 2,400 were casualties, the marines held a 4,000-yard
long beach-head, barely 700 yards deep in the north but
reaching 1,100 yards across the narrow southern end of Iwo
Jima to the west coast beaches, thus isolating Mount Suribachi.
The defences on the mountain slopes were more vulnerable
to naval gunfire than those on the northern plateau leading to
Motoyama village and resistance at the southern end of the
beach-head was consequently easier to overcome.

Although the Japanese garrison fought without air or naval
support, whereas the Americans had overwhelming superiority
of both arms, Iwo Jima was conquered only yard by yard.
Indeed, but for the air and naval support it might never have
been taken. Only a handful of Japanese aircraft flew any sorties
against the American shipping and few Kamikaze pilots were
active, although an attack before and after dusk on February
21 hit the veteran *Saratoga*, killing 123 and wounding 192 of
her crew and inflicting such damage that the carrier had to
retire to Eniwetok before proceeding home for repairs.

On the 23rd the marines reached the summit of Mount

Suribachi and there raised the Stars and Stripes. A second flag-raising, this time with a larger flag, took place a few hours later, and a photographer's picture of this incident became probably the most widely published photograph of the Pacific War. Not until 1800 on March 16 was the island officially considered 'secured', and even after the 26th, when its subjugation was declared completed, pockets of resistance still remained. In the capture of Iwo Jima the marines lost 5,931 men killed or died of wounds and 17,272 wounded, while the navy had 881 men killed or died of wounds and 1,917 wounded. By the end of May, when the last Japanese pockets had been eliminated, over 22,000 of Kuribayashi's garrison had been killed and 867 taken prisoners. Whether Kuribayashi himself was killed or committed *hara-kiri* is not known. On April 7 the first raid on Japan by Superfortresses escorted by long range fighters based on Iwo Jima took place, but the air forces found the island of less value than had been anticipated, except as an emergency landing field for crippled planes.

Strategic bombing of the Japanese mainland began with a daylight, high altitude attack on selected targets, principally Japanese aircraft industry, and engine factories, varied by occasional experimental incendiary raids on urban areas. The weight of the assault increased as more Superfortresses came into service and maintenance facilities improved, but the campaign failed to seriously curtail, much less to knock out, Japanese aircraft production and the results of the few incendiary raids seemed inconclusive. A fire blitz on Nagoya on January 3, indeed, caused so little damage that it created an exaggerated belief among the Japanese in the effectiveness of their fire prevention system. They were soon disillusioned.

The failure of high-altitude bombing brought about an American command change and the substitution of predominantly incendiary attacks. On February 4, immediately after the change in command, these destroyed or severely damaged 1,039 buildings in the south-western section of Kobe and left 4,350 people homeless. Five weeks later, as fire blitz techniques were improved, came the most destructive air raid of the entire war, either in Europe or the Pacific. On March 10 over 300 Superfortresses, surprising the Japanese defences by sweeping in at low altitude, dropped more than 1,600 tons of bombs, mainly incendiaries, on Tokyo. At little cost the raid wrought tremendous destruction. It burnt out an area of 15.8 square miles, razed 267,171 buildings—a quarter of the number in Tokyo—killed 83,793 people, injured 40,918 and left 1,008,005 homeless.

The fire blitz, in which napalm as well as incendiary clusters and a small proportion of explosive bombs were used, was directed at first against the larger cities, but was extended to smaller cities as the extent of the destruction, damage and loss of life became clear. In this way, some 66 cities were largely burnt out, with very heavy casualties, a lowering of civilian morale and a disastrous effect on war production. Japan in these weeks was ablaze from end to end, and she had no adequate reply to this form of attack. American losses were consequently light, being only 1.9 per cent.

Concentration upon the burning down of Japanese cities did not cause the air forces to neglect direct attacks on Japanese shipping. The Japanese merchant marine had always been a high-priority target both with the navy and the air force, and once the Americans closed in on Japan extensive mining of Japanese home waters began. Despite the success of the air campaign against shipping, submarines were the decisive factor in the attrition of the Japanese merchant marine. At December 1, 1941 Japan possessed 5,421,143 tons of merchant ships and 575,464 tons of tankers, but by December 1 1944 the former had fallen to 1,978,572 tons. Tanker tonnage then totalled 868,962 tons, but the remaining months of the war witnessed a sharp increase in sinkings and at the time of her surrender Japan had only 1,547,418 tons of merchant ships and 266,948 tons of tankers still afloat, mostly in distant waters.

In all, Allied submarines sank 1,150½ merchant ships, with a gross registered tonnage of 4,859,634. About two per cent of this total fell to British, Dutch and other Allied submarines, the remainder to United States submarines. The air forces sank 359½ ships totalling 1,329,184 tons. By the end of the war Japan had lost from all causes 2,259 merchant ships of a gross registered tonnage of 8,141,591, with a further 275 vessels (755,802 tons) so severely damaged as to still be unrepaired. The steady attrition of Japanese merchant shipping, which reduced her imports of bulk commodities from 22,039,600 metric tons in 1940 to 2,743,200 in 1945, was an important contributing factor in Japan's ultimate defeat.

As events turned out, the last and largest amphibious operation of the Central Pacific forces was that on Okinawa, which the planners expected to be merely preliminary to the invasion of Japan. This was the biggest island the Central Pacific command assaulted. It was defended by a force of over 100,000, of whom about 70,000 were army troops, under a resolute and able commander, Lieutenant-General Mitsuru Ushijima. The Japanese were well armed and equipped, having adequate artillery, mortars, automatic weapons, anti-aircraft and anti-tank guns and plentiful stocks of ammunition. Ushijima planned his defences skilfully, selecting for his main position difficult terrain that naturally lent itself to defence and then fortifying the entire area in depth.

With Spruance in overall command and Turner as Expeditionary Force commander, the invasion of Okinawa was entrusted to Lieutenant-General Simon B. Buckner's Tenth Army, consisting of Hodge's XXIV Corps (7th and 96th Divisions) and General Geiger's III Amphibious Corps (1st and 6th Marine Divisions), with four other divisions—three army and one marine—available for special tasks or as reserves. The invasion fleet comprised 1,300 vessels of all sizes and the total troops for the assault phases of the operation numbered 183,000. Sixty miles long and varying in width from two to eighteen miles, Okinawa was the largest and most central of the Ryukyu Islands and lay only 350 miles from the Japanese mainland island of Kyushu.

Protracted operations by the air forces of the Central Pacific and the South-West Pacific, as well as by the United States air force based in China, were undertaken to isolate Okinawa and neutralize Japanese air and naval strength. Mitscher's fast carriers were particularly active in hitting airfields on Kyushu, operations in which they lost 116 aircraft and the carrier

Franklin (27,100, 1944) was severely damaged, and 800 of her crew killed. Okinawa, especially its airfields, was attacked repeatedly.

On March 26 Major-General Andrew D. Bruce's 77th Division, assigned the task of seizing the Kerama Islands, fifteen miles west of southern Okinawa, landed on the beaches of Aka, Geruma, Hokaji and Zamami, the four central islands of the group. There was no resistance on Hokaji, and Geruma was secured within three hours, enabling a fifth island, Yakabi, to be also captured that day. There was stiffer resistance on Aka and Zamami as the troops moved inland, but by the 29th, with fifteen separate landings, the entire group was in American hands. Their possession gave the assault forces a convenient naval and supply base close to Okinawa and eliminated a potentially dangerous threat to the amphibious shipping by capturing no fewer than 350 wooden suicide boats—made of plywood to defeat radar—with their explosive charges. On the 31st Keise Shima, an island 11 miles south-west of the selected landing beaches on Okinawa's west coast, was occupied without opposition and here twenty-four 155-mm. guns were emplaced to provide direct artillery support for the assault.

While these preliminary operations were being carried out the usual pre-landing softening up was under way. The naval bombardment began on the 25th, but because of the need for extensive minesweeping the bombardment was at long range and largely ineffective until the ships were free to close their targets on the 29th. For the first time a British force operated with the Fifth Fleet. Its presence was due to Churchill's insistence. He was determined, for reasons of national prestige, that if Japan were to be invaded the invasion should not be a wholly American operation. The United States Joint Chiefs of Staff did not want British forces present. Technically, they had sound arguments on their side, as British ships, especially carriers, created difficult supply problems owing to their different requirements and their multiplicity of aircraft types, and, tactically, although less vulnerable, they were in some ways ill-suited to Pacific requirements, having too few aircraft. Nevertheless, the Joint Chiefs' primary objection arose from intense

nationalism, and it was only the determination of Churchill and
the understanding tact of Roosevelt which made possible the
presence of a British force at Okinawa.[2]

The force was commanded by Vice-Admiral Sir Bernard
Rawlings and comprised 2 battleships, the fleet carriers
Indomitable (23,000, 1941), *Victorious* (23,000, 1941),
Indefatigable (23,000, 1944) and *Illustrious* (23,000, 1940),
5 cruisers, 1 of which belonged to the Royal New Zealand
Navy, and 11 destroyers, 2 of them Australian. The four
carriers between them carried 218 aircraft—73 Corsairs, 65
Avengers, 40 Seafires, 29 Hellcats, 9 Fireflies and, for air-sea
rescue, 2 Walruses. Throughout the Okinawa operation the
British force kept the airfields in the Sakishima Gunto area
neutralized by air raids and naval bombardment, American
escort carriers performing this task when Rawlings had to
refuel. The British dropped 958 tons of bombs and fired 200
tons of shells, losing 160 aircraft, in the two months they
operated, and claimed to have destroyed 96 Japanese aircraft
and to have sunk or damaged 200 ships, mostly under 250
tons. They suffered their share of Kamikaze attacks, but
because of their armoured flight decks the carriers which were
hit remained operational. *Formidable* relieved *Illustrious* when
she developed defects due to Mediterranean service.

On April 1, after the heaviest concentration of naval gunfire
ever to support a landing—44,825 rounds of 5-in. and larger
shells, 32,000 rockets and 22,500 mortar shells—the Americans came ashore on beaches north and south of Hagushi, at
the mouth of the Bishi River, on Okinawa's west coast. Simultaneously the 2nd Marine Division made a feint. landing,
which it repeated next day, against beaches on the south-east
coast. Opposition to the main landings, which were made with
III Amphibious Corps on the left and XXIV Corps on the
right, was slight, Ushijima making no attempt to defend the
beaches. By nightfall the Americans held a beachhead 15,000
yards long and in places 5,000 yards deep, and they had
60,000 men ashore. Next day they had no difficulty in driving
through to the east coast, on the shores of Nakagusuku Bay.

Progress in northern Okinawa was rapid. As they advanced

northward the marines met only scattered resistance until they reached the rugged hills of Motobu Peninsula, where opposition hardened. Even so, it was quickly overcome after some heavy fighting and by the 18th northern Okinawa was officially considered secured. The island of Ie Shima, lying three and a half miles off the western tip of Motobu Peninsula and 20 miles north of the Hagushi beaches, was invaded on the 16th and secured by the 21st after some bitter fighting. There were still some Japanese pockets, but these were mopped up in the next few days. Possession of Ie Shima provided the Americans with additional airfields for the support of operations on Okinawa. The capture of Ie Shima cost the 77th Division 218 killed or died of wounds and 902 wounded, and, according to Bruce, the divisional commander, 'the last three days of this fighting were the bitterest I ever witnessed'. Japanese losses were 4,706 killed, including civilians who had been armed and given uniforms, and 149 taken prisoners.

The main Japanese defences were in the south, where Ushijima had constructed formidable fortifications amid the steep hills and narrow ravines around Shuri, north-east of Naha. The XXIV Corps, reinforced by the floating reserve, the 27th Division, was bloodily repulsed before these strong, well-defended positions, and it was May 21, after fierce fighting and slow progress, before the Americans broke through to the inner ring of Shuri's defensive positions. Then heavy rain—twelve inches fell in the last ten days of May—greatly hampered operations, so that practically no progress was made for some days. On the 31st, however, Shuri, the second town in Okinawa, was captured. It had been relentlessly shelled and bombed and the entire town had been reduced to rubble. The Japanese made an orderly withdrawal to organize another line of defence further south, and another month was required to dispose of them. By July 2 the Okinawa campaign was at an end.

While the operations on land were proceeding slowly to their inevitable conclusion, the Fifth Fleet and the shipping off Okinawa had been under frequent air attack, particularly from Kamikaze pilots. Spruance's flagship, the cruiser *Indianapolis* (9,800, 1932), was put out of action on March 31 and, after temporary repairs, had to sail for the United States. On April 6, when 355 Kamikazes flew missions, two destroyers acting as picket boats were sunk and others damaged, but the Japanese pilots were unable to get through to Mitscher's carriers. However, 200 reached Okinawa, where they blew up 2 loaded ammunition ships, sank two small vessels and damaged 22 naval ships. On this day the super-battleship *Yamato* (62,315, 1940), the light cruiser *Yahagi* (6,652, 1942) and eight destroyers headed for Okinawa, with insufficient fuel aboard, if they got as far as Okinawa, to make the return voyage. They were sighted and reported and early on the 7th Mitscher's carrier aircraft sank *Yamato*, *Yahagi* and two destroyers and drove the surviving vessels back to base.

Towards the end of May, because of the strain on commanders of continuous action, especially under Kamikaze attack, Halsey relieved Spruance and McCain took over from Mitscher, the fleet again becoming Third Fleet. By June 10 there was no need for Third Fleet to remain in Okinawan waters. Kamikaze attacks had declined sharply in the face of improved methods of meeting them and the reduced supply of suicide pilots, air power on Okinawa had been built up substantially, and the airfields of Kyushu were being neutralized by Superfortresses bombing from bases in China and the Marianas.

One unusual incident in late May, when the Japanese briefly stepped up their air attacks, requires mention. This was a suicide assault against Yontan airfield by about 70 commandos. Of the five aircraft carrying them, four, with the commandos still aboard, were shot down in flames, but the fifth made a belly landing on Yontan runway and as it came to a grinding halt about eight or ten commandos leapt out and began tossing grenades and incendiaries among parked American aircraft. They destroyed 7 and damaged 26 planes and set fire to 70,000 gallons of fuel. All the Japanese were killed.

Okinawa was the costliest operation in the Central Pacific. American losses were 12,520 killed—army 4,675, marines 2,938 and navy 4,907—and 36,631 wounded—army 18,099, marines 13,708 and navy 4,824. Non-battle casualties among the marines and army troops totalled 16,211. Thirty-six ships were sunk and 368 damaged, the majority by air action, and 763 American aircraft were lost in the three months from April 1 to July 1. About 110,000 Japanese were killed in the land fighting and 7,400 were taken prisoners.

While the fighting for Luzon and the amphibious assaults on Iwo Jima and Okinawa dominated the Pacific scene in the first months of 1945, there was also activity in the South-West Pacific and in South-East Asia. In the former theatre a series of campaigns was undertaken by the Australians against the by-passed Japanese garrisons; in the latter, following the Japanese disaster in front of Imphal and Kohima, Burma was recon-quered.

On Bougainville, where II Australian Corps relieved the Americans, there were some 42,000 Japanese in October 1944, comprising XVII Army (6th Division, one brigade and 6,000 naval troops). General Savige's II Corps comprised the 3rd Division (7th, 15th and 29th Brigades) and the 11th and 23rd Brigades. These forces, aided by native scouts and guerillas, gradually drove the Japanese back to their bases, where for the rest of the war they suffered starvation and illness. In the drive southward along the coastal corridor toward Buin there were occasional sharp clashes with Japanese rearguards entrenched in strong natural positions, and in late March and the first days of April, as the Australians crossed the Puriata River, the Japanese launched an eight-day offensive in which they lost 620 killed. Apart from this action fighting was on a small scale or confined to vigorous patrolling. On Bougainville the Australians lost 516 killed or died of wounds and 1,572 wounded, with 56 deaths from non-battle causes. Some 8,500 Japanese were killed and another 9,800 died of illness. When peace came 23,571 surrendered.

On New Britain the Japanese had 53,200 soldiers, 16,200 naval troops and 21,000 construction workers, but most of these were in and around Rabaul. Eighth Area Army comprised the 17th and 38th Divisions, five independent brigades or regi-ments, and the naval troops previously mentioned. The Ameri-cans were relieved by 5th Australian Division (4th, 6th and 13th Brigades, with some commandos and New Guinea infantry), which was commanded by Major-General Alan Ramsay until April and then by Major-General H. C. H. Robertson. The Americans had been in the Cape Gloucester area of western New Britain, with a smaller force at Cape Hoskins, on the northern coast. When the Australians went in, however, they elected to place their main strength at Jacquinot Bay, on New Britain's south coast, about 40 air miles south from the neck of the Gazelle Peninsula, at the northern end of which lay Rabaul. At the same time they sent a smaller force into Cape Hoskins, and by an advance along both coasts soon drove the Japanese, who were not very aggressive, into the peninsula and established firm control of the neck. Australian losses were light—53 killed, 21 dead from non-battle causes and 140 wounded.

There were some 35,000 Japanese based on Wewak in New Guinea, mostly survivors from the divisions which had been shattered in earlier fighting from Kokoda Track days onwards. These were the 20th, 41st and 51st Divisions, whose combined strength was still equal to about two full divisions, and they formed XVIII Army. The 6th Australian Division (16th, 17th and 19th Brigades) under Major-General Jack Stevens relieved XI United States Corps in the Aitape-Wewak area. The Americans, as elsewhere in the South-West Pacific, had been standing on the defensive, but the Australians took the offensive with a two-pronged drive along the coast and through the Torricelli Mountains inland. Except when interrupted by torrential rain the advances made slow but steady progress and on May 11 the Japanese base of Wewak was captured, the airfield being taken a few days later. Under cover of strong rearguards in the hills south of Wewak, the Japanese retreated inland. In these operations the Australians lost 442 killed or died of wounds and 1,141 wounded, while no fewer than 16,203 were admitted to hospital, 6,227 of whom were victims of malaria. About 9,000 Japanese were killed and 269 taken prisoners.

The largest and most ambitious operations carried out by the Australians in 1945 were those directed at Borneo. I Australian Corps, commanded by General Morshead, first seized Tarakan

Island with Brigadier D. A. Whitehead's 26th Brigade Group.
The invasion of Tarakan was made possible only by the provision of shipping by MacArthur, still in control, at least
nominally, of operations in the South-West Pacific. The 6th
United States Amphibious Group, commanded by Rear-
Admiral Forrest B. Royal, put the attacking force ashore under
cover of ships of the United States Seventh Fleet, including
an Australian cruiser and destroyer, and an American task
force commanded by Berkey. The R.A.A.F. and the United
States Thirteenth Air Force provided the air support. Tarakan
was bombed from April 12 and on the 30th Sadau Island,
in Batagau Strait, which separates Tarakan Island from the
mainland, was seized, so that artillery might be emplaced there
to cover engineers clearing 60-foot gaps in the underwater
obstacles protecting the beaches at Lingkas, the port of Tarakan. This task was successfully completed with the aid of a
smoke screen, a 20-minute naval bombardment and air strikes
lasting thirty minutes. Next morning, after a naval bombardment and air strikes, the troops landed unopposed on the
Lingkas beaches. Resistance from the Japanese force of about
2,000 stiffened as the Australians pushed inland, and mines,
booby traps and tunnel defences were encountered. The high
ground overlooking the beach-head was captured on May 4 and
next day both the town of Tarakan and the airfield fell. Fairly
heavy fighting inland continued until June 13, by which time
1,540 Japanese dead had been counted and 252 prisoners had
been taken. Another 300 surrendered after the cease fire. The
Australians had 225 killed and 669 wounded.

The primary purpose of the seizure of Tarakan was to secure
an airfield for further operations in Borneo, but because of
repair difficulties the airfield was not ready in time. Other bases,
including Tawitawi, which with Jolo Island was taken by the
Americans in April, had to be used to support the attacks on
Brunei Bay, on the north-west coast of Borneo, and Balikpapan, on the shores of Macassar Strait. Major-General G. F.
Wootten's 9th Division, which, with special units and R.A.A.F.
personnel, numbered 29,000 men, was put ashore at Brunei
Bay on June 10 by Royal's amphibious group, with naval cover

provided by Berkey and Barbey's Attack Force. The 24th Brigade went ashore on Labuan Island, off the northern end of Brunei Bay, and the 20th Brigade at Brunei Bluff, on the bay's south shore, and on nearby Muara Island. The landings were unopposed but there was occasional dogged resistance inland. The operations were carried out in sweltering weather. Brunei Bay, once it was completely secured, provided an advanced fleet base and Labuan Island an airfield. Australian casualties were 114 killed or died of wounds and 221 wounded. The Australians probably killed almost 1,400 Japanese and another 1,800 may have been destroyed in guerilla operations in North Borneo. The number of prisoners taken was 130.

The Balikpapan assault was the largest amphibious operation carried out by Australian troops. Including 2,000 R.A.A.F. personnel, Major-General E. J. Milford's 7th Division (18th, 21st and 25th Brigades) had a total strength of 33,446. Owing to the large amount of minesweeping necessary, intensive air bombing of the Japanese defences began twenty days before D-day. American underwater demolition teams, working under fire, cleared the beach approaches, and on July 1 the landing took place between Klandasan and Stalkudo, south-east of Balikpapan. The senior naval commander was Barbey, the Cruiser Covering Group was under Rear-Admiral Ralph S. Riggs and the Attack Group was commanded by Rear-Admiral Albert G. Noble. The landing, which illustrated the effective use of fire power of artillery and air forces, followed the familiar pattern of amphibious operations. The town of Balikpapan was captured on the 3rd and next day Manggar airfield was taken. By the 9th both airfields were firmly in Australian hands and by the 22nd Japanese resistance had been overcome. The cost to the Australians was 229 killed or died of wounds and 634 wounded. The Japanese had slightly over 2,000 men killed, of whom 1,783 were actually counted, and they yielded the Australians 63 prisoners.

The fighting in South-East Asia in 1945 was on a heavier scale than in New Guinea and Borneo, but, as with the Australian operations against the by-passed garrisons, it did not contribute directly to Japan's final defeat. In Arakan as the

United States Navy

American amtracs filled with assault troops head for the volcanic island of Iwo Jima after it received the heaviest sea and air pounding of any island in the Pacific

The last and largest amphibious operation of the Central Pacific was that on Okinawa. This picture shows the burning remains of two Japanese planes shot down while attacking American ships anchored off the island

United States Navy

Australian War Memorial

Had the allies recognised the sanctity of the Emperor of Japan and guaranteed that he would not have been tried as a war criminal, the Japanese may have surrendered earlier, making the atom bombing of Hiroshima, above, and Nagasaki, below, unnecessary

Australian War Memorial

monsoon eased there was some severe local fighting as both
sides reoccupied points of tactical importance abandoned when
the rain began. At first the Japanese were particularly aggressive but when the British began a general advance on December
14 1944 only slight opposition was met. The Japanese, having
decided they could not hold the coast or the Mayu Valley,
began to withdraw and, progressing rapidly, the British
occupied Akyab on January 3 without meeting resistance. On
the 21st an amphibious assault was made on Ramree Island.
There was no opposition on the beaches, but inland the
Japanese resisted strongly. The town of Ramree was not occupied until February 9 and it was the 17th before the island was
secure. The possession of Akyab and Ramree gave the British
airfields vital for the supply of troops engaged in the reconquest
of Burma.

On the central front the Fourteenth Army had by February 1
closed up to the Irrawaddy on a 140-mile front and had established bridge-heads across the river north of Mandalay. On the
northern front, where General Sultan now controlled operations, the advance from Myitkyina had been slow. Sultan's
command comprised an American brigade, in which the
Marauders had been incorporated, 36th British Division and
five Chinese divisions, shortly to be reduced to three.
By November 28, he had invested Bhamo, but the Japanese
garrison of 900, under cover of an attack against a Chinese
division protecting the rear of the investing forces, broke out on
the night of December 14-15, and, infiltrating the Chinese,
successfully reached Namhkam. Sultan's attack towards the old
Burma Road in conjunction with the Chinese offensive from the
Salween front compelled the Japanese to withdraw in the face
of such overwhelming force and on January 20 Sultan linked
up with the Yunnan armies. This opened land communications
with China and on February 4 the first convoy by the Ledo
Road reached Kunming.

It was now that the massive pressure of Fourteenth Army
began to first exert itself. Slim crossed the Irrawaddy in mid-
February. Focusing Japanese attention on Mandalay by clever
deception measures and inducing them to believe it was the

army's sole objective, he captured Meiktila by surprise on March 3. At the same time he was investing Mandalay from the north and south. By weakening the opposition against him these operations enabled Sultan to capture Lashio on the 7th. The Japanese launched an all-out effort to recapture Meiktila. On the 15th the British began to fly in reinforcements, but the airfield at Meiktila was under Japanese attack and, although only one of the 54 aircraft which landed was hit, it was obvious that landing was a hazardous affair. Next morning it was discovered that a party of Japanese had dug in during the night on the eastern side of the runway, and not until late in the afternoon was it possible to resume the fly-in. However, continued Japanese attacks then finally closed the airfield, and from the 18th supplies to Meiktila had to be air dropped. Heavy fighting, much of it at close quarters, followed but the Japanese attacks were repulsed with heavy loss and by the 31st, with the arrival of fresh troops, Meiktila was secure. Meanwhile, Mandalay had also been captured.

The Japanese, whose forces had been weakened by the withdrawal of troops to defend Indo-China, exposed to attack by the fall of the Philippines, were steadily driven back, and on May 3, after an amphibious landing combined with a parachute drop, Rangoon was occupied without opposition, the Japanese having evacuated it a few days earlier. There was further heavy fighting when the Japanese remnants sought to break out across the Sittang, but when the last battle of Burma had concluded only between 4,000 and 5,000 Japanese had succeeded in crossing the river. The remainder had been killed or captured. Japanese battle casualties, including deaths from starvation or illness, were high. The British and Indians, in the main actions alone, lost 4,115 killed or missing and 13,764 wounded.

As early as February or March the Japanese had put out peace-feelers to the Russians. They would have been better advised to have made a more direct approach to Britain and the United States through a neutral power, but although many high-ranking officers and officials in Japan were convinced by early 1945 that Japan was doomed, Japanese psychology was such that steps to bring the war to an end could not be taken. At all cost, if the approach for peace were to be initiated by the Japanese, there had to be some face-saving formula. The Russians appreciated this and since the seeds of the cold war with the western world were already being sown they refused to furnish the face-saving pretext. The Japanese approaches thus came to nought. On the Emperor's insistence they were renewed in July but were completely ignored by the Russians. Although the necessity for peace and its inevitability were appreciated by influential Japanese, the need to preserve face precluded immediate unconditional surrender.

Then, on August 6 an atomic bomb was dropped on Hiroshima. It destroyed 40,653 of the 50,160 buildings in the city proper and severely damaged a further 8,396. Casualties were estimated at 71,379 killed and 68,023 injured, without taking into account those resulting from the latent effects of radiation. The bomb destroyed 4.7 square miles. Thus, the first atomic bomb ever dropped neither caused as much destruction nor as many casualties as the March fire raid on Tokyo, but its psychological effects were probably much greater. Three days later, on the 9th, a second bomb was dropped on Nagasaki. On this occasion there was no wind to fan the flames and destruction was not as complete as at Hiroshima. An area of 1.45 square miles out of 3.84 square miles was destroyed. The Japanese estimated that 25,680 people were killed and 23,345 injured, but post-war American investigators considered these figures too low and raised them to about 40,000 killed and 60,000 injured.

The Russians, who had been transferring divisions to Manchuria for nearly six months, declared war on Japan on the 8th and next day attacked. There is no doubt their action was precipitated, firstly, by the dropping of the atom bomb and, secondly, by the knowledge that Japan was anxious to surrender. Stalin was determined the Soviet Union would be engaged in the war against Japan before peace came. The Russian operations were well planned and carried out with overwhelming superiority in numbers and weapons. They at once invaded Manchuria, Korea and southern Sakhalin, using airborne troops freely to occupy strategic points, and later moved also into the Kuriles. The Japanese forces, ill-equipped for large-scale open warfare, were soon crushed. On the pretext that there had been no formal capitulation of the armies opposing them, the Russians continued the fighting for a few days after Japan's formal surrender. The Russians claimed 594,000 prisoners and took 600 tanks and 1,565 guns.

Japan surrendered unconditionally on the 14th. Hiroshima and Nagasaki provided the face-saving pretext Japanese leaders had been seeking, and on September 2, in an impressive cere-mony attended by representatives of all the Allies, the instrument of surrender was signed on board the battleship *Missouri*. Similar ceremonies followed at intervals as the by-passed Japanese forces surrendered in behest to the Emperor's directions, some of these, such as that at Singapore, being invested with a symbolical significance because of their early victories over the Allies. For many months, in some instances for several years, small parties of Japanese and odd stragglers, unaware or unconvinced the war was over, lived a life of star-vation and privation in jungle or mountain fastnesses before finally laying down their arms. As Japanese forces were gradually repatriated to their homeland the sight of Japan's devastated cities and the presence of the occupation forces brought home to the returning soldiers, airmen and sailors the bitter fruits of defeat.

NOTES AND REFERENCES

1. S. W. Roskill, *The War at Sea, 1939-1945*, III; *The Offensive, pt 2, June 1 1944—August 14, 1945* (London, 1961), 211, says *Australia* was hit by a Kamikaze and that this was the first suicide attack on any Allied ship. This statement is supported by Rikihei Inoguchi, Tadashi Nakajima and Roger Pineau, *The Divine Wind: Japan's Kamikaze Force in World War II* (Annapolis, 1958), Appendix A, p.211, which lists two Kamikaze aircraft with one escort as having flown Kamikaze missions on October 21, 1944 with unknown results. Samuel Eliot Morison, *Leyte June 1944—January 1945* (English edition, 1958), 148 n., states the attack on *Australia* was not an organised Kamikaze attack. I believe that when the relevant volume of the Australian official naval history is published it will adequately prove the truth of the statement in my text.
2. On the politics of the participation of the British Fleet in the Pacific see B. B. Schofield. *British Sea Power: Naval Policy in the Twentieth Century* (London, 1967), 211-3.

FURTHER READING:

In addition to the official histories mentioned in the reading list for the previous chapter, the following should be consulted for the operations covered in Chapter 12: Whitman S. Bartley,

Iwo Jima: Amphibious Epic (Washington, 1954); Charles S. Nichols and Henry I. Shaw, *Okinawa: Victory in the Pacific* (Washington, 1955); M. Hamlin Cannon, *Leyte: The Return to the Philippines* (Washington, 1954); Robert Ross Smith, *Triumph in the Philippines* (Washington, 1963); Roy E. Appleman, James M. Burns, Russell A. Gugeler and John Stevens, *Okinawa: The Last Battle* (Washington, 1948), the last three being in the official history of the United States Army in World War II series; Gavin Long, *The Final Campaigns* (Canberra, 1963) and George Odgers, *Air War Against Japan 1943-45* (Canberra, 1957) in the Australian official history series; Samuel Eliot Morison, *Leyte June 1944-January 1945* (English edition, 1958), *The Liberation of the Philippines: Luzon, Mindanao, the Visayas 1944-1945* (English edition, 1959), and *Victory in the Pacific 1945* (English edition, 1960), these being respectively vols. 12, 13 and 14 of the *History of United States Naval Operations in World War II*; S. W. Roskill, *The War at Sea 1939-1945*, vol. 3 *The Offensive* pt 2 June 1, 1944-August 14, 1945. (London, 1961); and *Report to the Combined Chiefs of Staff by Supreme Allied Commander, South-East Asia, 1943-1945* (London, 1951). For the Battle of Leyte Gulf, James A. Field's *The Japanese at Leyte Gulf: The Sho Operation* (Princeton, 1947) and Stanley W. Falk, *Decision at Leyte* (New York, 1966) should be consulted. Rikihei Inoguchi, Tadashi Nakajima and Roger Pineau, *The Divine Wind: Japan's Kamikaze Force in World War II* (Annapolis, 1958) is illuminating on the Japanese suicide pilots. For the end of the war and Russian participation, Alexander Werth, *Russia at War 1941-45* (London, 1964) should be consulted. For general reading, Robert Sherrod, *On to Westward: War in the Central Pacific* (New York, 1945), Walter Karig, *Battle Report: Victory in the Pacific* (Washington, 1960), Richard F. Newcomb, *Iwo Jima* (New York, 1965), and John G. Glenn, *Tobruk to Tarakan* (Adelaide, 1960) can be recommended.

fourteen

AFTER THOUGHTS

The war in the Pacific certainly should have ended at least six months before it did. Japan had been defeated when the Tojo Cabinet fell on July 18 1944, and its successor, the Cabinet led jointly by General Kuniaki Koiso and Admiral Mitsumasa Yonai, could scarcely have had any illusions as to the war's outcome. Even if the loss of the battle of the Philippine Sea, the American capture of Saipan and the first bombing of the Japanese mainland since the Doolittle raid of 1942 did not convince them that victory could no longer be won, they could have been under no delusions once Leyte was lost and Luzon invaded. The fire blitz, at least after the disastrous March holocaust in Tokyo, underlined the inevitability of early defeat.

There was no peace, however, because of the intransigent decision of Roosevelt and Churchill that only unconditional surrender was acceptable. This applied both to Germany and to Japan and it prolonged the fighting both in Europe and the Pacific, at the cost of thousands of Allied and enemy lives and untold misery and suffering. Asian psychology, with its extreme sensitivity to loss of face, prevented any overtures from Japan without an acceptable excuse for ending the war, such as Hiroshima and Nagasaki eventually furnished. Despite all the reverses, the military and naval junta was still firmly in the saddle in Japan and was not prepared to admit that it had failed. The military leaders would not suggest unconditional surrender to the nation, and no civilian statesman, no matter how influential or how convinced he may have been privately that the war was lost and should be ended, could gird himself to oppose the militarists and advocate such a course—but the peace-feelers to the Russians show clearly enough that the Japanese were looking for a way out of the war they had so wantonly begun.

Perhaps no overture by the Allies would have succeeded, but at least the effort was worth making and should have been made. Only an approach direct to the Emperor, possibly ignoring normal diplomatic channels and protocol, would have produced results, and it may have been necessary to accompany it with a guarantee of the continued sanctity of the Emperor's sacred person. There certainly is some evidence for thinking that if the future position of the Emperor had been clarified at the time of the Potsdam Declaration, peace might have come sooner than it did. The question is intricate and involved, and cannot be determined with certainty. Yet a genuine and determined effort to bring home to the Japanese leaders the consequences of continued resistance—the devastation of their cities, the destruction of their shipping and the starving of the civilian population—and to provide an acceptable explanation for surrender might have ended the war in March.

President Harry S. Truman's decision to drop the atom bomb is a second question of paramount concern. Since it introduced nuclear warfare, the decision has been closely analysed and has provoked much controversy. When Hiroshima and Nagasaki were bombed Japan was already defeated, a fact which, as we have seen, her leaders knew but would not publicly admit. The fire blitz took heavier toll of life and property than the destruction wrought by the atom bombs, and the blockade, the dismemberment of her conquests and the sinking of her merchant ships were combining to bring Japan to the brink of starvation. At a time when the whole nation was organizing to resist an expected invasion, the bombing of Hiroshima and Nagasaki provided an immediate face-saving excuse for surrender. As the United States Strategic Bombing Survey stresses, the atom bombs 'permitted the Prime Minister to bring the Emperor overtly . . . into a position . . . to override the remaining objectors'.[1]

The alternatives to atomic bombing were not confined to a full-scale invasion of Japan or a continuation of the blockade and of orthodox bombing. The true alternative was the creation of conditions which would have made it possible for the Japanese to surrender before Hiroshima and Nagasaki were laid waste. If this could have been achieved, if the Japanese leaders could have been given a face-saving formula, then the decision to drop the atom bombs was morally indefensible. It is the fact that no attempt was made to induce Japan's surrender that justifies moral criticism of Truman's decision. This writer believes that if the Allies had shown an awareness of Japanese susceptibilities in respect of the sanctity of the Emperor's person, had guaranteed that his status would not be altered and that he would not be tried as a war criminal, but that these guarantees would not operate if resistance continued, an earlier peace might have been secured and a decision to drop the atom bombs rendered unnecessary.

If this premise is wrong, if no undertakings by the Allies would have prompted early surrender, Hiroshima and Nagasaki were justified. Truman's decision, however much humanitarians may deplore it, was correct, the result of a realistic appraisal of the situation. Invasion would have brought the war to an end, but despite Japan's parlous plight it would have been a frighteningly costly operation to the Allies and, more particularly, to the Americans. United States casualties in capturing small islands in the Central Pacific drive sufficiently indicate that the Japanese defence of their mainland would have been dogged and fanatical, and losses among the invaders, even with crushing superiority in the air and in *matériel*, undoubtedly would have been heavy. It is probable but not certain that reliance upon a continuation of the blockade and orthodox bombing would ultimately have resulted in surrender, but the process would have been slow and might have been prolonged, and would have caused the Japanese heavier casualties and greater suffering among civilians than the use of the atom bomb. From the Allied point of view, Hiroshima and Nagasaki were a more economical, effective and quicker way of bringing the war to an end than either invasion or reliance upon the blockade and orthodox bombing.

It was not known for certain until July that an atom bomb had been successfully contrived, and it was believed that an invasion of Japan would have to be carried out to bring the Japanese to surrender. In these circumstances, the assaults on Iwo Jima and Okinawa were necessary preliminaries. In the event, though the planners could not be expected to foresee this, both were unnecessary. Neither was used by the air force to the extent expected in the bombing of the Japanese mainland, and each contributed very little to the fire blitz on Japanese cities. This was the tragedy of these two costly operations; their contribution to ultimate victory was not commensurate with the casualties suffered in their capture. But if capitulation had not come, if it had been necessary to invade Japan, the capture of both islands would have been amply justified.

On the other hand, the final campaigns of the Australians in Bougainville, New Britain, New Guinea and Borneo were unnecessary, but in their favour it must be admitted they were relatively economical of life. Rather over 1,000 Australians were killed in their prosecution. However, the by-passed Japanese were effectively cut off from their homeland, many were underfed and suffering from diseases, and, for the most part, deprived of air and naval support, they were impotent, at least offensively. They could and should have been contained by purely defensive and harassing operations. The assaults on Tarakan, Brunei Bay and Balikpapan might have been avoided. They were dictated largely by political motives and international jealousy. There was no need to stage them when they took place, and if they had been postponed they would not have been required. The decisive theatre was the Japanese mainland,

and if it could be bombed and blockaded into submission, as was occurring, subsidiary operations elsewhere were valueless.

Victory in the Pacific was not, as, for example, MacArthur's propagandist communiques made it appear at the time, and as .many American writers have made it appear since the war's end, a wholly American victory. It was an Allied victory, although the United States played the predominant role, with its principal and decisive advance not MacArthur's drive to the Philippines but Nimitz' sweep across the central Pacific. Indeed, the first successes against Japanese troops were won by the Australians in the South-West Pacific. They held the arena after the fall of Malaya and the Indies as in Europe Britain had held the arena after the fall of France. However, the role played by the Australians was not solely a defensive one. They defeated determined Japanese offensives in Papua, and in both Papua and New Guinea, seizing the initiative, they followed up their successful defence by swinging over to the offensive. Although United States forces participated in certain phases of these offensives, they were essentially Australian victories and shattered a Japanese army. More than 100,000 Japanese died in Australian New Guinea. In Burma the British and Indians secured no parallel results until the closing months of the war.

Throughout the war in the Pacific, Japan had the Chinese war on her hands and she had also to guard her Manchurian frontier. These commitments absorbed never fewer than half her combat divisions, although as the war continued these were increasingly new and raw. Most of her veteran, battle-tried divisions fought, and fought well, in the Pacific.

Putting the facts in their true perspective, however, does not minimize America's contribution to victory. India, Australia, Britain, New Zealand and her other Allies put into the field almost as many as the twenty-seven divisions which the United States had in the Pacific when the war ended, but after 1943 these played relatively minor roles. The war with Japan could only have been won by the United States Navy and Army. America's immense man-power, enormous industrial resources, unrivalled flair for logistical organization, originality and imaginative thinking in solving the peculiar military, naval and air problems encountered in the Pacific—these were decisive factors leading to victory. From mid-1943 the Americans bore the brunt of the fighting, especially in the Central Pacific. They defeated the Japanese by superior numbers, superior equipment, and superior fire power. Their policy of saturation, of overwhelming the defence by sheer weight of numbers and *matériel*, were skilfully applied.

The Japanese soldier was hardy and courageous, skilled and obedient, willing, even eager, to die for his country. The quality of the Japanese command and administrative systems was inferior to that of the soldiers it directed and administered. Japanese military and naval planning was tortuous and rigid, without flexibility or originality. Once a plan was made it was seldom changed, no matter how circumstances varied. Supply services were rudimentary and often almost non-existent. These were defects which the heroism of the rank and file could not retrieve and they, along with the inadequacy of Japan's industrial resources for modern war on a great scale, were important contributing factors to Japan's defeat.

NOTES AND REFERENCES

1. United States Strategic Bombing Survey, *Japan's Struggle to End the War*, 13.

INDEX

398

399

400

Eora Creek: 200, 205.
Espiritu Santo Airfield: 224, 225, 230, 235.
Etorofu: see Kuriles.
Europe, war in: 151, 239, 344-5.
Ezaki, Col. Yoshio: 301, 302.
Fahey, James J.: quoted, 230.
Far East Command: 128.
Far Eastern Fleet: see under British Navy.
Farncomb, Commodore H. B.: 367.
Feldt, Lt.-Cmdr. Eric A.: 193.
Fergusson, Brig. Bernard: 336, 339.
Fiji: 151, 153, 154, 155, 212
Fiji Infantry Regiment: 280.
Finisterres: 298, 299.
Finschhafen: 249; Australians land, 258, operations at, 258-60; Japanese bomb, 258, 259, 260.
Fitch, Rear-Adm. Aubrey W.: 157, 158, 162, 163.
Flame-throwers: see Weapons.
Fletcher, Rear-Adm. Frank Jack: commands Task Force 17, 157, 160, 161, 162; raids Tulagi, 158; at Midway, 170, 174, 179; at Guadalcanal, 214, 218, 219, 220; dropped as carrier commander, 223.
Florida Island: 213, 214, 216, 220.
"Forgotten Armies": see under Burma.
Formosa: 52, 53, 55, 81, 263.
Four Power Treaty: 37.
French Frigate Shoals: 169.
Fuchida, Capt. Mitsuo: leads Pearl Harbour air attack, 22; at Midway, 173, 177; quoted, 173, 177.
Fuller, Maj.-Gen. Horace H.: 309, 311.
Funafuti Atoll: 274, 285.
Gali: 259.
Gap, The: 190, 195, 198.
Gandhi, Mahatma: 242.
Garrison Hill: 342.
Gavutu Island: 214, 216.
Gay, Ensign George H.: 177.
Gazelle Peninsula: 382.
Geelvink Bay: 308.
Geiger, Maj.-Gen. Roy S.: 280, 376; commands III Amphibious Corps, 318; at Guam, 318, Palaus, 322.
Gemas: 108, 110.
Georgetown: 104.
Germany: 37.
Gerow, Brig.-Gen. Leonard T.: 26.
Geruma Island: 377.
Getting, Capt. F. E.: 221, 222.
Ghormley, Adm. R. L.: 228; commands South Pacific, 188, difficulties, 214-5, confers with MacArthur, 212, estimates Japanese on Guadalcanal, 215, superseded by Halsey, 230, estimate of ability, 230-1.
Giffard, General Sir George: 329, 330, 335.
Gila Peninsula: 320.
Gilbert Islands: 46, 274, 280, 287, 289; Americans bombard, 148, bomb, 148,

Nimitz decides to capture, 274, raid by marines, 274.
Gili Gili: see Milne Bay.
Girua River: 207, 208.
Glassford, Vice-Adm. W. A., 117.
Gokteik Gorge: 126.
Gona: 204, 206; Japanese capture, 191, strength, 207-8, Allied estimate, 208, defences, 207, beach-head, 206-7; Allied operations against, 206, 210-10, casualties, American, 210, Australian, 210, Japanese, 210.
Gonzaga: 56-7.
Goodenough Island: 194, 206.
Gorari: 205.
Goto, Rear-Adm. Aritomo: at Port Moresby invasion, 157, 159, 162; Tulagi invasion, 157; killed, 228.
Goto, Maj. Ushio: 322.
Grande Island: 366.
Grasett, Maj.-Gen. A. E.: 82.
Green Islands: 278, 301.
Griswold, Maj.-Gen. Oscar W.: 266, 280, 365.
Guadalcanal: 204, 230, 231, 232; Allied invasion, 191, 192, 214-7, American forces for, 212, information lacking, 213, climate, 213, description, 213, Allied estimates of Japanese strength, 215, Allies bombard, 216, Allies bomb, 216, operations in, 217-38; Japanese bombard, 229, 231, 236, bomb, 217, 219, 228, 229, 231, 235, reinforce, 218, 223-4, 225, 226, 227-8, 229, 231, 234, 235, 236, 237; supply difficulties, 219, 224-5; Allies reinforce, 225, 229; naval actions off, 219-223, ship losses, Allied, 223, 225, 227, Japanese, 225; "Tokyo Express," 225, 226, 227, 228, 229, 235, 237; Japanese evacuate, 237; casualties, Allied, 216, 223, 225, 234, 237-8, Japanese, 216, 225, 226, 232-3, 234, 237.
Guadalcanal, battle of: 235-7.
Guam: 32, 145, 172, 303, 313, 314, 316; Japanese capture, 48, reinforcement attempts, 308; Americans invade, 318, casualties, American, 318, Japanese, 319.
Gumain River: 67.
Gunboats: 270, 290.
Gusika: 260, 297-8.
Gyaing River: 129.
Hagushi: 378.
Hainan Island: 38, 81.
Halewa Airfield: 31.
Hall, Maj.-Gen. C. P.: 366.
Halmahera: 307, 320.
Halsey, Vice-Adm. William F.: 166, 170, 248, 260, 323, 348, 371, 380; commands Enterprise Task Force, 154-5; flies off Doolittle raiders, 154; C-in-C, South Pacific, 230, 231, directives to, 248, 249, at Guadalcanal, 233; appoints deputy, 266;

404

406

409

New Caledonia: 150, 151, 154, 155, 185, 229.
New Georgia: 214; operations in, 260-2, 265-7, naval actions off, 262-4, casualties, Americans, 263, 266, 268. *See also* Rabaul.
New Georgia Occupation Force: 266.
New Guinea and Papua: 46, 153, 188, 296, 307, 320, 393; coastwatchers, 152; Allied need forward airfields, 183; reinforced, 185, 196, 203; weather, 201, 207, terrain, 198-200, 298, insects, 201, sickness, 201, 207; nature of fighting, 201-2, 255, Allied offensives, 250, 298-9, 308-9, 382, casualties, American, 210, 309, Australian, 210, 382, Japanese, 210, 250, 382. *See also* Buna, Finschhafen, Gona, Halmahera, Kanga Force, Kokoda Track, Milne Bay, Port Moresby, Salamaua, Sattelberg, Wewak.
New Guinea Force: 185, 193, 203-4, 210, 249.
New Guinea Volunteer Rifles: 152.
New Hebrides: 151.
New Ireland: 188.
New Zealand: 105, 106;
New Zealand Army: Divisions, 3rd, 268, 276, 301; Brigades, 8th, 276.
Newcastle: 190.
Ngakyedank Pass: 333.
Ngesebus: 321, 323.
Nggela Islands: 213.
Nichols Field: 55, 366.
Nicobar Islands: 106.
Nielson Field: 54, 55.
Nimitz, Adm. Chester W.: 188, 240, 248, 300, 323, 356; C-in-C, U.S. Pacific Fleet, 149-50, C-in-C Pacific Ocean Area, 150; directives to, 150, 188, 248, 249, 300, 303; directs Midway, 170; relieves Ghormley, 230; urges Central Pacific over South-West Pacific advance, 248; Marshall Islands strategy, 288-9; directed to aid South-West Pacific, 248, 300, South Pacific, 248, 300; visits Washington, 300; urges speed in Luzon, 365; promoted Admiral, 369.
Nine Power Treaty: 37.
Nishimura, Lt.-Gen. Takumo: 113.
Nishimura, Rear-Adm. Shoji: 117; at Leyte Gulf, 350, 351, 352, 353, 357.
Nishino, Commander: 355.
Noble, Rear-Adm. Albert G.: 384.
Noemfoor Island: 319.
Nomura, Kichisaburo: 25.
North Africa: 240.
North Pacific Area: 150.
Norris, Col. Kingsley: 198.
Novaliches Bridge: 366.
Noyes, Rear-Adm. Leigh: 214.
Nukufetau: 274.
Numata, Lt.-Gen. Takuzo: 309.

Obata, Lt.-Gen. Hideyoshi: 135; commands 5th Air Group, 57, 129; XXXI Army, 307; at Guam, 307.
Obayashi, Rear-Adm. Sueo: 313, 314.
Ocean Island: 164.
Ohnishi, Vice-Adm. Takijiro: 357.
Oivi: 205.
Olongapo: 56.
Oka, Col. Akinosuka: 232.
Okinawa: 370, 376, 393; air cover for invasion, 365, invasion postponed, 369; Japanese garrison, 376, American operations against, 377, 378-9, casualties, Americans, 379, 380-1, Japanese, 379, 380-1; Kamikaze attacks off, 379-80, Japanese commando raid, 380.
Okochi, Vice-Adm. Denshichi: 366.
Oldendorf, Rear-Adm. J. B.: at Leyte Gulf, 351, 352; Luzon invasion, 363.
Olevuga Island: 213.
Ominato: 170.
Omori, Rear-Adm. Sentaro: 276, 277, 278.
Operation A-GO: 310, 312.
Operation Watchtower: 212.
Operation Shoestring: 212.
Ormoc: 360, 361.
Osaka: 154.
Owen Stanley Mountains: 190, 204, 206, 250.
Owi Island: 310.
Oyen, Maj.-Gen. L. H. van: 120.
Ozawa, Vice-Adm. Jisaburo: commands Malaya Force, 142; First Mobile Fleet, 310, 312; at battle of Philippine Sea, 313, 314, 315, 316; at Leyte Gulf, 349, 350, 351, 355, 356.
Pa-an: 130.
Pabu: 260, 298.
Pacific Command Areas: 149, 150, 188.
Pacific Military Conference: 248.
Pacific Ocean Area: 149, 150.
Page, Sir Earle: 58.
Paidado Islands: *see* Owi, Mios Woendi.
Palawan: 368.
Palaus: 303; Allies bomb, 305; Combined Fleet retires to, 292, withdraws from, 305; Americans operations, 321-3, casualties, American, 323, Japanese, 323. *See also* Angaur; Peleliu.
Palompon: 361.
Palembang Airfield: 118-9.
Palmyra Island: 151.
Pampanga River: 66, 67.
Panaon Strait: 349.
Panay, 369.
Pandan: 57.
Paniguian River: 70.
Panjang Road: 113.
Pangkalanboeoen: 122.
Papua: *see under* New Guinea.
Paramushiro: 170, 271.
Paratroops, Allied: 256, 319, 367; Japanese, 107-8, 118-9.

410

411

Yorktown, 148, 157, 158, 160, 161, 162, 163, 164, 170, 177, 178, 179, 180, 218.

Battleships: *Arizona*, 31; *California*, 31; *Indiana*, 231; *Maryland*, 31; *Mississippi*, 281; *Missouri*, 388; *Nevada*, 31; *North Carolina*, 214, 227; *Oklahoma*, 31; *Pennsylvania*, 31; *South Dakota*, 234, 237; *Tennessee*, 31; *West Virginia*, 31.

Cruisers: *Astoria*, 220, 222, 223; *Atlanta*, 235; *Birmingham*, 351; *Boise*, 117, 228; *Canberra*, 347; *Chicago*, 161, 219, 220, 221; *Helena*, 31, 228, 263, 264; *Honolulu*, 31, 265; *Houston*, 118, 120, 121, 347; *Indianapolis*, 379-80; *Juneau*, 235; *Marblehead*, 117, 118; *Nashville*, 362; *Phoenix*, 301; *Portland*, 233; *Quincy*, 220, 222, 223; *Raleigh*, 31; *St. Louis*, 265; *Salt Lake City*, 271; *San Juan*, 220, 234; *Vincennes*, 219, 222, 223.

Destroyers: *Bagley*, 219; *Barton*, 235; *Benham*, 237; *Blue*, 220, 221, 225; *Buchanan*, 220; *Cassin*, 31; *Cushing*, 235; *Downes*, 31; *Duncan*, 229; *Farenholt*, 229; *Foote*, 277; *Gwin*, 264; *Helm*, 220; *Hoel*, 355; *Jarvis*, 217; *John D. Ford*, 117; *Johnston*, 354, 355; *Laffey*, 235; *Meade*, 237; *Monaghan*, 28; *Monssen*, 220, 235; *Mugford*, 217; *O'Brien*, 227; *Parrott*, 117; *Patterson*, 219, 221; *Paul Jones*, 117; *Peary*, 119; *Phelps*, 164; *Pope*, 117, 121; *Porter*, 234; *Preston*, 237; *Ralph Talbot*, 220; *Samuel B. Roberts*, 355; *Shaw*, 31; *Sims*, 161, 164; *Smith*, 233; *Strong*, 263; *Walke*, 237; *Ward*, 28, 34; *Wilson*, 220.

Destroyer-transports and Transports: *Colhoun*, 225; *George F. Elliot*, 217; *Gregory*, 225; *Little*, 225; *McCawley*, 262; *Pensacola*, 74, 144, 146.

Submarines: *Albacore*. 315; *Argonaut*, 274; *Cavalla*, 315; *Dace*, 350; *Darter*, 350; *Nautilus*, 175, 178, 274, 286; *S-38*, 61, 218; *S-44*, 223; *Sandlance*, 308; *Seal*, 62; *Sealion*, 56; *Tambor*, 180; *Trout*, 308.

Miscellaneous: *Antares*, target ship, 28; *Ballard*, seaplane tender, 169; *Condor*, minesweeper, 28; *Crossbill*, minesweeper, 28; *Curtiss*, seaplane tender. 31; *Langley*, aircraft tender, 121; *Neosho*, oiler, 157, 158, 161, 164; *Northwestern*, barracks ship, 171; *Oglala*, minelayer, 31; *PT 34*, motor torpedo boat, 71; *Thornton*, seaplane tender, 169; *Utah*, target ship, 31; *Vestal*, repair ship, 31; *William B. Preston*, seaplane tender, 52.

Australian: *Australia*, cruiser, 158, 161, 219, 220, 357, 363; *Canberra*, cruiser, 219, 220, 221, 222, 223;
Hobart (ex *Apollo*), cruiser, 121, 158, 161, 220; *Kuttabul*, ferry, 190; *Perth* (ex *Amphion*), cruiser, 120, 121; *Shropshire*, cruiser, 367; *Vampire*, destroyer, 95, 141, 142.

British: Aircraft Carriers: *Formidable*, 93, 378; *Hermes*, 141, 142; *Illustrious*, 378; *Indefatigable*, 378; *Indomitable*, 378; *Victorious*, 378.

Battleships: *Prince of Wales*, 93, 94, 97, 161; *Ramillies*, 140.

Battle Cruiser: *Repulse*, 93, 94, 97, 161.

Cruisers: *Achilles*, 264; *Ajax*, 264; *Cornwall*, 141; *Danae*, 121; *Dorsetshire*, 141; *Dragon*, 121; *Exeter*, 120, 121.

Destroyers: *Electra*, 94, 121; *Encounter*, 121; *Express*, 94, 97; *Jupiter*, 121; *Scout*, 103, 121; *Tenedos*, 94, 96, 121, 140; *Thracian*, 83.

Miscellaneous: *Anhui*, merchantman, 75; *Coast Farmer*, merchantman, 75; *Dona Nati*, merchantman, 75; *Dragonfly*, gunboat, 111; *Li-Wo*, auxiliary patrol vessel, 116; *Scorpion*, gunboat, 111; *Vita*, hospital ship, 141-2.

Dutch: *De Ruyter*, cruiser, 118, 120, 121; *Evertsen*, destroyer, 121; *Java*, cruiser, 120, 121; *Kortenaer*, destroyer, 119, 121; *Piet Hein*, destroyer, 119; *Tromp*, cruiser, 118, 119.

German: *Admiral Graf Spee*, battleship, 264.

Japanese: Aircraft Carriers: *Akagi*, 21, 173, 178-9; *Chitose*, 225, 356; *Chiyoda*, 315, 356; *Hiryu*, 21, 50, 173, 175, 179, 180; *Hiyo*, 315; *Junyo*, 170, 171, 180; *Kagu*, 21, 179; *Ryujo*, 170, 171, 180, 225; *Shoho*, 159, 160, 162, 164; *Shokaku*, 21, 160, 162, 163, 164, 165, 166, 234, 275, 313; *Soryu*, 21, 50, 178; *Taiho*, 315; *Zuiho*, 233, 234, 275, 356; *Zuikaku*, 21, 160, 162, 163, 164, 165, 166, 275, 315, 356.

Battleships: *Fuso*, 352; *Hiei*, 21, 235; *Kirishima*, 21, 237; *Musashi*, 41, 350; *Yamashiro*, 352; *Yamato*, 41, 380.

Cruisers: *Abukuma*, 21, 352, 353; *Aoba*, 221, 222, 228; *Ashigara*, 353; *Atago*, 350; *Chikuma*, 21, 234, 355; *Chokai*, 218, 221, 222, 355; *Furutaka*, 221, 222, 228, 229; *Jintsu*, 225, 264, 265; *Kako*, 222, 223; *Kinugasa*, 222, 228, 236; *Kumano*, 354, 355; *Maya*, 350; *Mikuma*, 180, 181; *Mogami*, 180, 181, 352, 353; *Myoko*, 350; *Nachi*, 352, 353; *Sendai*, 277; *Suzuya*, 355; *Takao*, 350; *Tama*, 356; *Tatsuta*, 308; *Tenryu*, 222; *Tone*, 21; *Yahagi*, 380; *Yubari*, 49, 159, 222.

Destroyers: *Arashi*, 267; *Asagiri*, 225; *Asagumo*, 353; *Ayanami*, 237; *Fubuki*, 228, 229; *Hagikaze*, 267; *Hat-*

414

415

holds, 338, death, 338, assessment of, 338-9.
Winterton, Maj.-Gen. T. J. W.: 134.
Woodlark Island: 159, 249, 253.
Wootten, Maj.-Gen. G. F.: 257, 383.
Wotje: 168, 169, 288, 289, 292, 371.
Yakabi Island: 377.
Yamada, Maj.-Gen. Eizo: 259.
Yamada, Rear-Adm. Sadayoshi: 157.
Yamamoto, Adm. Isoroku: 21, 164, 231; C-in-C, Combined Fleet, 21, 43, plans Pearl Harbour attack, 43; urges seizure of Midway, 153, 155, directs Midway operation, 166-181, Aleutians operation, 166-8, death, 251.
Yamashita, Lt.-Gen. Tomoyuki: 102, 103, 109, 110, 113; commands XXV Army, 93, Fourteenth Area Army, 348, defends Philippines, 263-4, strategy on Luzon, 364.
Yap: 313, 321.
Yaut River: 299.
Yellow River: 340.
Yokoyama, Lt.-Gen. Shizuo: 364.
Yokoyama, Col. Yosuke: 191.
Yonai, Adm. Mitsumasa: 390.
Yontan Airfield: 380.
Young, Sir Mark: 86.
Yunnan: 332, 335, 338, 341.
Zamami Island: 377.
Zamboanga Peninsula: 369.
Zanana: 262, 266.
Zedidaung: 243.

417